RURAL SOCIOLOGY IN CANADA

EDITED BY

DAVID A. HAY AND

GURCHARN S. BASRAN

Toronto Oxford New York

OXFORD UNIVERSITY PRESS

1992

Oxford University Press, 70 Wynford Drive, Don Mills, Ontario M3C 1J9

Toronto Oxford New York
Delhi Bombay Calcutta Madras Karachi Kuala Lumpur
Singapore Hong Kong Tokyo Nairobi Dar es Salaam Cape Town
Melbourne Auckland

and associated companies in
Berlin Ibadan

Canadian Cataloguing in Publication Data
Main entry under title:
Rural sociology in Canada
Includes bibliographical references and index.
ISBN 0-19-540818-7
1. Canada - Rural conditions. I. Hay, David A.
II. Basran, G. S.
HN103.5R87 1991 307.72'0971 C92-093019-0

This book is printed on permanent (acid-free) paper. ♾

Design: Marie Bartholomew

1 2 3 4–95 94 93 92

Printed in Canada by Webcom Ltd.

CONTENTS

LIST OF FIGURES

LIST OF TABLES

ACKNOWLEDGEMENTS

For the preparation and publication of this book we must offer thanks to many people. Our first acknowledgement is extended to our colleagues, the contributing authors. They all willingly accepted our request to contribute a chapter for the book, and graciously received our criticisms and requests for revisions. Needless to say, the book could not have been published without their scholarship, creativity, hard work and co-operation.

We are also grateful to the editors at Oxford University Press for their encouragement, support and understanding in bringing the book to fruition. In particular we wish to recognize the editorial work of Richard Teleky, Phyllis Wilson, and Olive Koyama.

Our sincere appreciation is also extended to Robert Cunningham and Jacqueline Andre for their assistance in reviewing and improving the content and readability of the material. Robert must also be thanked for his very efficient computer preparation of the manuscript.

INTRODUCTION

This text, unlike other contemporary writings on Canada, focuses on the rural sector of Canadian society. A number of images come to mind in relation to the term, rural: homogeneity; peace and tranquillity; a small farm, the little red school house, a tiny rural church, little rural village or hamlet. This may have been true in previous eras, but rural Canada today is characterized by considerable diversity of rural enterprises and occupations, resource bases, population numbers and characteristics, and historical patterns and traditions.

In academic and other discourses it has become somewhat routine to indicate that some important segment of society, some vital institution such as the economy, the family, the church, or the health and education system, is at a critical point in its development. In rural Canada such appears to be the case in relation to present-day farm, fishery, and other rural industry crises: the degradation and depletion of natural resources, the consolidation and closure of rural businesses and services, and the potential demise of rural trade centres and communities.

The essays in this book are intended to provide a more adequate understanding of historical and contemporary developments underlying the problems confronting rural areas and populations. These problems are the result of a multiplicity of intersecting social, cultural, economic, and political forces at the local, provincial or regional, national, and increasingly international levels. As a result we believe that it is necessary to focus on many relevant levels rather than on only one level (i.e., the locality, as is frequently the case) if the problems being experienced by the rural and other sectors are to be understood and addressed.

The relative importance of the rural segment of society in terms of population numbers and contribution to the national economy has diminished in comparison to earlier periods in Canada's history. In 1986 rural Canada did, however, include approximately one out of every four Canadians. Rural industries also continue to make substantial contributions to the direct employment of the Canadian labour force and, indirectly, to the employment of people in processing, transportation, and related activities of rural resources and products.

If an important component of our heritage is to be adequately understood and preserved, rural Canada is still a topic worthy of concern on the public and academic agendas. The problems presently affecting rural society are the result of a rapidly changing world: instantaneous communication, improved modes of transportation, and advanced technologies. The solution to these problems and the future viability of rural Canada will also necessitate further changes.

In a book such as this it is impossible to deal adequately with all facets and problems of rural life. The chapters and themes included have been selected to portray the diversity present in rural Canada in terms of the primary industries and their related technologies, rural communities and trade centres, and trends in population distribution and demographic characteristics of rural areas in Canada.

SECTION ONE

THEORETICAL PERSPECTIVES AND BACKGROUND DATA

In this section Basran's chapter deals with some theoretical perspectives used to examine changes in agriculture in Canada, and stresses that the crisis in agriculture can only be understood if we study the role of the state in Canada. Since 1867 the Canadian state has played an important role in the development of agricultural land, policies, and programs. If in 1991 fruit growers in the Niagara Peninsula in Ontario are experiencing some serious difficulties in maintaining viable operations, it is because of free trade with the US and not because of any inefficiency or lack of productivity.

To understand changes in rural Canada we must look at local, regional, national, and international issues. Social scientists have used various theoretical approaches to study rural Canada. The Adam Smith approach still dominates the work of most of the economists and agricultural economists. The staples model gained some popularity but did not pay adequate attention to the issues of who benefits from the control and exploitation of Canada's resources, or to Canada's position in the world capitalist economy. The Metropolis-Hinterland model has been used to discuss the crisis in agriculture in regard to US dominance of the Canadian economy.

There is a need to develop a theoretical perspective which will be based upon historical materialism as well as the everyday experiences of the people living in rural areas. Marxian and Political Economy models are discussed in this chapter.

Chapter Two, by David Hay, looks at trends and emerging developments in rural populations and industries. These trends and data provide background information with which to understand crises, changes, and present situations in rural Canada which are discussed in later chapters.

The rural population, in comparison to the urban population, is declining (76.5% urban in 1986) and the fertility rate is falling because of a structural adjustment in our economy, and changes in our values, traditions, and belief systems. In 1986 all provinces, with the exception of PEI and New Brunswick, were predominantly urban.

When the rural population is separated into farm and non-farm categories it is apparent that, with the exception of PEI and the prairie provinces, in 1986 a very small proportion of the provincial population was engaged in farming. The number of farms continues to decline. In 1986, over 57% of farms were located in the four western provinces. With the exception of BC from 1971 to 1981, the size of farms in Canada continues to rise.

There is a gradual increase in the proportion of farm operators over 55 years of age, and a decrease in the proportion of farmers in the younger age groups. There are some serious political, economic, social, and cultural implications when we find that in 1986, only four per cent of the Canadian population was employed in farming. Farmers may still play an important role in some provinces but nationally their relative influence has declined and will continue to wane. The Free Trade Agreement with the US may also result in the decline of certain kinds of farms (such as fruit and vegetable) in Canada.

CHAPTER ONE

CHANGES IN AGRICULTURE IN CANADA: THEORETICAL PERSPECTIVES

G.S. BASRAN

Agriculture in Canada is going through major crises. These crises are not new or unique to the 1990s—they are closely related to the historical development of agriculture in Canada. They are a significant part of our political and economic structures, and they must be viewed in the context of the position of Canadian society in the capitalist world economy.

During these difficult times federal and provincial governments have made various efforts to assist farmers. For example, in 1986 the Saskatchewan government provided about $25,000 in grants and loans to the average Saskatchewan farmer, and federal government programs offered an additional $8,000. So in 1986, total subsidies to Saskatchewan farmers came to more than $2 billion. In February 1991, the federal government's budget provided $1.3 billion to help the agriculture sector. While these subsidies may be viewed as unnecessary for the top third of the province's farmers, they proved to be inadequate for the bottom third who were struggling with heavy debts. McCreary and Furtan's research in Saskatchewan pointed out that land payments and deficiency payments based on production provided no more than 15% of monies to the poorest group, while they granted the wealthiest 20% of the families approximately one-third of the public funds. They

G.S. Basran is a Professor in the Department of Sociology, University of Saskatchewan.

concluded that if the government wishes to maintain farm numbers through government payments, then the most efficient method is targeted income supplements, which are much cheaper than the universal program (McCreary and Furtan, 1988: 64).

The percentage of farmers in Canada under the age of 35 rose from 15% in 1971 to 21% in 1981, but had dropped back to 19% by 1986. In 1986, 34% of farmers were aged 55 years or older. This is a higher proportion of older farmers than on any other census of agriculture in the post-war period. In 1986, about 40% of farmers were debt-free and most of them fell into the 'small farm' category—69% of those deriving less than $10,000 in gross sales were debt-free, while only 11% of the big farmers deriving $250,000 or more in gross sales had no interest expenditure. The value of farm land and buildings dropped 22% between 1981 and 1986 (from $90 billion to $80 billion). According to Statistics Canada, in 1986, 99.1% of the farm operations were classified as 'family farms', whether they were individual holdings, partnerships, or family-owned corporations. These farms produced 95% of gross farm sales (*Star Phoenix*, 4 June 1987).

The former Federal Minister of Agriculture, John Wise, predicted that the guaranteed price Ottawa paid for exported grain would fall 18% in 1986-87, on top of a 21% drop in price paid on the 1985-86 crop. On the other hand, the high costs of buying machinery and keeping it in operation are shown by the fact that in 1986 $391 million was spent on fuel, oil and lubricants and $305 million was spent on repairs and maintenance. Five years earlier the costs had been $241 million and $211 million respectively. Fertilizer and lime cost $310 million in 1986, compared with $167 million in 1981 (*Star Phoenix*, 5 June 1987).

The agricultural sector is generally subjected to fluctuating farm income, production, and prices and to worsening terms of trade. These fluctuations have serious side effects on the wheat economy of the West, as well as on the economies of other parts of Canada (Innis, 1956: 276). Realized net farm income in Saskatchewan fell from a peak of $489 million in 1967 to a trough of $202 million in 1969. Average per capita farm income fell from 93% of the national average in 1966 to 72% in 1980 (Pratt and Richards, 1979: 202-3). In July 1990, Agriculture Canada predicted that net farm income for 1990 would be down 22.5% from 1989, and net income in Saskatchewan was expected to be down by almost 67% in 1990 (compared to 1989). This loss of income is primarily because of subsidy wars between the US and the European Community, depressed grain prices, and loss of government aid for the farmers in 1990 (*Globe and Mail*, 12 July 1990).

Farmers are also subjected to a 'cost price squeeze': over the long run farm costs continually increase, while the prices of farm products remain relatively stable or at times decline or increase sporadically (Fry, 1979: 401). At the international level, according to the International Monetary Fund (IMF) figures, the price index of foodstuffs fell 14% in 1981 and was projected to decline 16% in 1982 (Brandt, 1983: 104). Thus, farmers experience production, export, and price fluctuations. The real commodity prices (non-fuel primary commodities) have been fluctuating and going down since 1970 (see Figure 1.1) (World Development Report, 1989: 11).

Figure 1.1 Real commodity prices, 1970–1988

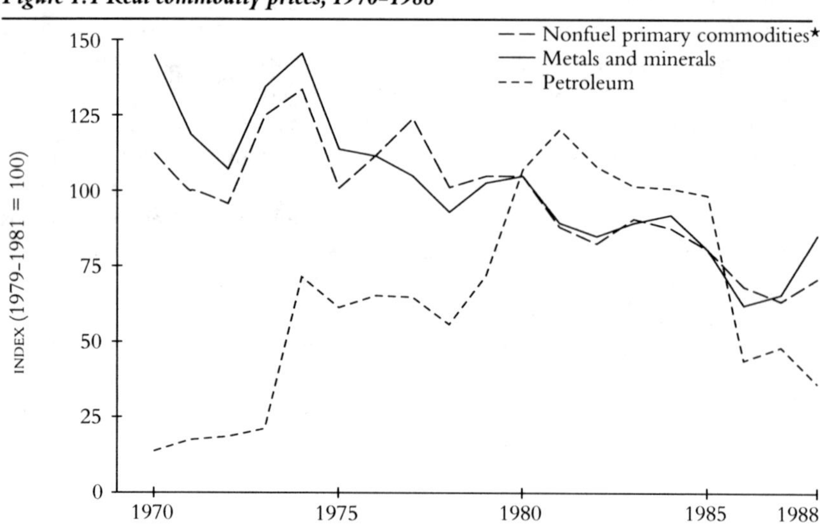

Note: Real prices are annual average prices in dollars, deflated by the annual change in the manufacturing unit value (MUV) index, a measure of the price of industrial country exports to developing countries.
*Based on a basket of thirty-three commodities.

Social scientists who have studied agriculture in North America have either presented the romantic and idealistic view of rural life or depended upon the theoretical insights of Adam Smith, who proposed that 'the greatest good for the greatest number was served when individuals pursued their own selfish objectives, constrained only by the unseen hand of competition'. The main objective of this paper is to discuss major theoretical frameworks which have been used to explain changes in agriculture in Canada. (For an excellent discussion on theoretical issues, see Buttel and Newby, 1980: 18-27; Philip McMichael and F.H. Buttel, 1990: 89-109; W. Friedland, 1991: 1-34.)

Before we discuss various theories in reference to agricultural changes, it is important to examine the role of the state. In the last three decades a fair amount of work has focused on the role of the state in capitalist societies. Our objective is not to address various theoretical issues but to point out the Canadian state's significant role in changes in the agricultural sector of our economy.

Role of the State

Historically, Canada's industrial growth has been paid for by public funds (Drache, 1977: 24). The Canadian state maintains its independence and mediates between conflicting interests in the society, but in the long run it serves the interests of the bourgeoisie as a whole. The Structuralist view of the state by Poulantzas is more relevant to understanding changes in agriculture in Canada than is Miliband's Instrumentalist view of the state (Poulantzas, 1974; Miliband, 1977).

As Leo Panitch points out (in Heron, 1977: 96–102) the state plays three conflicting roles in society. The *accumulation* role creates conditions under which profitable accumulation can take place—the state provides a favourable fiscal and monetary climate for economic growth through private enterprise and it can underwrite the private risk of production at public expense by providing grants, subsidies, fast write-offs, and depreciation allowances. For example, the state pays subsidies to farmers to survive the present crisis in agriculture, but at the same time the Canadian state has followed cheap food policy to appease the urban population as well as to help the agri-business corporations. In 1987, consumers spent about 12% of income on food prepared at home. (Disposable income spent on food, beverages, and tobacco was 29% in Spain; 24.6% in Switzerland; 23.3% in Sweden, and 18% in Canada, in 1987.) Moreover, J.W. Warnock and Agriculture Canada indicate that between 1949 and 1977, the farmers' share of the retail food dollar had fallen from 60% to 38%.

Since the state controlled the initial land development policies in the west, and continues to control immigration policies, it can provide cheap labour for the capitalist market. (See Ch. 15 in Fowke, *The National Policy and the Wheat Economy* [1973]: 281.) It can also absorb the cost of production and reproduction of labour by paying for some universal programs (including medicare, unemployment insurance, education, etc.) as well as other programs. The state also helps the accumulation process by providing infrastructures (roads, railroad lines, airports, means of communication, public utilities, etc.) for capitalist development. As John Conway pointed out, in exchange for building and operating a transcontinental railway, the CPR entrepreneurs received a massive Western empire, which laid the basis for the company's position today as the largest conglomerate in Canada. The terms of the contract still enrage Westerners. In addition to about $38 million worth of completed railway, the CPR received a $25 million subsidy and 25 million acres of prime Western land (Conway, 1983: 23).

In a democratic society like Canada, the state must also play the role of the *legitimizer,* creating stability and social harmony to allow the accumulation process to take place smoothly. Though historically the Canadian state did not emphasize this legitimation role as much as it emphasized the accumulation role, it became important after World War II. The Canadian state had to justify the ideology and operation of the capitalist system. It accomplished this by passing various social safety network legislations such as the Anti-Combine Legislation, the Unions Act, the Unemployment Insurance Act, welfare measures, so-called progressive income tax, old age pension, child care programs, medical care programs, etc. Discussing this role of the state, Poulantzas commented:

> The overall result is that certain specific policies of the state may produce 'short-term material sacrifices' by the bourgeoisie: being required to pay for the improved health and safety conditions of workers; contributing through taxation to public education, social security or unemployment benefits and so on. Still, these actions by the state really benefit the capitalists in the end, by defusing potential revolt, promoting a compliant and dependable work force and thus securing the 'long-term domination' of the bourgeoisie. (Grabb, 1984: 136)

The legitimation function is important to the state for political, economic and social reasons. The state can win political support by providing these services, and safety-net programs help the economy of the system by increasing consumption, employment and profits. The legitimation function provides social harmony and stability and humanizes capitalism. It controls and regulates dissenters' rebellions and protests (Skogstad, 1980: 66).

The Canadian state serves the interests of the bourgeoisie, which is primarily located in the central part of Canada. But the state cannot afford to alienate other parts of Canada too much, so it provides subsidies to the rural industries. The main objective of these subsidies is to help the capitalist farmers or fishers produce cheap food, to maintain political support for the state in order to win elections, and to discourage alienation. In 1980, a poll conducted by the CBC in Saskatchewan found that 10% would vote for a separatist party if one appeared on the hustings (Conway, 1983: 213). Of course, the separatist feelings are higher in Alberta than in the other western provinces. This may be partly explained by the Social Credit and Progressive Conservative parties' dominance of Alberta politics, and the programs, policies and philosophies which these parties have followed over the years.

The assistance provided to farmers and fishers is directed at suppressing rebellion and unrest and at creating harmony and stability. According to Skogstad's study of agrarian protest in Alberta:

> participants in protest activity tend to be characterized by current economic discontent, expectations of future financial deprivation, feeling of their own political powerlessness and perceptions of unresponsive (particularly federal) governments. (Skogstad, 1980: 66)

The third role of the state is *coercive*. Since it has access and legitimation to use the army, police, courts and other mechanisms, it can maintain law and order and can suppress disruptive elements considered harmful for the functioning of society. The Canadian state played the coercive role in reference to tight central control of Western settlement in the 1880s, suppression of the 1885 Northwest Rebellion, employment of troops against strikers in 1919, the War Measures Act in Quebec in 1970, and the use of force (police and army) to suppress the legitimate rights of Natives in the 1990s. Generally speaking, however, any democratically elected government is reluctant to play this role if it is left with any other option. Since the state controls important information and other structures in the society and the economic élites control the mass media and the functioning of other institutions, political and economic élites have been successful in legitimizing the ideology of the capitalist state. The state, therefore, rarely uses its coercive power since most of the individuals in the society have internalized the values, beliefs, norms and goals of the capitalist system.

Theoretical Approaches

In Canada, a number of theoretical frameworks have been used to examine the agricultural sector. Though the following list is not exhaustive, it covers some important perspectives.

Some social scientists have followed the Adam Smith perspective which emphasizes the free enterprise system in which open competition, demand and supply and the free market determine the prices of various commodities. According to this approach, various levels of government should not intervene in the agricultural sector and individual farmers should pursue their own selfish objectives, constrained only by the unseen hand of competition. This laissez-faire capitalism does not exist in reality, though a number of social scientists continue to conduct their research using this perspective.

Some private commodity groups which speak for the larger producers support the Adam Smith perspective. They have no romantic illusion about the 'family farm' and believe in open competition and the free enterprise system. They support some intervention from the state, but they do not want too much intervention from the national or international systems.

If we examine some of its recommendations it is clear that the Federal Task Force on Agriculture followed the Adam Smith perspective. The main principles underlying these recommendations are:

> The surpluses must be controlled and reduced to manageable proportions by reducing production drastically, if necessary. Where alternatives exist, production resources must be shifted to more promising market opportunities. Where such alternatives cannot be found, land and other resources must be retired.
>
> Governments should provide temporary, limited programs of assistance for the crop switching and land retirement, necessary to cut surplus production. At the same time this Report emphasizes programs to expand demand, particularly on the international scene.
>
> Agricultural subsidies and price supports that are not effective and efficient in achieving worthwhile high priority objectives should be phased out.
>
> Younger non-viable farmers should be moved out of farming through

> temporary programs of welfare, education and provision of jobs in other sectors of the economy. Older farmers should be given assistance to ensure that they have at least a 'liveable' standard of living. (Non-viable farms are those having incomes less than the poverty level of income.)
>
> Improvement of management must be encouraged by providing seed money for management training, provision of information processing systems, market price forecasts and other management tools.
>
> The organizational structure of agriculture both in the government and private sectors should be rationalized. Management by objectives, program planning and budgeting, cost-benefit analysis and other modern management techniques should be adopted. Every public policy should embrace these principles and procedures. (Task Force Digest, 1970: 2)

Theoretically and empirically, the free enterprise perspective is not of much use to explain and predict crises in agriculture. There is no open competition within Canada or at the international level; the free enterprise system is not free; supply and demand do not always determine the prices of commodities. The state has always played an active role in agriculture. Although some social scientists may make use of this theoretical perspective, politicians generally develop their programs and policies on the basis of political and practical considerations. Moreover, a theoretical perspective does not take into consideration subjective elements such as values, tradition, norms, goals, and sense of belonging to the community (see Hansen and Muszynski, 1990).

The second perspective which Canadian social scientists have followed with some diligence is the staples perspective. Harold A. Innis studied Canada's staple trades—the fisheries, the fur trade, lumber, wheat, and minerals—within the context of the world market. His main thesis was that Canada's economy was driven by the demands of the metropolitan markets of France, Britain, and the US for raw materials. The Canadian government has spent an enormous amount of money developing infrastructures to export and market these raw materials. And since the demand for our raw materials in other countries is beyond our control, we have on our hands a 'boom-bust' economy. Why have we not diversified away from our dependence on staples production? Why are we caught in the staples trap? Theoretically, some social scientists take the position that, considering the backward linkages (additional income created in industries that expand to provide inputs to the staple sector) and forward linkages (additional income in industries that, using the region's staple as inputs, transforms them further), it is not advantageous to diversify. We are more efficient in producing staples and should continue doing exactly this. The National Development Policy of the 1880s was an effort to escape the staples trap. The Canadian government decided to attract US branch plants to Canada in order to diversify the economy of the central part of Canada, and provided protection through tariffs to these US branch plants operating in the Golden Triangle (Windsor, Toronto and Montreal). The result of this policy was industrialization of the central part of Canada and the creation of hinterlands in the West and East. The National Energy Policy and the Foreign Investment Review Agency, which were created by the Liberal government in the 1970s, were half-hearted efforts to buy back Canada. Since 1984, under the PC government, Canada is for sale again. It is clear that the staples approach does not examine the forces and relations of production carefully. It is more descriptive than analytical. It also ignores the nature of power relations and particularly the question of who controls and benefits from the exploitation of resources, including agriculture.

A third perspective, that of the Metropolis-Hinterland, has been used to study the development or underdevelopment in Canada in general and in agriculture in particular. According to A.K. Davis, the metropolis signifies the centre of economic and political control located in the larger cities; the hinterland refers to an area or region which is underdeveloped and exports for the most part semi-processed extracted materials—including people, who migrate from the country to the city for better educational and work opportunities. There is always conflict between the metropolis and the hinterland because the metropolis continuously dominates and exploits the hinterland (Ossenberg, 1971: 12). This theoretical perspective is partly based upon A. Gunder Frank's work in Brazil and Chile. It is closely related to the Dependency Model and internal colonial perspectives. According to Frank, underdevelopment was and still is generated by the very same historical processes that generated economic development and the development of capitalism itself. Moreover, the hinterland will experience its greatest economic development if and when its ties to the metropolis are weakest. The most underdeveloped and feudal regions today are those that had the closest ties to the metropolis in the past (Frank, 1967). The main thesis of the Dependency Model is that surplus is extracted from the hinterland to the metropolis through unequal exchange relations. This causes the underdevelopment of the hinterland (West and East) and the development of the metropolis (central part of Canada). As Don Mitchell points out: 'The common problems faced by farmers in the West went far beyond the grief of struggle with wind, hail, frost, insects, crop diseases, weeds and prolonged drought' (Mitchell, 1975: 13).

In Canada, there is a debate among leftists as to whether Canada is a hinterland of the US or an imperialist country itself (see Moore and Wells, 1975). Those who believe that Canada is a hinterland of the US take the position that many of our problems in agriculture stem from our hinterland relations with the US. They believe that free trade with the US will have a disastrous effect on our horticulture sector, our cash crop sector and our marketing boards—it will create a further crisis in agriculture (see chapter in this book by Harold Bronson). Donald Smiley, discussing Canada's economic problems stated:

> Canada's position in both her trade and other financial relations with the outside world is largely that of her position in relation to the United States and the United

> Kingdom. This position is similar to that of a small man sitting in a big poker game. He must play for the full stakes, but with only a fraction of the capital resources of his two substantial opponents; if he wins, his profits in relation to his capital are very large, and if he loses, he may be cleaned out. (Smiley, 1963: 161)

S. Amin, G. Arrighi, G. Frank and I. Wallerstein have developed the Capitalist World Economy Model, which is an extension of the Metropolis-Hinterland Model (Amin *et al.*, 1982). This perspective is useful in understanding crises in the capitalist world economy and can be applied to the understanding of crisis in agriculture in Canada. Some of the important propositions of the Capitalist World Economy Model as articulated by Amin *et al.* are:

> 1. We believe that there is a social whole that may be called a capitalist world-economy. We believe this capitalist world economy came into existence a long time ago, probably in the sixteenth century, and that it had expanded historically from its European origins to cover the globe by the late nineteenth century. We believe it can be described as capitalist in that endless accumulation is its motor force. We believe that the appropriation by the world bourgeoisie of the surplus value created by the world's direct producers has involved not merely direct appropriation at the marketplace, but also unequal exchange, transferring surplus from peripheral to core zones.
>
> 2. We believe that we cannot make an intelligent analysis of the various states taken separately without placing their so-called internal life in the context of the world division of labour, located in the world-economy. Nor can we make a coherent analysis that segregates 'economic', 'political' and 'social' variables.
>
> 3. We believe that, throughout the history of this capitalist world-economy, there has been increasing organization of oppressed groups within the world system and increasing opposition to its continuance. The capitalist world system has never been under greater challenge. Despite, however, the unprecedented political strength of the world's working classes and peripheral countries, both the praxis and the theory of the world socialist movement are in trouble.
>
> 4. After World War II, the United States was the hegemonic power, having commanding power in the economic, political and military arenas, and able to impose relative order on the world system—a fact which correlated with the world's unprecedented economic expansion. We believe that this hegemony is now in a decline, an irreversible (though perhaps slow) decline—not, we hasten to add, because of any weakness of will among US leaders, but because of objective realities. This decline is manifested in many ways: the increased competitiveness of Western European and Japanese products, the frittering away of the old Cold War alliance systems and the emergence of a Washington-Tokyo-Peking axis, and wars among states in the periphery, including states governed by Communist parties.
>
> 5. We do not believe that the struggle between capitalist and socialist forces can be reduced to, or even symbolized by, a struggle between the United States and the USSR, however much the propaganda machines of both assert this. Nor do we think the analysis of the crisis can be made by looking at the core countries alone, as though the crisis were located only there. What is going on in the USSR, Eastern Europe, China, etc. is not external, or in contraposition, to what

> is going on in the rest of the world. The 'crisis' is worldwide and integral, and must be analyzed as such. (Amin *et al.*, 1982: 9–10)

If we use the Capitalist World Economy Model to understand problems of agriculture in Canada, we will consider Canada to be a semi-peripheral country, fallen under the economic and cultural influence of the US as a core society (Hiller, 1986: 46), and exploited by the US.

The main criticism of the Dependency Model, and to some degree the Capitalist World Economy Model, is that it puts too much emphasis on exchange relations between regions, rather than analyzing the relations and forces of production.

Our fourth theoretical perspective is based on the Marxist tradition. Some of the important propositions of this model are:

> 1. The economic basis of a society determines its social structure as a whole as well as the psychology of the people within it.
> 2. The dynamics of historical change are the conflicts between forces of production and the relations of production.
> 3. The class struggle between owners and workers is a social, political and psychological reflection of objective economic conflict.
> 4. Property as a source of income is the objective criterion of class. Within capitalism, the two basic classes are the owners (bourgeoisie) and the workers (proletariat) and class struggle between these classes is natural in a capitalist society. Exploitation of the proletariate by the bourgeoisie is a normal feature of the capitalist system. (Mills, 1962: 82)

From a Marxist perspective, regional disparity is a natural outcome of the workings of capitalism in any society. The goal of capitalism is not equitable distribution of wealth in all regions in Canada; rather, it is the accumulation of wealth by those who control the forces and relations of production. It is also the objective of capitalism to create a reserve army of labour in the peripheral or semi-peripheral areas, such as the western and eastern parts of Canada, and to use this workforce in the core areas, such as the central part of Canada (Matthews, 1983: 49–50). Moreover, the principal trend of capitalism is the displacement of small-scale production, both in industry and in agriculture (Lianos, 1984: 99).

Marx did not pay much attention to the study of rural societies in general and agricultural crises in particular (read Goodman and Redcliff, 1985: 231–47). He was more interested in the process of change from feudalism, to capitalism, to socialism, and finally to communism. Marx developed the concept of the Asiatic mode of production to understand the agricultural mode of production in India. He was critical of rural communities as oppressive, caste-ridden, and without history (Howard and King, 1975: 242). For Marx, farmers constituted a petite bourgeoisie class—they owned their own forces and relations of production and would eventually disappear into a proletariat or bourgeoisie class. As Wilfred Denis pointed out, Marx made certain assumptions discussing agricultural rent.

> The first assumption is that both agriculture and industry are fully capitalist. In both sectors surplus-value originates from identical relations of production. Marx also assumes, in this respect, the free movement of labour and capital between sectors, which means that the general tendency towards the equalization of the rate of profit exists in the economy as a whole. Secondly, he assumes a lower organic composition of capital in agriculture than in industry so that the production of value is higher in proportion to the capital invested in agriculture than in industry. Thirdly, he assumes that the supply of agricultural products is slightly inferior to demand. Fourthly, all agricultural production is wheat production and the production factors and costs for other agricultural commodities can be transformed into equivalents of wheat production. The final assumption is that the land owning class is separate from the capitalist farmers. (Denis, 1982: 128)

Lenin and Kautsky used Marx's ideas to examine the agricultural system (Buttel and Newby, 1980: 18-19). They found that the most important factors to consider are the forces and relations of production and the class relations in the capitalist system. According to this perspective, the ground rent is surplus, that is, a product from agricultural production acquired by the property holding of the land-owning classes (Buttel and Newby, 1980: 90). It is important to keep in mind that Marx's Ground Rent model is more relevant to peasant societies in which land is privately owned and is a scarce commodity. This is not the case in Canada. Most of the farmers are in the petit bourgeoisie and land was given to them for a nominal price. Moreover, there is an excess of production time over labour time because of the nature of agricultural production (Mann and Dickinson, 1980: 283). This means that capitalists in general are not willing to invest capital in this sector because the surplus which they can appropriate is not predictable or sufficient. According to a 1986 report commissioned by the Ontario Institute of Agriculture, return on capital on farm investment fell from 5.7% in 1975 to 2.1% in 1982. Returns were 3.2% in 1983 and 4.1% in 1984 (*Globe and Mail*, 4 June 1987). This does not take into consideration the decrease in asset values that occurred in the years from 1981 to 1986. In Saskatchewan alone, the value of farm land and buildings dropped 22% between 1981 and 1986.

In some respects it may be more useful for the capitalist state to encourage family farming; its production and reproduction of labour is cheap, and it creates maximum surplus and puts it at the disposal of urban capital (Whyte, 1979: 10). Mann and Dickinson's research addressed the question of the persistence of family farming into the era of late capitalism. According to them, non-identity of production time and labour time is considered to impede capitalist development. In addition, the perishability of commodities is not compatible with the requirements of capitalist production. Moreover, they take the position that the presence of wage labour is the fundamental criterion of capitalist agriculture. Mann and Dickinson's explanation of the persistence of family farming and the lack of penetration of the capitalist system into agriculture has been criticized by Patrick Mooney's work in the US (Mooney, 1982: 279-91). Farming communities act as places where a reserve army of labour can be accommodated. Family farms can also produce food in an inexpensive way to subsidize the production of food for urban residents.

The family farm has survived in Canada for several reasons. Family farms survive because there are no economies of scale (volume of production and cost per unit of output are not negatively related). Also, farmers are considered risk averters and are seen as satisfiers, rather than maximizers. Markets exist for farm products from even the least profitable farms. Politically conservative politicians draw their support from the petit bourgeoisie commodity producers. For example, the Saskatchewan CCF/NDP party consistently fared better in cities than in the countryside (Mandel and Taras, 1987: 372). It is hard to force out family farms in the way in which one can force out small industrial producers, because public investment in the form of subsidies, drains, irrigation projects, and transportation systems all contribute to the survival of family farms. Tax subsidies and direct farm income support payments from federal sources reached almost $3 billion in 1986. This does not include subsidies from the provincial governments, and marketing boards' protection for eggs, chickens, and turkeys. It was estimated that in 1987, federal and provincial governments provided about $4.7 billion in subsidies—virtually all of Canada's estimated net farm income (*Globe and Mail*, 22 April 1987).

Although the family farm survives, family farming is gradually ceasing as an independent mode of production (Buttel and Newby, 1980: 147). Moreover, the average size of the farm in Canada, as well as in the West, is increasing. (A farm is considered small if it is 240 acres or less, medium-sized if it is 241-1119 acres, and large if it is 1120 acres or more.) In Saskatchewan, the number of small farms increased by 31.2% between 1976 and 1981; the number of medium-sized farms declined by 21.1%; the number of large farms increased by 5.3% (Stirling and Conway, 1988: 73-83).

To examine changes in agriculture Canadian social scientists have also made use of various theories such as adoption and diffusion indicators, structural indicators, and ecological indicators. According to some research in the US these theories have not been very useful in understanding crises in agriculture, particularly the debt situation among farmers (for a detailed analysis see Murdock *et al.*, 1986: 406-35). Farmers and social scientists need sociological imaginations to examine changes in agriculture in Canada. Farmers and rural people should be involved in diagnosing and solving their problems. Any theory must be based on historical analysis. It should look at the role of the state, the relations and forces of production and exchange at local, regional, national, and international levels.

Readers will find that papers included in this volume represent all the theoretical perspectives discussed above.

CHAPTER TWO

RURAL CANADA IN TRANSITION: TRENDS AND DEVELOPMENTS

DAVID A. HAY

The early history of Canada was predominantly rural; the majority of the population were engaged in the primary extractive occupations, such as the fur trade, fishing, forestry, and farming. In 1871 when the first census of Canada following Confederation was completed, slightly over eighty per cent of the population lived and worked in rural areas.[1]

Since 1871, the total Canadian population, as indicated in Table 2.1, has increased in every decade. At the same time, the relative size of the rural population has exhibited a more or less consistent downward trend due to the technological displacement of labour in the primary industries and the subsequent migration of the rural population to the urban areas.

As a result of the concurrent processes of industrialization and urbanization occurring at varying rates throughout Canada's history, the rural-urban population distribution in 1971 was approximately reversed from the distribution one hundred years earlier. Over the period from 1971 to 1986 the relative size of the urban population appears to have stabilized at approximately 76%. Future trends in rural-urban distribution and the overall growth

---

David A. Hay is an Associate Professor in the Department of Sociology at the University of Saskatchewan.

of the Canadian population will be dependent on potential developments in internal migration, immigration, and the fertility and mortality patterns.

Table 2.1 Total population, per cent increase, and rural-urban distribution, Canada, 1871 to 1986

YEAR	TOTAL POPULATION (000s)	PER CENT INCREASE	PER CENT RURAL	PER CENT URBAN
1871	3,689	—	80.4	19.6
1901	5,371	45.6	62.5	37.5
1911	7,207	34.2	54.6	45.4
1921	8,788	21.9	50.5	49.5
1931	10,377	18.1	46.3	53.7
1941	11,507	10.9	45.7	54.3
1951	14,009*	21.7	37.1	62.9
1961	18,238	30.2	30.3	69.7
1971	21,568	18.3	24.0	76.0
1976	22,993	6.6	24.5	75.5
1981	24,343	5.9	24.3	75.7
1986	25,309	4.0	23.5	76.5

*Includes Newfoundland for first time.
Sources: Dominion Bureau of Statistics 1936, 1931 Census of Canada, Vol I., Table 2. Dominion Bureau of Statistics 1950, 1941 Census of Canada, Vol. I, Table 1. Statistics Canada 1978. Population: Geographic Distributions—Urban-Rural Distribution, Vol. I. Statistics Canada 1984a, Canada's Changing Population Distribution, Table 1. Statistics Canada 1988. Urban and Rural Areas in Canada, Provinces and Territories, Part 1.

Two of the periods presented in Table 2.1 are particularly noteworthy in relation to rural-urban population distributions: the Depression years from 1931 to 1941 and, more recently, the years from 1971 to 1986.

The 1931 census was the first in which the urban population exceeded 50% of the Canadian population. During the Depression the exodus from the rural areas was reduced as evidenced by the decline from 1931 to 1941 of less than one per cent in the rural population, in comparison to prior decades in which the changes were considerably larger. The relatively small loss of rural population during the 'Dirty Thirties' is generally attributed to the economic crisis and resultant lack of jobs in the cities. As a result, people returned to or remained in the rural areas, particularly on the farms where their livelihoods were more secure, at least in a relative sense.

Since 1971, Canada appears to have entered a new era in terms of the growth and distribution in the population. The increasing concentration of population in the urban centres up to 1971 tends to have slowed or even to some extent reversed. During the decade from 1971 to 1981, the rural population in all provinces and territories, with the exception of Saskatchewan and the Yukon, grew at rates above those for the urban and total Canadian populations. During this ten-year period the rural population grew by 1.8% per year in comparison to annual growth rates of between 1% and 1.2% for both the urban and overall population (Statistics Canada, 1984b: 2).

A portion of this rural growth was the result of natural increase and immigration, but according to Statistics Canada (1984b: 2) the more important factor was a reversal of the traditional rural-to-urban migration flows. As in the United States and other countries which have experienced a similar urban-to-rural migration, this was not a back-to-the-land movement such as occurred during the 1930s. Rather, the largest percentage of this rural revival or growth occurred in the fringe areas surrounding the larger urban centres as people attempted to escape or avoid the crowding, high taxes and land prices, and related problems in the cities (Statistics Canada, 1984b: 8–10).

The increase in the rural population may be a mixed blessing. It may be beneficial in terms of the potential growth and viability of some rural towns and villages whose existence were previously threatened by the out-migration of population and the loss of services. At the same time, it also increases the competition for and potential loss of farm land for residential purposes. The population increase also creates dilemmas for local government officials and administrators in attempting to satisfy increased demands for sewer, water, fire and police protection, and other services comparable to those in urban centres, while at the same time maintaining land taxes at a reasonable level (Rainey and Rainey, 1978: 126–40).

The results of the 1986 census presented in Table 2.1 suggest that the so-called 'rural renaissance' may have been short-lived, as has occurred in the United States and elsewhere. The relative size of the rural population again declined—albeit slightly—from 1981 to 1986. Future censuses will be necessary to determine if the rural growth of the 1970s was a short-term fluctuation or a more permanent pattern as people attempt to realize their life-style preferences in smaller rural centres or open countryside. These trends may also indicate that the relative size of the rural and urban populations may have reached respective plateaus of approximately 24% and 76%.

The two periods discussed above are also significant in their levels of population growth. During the 1930s Canada experienced an annual rate of population growth of only slightly over 1%. This was due to the effect of the economic crisis on immigration patterns and, more importantly, on the Canadian fertility rate.

During the more recent 15-year period from 1971 to 1986, the yearly rate of growth in Canada declined following relatively high periods of growth in the 1950s and 1960s resulting primarily from the baby boom. In the most recent five-year period from 1981 to 1986, the growth rate declined to the lowest level in Canada's recent history of approximately 0.8% per year. Dumas (1987: 1) indicates that the current slow-down in the growth rate is the result of low levels of fertility and immigration which tend to coincide with downturns in the Canadian economy. A number of socio-cultural variables, such as the increased entry of women into the labour force, the postponement of child bearing, and the declining importance of children as farm-family labour are also responsible for the fall in the fertility rate.

One of the major determinants of potential population growth is the fertility rate. During the first half of the 1980s, the Canadian fertility rate fell to its lowest level in history, including the 1930s rate of 1.7 births per woman. This is below the replacement level of 2.1 required to maintain the population. If these current fertility rates were to continue or decline even further in the future, Statistics Canada (1986: 3) predicts that in conjunction with present levels of immigration, the total Canadian population potential will peak or even potentially decline in the early part of the 21st century.

Provincial and Regional Patterns of Growth and Rural-Urban Distribution

The trends in the relative growth and rural-urban distributions of the Canadian population have not affected all provinces and the five geographical regions in the same way or to the same extent. In order adequately to discuss and understand the growth and distributional patterns in Canada, we must recognize provincial and regional variations. In general, these differences are indicative of the historical settlement and development patterns in Canada, agro-climatic and resource characteristics, and other relevant factors.

Table 2.2 shows that while the overall Canadian population has increased in every decade since 1871, its growth has not been evenly distributed across the provinces and regions. Rather, population growth has tended to accrue disproportionately to the more populous and urbanized provinces.

Approximately 62% of the Canadian population has resided in the provinces of Ontario and Quebec during the period from 1951 to 1986. The most densely populated area is a 650-mile corridor from Windsor to Quebec City (Statistics Canada, 1980: 2). The majority of Canada's larger urban centres, including the two largest cities (Toronto and Montreal), are located there. According to Statistics Canada (1980: 2): 'This concentration is not surprising since the corridor represents the line of earliest continuous settlement and includes the bulk of the nation's industrial production centres, most of the financial institutions and a strong growth potential.'

This highly populated corridor also includes the fruit-growing belt of the Niagara Peninsula which contains some of the most productive farm land in Canada. As a result of encroachment on this and other areas surrounding the urban centres by housing, transportation and other urban uses, the prime agricultural land base in Canada has been eroded (Burke, 1988: 33). The loss of the rural land base is particularly significant because less than 11% of Canada's land area is suitable for farming and less than 0.5% is prime land.

Table 2.2 Per cent distribution of total Canadian population by provinces

PROVINCE	1951	1961	1971	1981	1986
Newfoundland	2.6	2.3	2.4	2.3	2.2
Prince Edward Island	0.7	0.6	0.5	0.5	0.5
Nova Scotia	4.6	4.0	3.6	3.5	3.4
New Brunswick	3.7	3.3	2.9	2.9	2.8
Quebec	28.9	28.8	27.9	26.4	25.8
Ontario	32.8	34.1	35.7	35.4	35.9
Manitoba	5.5	5.0	4.6	4.2	4.0
Saskatchewan	5.9	5.2	4.3	4.0	4.0
Alberta	6.7	7.3	7.5	9.2	9.4
British Columbia	8.3	8.9	10.1	11.3	11.4

Sources: 1951: Dominion Bureau of Statistics 1953, 1951 Census of Canada, Vol. II. 1961: Dominion Bureau of Statistics 1963, 1961 Census of Canada, Population, Vol. I, Marital Status by Age Group, Catalogue No. 92-522. 1971: Statistics Canada 1973, 1971 Census of Canada, Population, Vol. I, Age Groups, Catalogue No. 92-715. 1981: Statistics Canada 1982, 1981 Census of Canada, Population, Vol. I, Age, Sex and Marital Status, Catalogue No. 92-901. 1986: Statistics Canada 1988, 1986 Census of Canada, Urban and Rural Areas, Canada, Provinces and Territories, Part 1, Catalogue No. 94-129.

The farm land base could potentially be expanded into new western or northern frontiers, but the replacement land is not of equivalent agro-climatic quality to the land being lost under urban pavement (Burke, 1988: 33). The urbanization of the farm land base, and in particular, the prime land, is of increasing concern to agricultural leaders, politicians and others if Canada is to maintain our position among the agricultural producing nations of the world. This issue will be pursued in greater detail in Chapter Twelve.

During the period from 1951 to 1986 the more urbanized provinces, with the exception of Quebec, increased their relative share of the Canadian population base. The other provinces and Quebec all experienced declines in their relative contribution to the overall Canadian population (Table 2.2).

According to Statistics Canada (1984a: 4), the largest proportion of the growth and increased urban concentration of the population in the provinces of Alberta, British Columbia, Ontario and Quebec has been the result of immigration, rural-to-urban migration, and the traditional east-to-west migration streams. However, the province of Quebec may not have benefited from these population movements to the same extent as did the provinces of Ontario, Alberta and British Columbia.

The diversity in the relative sizes of the rural and urban populations which has characterized the Canadian and provincial populations throughout our history is apparent from the data in Table 2.3. In 1986 all provinces, with the exceptions of Prince Edward Island and New Brunswick, were predom-

Table 2.3 Per cent distribution of population by rural-urban residence

	1951		1961		1971		1981		1986	
PROVINCE	URBAN	RURAL	URBAN	RURAL	URBAN	RURAL	URBAN	RURAL	URBAN	RURAL
Newfoundland	42.8	57.2	50.7	49.3	57.2	42.8	58.6	41.4	58.9	41.1
Prince Edward Island	25.1	74.9	32.4	67.6	38.3	61.7	36.3	63.7	38.1	61.9
Nova Scotia	53.7	46.3	54.3	45.7	56.7	43.3	58.1	44.9	54.0	46.0
New Brunswick	41.7	58.3	46.5	53.5	56.9	43.1	50.7	49.3	49.4	50.6
Quebec	66.5	33.5	74.3	25.7	80.6	19.4	77.6	22.4	77.9	22.1
Ontario	70.7	29.3	77.3	22.7	82.4	17.6	81.7	18.3	82.1	17.9
Manitoba	56.6	43.4	63.9	36.1	69.5	30.5	71.2	28.8	72.1	27.9
Saskatchewan	30.4	69.6	43.0	57.0	53.0	47.0	58.2	41.8	61.4	38.6
Alberta	47.9	52.1	63.3	36.7	73.5	26.5	77.2	22.8	79.4	20.6
British Columbia	68.1	31.9	72.5	27.5	75.7	24.3	77.9	22.1	79.2	20.8
Canada	61.6	39.4	69.6	30.4	76.1	24.9	75.7	24.3	76.5	24.5

Sources: 1951: Dominion Bureau of Statistics 1953, 1951 Census of Canada, Vol. II. 1961: Dominion Bureau of Statistics 1963, 1961 Census of Canada, Population, Vol. I, Marital Status by Age Group, Catalogue No. 92-522. 1971: Statistics Canada 1973, 1971 Census of Canada, Population, Vol. I, Age Groups, Catalogue No. 92-715. 1981: Statistics Canada 1982, 1981 Census of Canada, Population, Vol. I, Age, Sex and Marital Status, Catalogue No. 92-901. 1986: Statistics Canada 1988, 1986 Census of Canada, Urban and Rural Areas, Canada, Provinces and Territories, Part 1, Catalogue No. 94-129.

inantly urban. Considerable variability in the relative magnitude of the rural and urban populations which has characterized the provinces from 1951 to 1986 is also apparent in Table 2.3.

Of particular note are the provinces of Newfoundland, Nova Scotia and Saskatchewan which had rural population concentrations of approximately 40% or greater over the 35-year period (1951-1986). Over 50% of the population in New Brunswick and over 60% of the population in Prince Edward Island were classified as rural in each of the last five census years. In 1986, the other provinces had rural concentrations which ranged from 18% in Ontario to approximately 28% in Manitoba.

With the exception of the four Atlantic provinces, the decline in the rural segment of the Canadian population discussed previously has also affected the population distributions of the provinces. Considerable variability in the magnitudes of the rural population declines are apparent in Table 2.3.

Over the period from 1951 to 1986, Alberta and Saskatchewan experienced declines of over 30% in the relative size of the rural population. Quebec, Ontario, and British Columbia experienced declines of 11% to 12%, while the relative size of Manitoba's rural population decreased by approximately 16%.

The largest changes in the relative size of the rural populations generally occurred during the 1950s and 1960s with smaller decreases occurring during the 1970s and early 1980s. A notable exception to the general pattern of rural decline is the increase in the relative sizes of the rural populations which occurred in the provinces of Prince Edward Island, Nova Scotia, New Brunswick, Quebec and Ontario during the period from 1971 to 1981. This rural revival appears to be relatively short-lived as from 1981 to 1986 the rural populations in these provinces continued their previous declines.

As noted previously, the relative size of the rural population in the Atlantic provinces is considerably larger than in the other provinces. For example, the relative size of the rural populations in the Atlantic provinces in 1986 was approximately two to three times larger than the rural populations in the other six provinces, including those in the prairie region. In addition to the larger relative size of the rural populations in the Atlantic provinces, the data in Table 2.3 also suggest that the rural populations in these provinces may be more impervious to the concurrent urbanization and industrialization processes which have contributed to the overall decline in the rural population in Canada and the other provinces. Although varying to some degree, the rural concentrations in the Atlantic provinces remained relatively constant over the period from 1951 to 1986. This relative stability in the rural population segment may be the result of their smaller industrial base and relative absence of large urban centres in comparison to the other provinces and regions.

Rural Farm–Non-Farm Distributions and Related Trends[2]

Although the term 'rural' is generally associated with agrarian pursuits, such is not the case in the contemporary Canadian context as indicated in Table 2.4.

Table 2.4 Per cent distribution of population by rural-farm and rural non-farm

PROVINCE	1951		1961		1971		1981		1986	
	RURAL FARM	RURAL NON-FARM	RURAL FARM	RURAL NON-FARM	RURAL FARM	RURAL NON-FARM	RURAL FARM	RURAL NON-FARM	RURAL FARM	RURAL NON-FARM
Newfoundland	4.3	52.9	2.0	47.3	0.9	41.9	0.3	41.0	0.3	40.8
Prince Edward Island	47.5	27.4	33.0	34.6	18.9	42.7	9.8	54.0	8.1	53.8
Nova Scotia	17.4	28.9	7.6	37.9	3.3	40.0	2.1	42.8	1.6	44.4
New Brunswick	28.3	30.0	10.4	43.1	4.0	39.1	2.1	47.1	1.7	48.9
Quebec	18.9	14.6	10.7	15.0	5.1	14.3	2.9	19.5	2.2	19.9
Ontario	14.7	14.5	8.1	14.5	4.7	12.9	3.2	15.1	2.6	15.4
Manitoba	27.6	15.8	18.6	17.5	13.2	17.3	9.4	19.4	8.0	19.9
Saskatchewan	47.9	21.8	32.9	24.0	25.2	21.8	18.6	23.2	16.0	22.6
Alberta	36.2	16.0	21.4	15.2	14.5	12.0	8.5	14.3	7.5	13.1
British Columbia	9.4	22.5	4.8	22.7	3.4	20.9	2.2	19.9	1.8	19.0
Canada	20.2	18.2	11.4	19.0	6.6	17.3	4.3	20.0	3.5	20.0

Sources: 1951: Dominion Bureau of Statistics 1953, 1951 Census of Canada, Vol. II. 1961: Dominion Bureau of Statistics 1963, 1961 Census of Canada, Population, Vol. I, Marital Status by Age Group, Catalogue No. 92-522. 1971: Statistics Canada 1973, 1971, Census of Canada, Population, Vol. I, Age Groups, Catalogue No. 92-715. 1981: Statistics Canada 1982, 1981 Census of Canada, Population, Vol. I, Age, Sex and Marital Status, Catalogue No. 92-901. 1986: Statistics Canada 1988, 1986 Census of Canada, Urban and Rural Areas, Canada, Provinces and Territories, Part 1, Catalogue No. 94-129.

When the rural population is separated into farm and non-farm components it is apparent that, with the exception of Prince Edward Island and the three prairie provinces, in 1986 a very small proportion of the provincial populations was engaged in farming. As a result, the majority of the rural populations in the other provinces were occupied by primary activities other than farming, such as the fur trade, fishing, forestry, mining or combinations thereof.

These patterns are in general reflections of the historical settlement and exploration activities in these provinces, and the general unsuitability and inaccessibility of the land base for farming purposes. In addition, natural resource endowments—such as the proximity of the Atlantic provinces to the 'rich' fishing and fur sealing areas of the Atlantic Ocean, the mineral resources of Northern Ontario and Quebec, and the British Columbia forests and mineral resources—continue to determine the nature of the primary occupational structure in these regions. More extensive discussions on the Maritime fishing industry and the northern resource centres are provided in subsequent chapters by Sinclair and Bowles.

Due to the productive land base and favourable climate in Prince Edward Island, potato farming is one of the major economic activities. In 1986 slightly over 8% of the population in this province were in the rural farm population section; however, approximately 54% of the population in Prince Edward Island was engaged in primary occupations.

In the three prairie provinces, the data presented in Table 2.3 indicate that farming is an important activity for the respective provincial economies and for the employment of the rural population. In 1986, for example, the rural farm population represented 7% to 8% of the populations in Manitoba and Alberta and 16% of the population in the province of Saskatchewan. The rural non-farm segment of the population in these provinces is relatively small in comparison to the farm/non-farm distribution in Prince Edward Island.

The rural Prairie Region which contains over 80% of the arable farm land in Canada was initially developed as an agrarian region as the result of a number of initiatives by the federal government, the Canadian Pacific Railway, and other organizations. The Dominion Lands Act enacted by Parliament in 1872 offered 80 to 160 acres of land free to settlers if certain conditions were met (Fowke, 1978: 161). The Act also provided for the expansion of the initial land allocation after three years' residence, the making of improvements such as building a house and breaking the land, along with the payment of a small land registration fee (Kohl, 1976: 2).

The Dominion Lands Act, the expansion of the railways into the prairie frontiers, and the recruitment of settlers from Europe by land companies, the CPR, and other organizations were primarily designed to populate the fertile prairies with a large number of small family farm units for the production of grain, particularly wheat, for the export market. However, the purpose of these policies and related activities was not, according to Fowke (1978: 4), Davis (1971: 8), McCrorie (1971: 36) and others, to develop a rural agrarian society. Rather, the agricultural development of the West and to some extent in other regions was functional for, but subordinate to, the development of a national industrial and urban society. As a hinterland to the centres of economic and political power of the metropolis region in Central Canada, the above authors maintain, the prairies were to be primarily consumers of industrial products (machinery, fertilizer, etc.), the suppliers of resources including labour, and the providers of capital from export trade for development purposes.

Discussion of the relationship between the Western prairie hinterland and the Central Canadian metropolis is equally applicable to the relationship between the Atlantic provinces and Central Canada. As a result of their subordinate economic and political status, the hinterland regions are subject to exploitation by the metropolis areas (Davis, 1971; McCrorie, 1971). This introduces various conflicts and confrontations between the two regions. These antagonistic relationships have, it appears, been present in varying degrees and forms throughout Canada's history, as well as at the present time in farming, fishing, and other resource industries and in the political debates between the provincial and federal governments.

Farm Numbers, Size, and Related Trends

The provincial and regional variability in the relative size and nature of the

Table 2.5 Number of farms (000s), Canada and provinces, 1941 to 1986

PROVINCE	1941*	1951	1961	1971	1981	1986	PER CENT CHANGE 1941 TO 1986
Newfoundland	n.a.	3.6	1.7	1.0	0.7	0.6	-83.3
Prince Edward Island	12.2	10.1	7.3	4.5	3.1	2.8	-77.0
Nova Scotia	33.0	23.5	12.5	6.0	5.0	4.3	-87.0
New Brunswick	31.9	26.4	11.8	5.5	4.1	3.6	-88.7
Quebec	154.7	134.3	95.8	61.3	48.1	41.4	-73.2
Ontario	178.2	149.9	121.3	94.7	82.4	72.7	-59.2
Manitoba	58.0	52.4	43.3	35.0	29.4	27.3	-52.9
Saskatchewan	138.7	112.0	93.9	76.9	67.3	63.4	-54.3
Alberta	99.7	84.3	73.2	62.7	58.1	57.8	-42.1
British Columbia	26.4	26.4	19.9	18.4	20.0	19.1	-27.8
Canada	732.8	623.1	480.1	366.1	318.4	293.1	-60.0

*Newfoundland, Yukon and Northwest Territories not included prior to 1951.

Sources: 1941 to 1971: Statistics Canada 1973, 1971 Census of Canada, Agriculture Canada, Catalogues 96-701 to 96-711, Table 2. 1981: Statistics Canada 1982, 1981 Census of Canada, Agriculture Canada, Catalogue 96-901, Table 12. 1986: Statistics Canada 1987a, Census Canada 1986, Agriculture Summary Tabulations, Canada, Provinces, Table 1.

rural populations is also evident in relation to the number and size of farms located in the different provinces and regions. The differences in the characteristics of the farms in Canada to a large extent reflect variability in agro-climatic factors, the type of farm operations, and related considerations.

The number of farms in Canada, and in the majority of the provinces, increased up until 1941, at which time there were 732,832 farms in Canada (Table 2.5). Since 1941, the number of farms has decreased at varying rates in all geographical regions and provinces with the exception of the increase experienced by British Columbia during the 1971 to 1981 decade.

Significant differences in the rates at which the number of farms declined and the census periods in which the declines occurred are evident in Table 2.5. Over the period from 1941 to 1986, the number of farms in Canada decreased by approximately 60%. The largest declines (approximately 23%) in the number of farms in Canada occurred in each of the 1950 and 1960 decades. Statistics Canada (1989: 9-1) indicates that in the 1940s the number of farms declined by 15%, marking the beginning of major technological change in the farm industry. The downward trend in farm numbers has continued up to 1986 as a result of continuing technological developments in machinery, fertilizers, chemicals, and other farm inputs.

In all the provinces the loss of farms generally followed national trends. The four Atlantic provinces and Quebec experienced decreases above the national average, while the three prairie provinces and British Columbia had losses below the national average. While varying to some extent, the rates of decline for each of the ten provinces generally followed the national pattern, with the largest decreases occurring between 1951 and 1961 and from 1961 to 1971.

Table 2.6 Proportion of all farms in Canada by province, 1941 to 1986

PROVINCE	1941*	1951	1961	1971	1981	1986
Newfoundland	n.a.	0.6	0.3	0.3	0.2	0.2
Prince Edward Island	1.7	1.6	1.5	1.2	1.0	1.0
Nova Scotia	4.5	3.8	2.6	1.6	1.6	1.5
New Brunswick	4.3	4.2	2.4	1.5	1.0	1.2
Quebec	21.1	21.5	20.0	16.7	15.1	14.1
Ontario	24.3	24.1	25.3	25.9	25.9	24.8
Manitoba	7.9	8.4	9.0	9.6	9.2	9.3
Saskatchewan	18.9	18.0	19.6	21.0	21.1	21.6
Alberta	13.6	13.5	15.2	17.1	18.2	19.7
British Columbia	3.6	4.2	4.1	5.0	6.3	6.5

*Newfoundland, Yukon and Northwest Territories not included prior to 1951.
Sources: 1941 to 1971: Statistics Canada 1973, 1971 Census of Canada, Agriculture Canada, Catalogues 96-701 to 96-711, Table 2. 1981: Statistics Canada 1982, 1981 Census of Canada, Agriculture Canada, Catalogue 96-901, Table 12. 1986: Statistics Canada 1987a, Census Canada 1986, Agriculture Summary Tabulations, Canada, Provinces, Table 1.

The differential rates of decline in farm numbers have resulted in substantial shifts in the relative number of Canadian farms located in the provinces and geographical regions. The proportion of all Canadian farms located in the four western provinces, as revealed in Table 2.6, increased from approximately 44% in 1941 to slightly over 57% in 1986. In 1986, more than 41% of Canadian farms were located in the two provinces of Saskatchewan and Alberta.

The province of Ontario maintained a relatively constant proportion of numbers, but the eastern provinces all experienced declines in the relative percentage of Canadian farms. The largest change in the relative number of farms experienced by any province over the period under consideration occurred in Quebec, where the relative number of Canadian farms decreased from 21% in 1941 to 14% in 1986.

Concomitant with the decrease in farm numbers in the period from 1941 to 1986 has been a steady increase in average size of farms (Table 2.7). The one exception to this pattern is British Columbia; from 1971 to 1981 the average farm size decreased by slightly less than 15%. This was also the decade during which the number of farms in British Columbia increased by approximately 9%. This suggests that the increase in farm numbers during that decade was possibly due to a subdivision of existing farms and not to the development of new farm land.

Table 2.7 Average size (acres) of farms, Canada and provinces, 1941 to 1986

PROVINCE	1941*	1951	1961	1971	1981	1986	PER CENT CHANGE 1941 TO 1986
Newfoundland	n.a.	23	31	60	122	139	+504.5
Prince Edward Island	96	108	131	171	222	238	+147.9
Nova Scotia	116	135	178	221	228	240	+106.9
New Brunswick	124	131	187	244	266	284	+129.0
Quebec	117	125	148	176	194	217	+ 85.5
Ontario	126	139	153	160	181	192	+ 52.4
Manitoba	291	338	420	543	639	700	+140.5
Saskatchewan	432	550	686	845	952	1036	+139.8
Alberta	434	527	645	790	813	883	+103.5
British Columbia	153	178	226	316	269	312	+103.9
Canada	237	279	359	463	512	572	+141.3

*Newfoundland, Yukon and Northwest Territories not included prior to 1951.
Sources: 1941 to 1971: Statistics Canada 1973, 1971 Census of Canada, Agriculture Canada, Catalogues 96-701 to 96-711, Table 2. 1981: Statistics Canada 1982, 1981 Census of Canada, Agriculture Canada, Catalogue 96-901, Table 12. 1986: Statistics Canada 1987a, Census Canada 1986, Agriculture Summary Tabulations, Canada, Provinces, Table 1.

In 1986, the largest farms were located in the three prairie provinces with average acreages of 1036, 883, and 700 in Saskatchewan, Alberta, and

Manitoba, respectively. As with all averages, the figures tend to conceal the range of variability in farm sizes. In Saskatchewan, for example, in 1986, 14% of the farms were less than 240 acres and 17% were over 1600.

In accordance with the percentage change in farm numbers, the largest increases in farm size generally occurred during the 1950s and 1960s. These periods generally correspond to the substantial mechanization of farming which began in the 1920s and accelerated during the 1940s, and the general substitution of capital for labour (Wilson, 1981: 19). The transition to more capital-intensive farming has enabled the farm operator to increase the size and productivity of the farm. According to the Hall Commission:

> Over the past 100 years, the change has been from a labour-intensive, largely self-sufficient farm unit where each farm worker produced enough food for himself and three to five other people, to large scale capital-intensive units where the farm worker produces enough for himself and fifty other persons. (Hall Commission, 1977: 67)

The general correspondence between the decline in farm numbers and increase in farm size is, to some extent, indicative of the nature and type of farm operations in the different regions and provinces. In the western provinces, particularly on the prairies, there is a fairly close correspondence between the per cent increase in farm size and the per cent decrease in farm numbers indicating that the consolidation of smaller farms into larger units was one of the major factors involved (Whyte, 1970: 31). In the eastern provinces, Whyte indicates that farms previously occupied have been abandoned as a result of problems of accessibility and tillability, limited opportunities for expansion, and the loss of farm land to urban uses.

The magnitude and rapidity of changes in farm numbers at the present time tend to suggest that this is a relatively recent phenomenon, but the abandonment or consolidation of farm units has characterized the rural scene since the initial settlements. For example, Fowke (1957: 285) indicates that the intent of the Dominion Lands Act of 1872—to settle the prairie provinces with a large number of independently owned small farms—tended to be overly optimistic in relation to the area's physical and climatic capabilities. As a result of the short growing season, the necessity of summerfallowing to conserve moisture, and the relative isolation and loneliness experienced by the settlers, over 40% of the homesteaders did not register the title to their land.

A substantial proportion of the increase in the average size of farms has been increased reliance on the renting of land. Since 1911 there has been a decreasing proportion of completely owned and operated farms to larger, partly owned and partly rented farm units (Whyte, 1970: 32). This pattern is particularly apparent in the prairie provinces which also have the largest farms. Although outright ownership of the farm may still be a 'cherished value' as a result of the unfortunate experiences during the 1930s Depression, the trend suggests that with the passing of the older generation of farmers, younger farmers are more willing to lease land. In many cases, considering high capital requirements, high land prices, and high interest rates, leasing may be the only viable way to enter farming or to expand the size of the farm operation.

At the present time, the economic crisis in farming is exacerbating the effects of mechanization and the general substitution of capital for labour on the size and number of farms.

A widely recognized problem associated with farming in Canada is the instability of incomes adequate to meet farm expenses, an uncertainty resulting from shifting and often declining prices received for farm products and the increasing costs of farm inputs. This uncertainty, according to Wilson, in conjunction with the large capital requirements to enter farming is a prime reason for the reduction of farm numbers in all areas of Canada (Wilson, 1981: 59-60).

In addition, Wilson maintains that as a result of the escalating cost-price squeeze in farming, farmers have consistently lost ground in the quest for financial security. The result has been:

> the move of thousands from the land in search of a more stable financial future, a subsequent expansion in the land base of many farmers in an attempt to increase their income potential, and a rapid escalation in the debt load faced by farmers. (Wilson, 1981: 62)

Trends in Farm Operator Ages

Over the period 1966 to 1986, the age distribution of farm operators in Canada has been characterized by a considerable degree of variability. The most general trend, which tends to mirror the overall aging of the Canadian population, is a gradual increase in the proportion of farm operators over 55 years of age, a decrease in the proportion of farmers in the younger age groups, and an overall increase in the average age of farm operators.

From 1971 to 1981, the proportion of farm operators under 35 years of age increased from 15% to 21% but declined to 19% in 1986. The proportion of farm operators over 55 years of age decreased from 1966 to 1981 but increased to 34% in 1986. This is the highest in this age category in any census since World War II (Statistics Canada, 1987: 5).

Similar to other rural and farm trends, the aging process also varies by province or geographical region. For example, McSkimmings (1990: 21) indicates that the highest average ages and relative increase in the proportion of farmers in the over-55 category occurred in the western provinces between 1981 and 1986, while the proportion of farm operators in this older age category declined in the eastern provinces.

As in the general population, the aging process is the result of relatively low fertility and mortality rates in Canada. In the case of the farm population, however, a significant portion of the aging process, according to Wilson

(1981: 59, 101-2), is the inability of many young people to accumulate the necessary capital and other resources to enter farming. As a result, a significant percentage of these young potential farmers are forced to migrate to the towns and cities until they can obtain the necessary capital to enter farming, or until their parents are able and ready to retire. Many of these young people may intend to return to farming, but it has been found that they frequently do not. They prefer to remain in the urban centres with more certain and stable incomes and higher standards of living. This increasing age of farm operators is of concern to farm leaders and government officials as boding ill for recruiting future generations of farmers.

Summary

The rural scene in Canada, and the farm sector in particular, is characterized by a great deal of diversity and continuous and dynamic rates of change. The rural population may well stabilize or potentially increase, but it appears that the farm sector will continue to decline into the foreseeable future.

One of the most dramatic trends has been the decline of farm numbers and populations to the point where less than 4% of the Canadian population was employed in farming in 1986. In general, this is indicative of the relative efficiency and productivity of the Canadian farm industry, whereby a declining and relatively small percentage of the population is able to produce enough food and fibre to satisfy the domestic demands and provide a surplus for the export market.

Whyte (1970: 10) indicates that any alteration in farm trends is unlikely, and by the end of this century a very small proportion of the Canadian population will be engaged directly in farming. More dramatic changes as a result of future technologies accompanying Canada's entry into the information age are also likely to occur in coming years.

While the relative contribution of farming and other rural industries to the national employment patterns is declining, it is important to recognize that these industries continue to play an important role at the provincial and regional levels. For example, the relative size of the farm population (16%) in Saskatchewan in 1986 indicates the continuing importance of farming and agriculture to the provincial economy and to rural trade centres and institutions, whose future viability and longevity are dependent on rural clientele. This is also apparent in the Atlantic provinces and other areas with sizeable rural populations in which the continued existence of rural communities is being jeopardized by the effects of technology and the shifting patterns of employment in the primary industries. These related issues are more extensively discussed in the chapters by Diaz, Reimer, Bowles, and Sinclair.

In recognition of the above trends, Whyte (1970: 10) maintained that:

rural enterprises, although continuing to occupy a prominent position in the national economy, will be relatively less strategic in effecting the social welfare of the Canadian people, and that the urban-based enterprises will continue to employ more people and through them, extend a more pervasive influence over the institutional and cultural development of the nation.

Notes

[1]The definition of rural and urban used by the Canadian Census changed over the time periods under consideration. Some degree of caution should, therefore, be exercised in the interpretation of the rural and urban growth rates for successive censuses. Also the rural and urban figures only represent the respondents' place of residence on census day, therefore, do not reflect intercensus population movements.

The census definition of urban in the periods under consideration were:

1941—prior to 1951, the population residing within the boundaries of incorporated cities, towns, and villages regardless of size.
1951—all persons residing in cities, towns, or villages of 1000 or over whether incorporated or unincorporated as well as the population of all parts of census metropolitan areas.
1961—all cities, towns and villages of 1000 and over whether incorporated or not as well as the urbanized fringes of: (a) cities classed as metropolitan areas; (b) those classed as other major urban areas, and (c) certain smaller cities if the city together with the urbanized fringe was 10,000 population or over.
1971—all persons living in (1) incorporated cities, towns and villages with a population of 1000 or over; (2) unincorporated places of 1000 or over having a population density of at least 1000 per square mile and (3) the built-up fringes of (1) and (2) having a minimum population of 1000 and a density of at least 1000 per square mile.
1981—persons living in an area having a population concentration of 1000 or more and a population density of 400 or more per square kilometre.
1986—population residing in continuously built-up areas having a population concentration of 1000 or more and a population density of 400 or more per square kilometre based on the previous census. To be considered continuous, the built-up area must not have a discontinuity exceeding 2 kilometres.
In all censuses the rural population were those persons not classified as urban.

[2]The trends in farm numbers and related statistics must also be interpreted with a degree of caution due to changes in the definition utilized by Census Canada from 1941 to 1986:

1941—census farms were all holdings one acre or more in size if the production in the previous year was valued at $50 or more.
1951—a census farm was a holding on which agricultural operations were carried out and which was (a) three acres or more in size or (b) from one to three acres in size and with agricultural production during the previous year valued at $250 or more.
1961—a census farm was a holding of one acre or more with sales of agricultural products during the past 12 months valued at $50 or more.

1971—farm, ranch, or other agricultural holding of one acre or more with sales of agricultural products during the 12-month period prior to the census of $50 or more.
1981 and 1986—farm, ranch, or other agricultural holding with sales of agricultural products during the past 12 months of $250 or more. Operations with anticipated sales of $250 or more in the previous year are also included.

Some of the changes in farm numbers and related trends may be due to the different definitions used in the censuses of concern.

SECTION TWO

RURAL COMMUNITIES: THE IMPACT OF CHANGE

Canada is a part of the global village. We are a member of the capitalist world economy. Our position in regard to other economies determines the nature of the changes which we are now experiencing. It is true that our economy is closely tied to the North American economy, but we are also affected by the economies of other countries.

In this section Diaz and Gingrich examine crises and community in Saskatchewan. They ask the basic question, 'What is the future of the rural communities in Canada?' Sociologists in general, and rural sociologists in particular have difficulty in defining community. In Chapter Three, Diaz and Gingrich view rural community as a process and a product of historical and structural arrangements that define conditions in which communities must survive, as well as the manner in which members of the community react to those conditions. The second dimension of the community is its specific geographical location and the existence of one economic activity—agriculture. They discuss the history of the development of rural communities in Saskatchewan and the processes of change these communities experienced (from bonanza to crisis).

Earlier rural communities faced some problems but they survived because of their capacity to control conflicts. In the 1950s and 1960s the rural population and the number of small rural communities continued to decline. Various structural changes such as industrialization, centralization of goods and services, rail line abandonment, unstable agricultural prices, the increasing cost of farm inputs, and subsidy wars between the US and the European Economic Community have created a crisis in rural communities in Saskatchewan.

In the second part of their chapter, Diaz and Gingrich discuss networks of solidarity—systems of exchange for goods and services that are important for the reproduction of both community households and the community as a whole. Interestingly, they found that a network for mutual support seems to exist only in kinship, not in friendship. Secondly, they found community participation closely related to the size of the farms. 'Successful farmers' participate in community more actively than small farmers.

In Chapter Four, Reimer assesses the impact of technology on rural industries and populations. He looks at major technological changes in agriculture. Steam tractors became available in Canada at the turn of the century. Internal combustion tractors and the electrification of rural areas changed agricultural practices and rural communities in a fundamental manner. Changes in the transportation and storage of agricultural products resulted in the reorganization of the grain and dairy industries. Crop hybridization and, more recently, the use of biotechnology, expanded both plant and animal production. Technology also has had impacts on mining and petroleum, forestry, fishing, and transportation and communication.

In the second part of his chapter, Reimer assesses the effects of technology on the labour force, economic control, the demographic structure, and community life. Technological development will continue to play an important role in rural Canada. According to Reimer, there is considerable interaction between these developments and the social context in which they are used.

The chapter by Bowles focuses on the growth, decline, and death of single-industry resource communities in Canada's north. Bowles presents two case studies that exemplify northern resource communities: of Espanola, Ontario, a pulp and paper town located 72 km west of Sudbury, and of Schefferville, Quebec. He also provides an overview of literature on resource communities, and discusses resource communities throughout Canadian history. It seems that most of the industries now follow the pattern of temporary communities for resource development. Workers are flown to the site, work intensely twelve hours a day for a period of seven days and then are flown out to their own communities.

Core characteristics of resource communities are small size, remote location, economic dependence on a single industrial sector and rapid social change.

In the last chapter in this section, Sinclair focuses on the impact of change in Atlantic Canada's fishing communities. In Atlantic Canada fishing is a major industry in terms of employment and export from the region. Historically women have always played an important role in fishing. In 1990 they constituted about ten per cent of the actual fishing labour force and comprised over half of the processing-plant workers. In class relations, fishers may be subsistence producers, domestic community producers, petty capitalists, wage workers, or company skippers.

Sinclair examines the historical and structural reasons for the crisis of 1989-90 in the fishing industry. New technologies changed the social structure of fishing and made it possible for Canadian as well as foreign vessels to catch more fish.

At the end of the chapter, Sinclair looks at the impact of technological changes in two areas in Atlantic Canada. In conclusion he states that the Canadian state has not been able to regulate the fisheries, and the compulsion to fish more and more for profit is the root cause of many problems which fishers in Atlantic Canada face.

CHAPTER THREE

CRISIS AND COMMUNITY IN RURAL SASKATCHEWAN[1]

POLO DIAZ AND PAUL GINGRICH

What is the future of the Canadian rural community? This is perhaps one of the most important questions to which Canadian rural scientists must respond during the 1990s. The answer is not easy. Regional diversity, international price wars, shifting national and foreign markets, free trade, and lack of political leadership make predictions concerning Canadian agriculture and rural Canada uncertain.

This chapter offers a small contribution to developing an answer to the question. It begins with a very brief theoretical discussion of the concept 'community', followed by a description of the prairie rural community's historical development and of its present critical condition. The last section presents some survey data regarding patterns of mutual solidarity among farmers, and patterns of participation.

The survey data have been taken from a survey of farm families in four rural Saskatchewan communities, carried out in the summer of 1987. The communities studied were Coderre and Stewart Valley, both in the southwestern part of the province, and Naicam and Wishart, to the north of Regina. The four communities are broadly representative of farm communities in southern

Polo Diaz is an Assistant Professor in the Department of Sociology and Social Studies at the University of Regina. Paul Gingrich is an Associate Professor in the Department of Sociology and Social Studies at the University of Regina.

Saskatchewan, ranging in size from under one hundred farms to several hundred, including a range of livestock and grain production.[2]

The Concept of Community

Community is a concept in search of content. Its use in sociology has been characterized by ambiguity and vagueness, resulting in a multiplicity of definitions that impede a systematic understanding of the phenomenon.[3]

The first attempt to systematically develop the concept is found in Tönnies' work, who made the well-known distinction between *Gemeinschaft* and *Gesellschaft*, roughly translated as 'community' and 'association', respectively. Gemeinschaft refers to social relations that are warm, personal, face-to-face, and close, and that extend across many aspects of a person's life. These relations are relatively permanent, and take place in small social organizations. Gesellschaft refers to relations that are indifferent, impersonal, temporary, distant, and dominated by cold logic and rationality. These find their place in the institutions of modern society.

Tönnies' argument was that pre-industrial social life, characterized by Gemeinschaft, was being destroyed by the emergence of modern society and its Gesellschaft patterns of relations. In Tönnies' dichotomy we find an opposition to modern society, a nostalgia for the past, and the assumption that pre-industrial and industrial society are characterized by distinct types of social relations. This approach was emphasized even more by Simmel, who transformed Tönnies' dichotomy into a duality between rural and urban localities. For Simmel, the spread of urban society led to a destruction of rural Gemeinschaft life. This approach was elaborated even further by a group of American sociologists such as Sorokin, Wirth, and Redfield. In different forms, they developed the idea of a loss of community and the breakdown of social cohesion in the city, through the disappearance of primary social relationships.

A number of studies have found that these patterns were not so clear in the everyday reality of urban and rural life. These findings have led to constant variations in the theoretical approach, and the development of a variety of theoretical and empirical definitions of 'community'. Community has sometimes been understood as a group of people who share a defined geographical space, such as a neighbourhood; sometimes as a group of people who share some common traits that identify them as a unique group in society, such as the academic community; or alternatively, as the emotional and sentimental characteristics of a social group, providing a sense of identity to the members of that group. There have been, of course, attempts to combine these three approaches, as well as to make some of them more precise for empirical purposes. The result has been a myriad of definitions.

The concept disappeared from the main agenda of sociological research by the late 1960s. The definitional problems, the replacement of its main paradigm—functionalism—by conflict theory, and the hegemony of structuralist Marxism, with its emphasis on structural events and processes, contributed to the disappearance of the concept of community during the early 1970s. During recent years the issue has again become fashionable, as sociologists realize that structural analysis offers a limited understanding of micro events and processes such as community.

The new approach sees community as inserted into a structural framework constituted by the national political and economic structures. This implies that community is not independent of what is happening in the rest of society. In addition, the duality originally developed by Tönnies is asserted by those who distinguish between 'community as communion' and 'community as commodity'. 'Communion' refers to a set of meanings given to social relations, in which trust, friendship, reciprocity, and loyalty are essential dimensions. 'Commodity' refers to meanings of relations where exchange, calculation, and competition are predominant.[4]

Our discussion follows the new approach. However, we would like to emphasize two ideas. First, community is not a universal category that could be described according to given criteria. Rather, community is a process, a reality that acquires multiple forms, not just that of a simple duality. Communities are the product of both historical and structural processes that define the conditions in which communities must survive and the manner in which members of the community react to those conditions. The multiple possibilities of this encounter generate a variety of situations, all of them part of the process of 'community'. Second, rural communities have two characteristics that distinguish them from other types of communities. They are in specific geographical settings; this imposes certain conditions upon community life. Also, they are normally characterized by the existence of only one economic activity—agriculture—and one form of production—the farm—that gives the locality a commonality of experiences.

The Western Community: From 'Bonanza' to Crisis

Canada's western rural community was born under the shadow of the state and railway companies. From the beginning, its form and content were shaped by the Canadian state's desire to impose its sovereignty over the vast western prairie, to develop a market for eastern industry, and by the railway companies' insatiable hunger for profits.[5] To attain these objectives, thousands of settlers were persuaded to move to the new 'land of milk and honey'. They occupied the parcels of land established under the Dominion Lands Act and oriented their production to markets external to the prairies. Waves of people from Ontario, Quebec, the Atlantic provinces, the United States, and Europe moved onto prairie land. They created ethnic settlement patterns that varied from one locality to another, and with their traditions and cultural traits contributed to the formation of the rural community.

The creation of shipping points every seven to ten miles along railway lines, for the railway companies' control over the supply and outward movement of grain, also led to the emergence of meeting points for local farmers. Small towns and villages sprung up around the elevators, providing services and trading for local people. These small localities became the 'heart' of hundreds of rural communities that covered the prairies from Manitoba to the skirts of the Rockies. Their survival depended on the capacity of farm families to respond to the increasing demands of external markets.

Early community life was hard. The farm production process was labour-intensive and the short prairie summers demanded concentrated labour for seeding and harvesting. In spite of these limitations, social life was intense. Women and men participated in a myriad of local and regional organizations, and social, religious, and leisure events.[6]

By the 1910s the rural community was very alive in the Canadian prairies and over the next fifty years it grew and developed. The Great Depression of the 1930s constitutes an unpleasant exception, seriously affecting the stability of most communities and the viability of a few of them. The lack of all-season roads and private transportation along with the relative absence of mass media contributed to the development of a stable community. Railways played an important role in the community. Farmers' shopping and business patterns evolved around the train schedule. When the train came into the community, they collected their mail and freight and delivered their crops. It was during that day that farmers shopped and did what other business they had in town, a habit that regulated community life. This life was facilitated by the existence of a simple division of labour where all farm families were involved in similar activities and faced common problems. The similarity of experience facilitated community exchanges and relationships.

Relative isolation, 'similarity of experience', and physical closeness contributed to create what has been called a community spirit. Each community was able to develop its own ideas about community and people's involvement in community life. This created a common set of ideas that provided community members with a particular identity and each community with a collective consciousness. Thus, a web of social relationships was formed within the local community. Old traditions, the environment, the demands and impositions of the state and external markets, and the everyday life of the frontier contributed to the formation of community identity and to a sense of place. Undoubtedly this situation contributed to the formation of social bonds and to the creation of networks of solidarity. Based on these bonds and networks a plethora of collective behaviours emerged: barn raising, help with seeding, harvesting, round-up and branding, as well as nursing, midwifery and child care, and food co-operatives, in which mutual support among the members of the community was central.

Community relations were not always harmonious, as some of the romantic literature expresses.[7] Internal conflicts and tensions were also part of everyday community life. Community strife led to the formation of communities divided over a variety of political, cultural and social issues. These lines of division created a myriad of social networks, each with its own interpretation of community life and in constant conflict with each other, sharing only the willingness to maintain the community. Many communities survived due to their capacity to control conflict.[8]

By the beginning of the 1950s most of the rural communities had achieved a degree of stability. This consolidation was short-lived however; the 1960s brought an avalanche of events that profoundly dislocated that stability. These events are interrelated and are the expression of a larger process of reorganization of Canadian society and economy. Modernization of the Canadian productive structure and of its state and civil society, as well as the new patterns of Canadian integration into international markets, have directly affected western agriculture and indirectly influenced the rural community and its everyday life.

One of these events has been the depopulation of the rural sector, a pattern that is common to all societies in a process of modernization. Rural out-migration has been a characteristic of rural prairie communities since they were settled; it has not been confined to the last two or three decades. During the recent period, the process of out-migration has acquired new impetus due to road improvements and easy access to private transportation. Large cities have attracted those seeking better salaries and easier access to basic services and leisure. A continuous rural-urban migration has affected the stability of rural communities by removing from the locality large numbers of young and single people and, to a lesser extent, people of retirement age. To the best of our knowledge there are no empirical studies analyzing the effects of this migratory process upon the rural community. It is possible, however, to speculate that out-migration often involves the more highly qualified people of the community, hindering the community's potential for social and economic progress.

The extent of the decline in the farm and rural population of Saskatchewan over the last twenty years can be seen in Table 3.1. Some of the farm population has moved to neighbouring small towns. Even with this movement, however, the rural non-farm population of the province has barely held its own. Population data for the four communities surveyed in our study show the same process of depopulation. The rural municipalities in which the farmers live have experienced a population decline of 22% in the last 13 years, with the largest rural decline around Naicam and Wishart. The towns of Stewart Valley and Naicam have shown a small population growth, but the rural municipalities around these towns have declined precipitously.

A second event affecting the normal life of the rural community has been the centralization of the goods and services infrastructure and associated changes in the transportation of goods. Centralization has meant a reduction in the infrastructure and number of community outlets in the rural areas,

Table 3.1 Population of rural Saskatchewan, farm and non-farm (population in thousands of people)

YEAR	RURAL POPULATION FARM	NON-FARM	TOTAL
1966	280	207	487
1971	233	202	436
1976	193	217	410
1981	180	225	405
1986	161	228	389

Source: Saskatchewan Bureau of Statistics, Economic Review 1989, Table 4. Based on data from the Census of Canada.

along with the concentration of the remainder in fewer urban localities. Much of the centralization has been decided by private and public institutions existing outside the communities. The process started during the 1960s, when lumberyards, machinery and fuel distributors, and retail stores began to close their doors in the small communities and expand their services in larger urban centres (Mitchell, 1975). Later on, during the 1970s, and especially in the last decade, provincial and federal government services such as schools, hospitals, and post offices followed the same road (Olsen and Brown, 1975; Baker, 1980). Perhaps one of the most important blows to the local community was the decision by agricultural and railway corporations, supported by the federal government, to close many grain elevators and railway lines (Hall Commission, 1977; Gallagher, 1983).

Centralization of goods and services has become a dramatic experience for some of the communities. At the end of the 1950s the community of Coderre had a considerable infrastructure of goods and services: two restaurants, two retail stores, a blacksmith shop, two garages, two lumberyards, a hotel, a hardware store, a doctor, a Catholic and a Protestant school, and a branch of the credit union. By 1987 most of this infrastructure had disappeared. A retail store, a hotel, only one garage, a school and the credit union were all that were left. The rail line was still operating, but in a serious state of disrepair. It is expected to be abandoned by the CPR, a decision which will mean the closure of the local elevators. The school also faces a possible partial closure. By 1987, enrolment had dropped 20% from its 1977 level and its status was uncertain. The local residents expected to lose the high school portion of the school to a larger centre, Gravelbourg, within a year or two because of the lack of enrolment. This pattern reproduces itself to a lesser degree in Stewart Valley and Wishart. Naicam, on the other hand, has become a regional pole for the centralization of the goods and services infrastructure, and it has grown at the expense of other communities. The consequences of this process of centralization on most rural communities are obvious. To the extent that centralization forces farmers to take their crops to or to buy farm and household products in, other localities, it destroys the economic structure of the village that acted as the nucleus of the community.

The process, however, has been resisted in varying degrees by the members of the communities. In several communities rail line abandonment committees sprang up to fight against federal government decisions. In cases such as Naicam and Coderre, local communities have been able to maintain that service. In other cases, the issue of rail line abandonment served as a catalyst for a movement for the survival of the community. In the cases of Wishart and Stewart Valley there is a strong awareness of the importance of the community, a phenomenon undoubtedly strengthened by the conflict over the rail line, and perhaps by the fact that these two communities lost the fight to retain the line. People in Stewart Valley express this awareness in a strong commitment to the local structure providing goods and services, such as the co-operative store. Local people buy most of their goods at the co-operative even though a much larger centre, Swift Current, is only a few minutes away. Wishart's people have also had a long history of economic and social co-operation, creating in the process an organization that is relatively unique: Wishart Emerald Bankend Corporation (WEBCO). This organization was created in 1974 by bringing together a large number of community organizations. Its main function is to organize and carry out all types of community development and leisure activities. It has had a central role in the life of the community during the last ten years.

A third type of event that has affected the life of prairie rural communities is the unstable situation of agriculture with its negative effect upon farm life, the backbone of the rural community. Prairie agriculture has been characterized by continuous instability. Commodity prices have been fluctuating, creating a recurring climate of insecurity among farmers. Relationships between farmers and the markets have been characterized by a pattern of unequal exchange. Farm commodity prices have not kept pace with farm input prices. Financial hardships and farm bankruptcies have been a recurring feature of the agricultural scene. Net farm income declined during the 1980s, pushing many farm families below a minimum standard of living. Land prices went up in a spiral of speculation and high interest rates. The picture is undoubtedly dramatic and, to some observers, hopeless.

There are several causes for this long-deteriorating state of agriculture and they lie mainly in socio-economic and political structures rather than in the 'unpleasantries of nature'. First among them is the integration of prairie farmers into international markets, where a large number of factors—such as the recent price war between the United States and the European Economic Community—create a permanent instability in commodity prices. Second, the farm and non-farm sectors have a biased relationship that supports industrial and commercial development to the detriment of farming. These trends—which integrate farmers to the markets through patterns of marginality—are related to the political mechanisms that organize markets and the participation of the different economic sectors in them. The inability of the farm movement to influence the state and its policies is another important factor in the lack of stability of farm life.

The deterioration of prairie agriculture has been accompanied by changes in the traditional patterns of family farm agriculture. A process of differentiation is transforming traditional family farming in two directions: the creation of larger, more heavily capitalized farms, and the persistence of small farms. This process of differentiation has been accompanied by increasing specialization, more intensive use of non-farm inputs (machinery, fertilizers, pesticides, etc.), and a greater need for capital, resulting in a stronger integration to the markets. The logic seems to be that in order to resolve the problems created by markets it is necessary to become more active in them. Companion trends include a greater reliance on rented land and some changes with regard to labour inputs. In many cases paid family labour seems to be displacing unpaid family labour, and an increasing number of farm family members are engaging in off-farm labour.

The survey of the four communities provides dramatic evidence supporting our argument about the farm crisis. More than half (53%) of the interviewed households had a 1986 net farm income of less than $15,000, an income that is obviously limited. Forty-four per cent of the respondents recognized their incapacity to satisfy some of the basic needs of the farm, and almost 20% their inability to satisfy important family needs. In order to cope with their detrimental situation many of these farm families have been forced to adopt a variety of survival strategies, such as off-farm labour (see Diaz and Gingrich, 1989). A growing body of evidence indicates that off-farm employment has become extensive in prairie farm communities. Using this data and data collected in 1975 for the same four communities, Smith (1987) found that the proportion of farm households involved in off-farm employment had risen from approximately 33% to 60%. Analyses of census data have also shown the considerable significance of off-farm income for the well-being of farm families (Bollman and Smith, 1987; Agriculture Canada, 1982). All of this suggests that the strategy of off-farm employment has become deeply imbedded in the structure of prairie farming.

It is obvious that these low levels of income directly and indirectly affect the life of the rural community. Limited purchasing power has some negative effects upon local businesses, because farmers will either restrict their total purchases or buy elsewhere. The level of stress among those who suffer financial pressures makes their participation in community organizations unstable and sometimes conflictual. In addition, the process of differentiation among farmers might destroy 'the similarity of experiences' that characterized the old community, with consequences that are unpredictable.

To summarize, rural communities seem to be at a critical stage. A large variety of structural forces are undoubtedly affecting their everyday life. Is it possible, then, to predict the destruction of the community? It seems to us that this prediction could be too hasty. There appear to be forces of resistance within some communities, forces providing new fire to the spirit of community life. It is still unclear how important and widespread these forms of resistance are, but their presence means that the future of the community has not been definitely decided. In addition, as we will see in the following section, certain forms of community life are still alive, although transformed.

Mutual Support and Participation in the Rural Community

Two factors offer us to a deeper understanding of the current situation of community life. The first is the existence of informal kinship and friendship networks for mutual support in the community. These networks are very much an expression of the 'community spirit' or of Gemeinschaft. A second factor illustrates the patterns of integration of the rural community: the participation of farm families in community organizations and events. As we will see, these two forms of collective life are still part of the community, although transformed.

Networks of Solidarity

As noted by a large number of community studies, networks of solidarity act as systems of exchange for goods and services that are important for the reproduction of both community households and the community as a whole. Our analysis of networks of mutual support in our survey concentrates on community contributions to the local farms. Potentially, these contributions could come from other community members unrelated to the farm family, other relatives living in the community, or from the children no longer resident in the family household. In other words, kinship and friendship are the forces operating behind these contributions. Various types of contributions could be involved, such as labour on the farm or in the farm household, gifts or transfers of land, transfers of machinery, and financial transfers.

Contributions to farm families for the operation of farms from other community members who are not relatives is a long-standing tradition among prairie farm people. Informal interviews in different communities indicated that these help patterns persist, although they may be substantially reduced, and their forms have changed. However, our survey data indicate a trend that is slightly different. No survey respondents identified non-relative community members as making any contribution to their farms. The only contributors identified by respondents were relatives of the farm family, who were typically parents, aunts and uncles, or siblings in the recipient farm household. In other words, the networks for mutual support seem to lie only in kinship, not friendship.

About two-fifths of the interviewed farm families received help from relatives within the community; for half of these, the contribution was crucial, perhaps making the difference between successful reproduction of the farm and failure, or at least a very tenuous existence. Given the extent of this phenomenon indicated by the data, it seems likely that virtually every farm household has received such help at some point in their cycle of reproduction. Although the subtler aspects of the helping patterns await further study, the survey did identify many characteristics of the helped farms. There was a definite tendency for all types of contributions from the community to be directed toward younger farm families and, by implication, beginning farms trying to establish themselves. The helping pattern also carried on to older, established farms. When the contribution consisted of unpaid labour only, it tended to be directed towards farms with low or negative 1986 net farm income. If the contribution included or was exclusively capital (land or financial contributions), it tended to go to farms with higher 1986 net farm income. Nevertheless, since farms in all income categories received labour and capital assistance, the phenomenon does not appear to be simply a way of salvaging farm families that are 'on the ropes'. It is obviously evidence that the networks of solidarity in the rural community continue to be important.[9]

Community Participation

In the four Saskatchewan communities studied, local people appear to participate quite considerably in community activities. Of the households surveyed, just under 30% said that they contribute to community decisions. In general, these are also the people who are most active in the community, and one can speculate that these people could be considered to be the community leaders. Another half said they were active in the community, but did not contribute to community decisions. On the other hand, a fifth of the respondents considered themselves nonparticipants in community affairs. Of the latter, some were retired and no longer active in the community. Other households clearly did not participate in any of the activities and organizations in the local community. Of these, some had ties to other communities, and while they did not participate in local activities, they often did participate elsewhere.

The variety of organizations active at the local level is considerable. The following four types of organizations were frequently mentioned by respondents.

1. Churches and church-related organizations are important in the communities studied. Over a third of respondents attended church weekly, just under a third attended one to three times a month, with another third not attending church at all. Even of the latter group, a considerable number attended some church-related activities at some times during the year. Historically, the church often provided a focal point for community activities, and

this process continues to be of considerable importance for some communities. Those who attend church regularly are also among the more active participants in community organizations and events. When asked what organizations were important for the future of the community, considerable numbers rated the church as the most important.

2. Organizations, clubs and boards concerned with recreational and sporting activities were also important in community life. More respondents pointed to recreational facilities and boards than to any other type of activities, as the organizations that were most important for the future of the community. The feeling of many respondents was that these groups are important for planning community activities and keeping the community together. The level of participation in these organizations was certainly considerable. In addition, most households participated in many of these types of events over the course of the year. It may be that recreational and sporting activities are becoming a more important basis for community organization, perhaps replacing some of the functions formerly organized around the church.

3. Some farmers were heavily involved in boards or councils related to administration of local government or business, among them the formal municipal or town councils or the school board. Some respondents, although only a few in the four communities, were members of political parties. Other organizations of this sort relate more to the business sector, concerned with operation of the local co-operative or credit union. Some of these boards overlap with recreational and sporting activities. For example, there are recreational boards, boards to operate the skating or curling rink, etc. In Wishart, WEBCO is an umbrella economic and social development board which is involved in or co-ordinates the activities of many of the other organizations in the community.

4. Farm-related organizations also appear to be important for considerable numbers of households. Among these the Wheat Pool and United Grain Growers were the most important, with a number of households also participating in 4-H Clubs. The National Farmers Union does not appear to be an important organization in the communities studied. In spite of continued participation in these groups, respondents did not consider them of extreme importance for the life of the community.

People also participated in a wide variety of other organizations. Among those mentioned more than once in the communities were the Lions Club, the Canadian Legion, art or music groups, horticultural societies, etc.

Going out to bars or movies was a quite limited set of activities for the farm households in these communities. Most had not participated in these activities over the past month, and very few participated more than once. Going out to a restaurant was reported by considerably more. It is likely that the restaurants were not for the most part in the community, since there are few, if any, restaurants in these centres. In contrast, there was much more frequent attendance at recreational and sporting events, and at church.

Visiting in homes of friends or entertaining friends and relatives was a very common activity, with considerable numbers of respondents indicating visits more frequently than weekly. The community ties and the people were also the most common reasons given for what was most liked about the community. The respondents who entertained or visited friends and relatives frequently were also among the most active in the local community. Further, these same respondents tended to have a larger percentage of their close friends in the local community.

Those who had close friends or relatives in other communities did not seem so closely tied in to the local organizations and activities. Some of these latter households also do much of their business in other communities. In this case, whether the lack of close friends locally leads to a lack of local participation, or whether the direction of causation goes the other way is not clear. In addition, when asked what they liked least about the community, some respondents cited reasons such as cliques, intolerance, pushiness, and the lack of co-operation and community spirit. One other negative feature of rural community found in the study was that just over sixty per cent of the respondents indicated that stress in their life had increased over the last five years. If this is coupled with many respondents' beliefs that there are insufficient services in the community, and some respondents' opinion that there is a lack of community spirit and co-operation, it appears that members of a considerable number of farm households are discouraged and do not see the future as positive.

The emerging picture of the rural community is of a set of networks of friends and relatives who visit each other regularly, with many of the members of these networks being quite active in the local community. Then there is another set of residents who are excluded from these community ties either by choice or by intolerance. These latter residents are either more tied in to other centres, outside the area where they live, or participate little in any community.

The level of participation in the community appeared to have little relationship to age. On those farms where the respondents considered themselves to be among those who participate in decision-making within the community, the husband tended to be a little older than average. However, this difference was not all that marked. As well, some of the older farmers were essentially retired and no longer participated in the community.

The members of farm households that showed the greatest participation in the community tended to be among the more successful farmers, in terms of farm income and farm size. While many of the farmers having lower incomes do participate in community affairs, those whose farm incomes are greater are more likely to be members of organizations and also to participate in the various community events. Those who are more active also own and rent more land.

Since off-farm jobs have become essential to the survival of many farms, it might be thought that those who work at off-farm jobs might not have the time or energy to participate in community events. Such does not seem to be the case. Those households where neither spouse holds an off-farm job are less involved with community organizations and events than are those farms where one or both spouses have off-farm jobs. However, for those farms where at least one spouse has an off-farm job, those who are least dependent on off-farm employment are more likely to be involved in organizations and events than those who are more dependent on off-farm employment. The picture that emerges is that those farms where neither spouse has off-farm employment are the farms with the lowest level of involvement in the community. Those who have off-farm jobs are more involved in a range of community activities, but in some cases the off-farm employment may involve so much time and effort that it cuts into community involvement.

In conclusion, there appears to be a group of community decision-makers or community leaders who visit each other, are active in a variety of community activities, and are often among the more successful farmers. It is likely that these are the people who help to determine the future direction of the community. At the same time, some of the smaller and less successful farmers appear to be left out of the community. The image of a set of common interests and common experiences for all community members may be flawed. In at least some of the rural communities, there appear to be serious divisions within the community, both with respect to decisions concerning agriculture, and with respect to social and cultural activities, and the future direction of the community.

Conclusion

The discussion of the survey data in the last section of this paper shows certain patterns that are a 'bittersweet' mixture. Solidarity networks are still part of the community and that massive participation is still part of community life, patterns that sustain the picture of a rural community that is still alive.

However, there are some disturbing peculiarities in these patterns. One of them is the absence of friendship in the constitution of the networks for mutual support, networks that have always been considered part of the tradition of the prairie rural community. Help patterns persist in the community, but they are restricted to kinship. Most of the help for farmers comes from members of the nuclear family and from those who are part of the extended family and still live in the community. To this extent, the data seem to suggest that friendship is no longer a vital element in the organization of mechanisms of solidarity. If this is true, then there is a certain degree of dislocation of the everyday life of the traditional rural community, in which friendship was important. Is this an expression of a process in which the individualism of 'community as commodity' is becoming more important than the 'community as communion'? The data are too general to make a valid prediction, but the survey is methodologically solid enough for the development of hypotheses on this important issue.

The dimension of participation also presents some interesting patterns. Based on the data, participation is still alive in the rural community, with an increasing importance on sporting organizations, events, and activities. What is disturbing, however, is the fact that participation seems to be taking place mainly among 'successful farmers', those who generate the larger incomes and control the larger tracts of land. Marginal farmers, those with small farms and reduced incomes, seem to have a considerable lower degree of participation.

If this pattern is valid, then processes of class differentiation are forming in the life of the community. Those who have been able to succeed tend to play a major role in the community life and its power structures; meanwhile, those who lose in the frantic 'race to success' are being left out of community life. The dangers of this process for community life are obvious. To the extent that class distinctions are developed and incorporated into the everyday life of the community and its common sense, fractures can be expected to emerge, shattering the unity of the community.

Certainly, the survey data do not support the idea of an immediate destruction of the community. On the contrary, they indicate that the rural community is still alive, but with some dislocations of what has been considered the traditional patterns of the rural community on the prairies. Are these dislocations a sign of the impending destruction and disappearance of the rural community? Or are they a sign of a new type of community that in its forms and contents will be different from the traditional community? It is too early to make any prediction one way or another. What is clear, however, is that we need to carry out more research and develop a more solid sociological imagination in order to forecast the fate of the rural community in the next century.

Notes

[1]The data used in this chapter derive from a research project carried out under the auspices of the Canadian Plains Research Centre, the Department of Sociology and Social Studies, the Department of Political Science, and the Sample Survey and Data Bank Unit, all of the University of Regina. We gratefully acknowledge the assistance of our colleagues in those agencies, especially the important contribution from R.M. Stirling. The research was funded by the Social Sciences and Humanities Research Council of Canada.

[2]The formal survey had two parts. The first consisted of interviews with 304 families and dealt with a broad range of topics about farm, household and community relations. For the first part, total enumerations were done in three of the four communities, while a 50% sample was randomly drawn for the fourth community. The second part involved a mail-back questionnaire concerning the operation of the

farm, and community-use patterns. This was sent to all farm households in each community. Most of data presented here derives from a group of 128 persons who answered both the interview and questionnaire. Although the data are representative of the four communities and they are broadly representative of the region, we have made no attempt to estimate population parameters, or to treat the data as a basis for testing the statistical significance of relationships between variables. We think that the summary descriptions presented here reflect the broad trends to be found in prairie farming today.

[3]For a good and straightforward review of the concept of community and its applicability to different Canadian cases see Hale, 1990: 106-36. A more detailed analysis is found in Bell and Newby, 1971.

[4]There are some variations in this new approach. See, among others, Cox, 1981, Bell and Newby, 1976, and Jackson, 1980.

[5]For an historical account of this process see Fowke, 1957, and Conway, 1983.

[6]For a detailed account of the early rural community see Voisey, 1988.

[7]For an example, see Boyd, 1938. This emphasis is also found in certain theoretical analyses, such as in Redfield, 1947.

[8]For examples of forms of co-operation in the larger context of interfarm competition and dissent, see Friesen, 1987, and Voisey, 1988.

[9]For a more detailed analysis see Diaz and Gingrich, 1989: 16-24.

CHAPTER FOUR

MODERNIZATION: TECHNOLOGY AND RURAL INDUSTRIES AND POPULATIONS

BILL REIMER

In most cases, 'modernization' refers to the changes which occur as a society moves from a traditional form of organization to a modern one. This includes a transformation from the production of food for self-sufficiency to its production for sale on the market (Abell, 1966). It includes the change in communities from relatively self-contained units, to those which are integrated with and dependent on broader social organizations through trade, communication, and power relationships (Bowles, 1982). Modernization also includes the use of modern technology for economic production (Smucker, 1980). It is this latter characteristic on which we will focus.

Considerable discussion has taken place regarding the role of technology as a cause of change. Those who argue that technological development has been a primary causal factor in social change have been criticized by those who give it an important role, but neither a primary nor a causal one (Rosenberg, 1982). Others argue that the issue of technology has taken on an ideological dimension. Rather than remain a description of different tools and techniques used for production, they suggest that the concept is used for political purposes, and carries with it the suggestion that certain types of technology

Bill Reimer is an Associate Professor at Concordia University. The author would like to thank Valerie Morrison for her help with the background research, and Concordia University for their financial assistance.

are better or more 'advanced' than others. Technology, then, takes on the implication that larger, more complex, and more powerful technologies are to be preferred over smaller, simpler, and less powerful ones. In turn, those societies or groups of people who do not adopt the newer technologies are considered 'resistant' or 'backward' in their development (Hedley, 1976).

In order to avoid a detailed discussion of these debates, we will interpret technology in a highly descriptive manner, as the tools and knowledge that are used to produce goods and services for a society. This can include the wooden plough of early Quebec agriculture, the knowledge and techniques of the gold panner, the chain saw of the logger, the expertise of the geneticist, and the computer used in a hydroelectric generating station. These tools and techniques have had wide-ranging and profound effects on society.

We will not assume that technology influences social organization without in turn being affected by it. New technologies are imagined, developed, produced, and used within particular social contexts. These social contexts influence the direction of further developments. The technology to develop safer cars is well known, but few manufacturers have integrated them into their products, choosing instead to make them accelerate faster. Solar energy offers a solution to many of the problems associated with fossil fuels, yet relatively few financial resources are dedicated to developing this source of power. Enormous sums are spent on the development and production of arms, yet little is spent on health or pollution control. Few would argue that in each of these examples it is technology alone that drives the decisions.

Technological changes will therefore be discussed with a recognition that they are an integral part of the social organization of any society. Their importance derives not only from their existence but, in addition, from *how* they are used, and *by whom*.

In order to limit the discussion of technological changes, we have selected those which occur in the major economic sectors touching rural Canada. Most are related to the primary or resource industries: agriculture, mining and petroleum, forestry, and fishing. Since the communications industry has played an important part in changing rural Canada, it is included as well.

Major Technological Changes in the Rural Context

Agriculture

The technology of agricultural production in Canada has undergone major changes over the last hundred years. New inventions have transformed how we grow, harvest, store, transport, and market these agricultural products and in the process they have been a major part of the reorganization of the rural scene.

Many of these changes have been related to the development of new forms of power. At the time of Confederation, agriculture was dependent on human or animal labour for the heavy work of farming. Water and wind power were used to some extent, but they were largely limited to the processing of farm products, not for production. Irrigation was limited to sluices and ditches. It was only with the expansion of steam power, the internal combustion engine, and electricity, that power became more adaptable and major changes in the production of goods occurred.

Steam tractors became available in Canada at the turn of this century. Heavy and awkward, they were quickly supplanted by the internal combustion engine. By 1910 they had become obsolete. During the 1920s, western Canada provided the world's largest tractor market as the internal combustion engine became the most widely used power source for agriculture and, eventually, for personal and public transportation (Denison, 1949).

The electrification of rural Canada occurred at the same time as the expanded use of the internal combustion engine. Except for Ontario, which developed a farm electrification program in 1921, Canadian farms were relatively late in receiving electricity. By the mid 1950s, only 13% of Saskatchewan farms and 22% of Alberta farms had electricity (MacFarlane, 1972: 100-1).

The availability of internal combustion tractors and electricity were not equally advantageous for all types of farms. The expense of purchasing and maintaining these power supplies was such that only the larger farms were able to make the investment pay off by frequent use. Small family farms were disadvantaged since they could not do without the new power sources, but were unable to use it to economically prosperous ends (Friedland *et al.*, 1981).

The new power supplies also spawned extensive development of the agricultural implement industry. The new, more powerful tractors required machinery which could withstand the rigours of acceleration and high speed. This led to the redesigning of old equipment (ploughs, cultivators, threshing machines, water pumps), and the invention of new devices (the power train, pneumatic tires, hydraulic lifting equipment, and refrigerators) (Barber, 1971: 37-42).

Changes in the technology for the transportation and storage of agricultural products were instrumental in the reorganization of the grain and dairy industries. Trains and trucks made fast and easy transportation possible, and the design and construction of large and efficient elevators for grain facilitated the centralization of storage and the expansion of markets. The expansion of the pasteurization process and the development of refrigeration made it possible for dairy products to be sold far from the farm. Both of these technological developments made possible the increased centralization of the industry and helped move control out of the hands of the farmers (Mitchell, 1975).

The first steps toward crop hybridization were taken at the turn of this century. Hard or 'winter' wheats were brought to North America from Russia in the early 1900s; oats were imported from Uruguay in 1927 for their rust-resistant qualities; and 4000 varieties of soybeans were imported from Korea, Japan, and China between 1900 and 1930. By the late 1930s, the selection of special varieties gave way to hybridization: the search for specific genetic traits in plants that could be used for cross-breeding purposes. The results were a major improvement in crop yields, higher resistance to specific diseases, and better adaptation to Canadian climatic conditions (Kloppenburg, 1988: 78).

More recently, the use of biotechnology expanded to include the control of both plant and animal production. Hormone injections to enhance milk production, artificial insemination, embryo transfer, and gene manipulation are all used to increase production or control disease. Although Canada is not a leader in the development of this type of technology, we have been major exploiters of it for grain, dairy, and beef production.

Mining and Petroleum

New developments in mining technology have played a major role in shifting the industry from a labour-intensive to a capital-intensive one. During the early period of Canadian mining, human labour was used to extract the ore, usually from surface deposits. As the work moved underground, and deposits became lower grade, increased mechanization was required. Concurrent with this shift in the use of machines was an increase in the proportion of technicians in the labour force over those who operated as manual labourers (Patching, 1988). The cost of mechanization favoured the larger mining and petroleum companies for the same reasons that large farmers had the advantage in agriculture.

Technological developments in the processing of minerals also play a part in their social organization. The development of electricity-based techniques for the refining of aluminum, nickel, and other minerals gave considerable advantage to regions where there was an abundant supply of hydro power. This is particularly the case for Quebec, Ontario, and BC, where the availability of hydroelectric power often meant that raw materials were imported for initial processing.

Since the discovery and processing of minerals requires access to remote areas, the development of technology related to transportation has been a major component in the industry. Both the mining and petroleum industries depend on rail, road, and water transportation in addition to the pipelines used for the movement of oil. The remoteness of mineral sites also stimulated the development of housing and community organization technology to accommodate the large number of isolated and temporary communities.

Forestry

Like agriculture, the forestry industry has changed significantly as power sources moved from animals to the internal combustion engine. Heavier equipment gave easier access to more extensive terrain, the transportation of logs became easier, and the production of lumber or pulp became less dependent on water power for driving the mills. Technological developments in the cutting, transportation, and processing of logs permitted the industry to move toward larger (and fewer) mills, with a greater reliance on trucks.

The capital investment necessary to purchase the new machinery contributed to the concentration of the forestry industry. Pulp mills and sawmills have become larger, requiring a more extensive system of transportation. In many parts of the country the use of tree harvesters, shears, and mechanical felling machines has mechanized the felling of trees. Small operators are largely limited to the operation of trucks and small, relatively isolated sawmills, often working for larger companies on a contract basis (Marchak, 1983).

Fishing

Technological developments have had their greatest impact on the coastal fishing industry as opposed to inland fisheries. Just after the turn of the century, the introduction of steam-driven trawlers began to displace the traditional schooners. This trend to larger vessels continued and the development of better methods of refrigeration, transportation, and communication permitted the establishment of a year-round fleet of ships capable of operating for long periods of time without coming into port.

Changes in the technology of catching fish were also important factors for the social organization of the industry. The traditional methods using small boats operating from land required the existence of many small communities scattered throughout the coastal regions. As boats became larger and more powerful, proximity to a community was not as crucial since they could operate for longer periods at sea, and were able to reach fish processing plants at greater distances. The use of sonar and better communication techniques improved the efficiency of the catch to the point where overfishing has become a problem. The costs associated with the new technologies (for both catching and processing the fish) have worked against small independent producers and created considerable conflict between them and the larger operators. Only those regions such as British Columbia where co-operatives and unions are strong, have maintained a number of relatively independent operators (Gough, 1988).

Transportation and Communication

The remoteness of rural Canada has meant that technological developments in transportation and communication have affected most rural-based industries, and particularly the industrial sectors outlined above.

In the latter part of the nineteenth century, land-based transportation in ada was dominated by the railway. It could operate in winter and was far ...e flexible than water transport by river and canal, even though its capital costs were enormous. The train is still extensively used for the movement of bulk items, but its prominence as a means of transportation has been declining since the advent of automobiles and trucks. The development of heavy equipment facilitated extensive road building in Canada during the 1920s, and the improvements in road surfacing made the attraction of highway transport even greater.

Communication technology in Canada underwent a major improvement with the invention of the telephone in 1876. Up to that time, the electric telegraph (associated with the railway) was the major form of rapid communication. By 1920, coast-to-coast telephone transmission was possible. Communication to the more remote regions of Canada depended on radio and other forms of wireless transmission until the launching of the Anik series of communications satellites beginning in 1972. This newest technology promised easy communication for remote communities, a promise as yet far from fulfilled. Access to the system is controlled by a consortium of private companies, resulting in a system which is expensive for small communities to use, and oriented to the transmission of television signals from southern Canada and the USA rather than inter-community communication in rural Canada (Melody, 1988).

Social Changes Associated with Technology

To reflect the major areas of rural life which have felt the impact of new technologies, let us focus on four general areas: the labour force, economic control, the demographic structure, and community life.

The Labour Force

In general, technological developments have meant that rurally based industries have become more capital-intensive and less dependent on labour, with far-reaching consequences.

The best example of this process can be found in agricultural production. From 1951 to 1985 the value of machinery and equipment per farm rose from \$2,658 to \$54,793[1] in Canada. At the same time, the value of agricultural products sold per farm increased from \$2,794 to \$70,920,[2] the number of farms dropped from 623,000 to 293,000, and the average size of farms increased from 113 hectares to 207 hectares. Improved machinery, increased use of petrochemicals, biotechnology, and more extensive irrigation has made this possible.

The social impact of these changes on rural Canada has been enormous. With the dramatic drop in the number of farms and farm labour, the population of rural Canada has drastically declined and the labour force has shifted from a basis in agriculture to the service, manufacturing, and trade industries.

The increased use of technology has also meant that the organization of farming at the level of the household has changed. Machinery, fertilizers, specialty seeds, and production controls have required large capital expenditures. Only the larger farming operations have been able to take advantage of these new developments, and often the organization of their operation has shifted from that of a family farm to that of a business. This not only affects how the farm is represented to banks, government agencies, and supply or marketing companies, it has also affected the relationships between family members. A somewhat artificial separation of household and farm expenses is created, family members become employees, and the farm becomes viewed as a financial asset.

The investments required for equipment and farm inputs, and the demands of food processing companies have created pressure toward the specialization of farm products. A potato harvester, for example, is sufficiently expensive that its purchase must establish a commitment to produce potatoes over many years to make the investment pay off. Similar constraints operate for the purchase of milking equipment, combines, and poultry barns. The ensuing specialization has made farmers even more vulnerable to changes in market conditions (Mitchell, 1975).

Increases in mechanization also have a direct effect on the farm household. Rather than reduce the amount of labour input by household members, mechanization increases it in the long run (Reimer, 1984). The cost of new equipment places heavy demands on the household to pay the debt and to keep the machinery in use. To cope with these demands, women and children have been brought into the labour market, if not to help run the farm, then to seek employment elsewhere.

As the cost of purchases has increased, off-farm work has become an important source of income. This may include work on a neighbour's farm by household members, or work outside agriculture. These jobs are often used to supplement the financial demands of the farm (Bollman and Smith, 1988).

From the point of view of non-agricultural industries, the presence of a large number of farm persons who are available for employment creates a 'reserve labour market' (Connelly and MacDonald, 1983). Since farm households are considerably flexible in respect to the number of people they can support, they sustain their members in lean periods and supply labour during periods of expansion. This provides a source of short-term workers which local industry is able to use to keep wages low.

The patterns of relationship between agricultural technology and the labour force are repeated with some modifications for other rural industries. The fishing industry is perhaps the most similar since it has depended to a great extent on established communities. Mining and petroleum communities, on the other hand, have often experienced boom and bust periods since they are highly dependent on external markets and the availability of a non-renewable resource. As a result, they are more often treated as temporary establishments and a decline in labour demand is less threatening to long-established social relationships. Communities based on forestry are more likely to be mixed. Some of these communities are established mill towns. As the mills become more capital-intensive, the labour force tends to divide into manual workers and technicians, with a relatively low proportion of white-collar workers. A high level of unemployment is normal (Marchak, 1983: 115).

Control of Industry

The high costs associated with the mechanization of rural industries has meant that their control has moved to urban centres. This process has taken place through the requirement for capital, the demand for manufactured goods, and the increased dependence on external markets.

Mechanization requires considerable capital. Tractors, milking machines, fertilizer, and refrigerators all cost money, as do drill rigs, pulp mills, ocean-going boats, and canneries. In most cases, there is not sufficient capital in rural regions to pay for the new machines, so the farmer, miners, loggers, and fishers must seek it elsewhere. The usual sources are banks, corporations, or private capitalists, often with the aid of federal or provincial government backing. For farmers this may result in considerable debts to urban-based business, or exclusive contracts with companies that provide them with seed, support for machines, and the purchase of their products.

The manufacture of most farm machinery is also urban-based. The major Canadian manufacturers, originally located in southern Ontario, have since been eclipsed by multinational firms. The basis of control and manufacture for other technology used in rural areas shows a similar pattern. Most of it is imported from outside the rural areas, with only a small part originating in Canada (Barber, 1971: 387). This contributes to the pattern of net outflow of capital from rural areas, a lack of manufacturing jobs, and a general loss of economic control.

Technological development has also increased the commercialization of rural industries (Barber, 1971: 443f), and the market control has shifted away from the rural context. Most agricultural products are produced for urban dwellers. The centralization of marketing has meant that most of the goods produced are processed and packaged in larger urban centres. In this situation even farmers have had to buy much of their food from local supermarkets: food grown in rural areas is shipped to urban enterprises for processing and packing, then returned to rural areas for sale in stores owned by urban-based corporations. In addition, the regulations for this system are often under the control of government departments and officers based in urban centres.

The mining, petroleum, and forestry industries vary from this pattern only insofar as they are often urban-based to begin with. In most instances the search for mineral resources and the management of forest regions is initiated by urban corporations. The capital investment required for equipment and expertise has become so great that urban corporations are the only ones able to initiate and maintain such projects (Hayter, 1987).

One of the consequences of this shift in sources of capital is that there is a separation of large and small enterprises along urban and rural lines. The large industries tend to be controlled by urban-based interests. They have the capital base to pay for equipment, the contacts to gain access to the resources, and the economic resources to absorb variations in the market. Enterprises based in the rural areas tend to be smaller. This is particularly the case for the agriculture, forestry, and fishing industries. In addition, these smaller businesses are often more at risk than the larger ones. Through a system of contracts, for example, food processing companies, pulp mills, and fish canneries are able to lay off suppliers during lean periods, and rehire them when the market improves. This contributes to significant job instability in rural areas.

Demographic Structure

Rural depopulation has been one of the most widespread and influential trends since the turn of this century. As shown in Table 4.1, it continued throughout Canada until the 1970s, with only a slight indication of moderation or reversal during the last 20 years.

Table 4.1 Per cent of urban population, Canada, 1871 to 1986

YEAR	1871	1881	1891	1901	1911	1921	1931	1941	1951	1961	1971	1981	1986
PER CENT URBAN	18.3	23.3	29.8	34.9	41.8	47.4	52.5	55.7	62.4	69.7	76.1	75.8	76.5

Source: Censuses of Canada, 1871-1986.

The mechanization and rationalization of agricultural production has had an important role to play in this trend. As technological innovations made it possible to produce the same or even greater amounts of materials with the same labour, the need for large families declined, farms became larger to accommodate the larger machinery, and the farming of marginal land decreased. Many people, especially the young, left the rural areas to seek jobs, training, and an easier life in urban centres, leaving an older and smaller population.

Rural depopulation, in turn, affected the viability of the many smaller service centres throughout the country. Many of the smallest towns were bypassed as new roads and automobiles made it easier for people to travel greater distances. In order to survive, those merchants who were left were often required to enter into franchise arrangements with urban-based suppliers, resulting in a decrease in local control, and the standardization of merchandise. The standards were frequently established on national or provincial market criteria, resulting in the blurring of rural and urban distinctions, or the loss of local adaptations.

In recent years there is some indication that the rural depopulation trend is reversing. This is especially evident in those areas near the larger urban centres. More efficient transportation has made it possible for commuters to live farther from their place of work. Some people choose this option in order to obtain the benefits of rural living such as more green space and lower housing costs. Business enterprises have also been attracted to rural areas since they offer cheaper taxes, land, and labour costs. Improvements in communication technology have made this option possible. If these trends become widespread, they are likely to change the character of rural Canada even further, shifting it from its resource base to one based on service and possibly light manufacturing industries (Hodge and Qadeer, 1983).

Community Life

Technological developments have had both direct and indirect effects on many aspects of rural community life, among them social services, communication, recreation and leisure, and the quality of life.

The demographic changes related to technology have significantly affected the provision of social services to rural communities. With declining population, government agencies have moved to consolidate and rationalize their offices and organizations. Easier transportation has made the consolidation of education possible. There has been a massive increase in the number of children who are bussed to regional schools rather than sent to a school in their own community. This has meant not only that they are exposed to a more standard curriculum, but that they are introduced to contacts outside their local community, making eventual out-migration easier (Selby, 1977).

Technological developments in health care have improved the life expectancy of most members of society. Those living in a rural context have shared these benefits to the extent that they are able to make use of the general developments in transportation and communication. Since most health services are concentrated in the larger urban centres, travel to and from these centres is necessary for people to take advantage of them.

As with education and health care, most other government services are concentrated in regional urban centres. There is similar concentration of private service businesses in these centres. Consequently developments in transportation technology have become extremely important for rural citizens. Most of them are highly dependent on the automobile and its associated infrastructure of roads, fuels, and repair parts. The availability of transportation options has made possible the pattern of regional service centres which have been encouraged by government policy (Savoie, 1986).

Changes in the technology of communication have added to these trends. Radio, telephones, television, and newspapers have made rural Canada less and less isolated. Most of the broadcasting centres for these media are urban-based. As a result, the media have reflected urban values, urban problems, and urban locations. When communicated to rural areas, the media orient rural people to urban values and concerns, contributing to a blurring of differences between the two contexts, higher levels of mobility, and in some cases social conflict between urban- and rural-based values.

Recreation and leisure activities in rural Canada have also been influenced by changes in technology. As in an urban context, television, videos, citizens' band radios (CBs), home computers, and cars have become major elements of leisure activities. The impact of these on the more traditional recreational activities of rural people has not been well documented, but there can be little doubt that they have changed the way in which people spend their leisure time.

Technological developments have changed the quality of rural living in many less obvious but no less significant ways. The variety of goods and services available has increased, if not in one's immediate community, at least in the regional centre. At the same time, regional and community differences in values and life style have been reduced as consumer goods have become standardized, and markets have expanded. New technologies have made it much easier to relate to those outside of the local community, but they have also weakened the social support network of that community. They have made possible increases in production that allow us to feed and clothe more people with less work, but they have done so at the expense of many benefits of the rural environment.

Implications for the Future

Technological developments will clearly continue to play an important role in rural Canada. In offering some tentative suggestions regarding possible characteristics of that role, we emphasize that there is considerable interaction between these developments and the social context in which they are used.

In spite of the massive depopulation of rural Canada, we find that there is significant persistence of small rural towns and villages (Hodge and Qadeer, 1983). The reasons for this persistence are complex, but according to Hodge and Qadeer they include some of the technological developments that have made depopulation possible: better roads, telephone service, television, and electrical power (1983: 216).

Technology, therefore, can make it possible for rural communities to work together at the same time that it contributes to their diminution. The shape and organization of these communities will change. For example, the availability of a road network has made it possible for people to live in one small community, shop in another, and work in a third. Thus, these communities, although small, combine a number of specific functions into a large network.

The survival of rural communities and the rural population depends on the availability of employment. Once again, we find that although technology has played a part in reducing the number of jobs, it will also make possible the development of community networks with a mix of industry types. The availability of a wide variety of jobs, from resource extraction to manufacturing and service, is an important key to economic stability in the face of markets which are beyond local control. With easy transportation and efficient communication, access to this variety may be possible.

There is also some indication that rural communities are now attractive to manufacturing industries because of their low costs and cheap labour. Easy transportation and communication contribute to this attractiveness, since they make physical proximity no longer essential. This makes possible some growth in the rural population and the maintenance of community vitality.

With all of these changes, it is clear that the centres of power will remain urban-based. For this reason, the development of community power will be extremely important. Once again, the technology which has contributed to the blurring of regional and community differences, might also be used to develop and maintain the social interaction so important to local power (Flora, 1988). The particular conditions which make this possible are not all identified, but it is clear that the necessary conditions of interaction, co-operation, and co-ordination of activity can all be enhanced by the suitable use of technology.

Notes

[1]In constant dollars using the farm input price index, this is equivalent to a rise from $2,658 to $11,780.

[2]In constant dollars using the farm price index, this is equivalent to a rise from $2,794 to $18,876.

CHAPTER FIVE

SINGLE-INDUSTRY RESOURCE COMMUNITIES IN CANADA'S NORTH

ROY T. BOWLES

The industries which extract or produce natural resources have always been and will continue to be important in the Canadian economy. These industries include farming and fishing (discussed in other chapters), and forestry, mining, petroleum, and hydroelectric power. Each resource community has an economic base, and the organization of activities in the economic sector has important influences on community patterns and on social life. Each economic enterprise requires workers, and these workers and their families must have a place to live—a place where homes can be located, where the goods and services used in everyday life can be acquired, and where social life in its many forms can take place.

In what sense are resource communities 'rural'? Most are larger than the one-thousand-population Census Canada threshold for 'urban'. Most of the literature concerned with planning treats them as urban places. Where discussions of rural phenomena focus on agriculture, resource communities get no attention because they have little agricultural presence or history. However, much recent social science work shifts attention from individual communities to larger regions and the sets of communities within them. The fundamental distinction is between the 'metropolitan area', where the patterns

Roy Bowles is Professor and Head of the Department of Sociology at Trent University.

of urbanization characteristic of large cities are predominant, and the 'nonmetropolitan area', which contains no major city and which is far enough from major cities that daily commuting is not practical. Most resource communities are 'rural' in the sense that they are located in nonmetropolitan regions. As a group, they are important parts of the settlement system in nonmetropolitan areas of Canada.

Canada has a very large land mass but a relatively small population, and the population is highly concentrated. The phrase 'the ecumene' is used to refer to 'the area of Canada that supports a large population and an integrated transportation system' (Matthews and Morrow, 1985: 9-10). All large Canadian cities, most Canadian manufacturing, the vast majority of the Canadian population, and most Canadian agriculture are located in the relatively small portion of Canadian land where settlement is continuous across the landscape. Most resource communities are located outside the zones of concentrated settlement. They frequently appear as social islands connected by long threads of transportation and communication to other islands and to metropolitan centres. Thus they exist within a framework of *intermittent* settlement rather than a framework of continuous settlement.

This chapter is concerned with communities that provide homes and a home base for workers involved in logging, sawmilling, pulp and paper manufacturing, mining, mineral processing, oil drilling, and hydroelectric production. To cover such a broad set of communities requires some additional limitations. Most of the discussion will focus on communities established around a single industry (or related set of industries) and on communities which are outside the areas of concentrated settlement. More examples are drawn from mining than from other industries, but the principles discussed apply to various types of resource communities.

Two Examples of Resource Communities

Espanola, Ontario (Goltz, 1974; Morrison, 1989) is a pulp and paper town located 72 km west of Sudbury. In 1899 the Spanish River Pulp and Paper Company received a pulpwood concession from the Province of Ontario and agreed to build a pulp mill. By 1901 the mill was under construction and in 1903 the first houses in the company townsite were built. The first phase of life as a company town lasted from 1903 to 1928. Industrially, this phase was characterized by expansion, including the addition of a paper mill. Economically it was characterized by short-term fluctuations within an overall pattern of prosperity. The organized town in which the Company built houses, streets and utilities and within which it provided services grew to house those workers whose skills were in high demand. At the same time an unorganized fringe development grew to house most of the unskilled workers. Espanola was a new community and represented the first major Eurocanadian settlement in the vicinity. Merritt Township (the location of Espanola) had a population of 79 in 1901 and in 1921 a population of 2,750, most of whom were located in the townsite and fringe development.

In December of 1929 Abitibi Power and Paper Company, which had become the owner in 1928, closed the mill, and only minimal maintenance work occurred until 1946. Population remained in the area, but at one point 85% of the 1,925 residents were receiving government relief. During World War II the mill buildings were fenced and used as a prisoner-of-war camp, with prisoners and their guards adding about two thousand people to the community.

Using data available at various dates between 1930 and 1958, Goltz estimates that from 30% to 40% of the population near the mill were in the well-serviced company town, while most of the remainder were in the unplanned and poorly-serviced fringe. Thus, it would be a mistake to judge quality of community life associated with resource development on the basis of the quality of services available in those parts of settlements managed by companies.

After modernization, the mill was reopened in 1946 under the ownership of the Kalamazoo Vegetable Parchment Company. During this second company-town phase, as during the first,

> the company controlled the town, and built homes, sidewalks, sewer and water lines; provided schools, telephones and libraries; encouraged sports activities, formal and informal social organizations; made available medical and dental facilities, theatre, hotel and shopping conveniences. (Goltz, 1974: 101)

In 1958 Espanola, including the fringe development, was incorporated as a municipality, thus formally separating community government from industry management.

On various occasions pulp and paper operations came into conflict with environmental concerns. In 1947, tourist operators and commercial fisherman on the Spanish River brought suit and ultimately won an injunction prohibiting the company from polluting the river. In 1950, after pressure from the company and various community groups, the Ontario legislature passed a special bill 'which dissolved the injunction, and in effect allowed the company to continue polluting the Spanish River' (Goltz, 1974: 81). In 1968 another suit was launched against the company. Between 1970 and 1983 $50 million were spent on environmental improvements. In 1983 a spill from the company's sewer system resulted in a massive fish kill. In 1986 the company paid $122,000 in damages to a hotel owner in a suit relating to sawdust in the air. These environmental issues brought townspeople with a keen interest in the economic advantages of the mill and the jobs it provided into conflict with those with interests in the opportunities offered by the natural environment.

In 1986 Espanola had a population of 4,974, down from 6,045 in 1971. In 1990 the community appeared, based on this author's observations, to be increasing in importance as a regional and tourist centre.

Schefferville, Quebec illustrates the rapid social changes experienced by resource communities. Built in the 1950s, it had a short period of prosperity and maturity in the 1960s and early 1970s, and declined with the closure of the iron mine in 1983. Schefferville is located near the centre of the Labrador-Ungava trough, a long narrow geologic formation that straddles the border between Quebec and Labrador, and extends from Ungava Bay in the north to the town of Gagnon, Quebec in the south. Exploration in the 1890s identified iron deposits in the region. In the 1930s and 1940s mining corporations established the commercial potential of iron production. Through the 1950s and 1960s a number of new communities were established to provide labour for iron mines and ore-processing plants. (The discussion in this section draws on Bradbury, 1984a; 1984b; 1985a; Bradbury and St-Martin, 1983; Humphries, 1958; Ross, 1957; Montreal *Gazette* [various dates].)

The community of Schefferville is over 1,000 km by air northeast of Montreal. The Quebec North Shore Railway connects Schefferville to the community of Sept Iles on the St Lawrence River 620 km to the south. There were and are no roads between Schefferville and other communities.

Schefferville was built under provincial supervision, but as a company town. 'The Iron Ore Company of Canada (IOCC) retained ownership of all the land in the townsite (except for the commercial area, where it permitted private enterprise to enter) and also assumed responsibility for installing the utilities and building the houses, schools, community centre, and other structures' (Robinson, 1962: 57). Over the years IOCC reduced its direct involvement in community affairs. Following 1966 it insisted that duplexes and detached homes be purchased (but continued to own and rent other accommodations). In earlier periods the company subsidized heating fuel, electricity, and both passenger and freight transportations, but it cancelled these subsidies in later years. Over time, IOCC reduced the amount which it contributed, through taxation and direct subsidies, to the Schefferville municipal budget. While these changes had the positive effect of reducing company-town paternalism, they also had the consequence of reducing the company's financial responsibility when shutdown occurred.

The population of Schefferville had reached 3,178 in 1961 and remained over 3,000 in every census through 1976; it was 2,400 in 1981. While these figures obscure seasonal and annual variations, they do show that a viable population base for the community existed for two decades. The 1986 census gives the population as 276 and press releases for various dates after the closing mention figures of less than 300.

The optimism of the early period, which was widespread in the province of Quebec and the mining industry, was captured by geographer W. Gillies Ross (1957: 242, 247):

> Today at Knob Lake the orderly streets of the modern town of Schefferville run in arcs between symmetrical rows of brightly painted houses. Construction is

everywhere in progress; homes, a school, a church, a cinema, a bank, are triumphant, even arrogant, manifestations of man's conquest of nature.

Knob Lake is a mining area, and present estimates of ore reserves indicate a potential annual production of about twenty million tons for several generations. When, however, one considers the possibility of other large deposits in the area, and the probable exploitation of lower grade ores, it seems apparent that the life of Knob Lake will be very much longer.

Today settlement is filling in behind an advancing frontier of industrial development, a twentieth century method of colonizing vacant lands. It can honestly be said that the 'ice' of Labrador-Ungava has been broken.

On 2 November 1982 Brian Mulroney, who was then President of IOCC, announced that mining operations at Schefferville would be closed down. Press reports that follow indicate that employees were frustrated that termination and resettlement benefits would not pay actual relocation costs, that long-term residents were upset with the destruction of the community, and that most owners of private business were facing the loss of their income and investments

Over the years since the mine closure the Quebec provincial government has paid many of the costs of operating the town. It has considered bulldozing the buildings and closing the town completely to end these costs. It has attempted, unsuccessfully, to persuade the federal government to turn the town into a reserve for the two tribes of Indians resident in the area, and thus assume the operating costs. The Montreal *Gazette* captured the dilemma of municipal support:

After the Iron Ore Co. of Canada closed its mining operations here in 1983, the provincial government found itself supporting a municipal infrastructure costing millions a year, geared to the 5,000 population of Schefferville's heyday, for the benefit of fewer than 300 whites still living in the town and the roughly 1,000 natives on two nearby reserves. (Montreal *Gazette*, 1988)

The reporter described the community 'bust' situation in terms that contrast sharply with Ross' picture of the 'boom' in 1957.

By far the most overpowering presence in town is the row upon row of boarded-up buildings. Whole neighbourhoods which every soul has fled. . . .

It is easy to imagine the ghosts in the dank rooms behind the plywood-covered windows of the faded old company houses, laid out in gentle crescents, their lawns now wildly overgrown, the walkways pitted and crumbling. Or the heartbreak behind the abandoned United Church, with its shattered windows that once let in a glorious light on Sunday mornings, but now admit the scourge of a sub-arctic winter. . . .

The community centre, the curling rink, the bank, the Lions Club lodge, the arena, two schools, the hospital—all bolted shut and boarded up. Around them hangs an oppressive silence. . . .

Here and there are signs of habitation: a house with uncovered, unbroken

> windows; a snowmobile or two beached on the lawn;. . .But the overwhelming impression is of encroaching decay, of receding order, of a struggle being lost.

In 1991 most of the physical structures of the community and associated with the mine still exist. Caribou hunters, and tourists coming to see the caribou, provide some income to the community. In addition, even though Schefferville as a mining centre is now a ghost town, there is the potential of a renewed future. In 1988 the properties of the Iron Ore Company of Canada were purchased by La Foss Platinum, which has been exploring mineral deposits in the area and investigating the possibility of producing lump iron ore, manganese ore, and other products. On 11 June 1990 *The Northern Miner* published optimistic reports about the possibility of significant production in 1991, but this has not occurred. However, La Foss continues to explore the possibilities (personal communication).

The boom and bust pattern of Schefferville has been manifest in other communities in the Labrador-Ungava trough. The forces producing these rapid social changes in community life are located in world-wide economic and technological patterns, and in the strategies which corporations use to stay profitable in this economic environment. Over the brief life of Schefferville, which began with such optimism, depressions in the steel industry reduced the demand for iron ore. Changing blast furnace technology shifted demand away from the types of ore found at Schefferville, and corporations involved in iron mining and steel production were developing alternate sources of supply.

Brief Overview of Literature

There are common themes in the literature on resource-extractive communities, but different policy concerns and intellectual puzzles have guided work in different periods and it is important to be aware of the historical context from which a particular book or article emerges.

The Bunkhouse Man by Edmund Bradwin (1928, reissued 1972) is a study, based on extensive personal observation, of the work camps housing workers through the nineteenth and into the twentieth century. In 1953 the Institute of Local Government at Queen's University completed *Single-Enterprise Communities in Canada,* which noted the important transition from work camps for single men to permanent communities for families, identified problems with towns completely owned and operated by resource companies themselves, and articulated a need for improved urban amenities needed to recruit the skilled labour required in the post-World War II resource industries. Ira M. Robinson's *New Industrial Towns of Canada's Resource Frontier* (1962) provides a synthesis of concerns which were prominent during the fifteen years following World War II, sets issues in a 'comprehensive' community planning framework and explores these issues with discussions of four towns built in the 1950s: Kitimat, BC; Drayton Valley, Alberta; Elliot Lake,

Ontario; and Schefferville, Quebec. *Minetown, Milltown, Railtown* by sociologist Rex Lucas (1971) argues that small communities and resource-based communities continue to be important locations of social life for many Canadians, even though a large proportion of the society lives in major urban centres. A series of research projects conducted at the Centre for Settlement Studies, University of Manitoba (e.g., Matthiason, 1970, 1971; Riffel, 1975) began a strong foundation of empirical social science research on a variety of northern resource communities. Prominent concern of this research and other studies are quality of life in resource communities, and the need to maintain a stable workforce at the resource site. In *Little Communities and Big Industries* Bowles (1982) presents a cross-section of pre-1981 articles, including Stelter and Artibise's 'Canadian Resource Towns in Historical Perspective', Himelfarb's 'The Social Characteristics of One Industry Towns in Canada', and eight different community case studies. A broad range of issues which the expanded oil production and other social changes of the 1970s brought to the forefront are discussed by authors representing several disciplines in *Resource Communities: A Decade of Disruption* (Detomasi and Gartrell, 1984). *Mining Communities: Hard Lessons for the Future* (Centre for Resource Studies, Queen's University, 1984) reports the proceedings of a conference held to identify and explore ways to sustain the kinds of labour force needed at resource sites while avoiding some of the most critical problems evident in resource towns.

Among recent literature, Oiva W. Saarinen's 'Single-Sector Communities in Northern Ontario: The Creation and Planning of Dependent Towns' (1986) applies a comprehensive historical focus, examining developments from the 1880s to the present, in the Sudbury resource region. Bradbury (1983, 1984a, 1984b, 1985a, 1985b) and his associates have analyzed iron mining and the related communities (including Schefferville) in the Quebec-Labrador border region, where development began in the 1950s and winding down was occurring in the 1980s. They place regional and local developments in the context of world-wide economic processes.

Tumbler Ridge, established in the 1980s as a regional community to provide workers for a number of coal mines in northeastern British Columbia, is probably the most thoroughly researched and carefully planned resource town in Canadian history. Discussions of Tumbler Ridge which reflect very current concerns, particularly the attempt to plan for a resilient community which will provide a high quality of life, have been presented by many authors including Gill (1987, 1990), McGrath (1987), and Pagett and Walisser (1984). The recent strategy of using long-distance commuting to get workers to their jobs and thus to avoid a permanent town at the resource site has been discussed by Hobart (1982, 1984) and by Story and Shrimpton (1988, 1989). References to many other important works are found in the sources described above.

All of these works recognize that natural resource extraction is an important part of the Canadian economy, that it requires workers at various locations throughout the Canadian hinterland, and that the social arrangements used to provide a base for these workers shape patterns of daily life and quality of life for both workers and their families.

Resource Communities Throughout Canadian History

Given that most resource extractive communities are small, and the majority of the Canadian population now lives in major urban centres, it may seem strange to focus on such communities. If we consider the full sweep of Canadian history, however, we can see that small communities which serve the needs of big industries have been very important. (Material in this section is largely from Bowles, 1982.)

Beginning in the seventeenth century, fishing fleets from Britain, France, Spain, and Portugal visited the Grand Banks of Labrador and the Gulf of St Lawrence to fish for cod which was sold in various European countries. Some small settlements developed as stations for drying fish and performing other land-based operations directly connected to the fishery, but the fishery as a whole was organized and conducted from European ports and was substantially controlled by large firms.

The fur trade was the first major land-based economy in Canada. Through nearly all its history, the fur trade was controlled by large companies. These companies established extensive communication and transportation networks extending from Quebec City and Montreal deep into the interior of the continent to trade European-manufactured goods for furs. Focal points in these networks were trading posts. Many of these remained small and served only as points of storage, trade, and transshipment. Others, the best example being Red River, developed as essentially complete communities occupied by families and producing goods both for subsistence and to supply the fur trade. The fur trading posts that operated in Canada from the seventeenth century onward can be treated as little communities serving the needs of a big industry.

The timber trade between Canada and Great Britain began early in the 1800s and was significant throughout that century. Major points of Canadian control were in Quebec City and Montreal. Other communities, Ottawa being a good example, were largely established as points of supply for camps and transshipment of timber. Settlements whose economic function was linked to the timber trade varied in size and permanence. One might include, at the extreme, the numerous 'shanty towns' or camps in which small groups of men spent the winter months so that they might get the logs out of the forest. Many small 'permanent' villages established to serve the timber trade did not diversify into other activities and declined when lumbering declined locally. The Canadian timber trade was a large industry which gave rise to many small communities, some of which grew larger while others disappeared.

The export of wheat has been another large industry. Wheat was and is grown by many farmers but its collection and export have always been controlled by a relatively small number of companies and organizations. In the first half of the nineteenth century numerous small communities came into being on the lakes in Upper Canada (now Ontario) to serve as ports for the export of wheat and the forwarding of supplies. In the late nineteenth and early twentieth centuries when the transcontinental railroad was established, in large part to open the West for the production of wheat as an export staple, many railway towns and farm service centres were created. The well-being of residents of such communities was closely tied to developments in a single industry.

The new industrialism of the late nineteenth and early twentieth centuries saw the development of hydroelectric power, the expansion of mining, and the growth of pulp and paper manufacturing. Each of these industries was large in that it employed major concentration of capital, was dominated by large companies, and employed complex technologies. Each created small communities, many of them distant from other settlements, to supply labour required for production.

In the post-World War II era the resource industries continued to expand and to produce new communities. Perhaps the most dramatic developments have occurred in energy resources since the early 1970s when the first of recent oil crises occurred. There are deposits of petroleum, uranium, coal, and other valued resources at many locations in the Canadian hinterland. Canadian and world demand for energy makes it virtually inevitable that large industrial projects will be constructed to exploit these resources, that communities will be established to supply the needed labour, and that circumstances of life will be dramatically changed in existing communities.

What implications can we draw from this overview? In every period of Canadian history there have been large industries in the sense of large economic organizations controlling substantial amounts of capital and exercising dominance within economic processes. In each period there has been a demand for labour at various dispersed locations to develop, process, and export resources. Little communities have come into being to supply this labour. The core consequence is this: in every period of Canadian history there have been small settlements in which the circumstances of daily life have been clearly dependent on the economic patterns within and the decisions made by directors of big industries.

Generations of Resource-Extractive Communities

If focus is on the workers and their lives, it is useful to think of 'a community as the base camp or general headquarters where individuals engaged in work meet (as best they can) their daily needs for shelter, food, and rest so that they may work again another day' (Bowles, 1982: 2).

Different arrangements have been made to house the labour force employed in resource-extractive industries during different periods and circumstances. The idea of 'generations' of resource community types can organize this discussion, as long as we remember that there is much overlap.

Throughout the nineteenth century work camps designed for men only, and providing few services, were more common than permanent communities. While individual camps were temporary, the organizational form appeared again and again (Bradwin, 1928). Although permanent towns became more numerous as the twentieth century progressed, work camps continued to be important. Rolf Knight (1975: 7) provides a useful overall characterization:

> Work camps are typically all-male settlements of workers engaged in isolated primary resource industries and on construction projects. Specific camps are established and operated by a single company and provide barrack housing and board at isolated work sites. Most camps are relatively impermanent, lasting from a few months to a few years, and frequently marked by a certain seasonality of operation. Workers in them usually 'sign on' for a limited duration, after which they may return or try another camp. At one time, a large proportion of camp workers were single men. Today however the normal percentage of men working in camps have families, often resident in towns and villages. Camp workers generally have homes or home bases from which they enter and leave camp work. The bunkhouse is for most not a home.
>
> Industries relying on work camps have been, above all, logging, railway and other heavy construction projects in isolated areas. There are also drilling camps of oil rigs, camps attached to small saw mills and camp-like settlements around the fishing stations and canneries of the immediate past. Some mining camps, as distinct from mining towns, also continue to exist.

In the late 1800s when mining began to develop in northern Ontario, for example, somewhat more permanent communities began to emerge. At first, however, 'they were merely appendages of a company's mining and smelting operations and were hardly more than collections of hastily constructed bunk houses often scattered haphazardly near the mining and smelting facilities' (Stelter, 1974: 8).

Most twentieth-century resource centres in Canada have been planned (McCann, 1978, 1980; Stelter and Artibise, 1978), in the sense that a small group of identifiable people have made decisions about the physical structure of the communities. Most of this planning has been linked to the need to recruit, house, and retain a labour force to operate the industry. Prior to 1920 most of this planning was done by company managers in connection with the development of a particular mine or mill, and the company continued to own the town. In this *additive planning* there was little sense of a community separate from the mine or mill. Housing and services for workers would be added to the industrial plant itself, using some sense of order such as a gridiron layout of streets.

Holistic planning, which guided the construction of many towns in the years between World War I and World War II, did have an integrated conception of the community as a physical site. This planning 'envisaged the creation of self-contained, unified communities which utilized such integrative measures as land use separation, the matching of physical layout to topography, and greenbelt that protected towns from sprawl development' (McCann, 1978: 47); applying ideas from the metropolis—the City Beautiful Movement and the Garden City Movement—to shape environments in hinterland communities. Many of the communities built within this framework were closed company towns.

In the decades after World War II the rapid expansion of resource industries required a larger labour force, and the more sophisticated technology demanded some workers with high levels of occupational skill. Industrial opportunities were increasing in the growing urban centres. The quality of services such as health and education were improving. These societal changes contributed to the emergence of new planning perspectives for resource communities. Concern with quality of life gave rise to *comprehensive planning*, which attempted to incorporate broader 'social and economic principles into the fabric of physical planning' (McCann, 1978: 48). Elliot Lake, Ontario and Kitimat, BC, as well as other towns planned on this model, had separate areas for the basic resource zone, the town centre, service industries, and residential neighbourhoods. The design of houses and the layout of neighbourhoods in these communities were very similar to those in southern Canadian suburbs constructed during the same period.

Recognition that support for modern services requires a large population, and that a community associated with a single mine or mill would lose its economic base if the industry closed, produced an effort to build regional centres separate from any particular resource site and that could house the workers from several different mines or mills. For example, Elliot Lake was planned as a community to serve several uranium mines. Concerns with the 'industrial feudalism' which sometimes occurred in closed company towns led to the belief that each new resource town should be an independent entity, separate from direct ownership by a resource company and having its own municipal government. The framework of comprehensive planning is manifest in provincial legislation pertaining to new towns (Bradbury, 1980).

Through the 1980s there was sustained concern with communities based on resource-extractive industries and the problems they face. This has been manifest in three ways. First, town planning has been seen as a tool for developing healthy communities with sustained life. This is best illustrated by the elaborate planning processes applied in the case of Tumbler Ridge, BC. Second, there has been increasing interest in the 'no town' option for developing resources. This often involves long-distance fly-in commuting by workers. Third, there has been increasing concern with economic decline in resource industries, community and other problems associated with decline, and strategies for maintaining sustained economic well-being in the face of decline in the resource extractive sector. These concerns were the focus of the Task Force on Mining Communities (Canada, 1982) which was jointly sponsored by provincial governments and the federal government (Robson, 1988).

A consideration of the 'no town' option will reveal some of the assumptions now being employed by decision-makers in the resource industries. In 1986 the Institute for Research on Public Policy sponsored a conference under the title *Towns, Wheels or Wings? for Resource Development.* Behind this title were several observations and questions about the social arrangements which can provide labour resource development. The difficulty and expense of sustaining high quality services and living environments in single-industry towns was recognized. Most importantly, participants explicitly recognized the volatility and unpredictability of resource industries, and the associated instability of communities based on resource extraction. Key personnel involved in the development of Canadian resource industries were asking: can we recruit and maintain the needed labour force without building and operating communities for these workers and their families? Barbara L. Hodgins (IRPP, 1986: iv) wrote:

> Evidently the preferred choice for resource development is wheels or wings, not towns. Short and long-distance commuting by workers has, bucking the Canadian tradition, replaced the new town as the means for natural resource development, in western Canada and the North. Tumbler Ridge, built to support the Northeast coal development in BC, may have been the last new tailor-made resource town.

Storey and Shrimpton (1988; 1989: 20) have thoroughly reviewed the literature on long-distance commuting (LDC) in mining and summarize two sets of conditions that support this policy.

1: changes in absolute and relative cost factors, including:

- –improved quality and absolute decline in air travel costs (measured in current dollars)
- –increase in requirements and costs of developing resource towns
- –cost and availability of capital for resource town construction
- –increased capital and operating costs of resource towns because of increased demands from residents
- –increased costs associated with resource town closure
- –increase in the price of gold and greater profitability in developing smaller, more remote, short life-span resources
- –increased labour costs associated with high absenteeism and turnover rates

2: changes in attitudes towards work and well-being, including:

–increased demand for services and facilities (especially education facilities) which cannot be provided in small single industry resource communities
–increased demand for a greater range of employment opportunities as two-income households become the norm
–overall worker and family preference for LDC mining among those who have experienced both LDC and mine communities
–lower vulnerability of LDC workers and families to boom-bust cycles and mine closures
–opportunities for some LDC workers to be involved in other occupations and leisure activities in their free time

These factors and others, including a regulatory environment which tends to encourage commuting rather than new town development, have contributed to the growth in the use of LDC and a decline in the traditional approach to mineral development which was through the construction of mining communities. Indications are that these factors will increase in importance in the foreseeable future, and thus the use of LDC is likely to increase.

In a typical long-distance commuting arrangement a group of workers are flown to the site, work intensively for a period (e.g., twelve hours a day for seven days) and then are flown out to their home communities. While at the work site they eat, sleep, and spend such leisure time as they have in a modern version of a work camp. The 'hot bed' arrangement practised in some camps indicates the intensity with which camps may be used and the kind of home base they supply. In this arrangement two workers share one bed, each sleeping while the other is at work.

Most discussions of long-distance commuting are written in the perspective of administrative economics, with a central concern for the cost of supplying labour. Once the 'no town' option is accepted, little attention is directed to community phenomena. For those interested in community studies, however, there continue to be concerns. First, the communities where the families of workers live, and to which workers return when not at the resource site, are affected by the work and the work rotation. They must, for example, provide social services for families who experience major stresses arising from the combination of prolonged separateness and intensive togetherness. Second, modern work camps are 'communities' in the sense of being places where people together spend significant parts of their daily lives. Work camps of the 1980s are different from those of the 1880s because of, for example, hot showers and satellite TV. They are similar in that they are specialized living arrangements for workers engaged in resource extraction.

The importance of resource communities in each of the periods discussed arises from the persistent need for a labour force to develop resources. The particular form and social arrangements which characterize the communities in a given period are a product of the cultural assumptions which guide the decision-makers of the time.

Resource Communities as the Settings of Daily Life

A central argument of much of the literature on resource settlements is that residents of such communities generate a set of experiences, or a set of challenges, which differ in some important ways from those experienced by residents of other communities in the society. Conceptualizing local community as the setting of daily life for family households will give us a framework examining this argument.

For individual family members and for the family household as a social unit, the local community in which a family lives is the tangible context in which much daily activity and experience occur (Bowles and Johnston, 1987). Each family household has an agenda or general schedule of activities within the household and pattern of participation by household members in other settings. As an operating unit it has a set of needs or demands for goods, services and opportunities. In a very elemental sense, a household is a base camp from which members, individually or together, depart to participate in other settings such as work, school, medical services, and recreation, and to which they return periodically to rest or restore supplies. Members live out their daily lives in the particular community where the household is located and those other communities that are accessible from it. The opportunities available in the community are those from which most families will choose most of their experiences. The resources available in the community are those which a family must use to meet most requirements. Most of the other individuals and families with which a family and its members maintain face-to-face association on a regular basis will be found in the same community. If a family has a need for some service that is not available in the community, e.g., specialized medical treatment, then it must find some way to access it. The transportation network surrounding the home community will shape the arrangements required. In summary, a community is the habitat of the families who live in it.

Qualifications are needed to prevent overstatement of this perspective. There are many forces in modern society which produce similarities of behaviour and experience between different communities. The television and the other mass media, consumer products, government services, work patterns associated with large organizations and with industrial production, the regime of school systems, the architectural design of houses and even the planning models that shape the physical community all are homogenizing forces which tend to produce similarities in and between communities. Most people travel outside of their home communities on some occasions, and some travel extensively perhaps to work at other sites. It is the contention of this author, however, that 'local community' or 'local area' remains an important habitat for most people.

Rex Lucas, in his classic *Minetown, Milltown, Railtown* (1971: 20), emphasized the modernity of Canada's single-industry communities and the up-to-date orientations of their residents, that is, the ways in which resource communities are integrated with modern society:

> Canadian communities of single industry are twentieth-century products of an age of industry and technology. . . . They are new communities and their very existence depends upon advanced technology, a complex division of labour, and a sophisticated system of exchange. With few exceptions, they have a short past, because they were born of technology; the oldest of the communities are products of the coal and rail ages; the newest have been created to supply industrial metals. Their inhabitants have no lingering myths of days gone by; they know that their community, jobs, and lives depend on twentieth-century science and technology. They know that their situation is bounded by bureaucracy and a precise division of labour which in turn depends on a complex national and international division of labour. They know that their future depends upon impersonal forces outside their community such as head office decisions, government policies, and international trading agreements.

Lurking behind Lucas' characterization is a somewhat romanticized image of noble, if modern, pioneers, but his statement can still serve as a beginning point for analyzing community characteristics. The industries that form the basis of many resource communities—mining and mineral processing, pulp and paper manufacturing, oil drilling and refining—do depend on advanced technology and the research that supports it. As new processes are developed, often through elaborate research, it becomes possible to exploit new resource deposits and new communities are needed. Fort McMurray, based on the production of petroleum from oil sands, illustrates this. The work environments of resource communities are industrial and, at least at plant start up, use very modern machinery and work processes. A new wood pulp plant, for example, is typically built with the most recent equipment and with 'modern industrial' work environments much the same as a new factory in southern Canada. The situation of residents of resource communities is 'bounded by bureaucracy' in several senses. The corporation that employs workers, the provincial and federal governments that regulate the industry, and the provincial ministry that is important in planning and overseeing the town are all large rule-governed organizations whose policies shape work and community life. The issue of 'impersonal forces outside the community' most centrally involves international markets which produce local bounty when they are healthy and local distress when they are depressed. Lucas is quite correct in saying that important forces at work throughout the society are also shaping life patterns in resource communities.

Core Characteristics of Resource Communities

Four core characteristics of resource communities are small size, remote location, economic dependence on a single industry, and rapid social change. These characteristics working together produce patterns which distinguish resource communities from many other settlements. They impose special demands on families who live in resource communities.

Population data on a set of resource towns can help illustrate these community features. McCann (1980), drawing information from several sources, presents a list of 93 resource communities having populations in excess of a thousand residents in 1971, together with populations size in 1961 and 1971. The present author has checked population figures where they are available in the 1981 and 1986 census reports. For simplicity in reading, numbers have been rounded to the nearest 100.

Small size

Most resource communities are small. The issue of community size relates to the question of what is an 'urban' environment in today's society. Rex Lucas argues that the census classification of communities with 1,000 population as 'urban' as far too low. He suggests that communities with less than 30,000 population lack the qualities which scholars have associated with urbanism as a way of life. Hodge and Qadeer, in *Towns and Villages in Canada* (1983), define urban settlements as those places with a population of more than 10,000, and focus their study on smaller communities. The largest of the communities identified by McCann (1980) was Corner Brook which had a population of 26,300 in 1971, and only Fort McMurray (with 34,900 in 1986) surpassed this number in any of the four census years. In 1971 (when data are available for all 93 communities) the number of communities in different size classes were:

1,000	to	1,999	29
2,000	to	4,999	30
5,000	to	9,999	16
10,000	to	19,999	9
20,000	and	over	3

In addition, there was an unknown number of resource communities with fewer than 1,000 population. While some of the communities had grown by 1981 or 1986, others had declined. Relatively few communities showed a pattern of regular growth over the 25-year period. The generalization that resource communities tend to be small is still very applicable. (One change that produced a more urban pattern for some communities was the incorporation of a number of small mining communities into the city of Sudbury.)

A graphic illustration of the consequences of small size is presented in an advertisement which United Keno Hills Mines Ltd placed for a family practice physician for the community of Elsa, Yukon Territory (Toronto *Globe and Mail*, 9 December 1985). It read in part:

> Elsa is a modern city with excellent school and recreational facilities. There is regular air service and road connection to Whitehorse. A hospital staffed with a physician is within a 1/2 hour drive. This is an ideal position for a physician interested in both private practice and the supervision of occupational health service. The new, fully equipped Elsa clinic is staffed by a registered nurse.

A small community can support only a limited set of services, and cannot support the variety of services available in the society as a whole. Residents of a city of 60,000 might expect to have a hospital with specialized wards, choice between several general practice family doctors, and availability of several types of medical specialists. Residents in a community of 6,000 or less will have local access to very few physicians and only very basic services. High school students in a city of 60,000 have choice between many different programs. A high school which draws its students from a population of 6,000 will provide much less choice of specialized curricula and much less depth in those it does offer. The same patterns hold in such things as commercial recreation opportunities and in opportunities for participating in special interest community organizations. Other opportunities, such as outdoor recreation and access to the natural environment, may be more readily available to residents of some small communities than they are to those in larger communities.

Remote location

Resource communities are frequently described as 'isolated', but *remote* is a more useful word. Modern telephone systems, satellite television transmission, and today's patterns of air travel make it possible for residents of resource communities to stay in contact with and to spend time in other parts of the country. There is frequent communication of local managers with personnel at corporate headquarters through travel, telephone, and written correspondence. Local union officials also can communicate with national and even international headquarters as frequently as they feel the need. In short, modern technology for communication and travel help resource communities avoid isolation.

Many resource communities are located in intermittently settled parts of Canada. In these regions communities tend to be small and separated from each other by long distances. This means that residents have access to few services and opportunities located outside of their home communities. Hodge and Qadeer (1983), in terms applicable to continuously settled nonmetropolitan regions, have suggested that in some parts of Canada the set of small communities taken together may be understood as a 'dispersed city', which supplies a broad range of services and employment opportunities. Because driving times between communities are short, residents can get access to services and opportunities with about the same time and effort that they would spend in an urban centre. A village of 3,000 in southern Ontario may actually have fewer local services than a community of the same size in northern Ontario. However, residents of the southern community can usually make short to moderate car trips to several other small communities and often have similar access to larger towns and cities. Many resource communities are remote from other small communities, as well as from larger towns and cities. As a result residents must exert considerable time and effort if they want to use the services and opportunities of communities other than their own. This is especially true in communities like Schefferville which have no road connections.

Economic dependence on a single industrial sector

The characteristic which most distinguishes resource-extractive communities from other communities is economic reliance on a single resource sector. This is most pronounced when there is only one company and only one mine or mill. But even when there are a number of companies and a number of mines or other projects, as in the case of Elliot Lake where there were several separate uranium mines, the ups and downs in a single market have consequences for community life.

Rapid social change

One of the most important consequences of reliance on a single industrial sector is the rapid social change which resource communities experience. These communities often grow rapidly, experience dramatic rises and falls in the size and economic well-being of their populations, and then decline and are closed. It is this pattern of rapid social change which gives rise to frequently used terms such as 'boom town', 'instant town', 'ghost town', and 'boom and bust cycle'. Lucas (1971) in an attempt to capture changing social conditions identifies community life-cycle stages of construction, recruitment of citizens, transition, and maturity. Bradbury and St-Martin (1983) in their study of Schefferville, emphasizing that many resource communities experience rapid decline, add the stages of winding down and closure.

There are a number of reasons for fluctuations in a resource industry, and these can be illustrated with examples from mining. Ore bodies run out. New ore bodies may be discovered in other Canadian locations or other parts of the world, and these may be cheaper to exploit. New technologies for mining or processing metals may be developed and these can make it difficult for an established operation using older technologies to compete. Most mineral products are sold on an international market in competition with supplies from all over the world. Prices fluctuate quite dramatically because of variations in supply associated with the opening and closing of mines elsewhere. Changes outside the industry also have consequences for the economic viability of a Canadian mine. If the Canadian dollar rises in value in relation to other world currencies, the cost of the Canadian product rises on the international market. Environmental concerns that relate to the industry may suppress demand. For example, the increasing concern about the safety of nuclear power plants has reduced the world demand for uranium. In brief, reliance on a single product sector produces dramatic changes in the local economic base of a resource community.

Several observations about the population data presented by McCann (1980) illustrate rapid community growth. Eleven of the communities on the 1971 list were established in the 1960s and an additional 14 were established in the 1950s. Some examples of dramatic growth were Fort McMurray, Alberta (1,200 in 1961 to 34,900 in 1986), Thompson, Manitoba (3,400 in 1961 to 19,000 in 1971), and Labrador City, Newfoundland (386 in 1961 to 14,700 in 1981).

Two communities which show both rapid growth and rapid decline are Uranium City, Saskatchewan and Schefferville, Quebec. Uranium City was established in 1952, had its largest census year population of 2,500 in 1981, and had only 159 residents in 1986. Schefferville was established in 1954, had just over 3,000 residents in 1961 and 1971, but only 276 residents in 1986. Ocean Falls, British Columbia, is an older community which showed rapid decline. It was established in 1909, had a population of 4,200 in 1971, but only 12 residents in 1986.

The general tendency toward instability, or fluctuations, in resource communities is indicated by the frequency of population decline. Data for all four census years (1961, 1971, 1981 and 1986) were available for 71 communities. Sixty-three communities experienced population decline in at least one of the three intercensus periods, while only eight never experienced a decline. While some of the declines were relatively small, many were large enough to affect community services, organizations and businesses in important ways. Some examples are Fraser Lake, BC (1,500 in 1981 to 1,200 in 1986), Atikokan, Ontario (6,100 in 1971 to 4,400 in 1981), Flin Flon, Manitoba (11,100 in 1961 to 9,300 in 1971) and La Tuque, Quebec (13,100 in 1971 to 10,700 in 1981).

Rapid growth, rapid decline, and fluctuating patterns have tangible consequences for residents of the specific communities in question. They have more general consequences for residents of all resource communities. The knowledge that such frequent and often dramatic changes occur in many communities becomes part of the culture common to all resource communities, and contributes to an atmosphere of insecurity with which residents of all such communities must live.

Bradbury (1984a: 311) effectively captures the links between the cyclical nature of the mining industry and demands on families:

> The mining industry is subjected to strong cycles of upswings and downswings which have both dramatic and traumatic impact on the population of mining regions. In periods of prosperity labour migrates to townsites and in downswings it must move to locations to find alternative jobs or to wait out the decline. The mining industry would not be able to operate or survive without this form of specialized, segmented, mobile and pliant labour force. The rhythm of business cycles, closures and uncertain and indefinite periods of work is incorporated into the everyday lives and lifestyles of the population. Men, women and children must adapt, and be ultimately adaptable to this form of uneven temporal working life.

To sum up: the extraction and processing of forest products, minerals, and energy resources have been and will continue to be important to Canada. Nearly all of this resource-extractive activity occurs in nonmetropolitan Canada, and most of it occurs in the intermittently settled parts of the country rather than in areas where settlement is continuous across the landscape. Each resource project requires a labour force, and this labour force requires a home base where they can eat, sleep, spend leisure time, and meet other needs. In every period of Canadian history the communities that have housed and provided an operating base for resource industry workers and their families have been important parts of the settlement pattern in many nonmetropolitan areas of Canada. Thus, a comprehensive sociological understanding of rural, or nonmetropolitan, Canada requires the study of resource communities.

The core characteristics of resource communities are small size, remote location, dependence on a single industrial sector, and rapid social change. These characteristics have consequences for families.

Each community serves as the habitat of daily life for the families and individuals who live there. Small size and remote location mean that a family in a resource community has local access to a limited range of the goods, services, and opportunities available in the broader society. Any small community by itself can only support a small set of retail stores, medical services, recreational outlets, and so on. In a community that is remote from other settlements, families cannot easily expand their access by using opportunities in nearby communities. Families wanting or needing to access the more specialized services and opportunities must make more complex arrangements than would those in larger communities or even those in small communities in the continuously settled parts of Canada.

Family households are units of economic adaptation. Those located in resource communities must often adapt to the changing economic fortunes of one of the major companies operating in the community. Many households develop an economic strategy based on two incomes derived from employment of both husband and wife. If one person is laid off, the other income continues. Frequently, this strategy is not possible in a resource community because it is too small to support a range of other businesses which provide employment and because it is too far from other communities for one person to commute to work. It does appear that more resource companies are hiring larger numbers of women for a more diverse set of jobs than has previously been the case, so husband and wife may both work for one of the major companies. This means they may both experience lay-off in a major slump. Job loss is a frequent experience throughout the society and many who are in other communities must adapt to it. For those in cities, or even in smaller communities in continuously settled regions, it is often possible to locate new employment while staying in the same home and commuting to a new place to work. One principal mode of adaptation to economic decline in a resource community is migration to some other community. This often involves major economic costs, such as loss of equity in a home and extra expenses in establishing a new household.

CHAPTER SIX

ATLANTIC CANADA'S FISHING COMMUNITIES: THE IMPACT OF CHANGE

PETER R. SINCLAIR

As this chapter is being written, the people of Atlantic Canada's fishing communities find their lives in disarray — not for the first time. Fish plants are closing and vessels are being withdrawn from the fishery. Many fishing people wonder if they will be able to remain in the communities where they want to live. Powerful state agents would prefer them to move, and a new program of aid to the industry is partly an aid to relocation. The present I describe is but a frame in an endless series of frames. It is the impact of change and it is part of the process of change.

Before locating contemporary problems in the changing structure of the fishing industry, I want to set out why the fate of the industry is so important in Atlantic Canada, and to alert the reader to its social complexity. The core of the ensuing analysis is a discussion of how present problems are rooted in the competitive struggle for fish and the technological change associated with that struggle. An important contributing factor has been the Canadian state's inadequate response to earlier crises in the industry. In this chapter the concept of community is treated more in a geographical than in a sociological sense. What people of a community actually have in common may be no

Peter R. Sinclair is a Professor in the Department of Sociology, Memorial University, St John's, Newfoundland.

more than place of residence or work. I am unwilling to assume common values and sense of identity among those who live in the same 'community'. Differences in identity and values may overshadow what people within a given territory share.

The Importance of the Fishery

Does it matter what happens to the fishery? In Atlantic Canada, fishing (including processing as well as harvesting) is a major industry in terms of employment and fish products are important exports from the region. About one-quarter of the population lives in small fishing communities (including places with up to 10,000 persons) and the fishing industry is the only or the core employment sector in well over half of these communities. In Newfoundland, 50.4% lived in such centres in 1981 (Canada, 1983: 70-2). Fishing and processing occur all around the coasts of Newfoundland and Labrador, even in St John's. All the Atlantic provinces have substantial fisheries and so does Quebec around the Gaspé and lower north shore of the Gulf of St Lawrence. The fishery obviously does matter.

How many people are at risk when the industry is in trouble is, however, a matter of speculation. The number employed in the fishing industry is not easily determined, even for the present, let alone the past. The number of licences issued by the federal Department of Fisheries and Oceans (DFO) is an unreliable measure because not all licence holders actually fish. Roughly half of Atlantic Canada's fishers[1] hold part-time licences. In 1981, it was reported that 27.8% of these part-time licences were never used (the number reached 45% in Labrador and northeast Newfoundland) in contrast with 3.4% of full-time licences (Canada, 1983a: 48-9). Some people appear to have purchased part-time licences in order to maintain the right to fish, even if they do not expect to use it. Fishing is also a secondary occupation for many other part-time fishers, judging from evidence that only about 25% of part-timers earn from fishing an amount equivalent to even the less successful full-time fishers (Canada, 1983a: 48). Clearly, the number of fishers listed by DFO overestimates the number for whom fishing is important and can give a misleading impression of overcapacity.

An alternate source is the census, which asks what the respondent worked at in the week prior to the census. If unemployed, the occupation of longest duration from the start of the previous year is requested. The census is conducted in early June. Because the groundfish season is not yet under way in most of rural Newfoundland, this date will exclude many inshore, part-time fishers, whose main employment at other times would not be in fishing. However, most full-time fishers will be included on the basis of their employment in the previous year and a half. A comparison of census and DFO data in the Atlantic region for 1981 shows by far the greatest discrepancy for Newfoundland, where the DFO total exceeds the census by 58%. This may be explained by the particularly high percentage of unused licences in Newfoundland and by the late start to the inshore season.

To establish how many people depend on fishing as their most important source of earned income, probably the best procedure is to take the number of full-time fishers and add 25% of the number of part-time fishers, assuming that the income relationships established in 1981 are still more or less operative. This procedure gives a total of about 35,000 for 1985. The disadvantage of this approach is that no long-term trend can be identified because the necessary data do not exist prior to 1980. Thus for historical series, it is preferable to follow the census, despite its underestimation of numbers in Newfoundland.

It is equally difficult to determine the numbers employed in fish processing. For 1980-81, several different sources are available and it is discouraging that they vary so much. The Task Force on Atlantic Fisheries surveyed over 500 plants (excluding only some of the smaller ones) and estimated that there were 48,000 processing jobs in the region in 1980 (Canada, 1983a: 67). This is about 5,000 fewer than the census figure for 1981. The annual census of manufacturers (reported in DFO publications) collects data on the average number of employees. For 1981, the Atlantic region total was 23,278 (Canadian Fisheries Annual Statistical Review 1982, Table 79)—far fewer than the census total for fishing industry occupations.

If our concern is to identify the number of people who are affected by the state of the fishery rather than the total or average employment that the industry generates, the census industry data should be used. Based then on the census, Table 6.1 gives the number of persons employed in the fish products industry in Atlantic Canada from 1971 to 1986. It should be remembered that much of this work is seasonal, especially in Newfoundland. That having been noted, the data still show a marked expansion in fish processing work since 1971 and an upward trend in the percentage of women who now constitute about half the labour force in this sector. Table 6.1 includes both manual and white-collar workers, but we know that women are unevenly distributed among the fish processing occupations. Other occupational data suggest that women are more likely to be employed in processing jobs. Thus of 13,275 employed in 1986 in Newfoundland as fish canners, curers or packers, 58.8% were women. Clearly any reduction in fish processing in the region will be especially serious for women, even though their work is often arduous, seasonal, or part-time, and involves little chance of promotion.

Gender and Class

Until recently, social research dealing with fisheries ignored gender relations (see Porter's [1987] critique), perhaps because they were invisible on the boats where most male researchers focused their attention. But women have always been involved in fishing economies (Nadel-Klein and Davis, 1988) in such

Table 6.1 Employment in fish-processing plants

	NUMBER OF EMPLOYEES			PER CENT WOMEN		
	1971	1981	1986	1971	1981	1986
Newfoundland	8,015	22,890	23,235	18.6	40.8	45.3
PEI	1,620	2,460	2,510	48.1	55.7	61.0
Nova Scotia	7,675	12,405	11,280	27.2	36.8	40.3
New Brunswick	5,545	10,030	10,415	52.0	62.6	60.8
Quebec	2,445	5,840	5,780	31.1	39.3	45.8
Total	25,300	53,625	53,220	31.6*	44.5*	48.1*

* Weighted average
Source: Calculated from Statistics Canada, cat. no. 93-152, Table 2.

activities as preparing gear, processing, marketing, and providing for the male fishers. Today in Atlantic Canada, women approach ten per cent of the actual fishing labour force and comprise over half of the processing-plant workers.[2]

As MacDonald and Connelly (1989) demonstrate, gender and class in the fishing industry are interconnected in complex patterns. They found that about half the wives of boat owners in their Nova Scotian study worked for pay at some time, about one-quarter in fish plants, but they noted a trend away from paid work for wives in larger ports. Regardless of their paid work patterns, more than half the wives of boat owners contributed to the enterprise through bookkeeping, while about one-quarter arranged sales, cooked meals, and fished. Husbands of fish-plant workers in larger ports typically worked for wages, many also in the fish plant. In smaller centres, husbands were more likely to be fishers. Younger couples were more likely both to be wage workers.

Class relations are defined here in terms of ownership and control of the means of production. People with the same class position share a common interest that potentially can generate a common consciousness and collective action. One of the fascinating features of the fishing industry is that class relations vary considerably even within the one area and many individuals have such complicated work and family relations that their class position is ambiguous. Recognizing that individuals may move from one category to another over their lifespan or even within the course of a season, it is still worth setting out the types of class position that fishers may hold.[3]

1. Fishers may be *subsistence producers* who own or rent means of production to produce fish for their own consumption. Commercial production is a secondary aspect of their labour, if present at all.
2. Fishers may be *domestic commodity producers*, also known as simple, petty, or independent commodity producers. Domestic commodity production signifies a form of production in which household members who own the means of production (boat and gear) supply the labour to produce fish for sale. Work and

kinship relations overlap. Goods are sold in order to acquire means of subsistence. Accumulation of capital is not impossible in fortunate circumstances, but it is not the driving force of this economic activity.

3. Fishers may be *petty capitalists*. In this case, they are small-scale owners of vessels who hire labour without special concern for kinship ties, and attempt to produce for profit. The owners of small trawlers fit into this category. Both domestic commodity producers and petty capitalists may form co-operatives to market or process their fish. In that case they are also acting as what Clement (1986) calls cooperative commodity producers.

4. Fishers are often *wage workers*, both as sharemen (people who work for a share of the catch) in small boats and as more conventional labourers in deep-sea vessels. In this situation, they do not own the vessels and gear. Their share of the catch is exclusively a payment for their labour.

5. A final category is the *company skipper*, who combines some of the features of capitalists and workers. Controlling and sometimes hiring labour, in charge of the vessel's routine operation, the skipper enjoys the rights of capital to that degree. But the company skipper does not own the vessel and, like the workers, sells his labour (I know of no women skippers).

It seems clear that the term fisher cannot alone identify the social position of those who fish, and that the experience of men and women in the fishing industry differs dramatically according to both their own work activity and that of the other adults in their household. The structure of the industry varies a great deal for other reasons. There are many different commercial species of fish distributed unevenly around our coast. The fishing industry produces many distinct products, the combination of which varies from enterprise to enterprise, from community to community. The class composition of the industry is fluid and again exhibits wide regional diversity. Thus the rough general account that follows should be read with this awareness.

The Crisis of 1989–90

Lobster are the most important species around Prince Edward Island, parts of New Brunswick and southwestern Nova Scotia. Scallops are the most important shellfish in Nova Scotia. Shrimp are a highly valued species in parts of the Gulf of St Lawrence and off Labrador. Capelin roe has become important in recent years. Many species of groundfish (fish that swim near the ocean floor) are caught. None, however, approaches the importance of cod, which is usually worth about a third of the total value of the catch in the region and about one-half in Newfoundland. Consequently, if the major cod stocks are in trouble, it is particularly serious for most communities.

Haddock, redfish, and cod, the major groundfish species, have in fact been seriously overfished. The gravest problems are with cod in the eastern Gulf of St Lawrence and in the Atlantic, off Newfoundland. Since 1977, Canada has claimed a fisheries jurisdiction zone up to 200 miles offshore and has imposed quotas on the major stocks, of which northern cod is the most important.

Because of inaccurate information, in the last decade quotas have been set too high to permit rapid rebuilding of the stock. Indeed, high quotas and illegal, wasteful fishing practices by Canadian and foreign vessels mean that the northern cod may even be in decline at present. Rather than catching a reasonable 20% of the biomass of cod, it appears that something in the region of 45% has been harvested annually (Canada, 1990). Recognizing that the fishery was endangered, scientists have recommended major cuts in the total allowable catch (TAC) in recent years, and the state has gone along to some extent with reductions from 266,000 tons in 1988 to 235,000 in 1989 and 197,000 in 1990. The Harris report, however, recommended an immediate reduction to 125,000 tons (Canada, 1990).

The size of the formal allowance is largely irrelevant to the many thousands of fishers who must remain close to shore because their boats and gear do not permit them to catch even what has been officially set aside for them. For the last decade or so, the total inshore catch in Newfoundland has only been about two-thirds of its level in the 1950s and in some areas it has plummeted far below normal. Quota reductions do force the larger vessels, both fisher- and processor-owned, to cut back their landings in the short term and this has meant that plant operators have less raw material and in some cases must shut down.

Although there are hundreds of small groundfish-processing plants in Atlantic Canada, the industry is dominated by two giants, National Sea Products and Fisheries Products International (FPI). Between them, these two companies also own most of the deep-sea trawlers that fish year round. With declining stocks and the major companies losing money in 1989, it was no surprise that they should announce plant closures and fleet reductions. National Sea Products, the world's largest fish company, announced that its major plant at Canso, NS, which employed up to 700 people, would be closed as would the trawler port in St John's, Nfld. FPI wanted to close four plants and retire 13 trawlers. In southwest Nova Scotia, skipper owners demonstrated against quota reductions, while workers at small plants in the Digby area wondered how they could survive closure. Newfoundland's small scale fishery was in a state of despair, especially on the south and west coasts, where in the winter of 1990 hardly any fish were landed. Wherever one looked, problems appeared. Thousands of men and women were faced with unemployment, dependence on welfare, or the need to move. Communities that had lived from fishing for hundreds of years would no longer have an economic base.

Faced with a major problem, the federal government first established a high-powered task force to advise it what to do about the northern cod situation and then announced an adjustment program costing $584 million over five years. Although extremely vague in critical details, the plan was to promote rebuilding the stock, foster economic diversification within and outside the fisheries, tighten control over participation in the fisheries, and encourage exit from processing work through training programs. Notably absent was any direct aid for the inshore fishers. Indeed, the proposal to introduce individual transferrable quotas promised a reduction in the number of fishers. In such a system the TAC is divided among the enterprises according to some formula. They are then free to fish the quota or to sell it. Although limits on ownership of quota might be introduced, it seems at present that the potential for concentration of quota among a small number of well established skippers is high. There are no concrete plans for diversification as yet, no sign that the failures of the past in this respect can be overcome. In that case, training programs for those who wish to leave the fishery imply the need to migrate.

Roots of Social Change

The fundamental problem at present is that not enough fish are being caught to maintain employment. The principal cause is that recent technologies have led to catches of so much fish that some key stocks have declined. And behind the introduction of these technologies is the social process of competition that leads enterprises to search out and introduce more efficient technologies in order to outperform their rivals.

Until the late nineteenth century, fishing was a passive or waiting activity. Nets were set or hooks and lines placed in the water in the hope that fish would come to the gear and be caught. Late in the nineteenth century, steam power made it possible for fishing to become a hunting process in which the gear was active or mobile. Motor-driven vessels had sufficient power to drag nets through the water and then haul them back, ideally full of fish. This type of technology required far larger investments than could be undertaken by the poor fishing households in most of Atlantic Canada. It was only fish merchants and processors who might, if the returns appeared good, be prepared to invest in the deep-sea trawler. In the 1920s in Nova Scotia, powerful trawlers were already contentious, a source of division among fishers. By the Second World War, the old salt-fish industry based on household production appeared doomed, even in Newfoundland, and the state actively promoted the introduction of trawlers and fish-processing plants with freezing capacity. Expansion was rapid. By 1945, there were 18 trawlers and 13 freezer plants in operation with most production going to Britain (Sinclair, 1987: 34). Exports dropped briefly once Britain was able to meet its own needs, but the American market soon became important and frozen fish products increased in importance until they became the dominant component in the Newfoundland industry. This change is clearly evident in the proportion of landed cod that went to different end products (Figure 6.1). Figure 6.2 shows that the landings by offshore vessels approached those from the inshore fleet by 1965 and far surpassed them by 1970. By that time Nova Scotian trawlers, an insignificant factor until the late sixties, accounted for about 30% of all landings in Newfoundland.

Figure 6.1 Principal uses for cod, selected years, 1953–1970

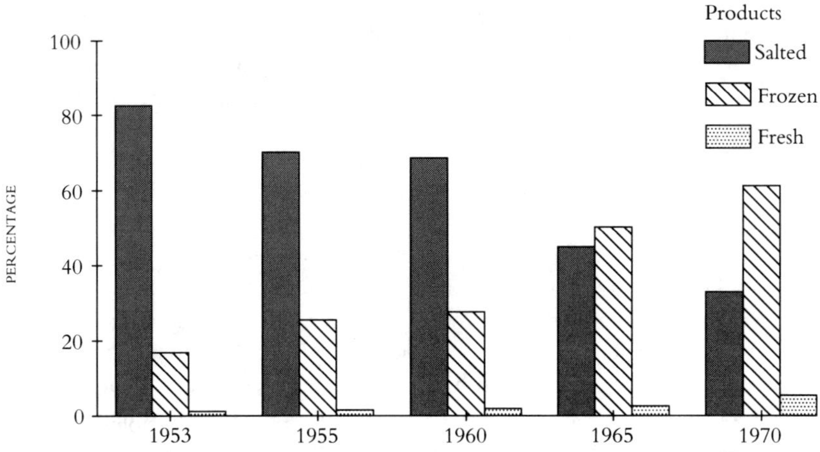

Products
Salted
Frozen
Fresh
100
80
60
40
20
0
PERCENTAGE
1953
1955
1960
1965
1970

Source: Copes (1972: 212)

Figure 6.2 Landings in Newfoundland—inshore vs offshore (% of weight)

Type of Vessel
Inshore
Offshore
100
80
60
40
20
0
PERCENTAGE
1953
1955
1960
1965
1970

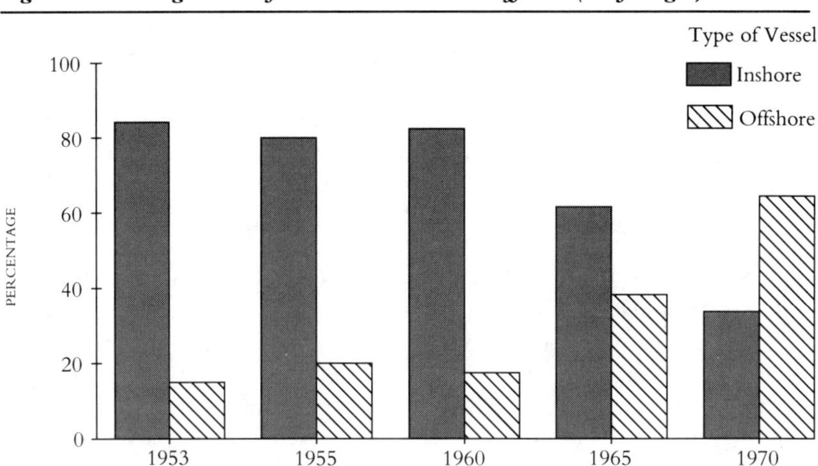

Source: Copes (1972: 199)

The new technology resulted in significant changes in the social relations in the fishery as the industry underwent a process of capitalist industrialization. In the first three centuries of fishing in the North Atlantic, the fishing was conducted by large vessels whose owners hired wage or share workers for the season. Each year the fishing ships crossed the Atlantic in the spring and then returned later in the year with their catch of salted fish. The actual fishing technology, however, was simple and most fish were caught close to shore. Eventually, settlers proved effective competitors to the fishing ships and fishing in much of Atlantic Canada became a form of household enterprise—domestic commodity production. Fish were caught from small, open boats close to shore, although schooners, outfitted and sometimes owned by merchants, sailed with crews of six to ten from many island harbours to the Labrador coast where fishing and initial curing took place during the summer.

Resident settler families, because they relied on the unpaid labour of household members for most of their subsistence needs, could catch and cure fish more cheaply than merchants who had to hire wage workers. The formally independent fishers could not push up the price for their fish except in the few areas where there was competition among merchants. Usually, the price they received for their season's catch was just enough to cover the debts they had previously incurred with the merchant for essential supplies.[4]

Whereas salt cod was produced by thousands of separate households using family labour, frozen fish was produced in a capitalist, factory-based form of production. Small-boat fishers sold fresh fish to the plants where it was processed by wage workers, among whom women came to form a growing proportion. Prior to unionization, wages were low and working conditions frequently unpleasant or harsh. The trawlers were owned by the processing companies and their crews were unorganized, semi-skilled workers who were paid on a share system that typically generated such low incomes for the physically demanding labour that turnover was high (Sinclair, 1987: 48). This situation improved after unionization in the early 1970s.

The inshore fishery itself began to lose its homogeneous character as some fishers acquired more advanced and expensive technologies. Longliners were introduced in some areas in the early 1950s (and before that, in the Maritimes) and, with government assistance, quickly took a prominent place in many fishing settlements. In some areas of Newfoundland, beginning on the west coast of the Great Northern Peninsula, these boats were adapted for dragging scallops, shrimp, and—once powerful engines had been acquired—groundfish. Off the east coast, crab grounds were discovered that were suitable for this size of vessel, which also fished mackerel and herring when they were available. In the 1980s, purse seine fishing for capelin became important as well. The coming of the longliner led to more contractual type relations between skippers and crew, and less dependence on kinship as the basis of crew formation (Stiles, 1979; Sinclair, 1985). Many longliner skippers functioned more as small capitalists than as leaders of a household production unit. Much more than in the past the skipper was a clear source of authority with the right to make fishing decisions.

The new structure of the fishery was evident in landing statistics. By 1980 in Newfoundland, trawlers were taking 35% of the catch of all species, nearshore longliners and draggers 30%, and the mass of small open boats the final 35% (Canada, 1983b: 57). Lobster and salmon catches helped give the small boats a somewhat larger share of total value. The fishery had become more diversified in technology, in social organization, and in the species caught.

As the competition for fish increased, vessels became more powerful and hauling gear more sophisticated. Electronic navigation and fish-finding equipment made it possible to pinpoint large concentrations of fish. Machine cutting and computer-controlled processing have also entered the fish plants in recent years. Yet, what proved particularly problematic for Atlantic Canada was the revival of large-scale transatlantic fishing fleets, that entered the major fishing grounds in the 1950s. Freezer trawler fleets from eastern and western Europe expanded their efforts to the point that they far exceeded the total catch of cod taken by Canadian vessels on the main fishing grounds off Newfoundland and Nova Scotia. Total landings of northern cod peaked in 1968 at 783,000 tons, after which they declined despite sustained fishing effort. The worst year for Newfoundland landings was 1974 when only 36,000 tons were caught.

After years of complaint, hesitation, and long negotiation sessions with other countries, Canada finally declared a 200-mile fishing zone, effective in 1977. Temporary subsidies had bailed out the industry and now a long-term management plan based on the 200-mile limit was intended to put everything in order for a prosperous future. To rebuild the stocks and control fishing effort a system of quotas and licences was introduced. Entrepreneurs, banks, fishers and governments all invested heavily in the industry. For example, in Newfoundland from 1976 to 1981 plant capacity rose by 230%. Since 1977, the government of Canada has been the manager of the fisheries. Instead of fish being a resource available to anyone with the means to catch them, they became state property the rights to which were delegated in the management plans. Therefore, the management policy of the Canadian state has become a major factor in the condition of the industry since that time.

For the first few years of extended jurisdiction, stock recovery and fish market conditions were encouraging, but by 1980 more trouble was in sight. That year saw bitter strikes in the inshore and offshore sectors. Within two years, plant closures and extended lay-offs had been announced, while the largest vertically integrated companies teetered on the edge of bankruptcy. By the end of 1981 a high-powered federal task force chaired by Michael Kirby was appointed to investigate the situation and recommend policy.

The task force (Canada, 1983a) located the causes of the new crisis in high debt loads as a result of excessively optimistic investments coupled with unexpectedly difficult economic circumstances. Fish were allocated to specific types of vessels, but not to specific enterprises. Thus companies struggled to acquire the capacity to catch and process as much fish as possible before their competitors could do so. Much of the expansion had been based on borrowed money such that debt-capital ratios were excessively high. Then slow markets and high short-term interest charges put fish companies under more stress. To illustrate more concretely, the real value of all fish landings fell in 1981 and 1982 when they were worth only 80% of the 1979 catch. The decline in the real value of fish products was somewhat less (Sinclair, 1987: 114).

Although the Kirby task force recognized that the small, 'flexible' plants performed better in this crisis than did the large companies, political pressures (of which the strongest was probably that of the Bank of Nova Scotia, a heavy investor in the fishery) brought forth public funds to save National Sea-Nickerson, Fisheries Products International, and the Lake Group. The short-term result was a state-supervised centralization of production and new ownership. In Newfoundland, the Bank of Nova Scotia's investments were protected as both provincial and federal governments combined with it to form FPI out of the remnants of the old companies. With new management and favourable economic conditions, FPI was soon able to report a profit and was returned to the private sector in 1987. This brings us back almost to 1989-90 and our newest resource crisis.

I have argued that underlying the crises of the fisheries are the acquisitive and expansionist drives of competitive capitalism, although the unrestrained pursuit of fish by socialist state vessels also played an important part in the period 1955-1975. Since 1977, inefficient state management of competition for the resource has contributed to continued problems. Let us now look at two case studies of the social impact of technological change and management strategies on the industry and the people of Atlantic Canada's fishing communities.

Technology and Social Structure in Northwest Newfoundland[5]

The outports along the west coast of the Great Northern Peninsula of Newfoundland were settled only in the nineteenth century. For roughly a hundred years the settlers' fishery for cod, salmon, and lobster was conducted from open boats using household labour. There was always competition from visiting schooners, and by mid-twentieth century, from deep-sea trawlers. Nevertheless, the outports themselves were socially homogeneous based on a common technology, dominated by merchant suppliers, and thus in a situation that allowed no one to accumulate capital.

By the early 1960s, the survival of households was based on fishing, subsistence production, and various state transfer payments. All able-bodied household members contributed their labour in some way to this process. Women attended both to domestic tasks—the housework, child care, and gardening—and assisted in the processing of salt fish. Family allowance cheques were paid to the mothers. Men cut and hauled wood in winter and repaired boats and homes, while collecting unemployment benefits. Some worked for pay for logging companies. In late winter, sealing was usually possible. In the spring, lobster were caught inshore along the southern part of the coast. By June, capelin and cod moved close enough to be caught by traps, hand-lines and gill nets. Homes were built and gardens maintained where the soil allowed (Firestone, 1967).

Between 1965 and 1980, technological changes brought social changes to the area. Beginning in the early 1960s, the social structure became more differentiated as some enterprising fishers managed to purchase or build bigger boats of 12 to 14 metres in length. These innovative fishers were no longer prepared to toil like their fathers, fishing lobster in miserable conditions for next to no income. By the early 1970s, scallop and shrimp dragging had started with Port au Choix as the primary centre. Gradually, vessel sizes and horsepower increased, as fishing success encouraged more investment. Today, the best equipped, steel-hulled draggers cost about $1,250,000.

With the emergence of the draggers, the fleet structure has become more complex. There are now about 80 active, mobile-gear vessels based on the west coast of the island of Newfoundland and the southern part of Labrador. Under fisher ownership for the most part, and crewed by about 250 hired sharemen, they are essentially small capitalist enterprises. Most of the other 2,400 fishers in the region work from open wooden boats powered by outboard motors and roughly 5 to 8 metres long. They fish with traps, gill nets, baited lines and jiggers (lure and unbaited hook attached to a line) in waters close to shore. A few larger vessels have inboard diesel engines. About 700 fishers have lobster licences, while half that number have commercial salmon licences.

As the early draggers became better equipped, their skippers more knowledgeable and their catches improved, others were attracted to the fishery. It was at this time that the state also became more involved as a manager. By the mid-1970s, Canadian fisheries managers had become convinced of the validity of the economists' attack on the evils of common property—principally that it promoted excess capacity, economic inefficiency, loss of resource rent, and overfishing of the stocks. The result in the Gulf of St Lawrence was the creation of limited-access licensing to fisheries of relatively high value.

In 1983, the licensing system changed in response to concerns over poor quality and over-capitalization as draggers scrambled to get the largest possible share of the quotas allocated to their fleet sector. The mobile-gear fleet was technically capable of catching much more than its season quota, which meant that there was a strong incentive for all skippers to catch fish as quickly as possible. This rush led to gluts of poor quality fish, due to improper handling on board, especially in the winter fishery off southwest Newfoundland where the fish tend to be densely concentrated.[6] At times, either the buyers or the federal government imposed daily trip limits, but the most interesting step was the introduction of seasonal, non-transferrable quotas attached to a specific vessel. This system appears to have been accepted by the skippers and remains in force.

In practice, licensing and quota policy favour the small dragger fleet. The vessel and gear licensing system restricts access to the most productive technology in the name of economic efficiency and thus protects a class of affluent skippers and draggermen at the expense of those who have to rely on older technologies.

Figure 6.3 Cod landings, areas 4RS and 3Pn, eastern Gulf of St Lawrence

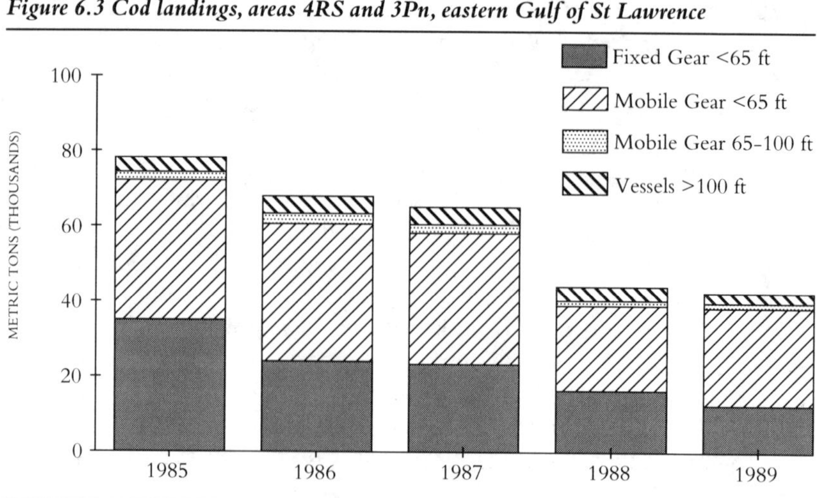

Source: Canada (1990: 24). Data for 1988 and 1989 are preliminary.

It is now clear that the control strategy of the last fifteen years has not protected the resource from overfishing. The strategy generates social conflict and threatens the viability of many household enterprises, which are denied access to fish. As indicated in Figure 6.3, the catches of small fixed-gear vessels, on which the majority of fishers depend, have collapsed since 1985. Because the social inequalities are buttressed by state policy, they are particularly resented by those who cannot benefit. Social resentment is created not simply because one group is well off, but also because the fishing élite is thought to behave illegally and treat other fishers unfairly by catching so much that there is next to nothing left for open-boat operators. There is no point in small-boat fishers receiving a quota if the fish don't reach their nets any more.

State policy at present clearly supports the petty capitalist dragger fishery against the household or domestic commodity form of production that is represented by the open-boat fisheries. But the management policy is also relevant to the very survival of villages in the area, because the privileged fleet is concentrated in only a few harbours: Port au Choix, Port Saunders and Anchor Point. When the small-boat fishers are deprived of fish, the culture and structure of their villages are threatened. They are increasingly becoming rural welfare ghettos. Parsons Pond, for example, is a small fishing community in which government transfer payments accounted for 48.6% of total income in 1986 (data supplied by Statistics Canada).

Digby Neck and the Islands

The experience of people in northwest Newfoundland is by no means unusual in Atlantic Canada. Consider the case of Digby Neck and the Islands, situated in southwest Nova Scotia between the Bay of Fundy and St Mary's Bay.[7] The Acadian settlers of this area survived by integrating marine, agricultural, and forest resources in a household economy similar to that on the Great Northern Peninsula, although in this region fishing is possible year-round. For much of the twentieth century the coastal fishery for lobster, cod, and pollock was based on day trips in partially covered vessels of about 13-14 metres in length, i.e., more substantial than the inshore Newfoundland fleet. In 1955, small draggers were introduced under fisher ownership. This sector of the fleet expanded from 10 in 1957 to 35 by 1983, while the number of fishers declined from 550 to 367. Whereas in Newfoundland the dragger and small-boat fisheries both expanded over this time period, the Digby Neck draggers have reduced others close to the point of extinction, at least to a part-time, seasonal activity dependent on lobster. That the draggers may also eliminate themselves by overfishing is a distinct possibility.

Until recently, it is clear the limited-entry licence to dragging had become a valued possession, a key to relatively high incomes. The boat share provided the source of capital accumulation and the division of labour became more impersonal. Skipper-owners could provide their children with a chance to enter the fishery that remained unavailable to others. As in northwest Newfoundland, the result is a sharply divided community structure in which divisions are guaranteed by state licensing policy. The resentment of those excluded from the licences and rewards is strong.

As the fishery has changed, population has become concentrated in the dragger ports and processing centres, the only communities to retain any sense of vitality. And as in other areas, fish processing has become a factory-based activity organized on capitalist principles. Here too there has been concentration as the number of processing establishments in the area fell from 23 in 1961 to 10 in 1984, by which time freezers and machine processing had become normal. Plant owners are also involved in the harvesting sector as they try to ensure supplies of fish by helping to finance the new draggers. Women now form an important segment of the plant labour force, but are concentrated in the casual, less skilled and less well paid jobs. Paid work in the fishery is clearly gender-segregated.

Conclusion

The competitive struggle to acquire valued fish resources is the underlying dynamic force behind the ecological and economic crises of so many of Atlantic Canada's fishing communities. Highly efficient fish-hunting technologies introduced in this competitive situation provide fishing enterprises with the capability of overfishing. Our knowledge of relevant marine biology has proved too incomplete and the attempts of the state to regulate the fisheries have failed to prevent the problems described in this chapter.

Notes

[1]This old, gender-neutral word is preferable to 'fisherman'.

[2]A detailed account of women's work in three Newfoundland plants is provided in Neis (1988).

[3]This review is based on Sinclair (1986: 33-4), but see also Clement (1987: 63-5) for a similar presentation.

[4]For an excellent account of this system in the Gaspé and how it inhibited development see Ommer (1981; 1989).

[5]Parts of this section are drawn from a recent paper (Sinclair, 1990). For a fuller discussion of this region, see Sinclair (1985).

[6]Every year in December the small trawlers head south in preparation for the winter fishery based on Port aux Basques.

[7]The following paragraphs summarize some key points in Anthony Davis' (forthcoming) study. See also Davis and Thiessen (1988). Another interesting case study, thoroughly researched, is of the lower north shore of Quebec (Breton *et al.*, 1988).

SECTION THREE

RURAL LIVING: PROBLEMS AND ISSUES

The chapters in Section Three discuss the substantial changes and challenges that modernization of rural industries, trends in fertility and mortality, and immigration patterns present to rural areas.

The first chapter examines the problems faced by contemporary rural educational systems. Declining fertility rates and the out-migration of younger rural families have caused declining enrolments in the rural school systems. The typical response to this problem, while at the same time attempting to maintain or increase the quality of education, has been closure of the smaller rural schools and their consolidation into larger school divisions or districts. According to Randhawa the process, rationale, and effects of school consolidation have not been adequately researched prior to actual consolidation. The potential benefits and optimal size of larger schools should in future be more systematically studied, and the populations affected by school consolidation should be more adequately consulted and involved in the realignment of rural school systems.

In the second chapter of this section, Schissel discusses trends in rural crime rates. Rural areas have traditionally been viewed as havens of security, peace, and tranquillity. However Schissel indicates that the rates of criminal activity in rural areas tend to be keeping pace with and — for certain types of crime — exceeding the rates evident in urban areas. Certain age groups' fear of being victimized by crime is approaching the fear of crime experienced by urban residents.

The chapter by Keating outlines the experiences and problems of older rural Canadians. In addition to the aging of the population due to declining fertility and mortality rates and the out-migration of the younger families, many rural towns and villages also serve as retirement centres for the surrounding population. As a result rural centres have a larger proportion of aged populations than is apparent in the overall Canadian or provincial populations, and are faced with the problems of providing the services required by this age group.

The invisible and generally unrecognized and undervalued contribution of women to rural (especially farm) enterprises is discussed in the chapter by Smith. The typology developed by Smith highlights the many ways in which women contribute to the maintenance of the farm, the household, and the family. In addition to the involvement in farm activities, an increasing number of farm women are also involved in off-farm work. Women also provide the necessary leadership and volunteer activities to community organizations.

CHAPTER SEVEN

RURAL EDUCATION: OPPORTUNITIES AND ISSUES

BIKKAR S. RANDHAWA

Demographic changes in Canada in the past 25 years have been as variable as the regions themselves. For example, in most provinces the trend toward urbanization has in the last decade not only discontinued but there has been a net gain in urban-to-rural migration; in Saskatchewan and Manitoba the rural depopulation continued (see Table 7.1). With the change in population demography in Canada, there have been concomitant changes in educational services and opportunities.

A general description of demographic changes in Canada clarifies the mistaken notion of general rural depopulation while, in fact, the rural population in absolute terms increased in every decade since 1901 except two, 1941–1951 and 1961–1971. Even though the proportion of rural population has been decreasing, in 1986 Canada had the largest ever number of rural residents.

Demographic Changes in Canada

In 1851 only about 13% of the Canadian population lived in urban areas. Today more than 75% of all Canadians live in urban areas; 75.5% and 76.5% of

Bikkar S. Randhawa is a Professor of Educational Psychology at the University of Saskatchewan.

the Canadian population lived in urban areas in 1976 and 1986, respectively (Statistics Canada, 1979; 1987). Indubitably, the trend toward disproportionate urban growth continues. Moreover, Ontario is the most urban province, 82.1% of its residents lived in urban centres in 1986. Other provinces which had higher percentages of the residents living in urban areas in 1986 than the national average were Alberta (79.4%), British Columbia (79.3%), and Quebec (77.9%). Figure 7.1 shows the percentages of rural population in Canada, the ten provinces, and the two territories in 1976 and 1986. PEI is the most rural province; 82% of its population lived in rural areas in 1986. This province recorded an approximate proportional drop of 1.6% in its rural population between 1976 and 1986. However, it must be clear that the number of rural residents in the province actually increased. This suggests that the growth patterns of rural and urban areas were disproportionate. That is, as there was a slight increase in the total population of the province in the time interval between the two censuses, the absolute population increase of the urban centres was more dramatic than those of the rural areas. This is illustrated in Table 7.1.

The Atlantic provinces were the four highest in the proportion of rural population among the Canadian provinces in 1986. Moreover, among the three prairie provinces, Saskatchewan had the largest proportion of rural population in 1986 (39%) and in 1976 (44.5%). From 1976 to 1986 Saskatchewan lost about 5% and Manitoba lost 3.5% of their rural populations, mostly to urban centres within and outside the province. The growth in the urban population of Manitoba (7.3%) was not as dramatic as that of Saskatchewan

Table 7.1 Net percentage change in the total, rural, and urban population of Canada, provinces, and territories between 1976 and 1986*

JURISDICTION	TOTAL	RURAL	URBAN
Canada	10.1	5.7	11.4
Newfoundland	1.9	1.8	2.0
Prince Edward Island	7.1	5.4	10.0
Nova Scotia	5.4	10.0	1.8
New Brunswick	4.8	11.2	-1.2
Quebec	4.8	10.9	3.2
Ontario	10.1	4.9	11.3
Manitoba	4.1	-3.5	7.3
Saskatchewan	9.6	-5.0	21.3
Alberta	28.7	6.3	36.2
British Columbia	16.9	5.1	20.4
Yukon	7.6	-2.6	14.2
Northwest Territories	22.6	30.7	14.4

*Adapted from Statistics Canada (1979), Catalogue no. 98-802 and Statistics Canada (1987), Catalogue nos. 92-109 to 92-120.

Figure 7.1 Percentages of rural population (1976 and 1986) for Canada, provinces, and territories

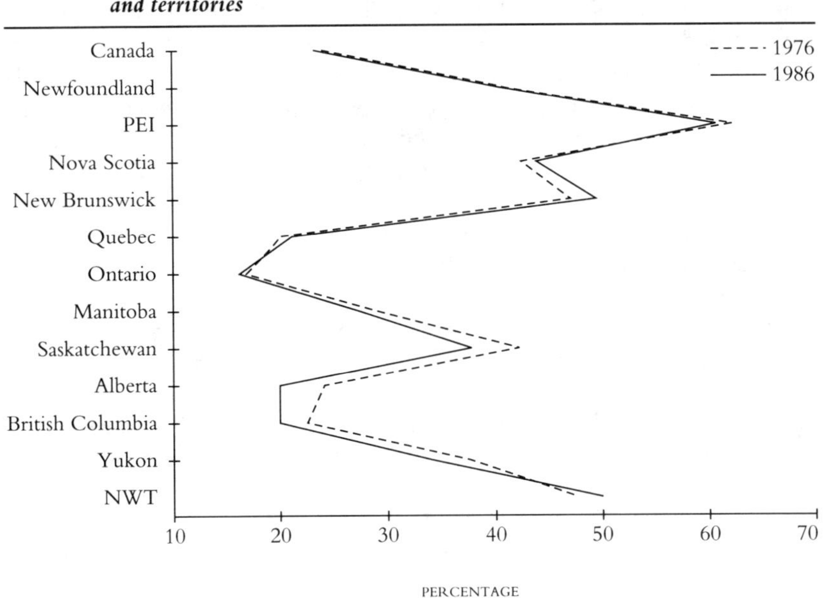

(21.3%). Overall, Saskatchewan and Manitoba experienced a population growth of 9.6%, and 4.1%, respectively, in the ten-year period 1976–1986.

In Ontario, Alberta, and British Columbia the total rural population during the 1976 to 1986 decade increased, although the proportional rural population had decreased. This scenario is similar to that discussed for PEI. Interestingly, New Brunswick was the only province experiencing a net decline of 1.2% in its urban population and a net gain of 11.2% in its rural population during this period, with an overall net increase in its population of 4.8%.

Although Statistics Canada (1984), on the basis of comparisons of 1976 and 1981 populations, concluded that urbanization was on the rise in the Prairies and the Yukon, but was declining in all of the other provinces, there was a decline of only 0.4% in the rural population of Saskatchewan. Manitoba, on the other hand, had a slight, 0.1%, increase in its rural population. The next five years took their toll on these provinces because their rural populations declined substantially, 3.5% in Manitoba and 5% in Saskatchewan, between 1976 and 1986. These losses in the rural populations of these two prairie provinces were in sharp contrast to the 5.7% growth nationally in the rural population during this decade. In fact, increased urbanization (a net percentage change in population was higher than the total net percentage increase) was observed in all provinces except Nova Scotia, New Brunswick, and Quebec.

Changes in the School-Age Population

Statistics Canada (1978 and 1988) provided the school-age populations for the last two mid-census years. Unfortunately, the school-age definition was not the same in these tabulations. The data for the 1978 census defined as school-age those individuals who were between and including the ages of five years and 19 years; for the 1986 data, the school-age group comprised those people who were between and including the ages of six years and 17 years. Despite this variability, it is assumed for the purposes of this chapter that proportional distributions of these groups in rural and urban centres of Canada and the provinces would be comparable and that comparative judgements can be made without prejudice.

The aggregated rural school-age population in Canada remained virtually unchanged at 27.7% between 1978 and 1986. However, when the rural population is broken down into non-farm and farm groups an interesting picture emerges. While the non-farm school-age population increased by 1.2%, there was a corresponding decline of about 1.2% in the farm school-age population. This might suggest that any net population increase in the rural sector during this decade was limited to the non-farm rural sector. No infusion of new school-age children either of new settlers or of those from the internal migration group took place in the farm sector. If anything, in some of the provinces there was a slight downturn in the number of school-age children who lived on farms. It might also suggest that the rural farm sector population is aging and the proportional contribution to the school-age population of this sector is decreasing. Taken together, these two factors would affect school enrolments in small rural farm-based schools. More school closures and a concomitant economic decline and business disruption could be the result. Scharf (1974) pointed out that rural schools provided stable economic and social activity for rural communities. With the closing of the rural school, substantial domino effects on economic, social, political, and cultural domains have been noted (Sher, 1981; Sher and Tompkins, 1976). In fact, rural school closure is not a new phenomenon in Alberta, Saskatchewan, Manitoba, and elsewhere (Marshall, 1985). The reasons for closures have been varied. Among the most common are educational and economic benefits. These assumptions of consolidation were questioned several years ago (Barker and Gump, 1964), and debate on such emotional issues can never be dispensed with on the basis of rational and objective evidence.

Currently, even in those provinces where rural population has been increasing, the increase has usually been in areas adjacent to the urban centres. People left the urban core centres and moved to the fringes of the large and moderate-sized cities. With the exception of Alberta, Saskatchewan, and Manitoba, all other Canadian provinces recorded a net positive migration in 1981 from cities to rural areas (Statistics Canada, 1984). In fact, a substantial proportion of rural population growth was from this internal migration. For example, 85.7% of the rural growth in Ontario in 1981 was due to the urban-rural migration. The corresponding percentage for Canada was 51.1. Due to these migrations, the rural school districts adjacent to the cities have shown steady or improved enrolments. But that does not mean that these school districts did not face consolidation problems and other educational challenges.

Rural School Development and Consolidation: A Saskatchewan Focus

The development of Canada as a federal state is marked by the unique educational, social, and cultural history of each of the provinces as they joined Confederation. It is a challenging task to review the rural education development and consolidation of each province. To reduce the challenge and for the economy of space a brief history of the rural school in Saskatchewan is undertaken here. Presumably, parallel developments in the other provinces of Canada can be assumed without specific reference to the dates, documents, and legislation mentioned here.

In 1905, as Saskatchewan became a province of Canada, there were about 900 school districts already in existence. In most instances, these school districts were comprised of only one school. Between 1905 and 1930 Saskatchewan witnessed a phenomenal growth in population. The new settlers were keen to provide a better life for their children and the means for achieving this was thought to be education. Hence, there was a tremendous increase in the number of elementary schools in the southern belt of the province where newcomers lived in ethnic settlements, 'which differed one from the other in language and culture' (Saskatchewan Education, 1981: 20). This necessitated legislation for the development of a system of schools, school districts, and local school boards. There was both quantitative growth and development of elementary education in the province. Also, the objectives and the scope of provincial jurisdiction were expanded to include a system to provide secondary education in urban centres (The Secondary Education Act, 1907); free text books (The Free Text Book Act, 1908); education of blind and deaf children (1924; 1928); and correspondence school education (1925).

The Depression and war years (1930 to 1945) had a serious impact on the educational developments in the province.

> Education allocation by the province dropped from about $17 million in 1929 to $8.5 million in 1935. To compensate for the serious problems faced by the small school boards, the province introduced the concept of equalization grants which in 1939 amounted to $100 a year to rural and village districts. (Saskatchewan Education, 1981: 21)

In 1944, The Larger School Unit Act initiated a restructuring of rural education. School district boundaries were redrawn and consolidation began in earnest. The consolidation direction implemented through this legislation was supported by the 1956 Province of Saskatchewan Royal Commission report entitled *Rural Education.* The report recommended the continued consolidation of school facilities in villages and towns in order to improve 'standards of education'. The construction of comprehensive schools in the province was completed in the early 1970s, marking the end of many small rural high schools.

The impact of this development continues to be felt to the present time. This is partly illustrated by the enrolment in grades 1 to 12 in the province between 1979 and 1983 as shown in Figure 7.2. The figure shows a marked decrease in enrolment in high school grades (10 to 12). Not only did grades 10 to 12 have an unusual drop in their enrolment but grades 8 and 9 were also affected. This might be due to the fact that if an older sibling is driving or riding a bus to a city or a large town comprehensive school the younger sibling(s) might also accompany him/her to the same or another school. At least, this is how such a large discrepancy in enrolments between 1979 and 1983 could be explained. The actual 1979 enrolments in the three cohort groups (grades 6, 7, and 8) four years later, in 1983, would be in grades 10, 11, and 12, respectively. Differences in birth rates and other factors do not seem to fully explain these enrolment trends.

Figure 7.2 Actual enrolments for 1979; projected enrolments (accurate within ±1% to the actual) for 1983 and 1987, by grade, in rural Saskatchewan

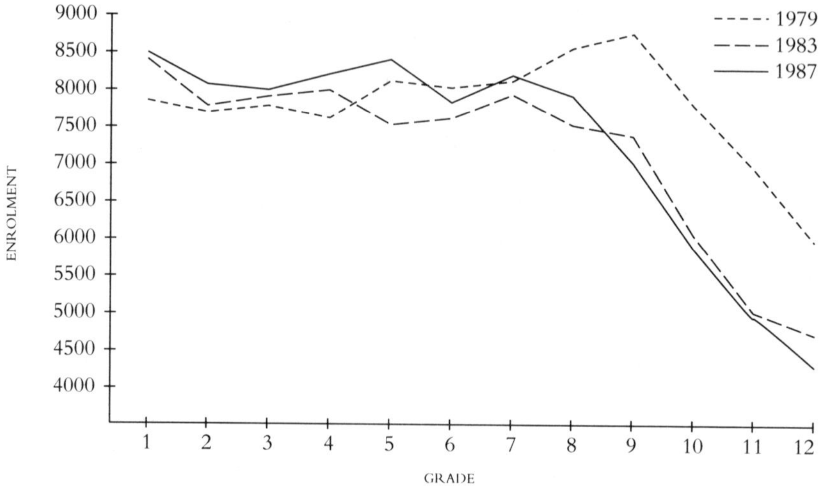

Source: adapted from *Saskatchewan Education* 1981: 3, Figure 1

Whether the quality of education, measured on objective criteria, offered in these huge and well equipped comprehensive high schools is better than that was (is) in the (remaining) small rural high schools has not been substantiated.

Issues and Effects of Demographic Changes on Educational Opportunities in Rural Sectors

Any major or minor demographic changes in school-age population have had educational, economic, social, and cultural ramifications in the affected communities and school districts (see Scharf, 1974; Lucas, 1982). Declining school enrolments and closure have been typical of rural, agricultural areas in North America almost since this continent was settled by the early colonists. A brief survey of contemporary issues with regard to changing demography and its effects follows.

Inevitability of School Closure and Futility of Local Protest

The fact of chronic rural population decline and school closure may have led to the assumption that it was irrevocable (Lucas, 1982). Lucas attributes the futility of much of rural protest against school closure to such an assumption. Indeed, he outlined two central issues in regards to these protestations and conflicts:

> Two central issues were evident in these conflicts, with some variations in intensity related to particular community circumstances. First [,] it is almost the sole defence available to many small rural communities to assume that there will be an impact upon the traditions, social identity, and ultimate survival of the community. The second issue, closely related, concerns the quality of education that such communities are able to provide under restricted circumstances; school authorities may offer alluring educational opportunities in transfers to larger schools in larger communities. On these two issues it is difficult, and probably dangerous, to draw the line between 'subjective' and 'objective' data. (Lucas, 1982: 251)

It will be shown that there is objective evidence on the issues of school closures but it is often ignored by policy-makers and bureaucrats with preconceived notions that 'bigger' is better (Haller and Monk, 1988). Earlier consolidations resulted in the closure of many one-room schools and small school districts. That consolidation, whether good or bad, took place under the perceived belief of achieving better efficiency and equity and equality of educational opportunity (for a clarification of the distinction between equity and equality, see Randhawa, 1991: 140–2). It is not evident that the stated or implied objectives were realized because those closures took place under the theoretical belief of consolidation without any supportive empirical research on educational outcomes and on the social and economic advantages and disadvantages of the resultant amalgamations. Interestingly, what is happening now is that the available research is often ignored by those commissions or consultants appointed to advise on consolidation of schools or school districts, because an overwhelming amount of evidence points against the larger schools or school districts (see Sher, 1986). For example, in North Carolina, the State Education Department prepared a document recommending an encompassing, mandatory reorganization of schools in the state. It concluded that recent research showed that school districts in the state should serve at least 5,000 students and that the optimal number was 10,000. Haller and Monk (1988) pointed out 'had the authors of this report relied upon earlier research, they would have found even larger numbers'. Hanson (1964) concluded, on the basis of a study of nine states, an optimal size of 20,000 students, the smallest in the nine states involved, for a school district in Nebraska and of 180,000 students, the largest, in New York. Sher (1988) pointed out that the North Carolina report did not seem to have relied on any research conducted after 1971 and it even failed to acknowledge one study conducted by an official of the department. Sher also found that when department officials conducted studies of the feasibility of specific mergers of school districts, they always found in favour of the proposed consolidation.

Analysis of Costs and Benefits

Enrolment shifts take place in all school districts, rural and urban. However, when enrolments decline below a magic number, regardless of how it is derived, since the strident move to consolidation began in the 1960s, the only solution has been to consolidate that school or district with one or more schools or districts. There has been no systematic research which has unequivocally demonstrated the systemic costs and benefits of school closure or of school district consolidation as a function of size. Nor have other viable alternatives been explored. Usually the word comes down the bureaucratic hierarchy and the public is made aware of the proposed action. Protests begin, commissions or committees are appointed, and schools close or are consolidated anyway (Haller and Monk, 1988). It is no wonder that the public has become cynical of politicians and bureaucrats.

What should be expected in the future? The same, unless administrative practices and attitudes change; taxpayers become better informed and more active; and proper study by independently appointed experts or committees is undertaken to fully assess the costs and benefits of a school closure or district consolidation. The economy-and-efficiency argument does not seem to stand rigorous scrutiny. For example, Barker and Gump (1964) demonstrated that larger schools were more impressive on the outside, but on closer examination the smaller school provided a higher quality of education. They called this the inside outside perceptual paradox. Similarly, Hind (1979) determined that most school closures were not as economically efficient as originally proposed.

Size of the school or school district is often only the surface pretext; there are usually a number of explicit and implicit motives for a proposed closure. Burns, Taylor, and Miller (1984) identified a few, among them availability of space in a neighbouring facility; viability of the program being offered; better physical facilities accessible elsewhere; and contemplated district or program reorganization.

School Closure Policy

Not all provinces operate without a formal policy on school closure. Ontario, for instance, requires school boards to provide for public input in the process of considering of school closure. Also required in the Ontario school closure policy is provision of a realistic time frame from the date of announcement of intention to close a school to when the school is actually closed. Burns *et al.* (1984) found, however, that the intent of these policies is rarely followed. They also found that the views of the community were usually ignored by the board; that the involvement of parents and the community in the process was a reaction to closure, not a part of the process; that greater planning for closure resulted in greater opposition to closure; and that the intent to close a school was rarely reversed by community reaction. The study concluded that school boards did not seem to need help in the process of school closure, but they needed assistance in conflict management.

Quality of Programs

The most fundamental concern of any parent for the quality of a school is the program and its delivery. It is not surprising, therefore, that when a school closure is contemplated by bureaucrats, a primary reason advanced is the program quality and its breadth. Is this a coincidence or do the planners know that such a rationale would be a proper defence against the emotional uprising of the community that is to be anticipated? Most administrators have been trained with a strong theoretical belief that bigger schools offer better program alternatives and that the staff's academic and professional strengths can be more fully exploited. This argument may look acceptable on the surface, but what are the outcomes of larger and smaller schools in terms of the quality of education? It is implied in the proposed rationale that students will be more satisfied with the school, and, since the instructional work will be carried out by more competent professionals, the student will learn more in larger comprehensive schools. However, the available research does not seem to bear out this theoretical expectation. For instance, Randhawa (1991) found that small rural schools had a lower percentage of dropouts than the big urban schools. In another study, Randhawa and Michayluk (1975) demonstrated that there were no significant differences in the intellectual ability of rural and urban classes; however, they noted that, in terms of the perceived learning environments, rural classes rated their learning situations on a number of dimensions to be more favourable than those rated by the urban classes.

Furthermore, it can be concluded from the past available research in the US that 'large schools have adverse effects on certain aspects of education and social development of youth' (Haller and Monk, 1988: 471). Since the publication of the comparative analysis of the outcomes of smaller and larger schools by Barker and Gump (1964), it is becoming clear that 'students in smaller schools participate more actively in the extra-curriculum, have better self concepts, and exhibit lower levels of alienation' (Haller and Monk, 1988: 471). Hamilton (1963) has an excellent review of such social consequences of schooling in different situations. Moreover, there is an indication that smaller schools are more affiliated with their communities (Carlsen and Dunn, 1978; Kay, 1981; Peshkin, 1978) and have less hierarchical, more collegial decision-making mechanisms than larger schools (Dunn, 1977). Goodlad (1984) found big schools a source of undesirable outcomes. Boyer (1983) discovered that big schools were the source of a dilemma wherein possibilities for enlarged curriculum must be balanced against the drawbacks for student social development or increased parental involvement.

Social Costs and Survival of Rural Community

The social costs of consolidation must be properly weighed before the existing few small rural schools vanish from the scene. A broader alternative perspective than the economic, which is tenuous at best, and the illusory enlarged curriculum advantages, appears to be necessary in this sensitive area. As we continue to make our urban centres less desirable to inhabit, there might be increased population migration back to the rural areas. We may need these institutions in the near future, perhaps in a more numerous form.

Currently, however, the population decline in rural communities and the concomitant enrolment drop in those communities' schools threaten not only the school but the community itself. It has been observed that the closure of a school, which might in the first instance be the result of the shrinking population in the community and the surrounding farms, would speed up the decay and closure of the community. In fact, many ghost towns in the prairies and elsewhere bear witness to this phenomenon.

Lest the above gives the impression of cause and effect such is not the case. For example, imagine the scenario where a small rural town is witnessing an out-migration at a tremendous rate. Businesses are closing down or threatening to close down if some action is not taken quickly. What can be done? Some would argue that it is a natural process of the emerging demographic pattern. People cannot be kept hostage in a community. They have the right to live wherever the opportunity presents itself. They have the right to support the local institutions and businesses or to do their business elsewhere.

Lucas (1982) speculated that 'small rural communities are to some degree the victims of an empirically-based demographic theory predicting their eventual and inevitable demise in a society evolving steadily toward urbanization' (Lucas, 1982: 257). He characterized this theory as the 'resettlement idea', in that the declining rural small communities are essentially insignificant and are, therefore, destined for ultimate disappearance. Two implications derive from this theoretical perspective: (1) let the resettlement forces influence the natural course of demise; and (2) decide either to withhold resources from the 'doomed' communities and thus speed up the process of demise or to distribute resources to communities which are expected to survive and thus pave the path for the emerging demographic landscape which will eventually contribute to the disappearance of the less viable communities.

A formal policy may not govern the deliberate action of the bureaucrats but there appears to be operational evidence demonstrating that deliberate actions might indeed have been at work to speed up the process of rural depopulation. For example, establishing a modern comprehensive school in a larger community—with all the accompanying promises of provision of up-to-date, in breadth and depth, programs, unparalleled by any in even larger cities—could very well be a case of differential allocation of resources to communities. The additional resource may act as a magnet for smaller communities to begin to use it at the cost of the local secondary schools. Lucas (1982) cites another example in which the school board's adamant refusal to commence kindergartens in rural community schools was interpreted by the community pressure groups as a deliberate act of withholding resources 'which would serve community educational needs and also bolster declining enrolments' (Lucas, 1982: 257). In another instance, the school board insisted on bussing students from a closed small rural school to a town school, rather than to a school in a neighbouring community which was much closer than the town. Unless such interventions and attitudes change, we look with dismay toward the day that some rural communities in Canada have been made a thing of the past.

The growth of industry in larger cities, and also only in some but not in other regions, has not taken place randomly and without intervention by local, provincial, and federal governments. It is not the outcome of historical accident. It can be demonstrated that industrial growth benefits from the differential allocation of resources by authorities. The outcome of authoritative actions and discriminations in the provision of supplies and services is evident. The railway freight rate differentials are another example of authoritative action. Currently, the closure of railway lines to rural communities would further hasten the decline of these communities, and their educational services would, as a consequence, also wither away if not totally disappear.

Rural communities and their institutions can survive only if the inequities of the past are reversed and corrected. These communities have to be seen as valuable and deserving of support for the ultimate equal and equitable distribution and provision of services. A possible national small rural community network could embark on effective and co-ordinated political action against future inequitable distribution of resources and protect and enhance the small rural communities of the nation.

Conclusions

It has been demonstrated that there is an emerging shift in the demography of Canada. Except for the Prairies, it is evident that at least the fringe towns in the shadows of the large cities have shown population growth in the last decade. Still small rural communities are in danger of demise unless a new strategy is developed; the past discriminatory practices in allocating resources to communities cease; and corrective actions are taken.

The issue of rural education is very sensitive and an irrational approach to school closure should no longer be allowed. Rural communities must develop political and cohesive strategies to protect their schools and the interdependent survival of their communities. In the face of a school closure, if the rural community chooses to protest, in spite of the past perceived futility and the irrevocability of school closure, its protest must be well orchestrated and effective. A rural small community network for a collective and co-ordinated political action might be an alternative the potential of which has not been fully explored.

CHAPTER EIGHT

RURAL CRIME, POLICING, AND RELATED ISSUES

BERNARD SCHISSEL

It is difficult to discuss issues of crime and justice in modern-day rural Canada within the narrow confines of law-breaking and law-enforcing. While Canada's legal system assumes a monolithic society, rural Canada is distinctly heterogeneous. Region-specific issues such as rural depopulation, dwindling agriculture and fishing economies, hinterland development, and ethnic and class discrimination are indicative of regional diversity and are linked by the common thread of economic and political marginality. These issues are central to discussions of crime and the administration of justice in rural areas.

Large-scale prairie agriculture, the BC fruit growing industry, Quebec and Ontario mixed farming, the Atlantic and west coast fishing industry, and the northern hinterlands have all experienced 'boom and bust' times. As a result, the cultural and social life in these essentially rural areas has been in a constant state of change. There is little Canadian research documenting the impact of urbanization and industrialization on actual crime committed. American studies, however, have shown that with urbanization, crime increases in the rural setting because of a diffusion of criminal activity from the city to the country, or structural changes (unemployment, poverty, and gun ownership)

Bernard Schissel is an Assistant Professor in the Department of Sociology at the University of Saskatchewan.

that are conducive to criminal activity (Carter and Beaulieu, 1984; Fischer, 1980). As well, with hinterland development rural communities become more transient and, as a result, informal mechanisms of social control may become eroded (Boggs, 1971). However, it is ironic that in the face of a rapidly changing industrial society, rural residents in Canada and the United States fiercely defend rural life as a safe haven from the evils of urban society (Linden and Minch, 1985; Smith and Huff, 1982).

Changes in official and unofficial crime rates in non-urban areas can be partially attributed to the changing economic and demographic nature of these areas, to the nature of justice as it is applied to generally disempowered peoples, and to a collective sense of political and economic helplessness. There is a vast body of North American literature which addresses the issue of crime in declining economies (Currie, 1985; Wright, 1981). Its overriding theme is that criminal activity is correlated with high inflation, high unemployment, and low productivity, and that these economic indicators are reflective of a system which may produce economic hardship for the individual and make the acquisition of an adequate livelihood difficult by legal means. Such explanations address only a part of the problem of crime in economically marginal areas in Canada.

The Nature and Extent of Rural Crime

Traditionally, rural society has been depicted as a sanctuary of security. In marked contrast to its urban counterpart, the rural context has always been perceived as a secure refuge where crime is evident but minimal. The need for formal control has been obviated by low rates of crime and by informal mechanisms of social control which derive from extended family ties and mutual economic and social interests. Low official crime rates, characteristic of some rural regions, have been shown to result from informal community control of offenders rather than from less crime committed. The specific crimes that are dealt with informally tend to be property crimes and petty theft; in non-urban areas, these crimes go largely unreported to police (Shapland, 1983).

The changing nature of the agriculture and fishing sectors, and the resource exploitation of rural areas in Canada have altered the nature and extent of rural crime. While rural areas may not be substantially more criminogenic than before, they are perceived as such by constituents and social control agents. Increased citizen participation in crime prevention and control in rural areas is evidence that security is presently an overriding concern in non-urban societies (Linden and Minch, 1985).

Unfortunately, one of the major obstacles in analyzing rural crime in Canada is the lack of information; rural crime has largely been ignored by researchers, and has been given low priority by government agencies. As a result, we are relegated to using available aggregated statistics that reveal very little about the rural context other than that it is not urban. The available official statistics do show that the urban crime rate exceeds that of rural areas, and that over time, the difference is diminishing only marginally. The trends in overall criminal offences are illustrated in Figure 8.1.

Figure 8.1 Total criminal code rate by demographic area, Canada, 1977-1989

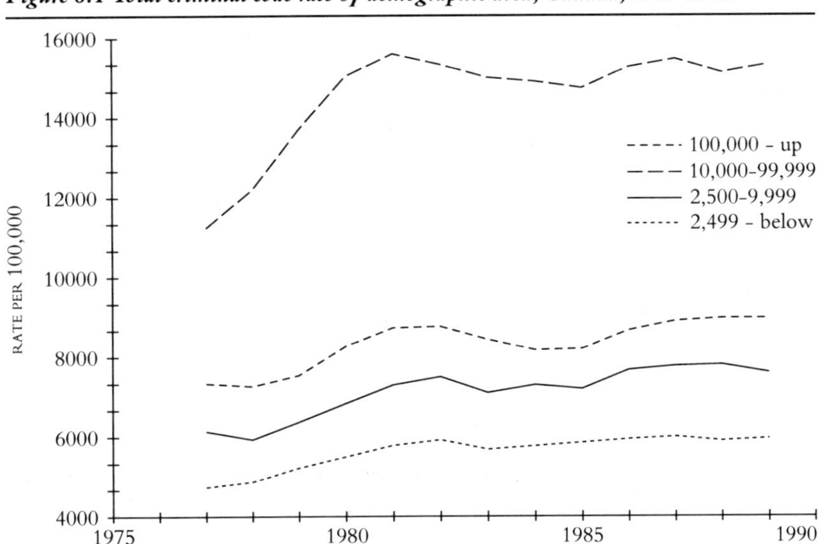

These findings suggest that while the smallest, most rural communities (under 2,500) experience the least official crime, the communities with the highest rates of crime are the small urban centres and not the large, highly urban communities. These data also illustrate the enduring crime rate difference between rural and urban areas. However, a closer look at different categories of crime reveals that the trends depicted in Figure 8.1 are somewhat misleading. The selected crime categories here are homicide, total violent offences, and property crimes.

Figures 8.2, 8.3 and 8.4 depict homicide, violent crime, and property crime rates respectively for different community sizes in Canada.

In Figure 8.2, we see that the large urban centres have relatively low rates of homicide compared with most rural communities. The findings in this figure, however, must be viewed with some scepticism because there are relatively few homicides in Canada per year and an unexpectedly high number of homicides in one area in one year may skew the graphs significantly. For example, in the line graph for large rural communities, the relatively stable homicide rate is affected dramatically for the years 1978 and 1980.

Figure 8.2 Homicide rate by demographic area, Canada, 1977–1989

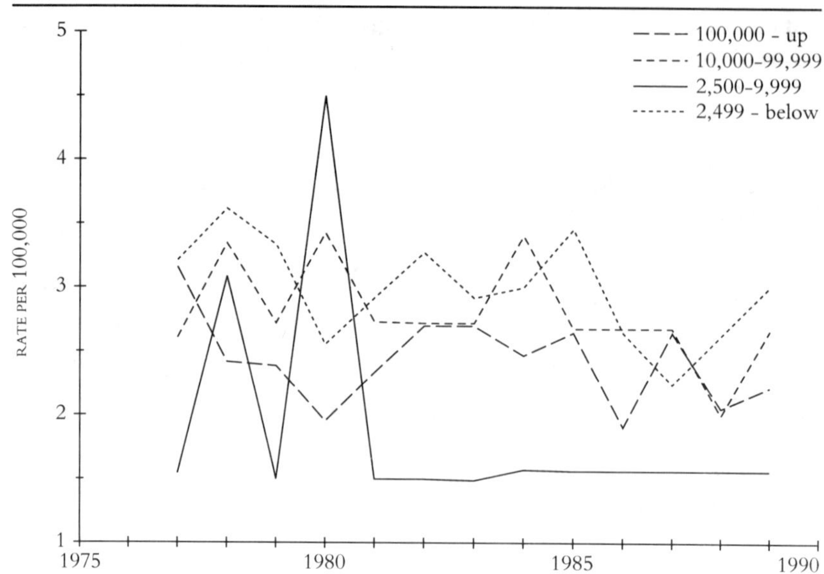

The violent crime rates graphs give a clearer, less fluctuating depiction of crime by community size. Figure 8.3 illustrates that officially, the most violent crime-ridden communities are once again not the largest urban centres, but the smaller urban communities.

The two types of rural community appear to be relatively immune to violent offences. If we contrast this graph with the previous homicide graph, we see substantially different crime trends for the small rural community; such communities have high homicide rates and low violent crime rates. We might argue that given the unstable nature of homicide statistics, the violent crime rates more accurately reflect the criminogenic climate (assuming that official statistics accurately reflect the amount of crime in society and not merely the amount of crime detected).

Figure 8.4 presents property crime rates for the four designated community sizes.

Similar to the rates for violent crime, official property offence rates are highest in small cities and lowest in the small rural areas. Once again, the official data illustrate the greater susceptibility of small cities to criminal activity, compared to large urban centres and smaller rural areas. The explanations for this phenomenon, although speculative, may involve the types of communities characteristic of remote areas where resource exploitation is occurring. Communities in areas such as the James Bay area in northern Quebec and the tar sands area in northern Alberta generally fall into the

Figure 8.3 Violent crime rate by demographic area, Canada, 1977–1989

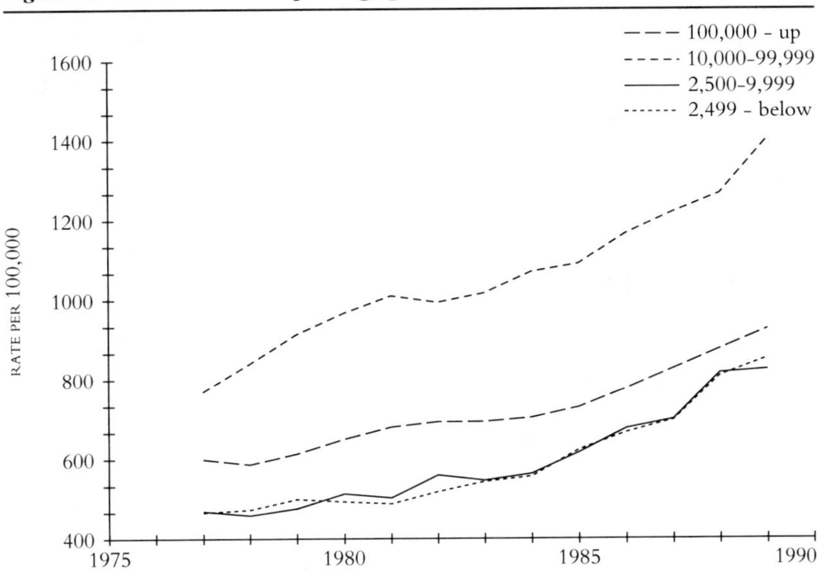

Figure 8.4 Property crime rate by demographic area, Canada, 1977–1989

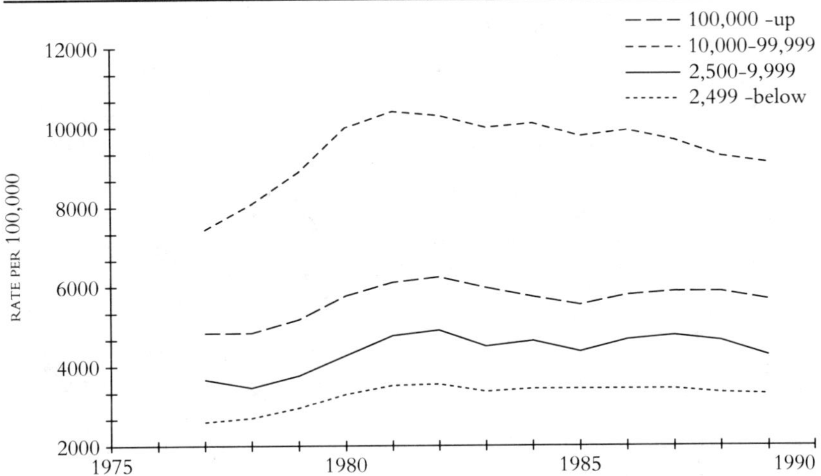

medium-sized urban range. These communities may be more criminogenic as a result of economic and demographic fluctuations, and, as we shall see in the sections on rural policing and justice, may be more closely scrutinized by official social control agents.

Figure 8.5 Criminal code offence rate in rural Canada, 1977 and 1988

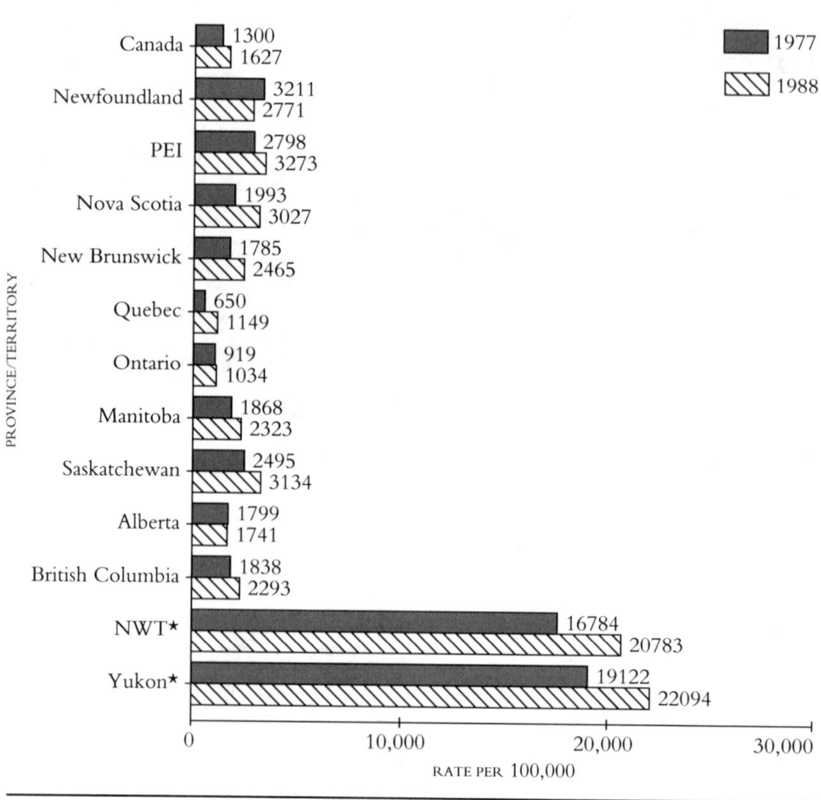

*Given that there are no municipal police forces in Yukon and the Northwest Territories, data from these areas include all offences, not just those occurring in rural areas.

Figures 8.5 through 8.7 illustrate the changes that have occurred in rural crime rates for specific regions in Canada from 1977 to 1988. Unlike the previous four graphs, the rates for the following graphs are calculated on a provincial basis, and we therefore do not get an indication of crime relative to community size. Also, given that there are no municipal police forces in the Yukon and Northwest Territories, the data from these areas include all offences that have occurred in the entire area, not just the rural areas. The bar graphs for the two territories are intended to show only the changes that have occurred over time in these areas and not the absolute rural crime rates.

Figure 8.5 shows the total crime rate for the years 1977 and 1988.

Rural crime rates have increased over time in all regional jurisdictions with the exception of Newfoundland, which has experienced a decrease over time, and Alberta where the rate has remained constant. When we compare the trends to those for violent offences (Figure 8.6), we see that rates for violent offences have increased for all rural jurisdictions, with only slight increases in Alberta and the territories.

Figure 8.6 Violent crime rate in rural Canada, 1977 and 1988

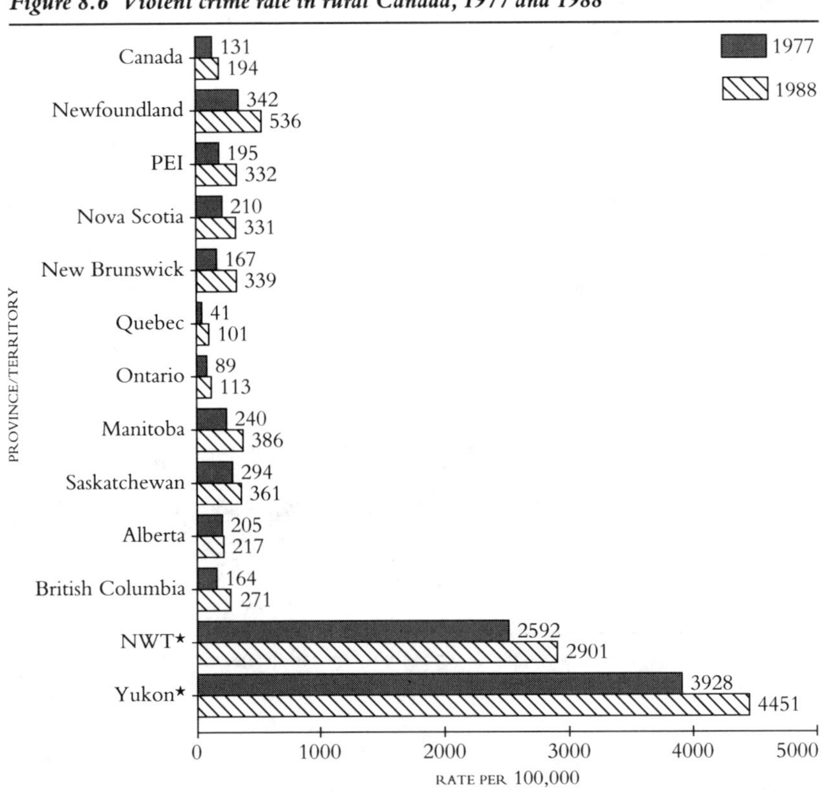

*Given that there are no municipal police forces in Yukon and the Northwest Territories, data from these areas include all offences, not just those occurring in rural areas.

It is significant that the violent crime rate has increased much more dramatically than the overall crime rate. The explanation for this phenomenon lies primarily with the effect that the property crime rate has on the overall rate. The decrease in the property crime rate neutralizes the increases in violent crimes when both are combined into the calculation of the overall crime rate. Figure 8.7 illustrates that for the years 1977 and 1988, the property crime rate increased only slightly for most of the areas and decreased for Newfoundland and Alberta.

The rather negligible increases in property crime rates is evidence of (a) the

Figure 8.7 Property crime rate in rural Canada, 1977 and 1988

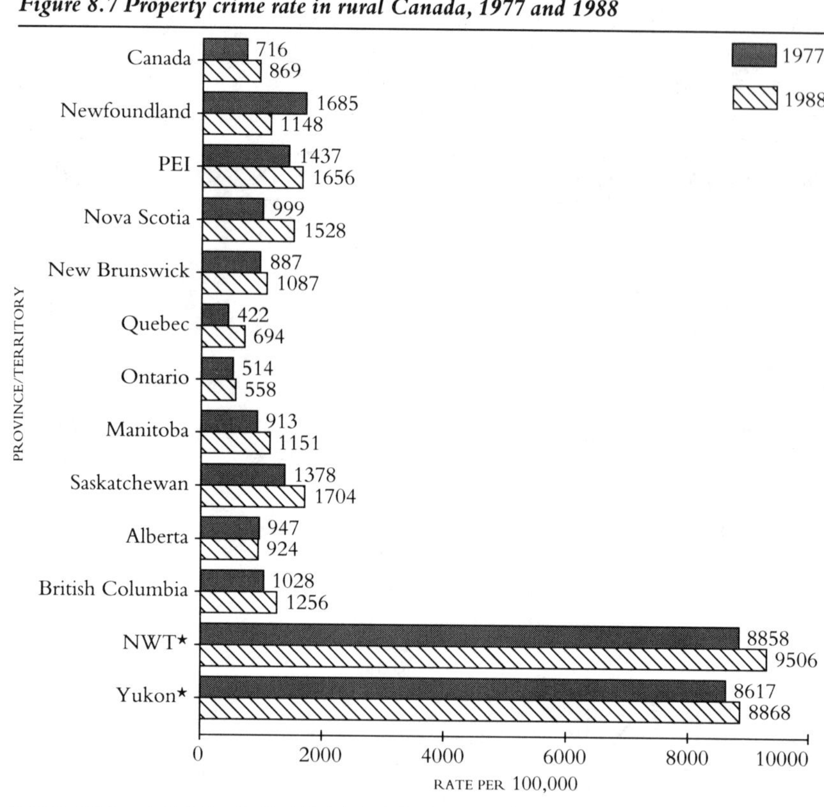

*Given that there are no municipal police forces in Yukon and the Northwest Territories, data from these areas include all offences, not just those occurring in rural areas.

increase in community policing that is currently characteristic of most rural areas; (b) the effectiveness of community policing as a crime prevention strategy, especially for property crime; and (c) an increased awareness on the part of rural residents in ensuring the security of their property.

Rural depopulation has become a major concern among social commentators who bemoan the demise of rural societies, and recent analyses have shown that rural depopulation is widespread in most regions and especially pronounced in the western prairie region (see Chapter Two). When findings that rural areas are experiencing more violent crime and less property crime are set against the backdrop of demographic changes in these areas, a rather obvious conclusion may be posited. The increases in crime rates in rural areas, especially violent crime rates, suggest an association with the depopulation of rural society. The initial four graphs in this chapter show rural violent crime rates are increasing in proportions equal to or greater than those in urban areas, and this might suggest that rural depopulation is related to changes in the criminogenic nature of both the supplier and the recipient communities. It may be argued that an increase in crime results from both the economic crises and the social disruptions that accompany rural depopulation.

S.D Clark, in his landmark study on rural migrants in Canadian cities (1978), comments on the social disruption that population displacement causes. Clark describes the effect of rural impoverishment on population shifts and the impact of privation and cultural collision on the rural and the urban community. I would argue that much of the change in criminal activity in rural Canada over time is the result of rural impoverishment—a consequence of the crisis of agriculture and the instability of resource-based economies—and the resulting population disruptions.

Rural/Urban Policing in Canada

While official crime rates are often used to indicate criminal activity, they reveal little about the nature and extent of policing and the administration of justice. Regional disparities in police activity and expenditure may reveal not only the extent of crime in an area, but also the degree of public resources devoted to crime control.

Policing in Canada is the responsibility of three levels of government: federal, provincial, and municipal. Most provinces require that cities and towns maintain their own municipal police forces (based on a minimum population size between 1,500-5,000, depending on the province). Generally, municipalities smaller than these minima are policed by the provincial police forces. Much of the policing of rural communities is maintained by provincial contracts with the Royal Canadian Mounted Police. As Figure 8.8 illustrates, wide disparities in the type of police force exist by region in Canada, and these disparities are somewhat, but not entirely, dependent on the rural/urban nature of the region.

For example, the Maritime provinces are primarily rural and their police forces contain a substantial number of municipal/urban police, unlike the Northwest Territories and the Yukon which are policed by the RCMP exclusively (under federal or provincial contract). The impact of this phenomenon is twofold. Firstly, as Kueneman *et al.* (1986) have suggested, inadequate facilities, inordinate time demands, and the geographical remoteness of some communities result in RCMP personnel feeling unable to conduct adequate police investigations. The low levels of job satisfaction that exist among the RCMP in remote areas result in part from the constraints placed on the police officer in the untenable position of having to administer the law with a minimum of information. The tendency for the police in such cases is to deal in an overly formal manner with offenders, to assume the role of crime

Figure 8.8 Policing expenditures by level of policing, Canada: provinces, and territories, 1988

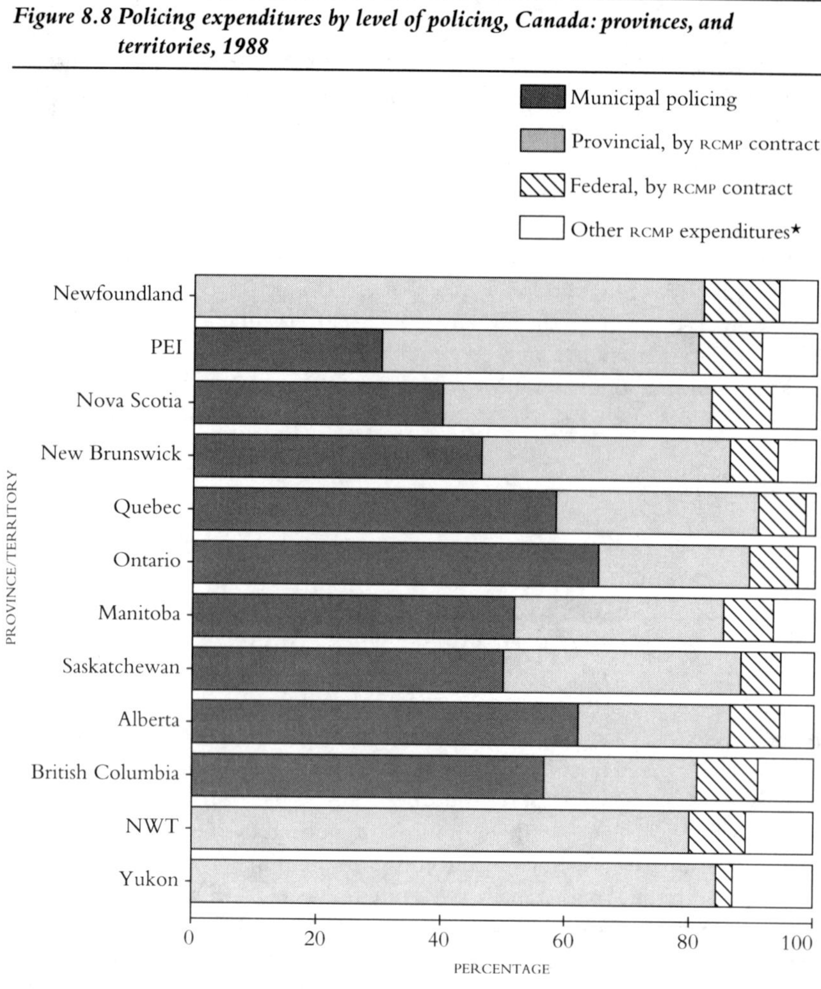

*Includes RCMP Division administration, overhead costs, and Canadian police services. Excludes Department Administration and Training Academy which are centralized and not allocated to any one province.

control agent rather than peace officer. Secondly, the low level of economic development that is characteristic of isolated areas limits work opportunities for the family members of police officers as well as for permanent residents. Furthermore, the length of assignment for RCMP officers is shorter than that for municipal police officers; the RCMP officer is relegated to the status of temporary resident. These conditions dispose officers to a lower level of commitment to the community, and to a continual adjustment to new social and cultural systems. As has been shown for judges in circuit courts, non-resident social control agents, being in a position of relative social and cultural unawareness, administer the letter of the law with little discretion (Kueneman *et al.*, 1986; Hagan, 1977). Harsh justice may result from the police rigidly administering the law with little consideration for the situational and cultural context of the rural offender.

Policing differences exist, as well, across regions with respect to per capita spending on policing and to per capita size of the police force. Figures 8.9 and 8.10 show the population per police officer and the per capita cost of policing by region.

These graphs illustrate once again the disparities that exist in criminal social control in Canada. The northern regions have inordinately high police costs, and although some of these costs can be attributed to the high cost of living and to costly administration services, the ratio of population to police officer indicates that these costs are, at least in part, the result of heavier policing. The other predominantly rural regions, especially the Maritimes, experience the opposite phenomenon with low expenditures and high population to officer ratios. In part, this low level of policing can be attributed to the nature of society, especially the small physical distances, and the permanent traditional

Figure 8.9 Population per police officer by province and territory, 1988

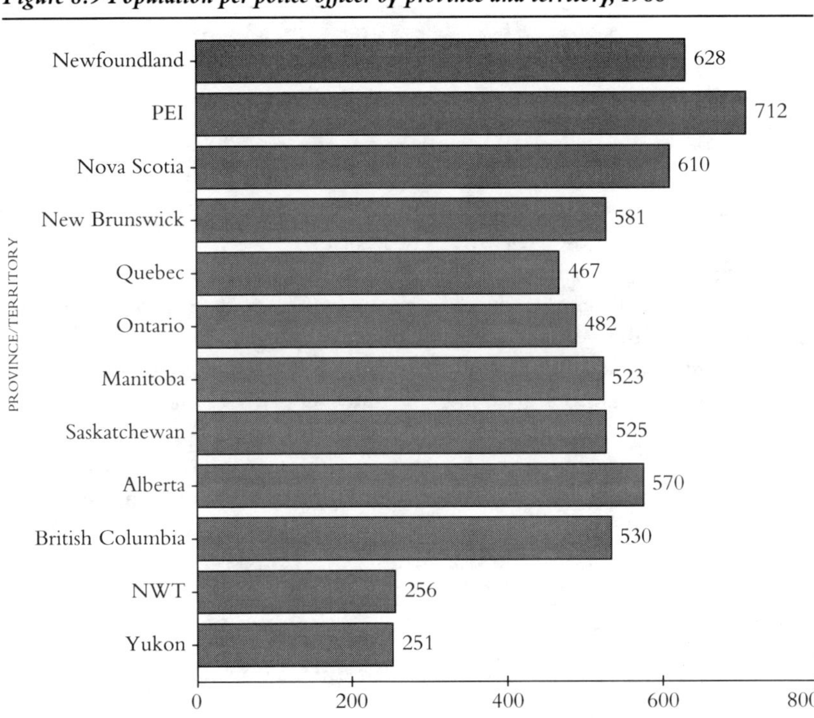

Figure 8.10 Total per capita cost of policing, Canada: provinces, and territories, 1988

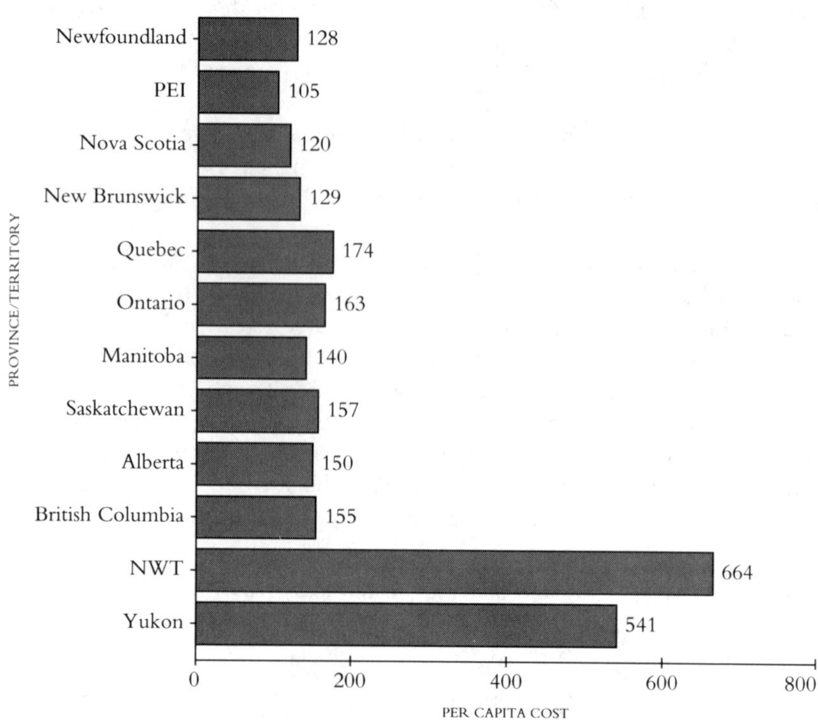

communities that are characteristic of the Maritimes. Whatever the reason for these large disparities in policing in rural areas, it is likely that the result will be greater scrutiny of certain class, racial, and ethnic groups situated in highly-policed areas, such as the Northwest Territories.

The foregoing information might suggest that part of the reason for the exaggerated official crime statistics in certain rural regions and not in others in Canada may be the result of greater official policing. It may be argued that frontier societies like the Territories, given their precarious economic and social character, are more criminogenic and therefore require greater policing. This does not explain, however, why other frontier-like areas, like the northern regions in Alberta and BC that are characterized by population and economic changes, expend relatively little human and economic resources on policing. Given the great disparities that exist, it is difficult to talk about a rural/urban policing agenda in Canada.

Justice in Rural Canada

Like the studies of rural/urban crime patterns in Canada, research on the administration of rural justice is alarmingly absent; the complexity of rural Canada renders this type of research difficult. The majority of Canadian research on rural justice has centred on issues of race and culture. While issues of demographic and cultural differences among rural areas in Canada are important, there are enough problems in common to all rural jurisdictions to discuss issues of rural justice in general.

The problems of the rural justice system appear to derive from the circuit nature of rural courts. Kueneman *et al.* (1986) have studied Manitoba's northern and rural juvenile courts, and reveal a system which is compelled to deal formally with the accused. Judges who travel the circuit are temporary residents and are removed from the social and cultural context of the violation. As well, circuit court work places inordinate demands on the court official's time, and as a result, job satisfaction among judges, lawyers, and court workers is relatively low. This situation is exacerbated by inadequate physical facilities which place emotional and physical restrictions on both the accused and the court official. Despite the pressures of rural courts, Kueneman *et al.* (1986) have found that justice in juvenile courts is administered primarily on the basis of legal concerns and that cases across jurisdiction are handled uniformly. Inadequacies occur, however, at the structural level where humane and accessible detention facilities are inadequate, where experienced legal counsel is lacking, and where supervisory personnel are absent.

Hagan's (1977) research on rural and urban courts in Alberta illustrates the persistent problems in rural jurisdictions. Again, problems of geographical isolation, overworked court officials, and inadequate facilities combine to produce sentencing decisions by the judiciary and probation officers that are based not on legal considerations but rather on social and cultural stereotypes and on the capacity of the prison system. Native offenders are more likely to receive immediate prison dispositions than their non-native counterparts, and are more likely to be imprisoned in default of fines.

The previous research findings present something of a paradox when analyzing rural justice. The structural and social characteristics of the system dictates that judgements be made on the basis of official (legal) information only, and in an ideal world this system would prove to be the most just. However, as critical criminologists have suggested, formal justice systems have a built-in advantage for those who can afford to use the system (Chambliss and Seidman, 1971; Turk, 1976). If the formal system is flawed, and if informal sentencing and parole decisions result from the structural inadequacies of the rural system, then, as Hagan (1977) has documented, rural courts are inadequate.

The problems of rural justice have been linked to structural conditions by researchers such as Cruikshank (1981) and LaPrairie (1983) whose investigations of northern Canadian rural courts help explain the application of discriminatory justice against rural and native Canadians. Cruikshank suggests that rapid industrialization of frontier areas results in the geographical and cultural disruption of rural families. As a result of industrial pressure and cultural hegemony, Native rural families are becoming increasingly matrifocal—the male parent is often a temporary member of the family. Single-parent families are not necessarily criminogenic, but are generally seen as unacceptable by social control agents. LaPrairie (1983) presents data from northern rural juvenile courts that describes how discrepancies in juvenile justice are related to court biases in favour of two-parent families. The reasoning is that the police, prosecution, judges, and court workers feel less threatened by single-parent families, perceive them to be less stable than conventional two-parent families, and accordingly administer harsh justice.

While the few studies of rural justice in Canada concentrate primarily on northern areas, the implications for all isolated rural areas warrants discussion. First, the circuit court nature of rural justice dictates that justice officials have little insider's knowledge of the social and cultural context, and as a result, depend on police information and official evidence for judgements. Such a judicial posture disallows mitigating social, cultural, and structural considerations. Secondly, rural court facilities appear to be somewhat inadequate, and inordinate demands are placed on rural court workers. These physical realities prohibit the administration of considerate and humane justice. Thirdly, many rural areas in Canada are characterized by fragile marginal economies where the temporary nature of labour and community results in family disruption. In the courts, the nature of the family becomes a focal point for administering justice, and it may be argued that this somewhat arbitrary criterion for making judicial decisions further victimizes already afflicted families.

Fear of Crime in Rural Areas

The perception by rural residents that their communities are safer that urban communities seems to persist, despite some evidence that rural crime is increasing. American research (Huff, 1982) has shown that despite evidence to the contrary, rural residents perceive their lives as safer than their urban counterparts. In Canada several community studies (RCMP, 1984; RCMP, 1981) have shown that rural residents feel relatively secure in their environs. However, Lee (1982) has introduced an important qualification that shows that fear of crime is dependent on the size of the community; fear is greatest among inner-city urbanites and farmers and lowest among suburbanites and small town dwellers. Similar findings are presented by Boggs (1971) whose earlier researches revealed again that central city and isolated rural residents, specifically farmers, have relatively high levels of fear of crime. Kennedy and Krahn (1984) have illustrated another important aspect of rural life and security. Ironically, they have found that the feeling of security that results from growing up in a rural area translates into greater levels of fear of crime upon migration to an urban area, especially for the elderly sector of the population. We may surmise that rural life may not adequately prepare individuals for migration to urban society.

While the research is inconclusive, the increasing anxiety of rural residents over the criminal potential of the changing community is evidenced by the increasing prevalence and preoccupation with crime prevention and self-policing. Crime-prevention programs such as Rural Crime Watch, which consists of a number of different programs in rural areas across Canada, is one indication that rural residents are anxious about the increasing potential for crime. These programs involve co-operation between the police and the community in establishing programs for securing property and for patrolling remote areas.

The Statistics Canada General Social Survey (1988) has attempted to document victimization and fear of crime rates for urban and rural areas in Canada. Table 8.1 presents actual victimizations rates for different types of crimes by area, gender, and age. Generally, these data reveal that the likelihood of victimization in urban areas is slightly higher than in rural areas, but not appreciably so. In fact, for certain categories of age and gender, victimization is higher in rural contexts. For example, for both total personal victimizations and total violent victimizations, 15- to 24-year-old men are more vulnerable in rural areas. On the other hand, women of this age group are slightly more vulnerable in urban areas. Given these rather inconsistent findings, it is interesting that feelings of potential victimization have little relationship to the actual victimization rates.

Table 8.2 presents an analysis of fear of crime (indicated by degree of safety felt walking alone in own neighbourhood after dark) broken down by area, age, and gender. The overwhelming trend in these data is that rural residents, both male and female, feel safer than their urban counterparts, and that these differences are consistent across age categories. The only anomalous finding involves the percentage of elderly men who feel very unsafe in their neighbourhoods; a greater percentage of rural men between the ages of 45 and 64 feel unsafe than do their urban counterparts. This finding is consistent with the research by Lee (1982) and Boggs (1971) who find that elderly male farmers and elderly male non-farm rural residents reveal inordinately high levels of fear of crime. Neither author offers an explanation for this phenomenon although it may be speculated that increased infirmity coupled with physical isolation disposes elderly rural men to some degree of psychological trauma.

What is apparent in the data on fear of crime is that rural and urban residents fear being victimized by different types of crime. Urban people fear attack or the threat of attack more than do rural people. On the other hand, rural people appear to be more fearful of theft or damage to personal property. These differences certainly are relevant when discussing the psychological impact of fear and the influence that such fear has on life-style and daily routine; it is undoubtedly more psychologically debilitating to fear personal

Table 8.1 Victimization rates per 1,000 population, by type of personal victimization incident and area, gender, and age

PERSONAL VICTIMIZATION RATES

AREA, GENDER, AGE GROUP	TOTAL PERSONAL VICTIMIZATIONS	THEFT OF PERSONAL PROPERTY OR ATTEMPT	VIOLENT VICTIMIZATIONS		
			TOTAL VIOLENT	ROBBERY OR ATTEMPT	ASSAULT
ALL AREAS					
Women	138	61	77	10	6
15–24 years	287	126	161	—	124
Men	148	58	90	17	74
15–24 years	335	121	214	49	166
URBAN AREAS					
Women	161	74	87	12	70
15–24 years	306	136	170	—	128
Men	155	65	89	16	74
15–24 years	322	128	194	—	159
RURAL AREAS					
Women	93	39	54	—	47
15–24 years	277	—	159	—	129
Men	135	53	83	—	65
15–24 years	354	125	229	—	153

Source: General Social Survey, Statistics Canada, 1988.

Table 8.2 Feeling of safety walking alone in own neighbourhood after dark, by urban/rural area, gender, and age group, 1987

AREA, GENDER, AGE GROUP	HOW SAFE RESPONDENT FEELS WALKING ALONE AT NIGHT IN NEIGHBOURHOOD					
	VERY SAFE %	REASONABLY SAFE %	TOTAL UNSAFE %	SOMEWHAT UNSAFE %	VERY UNSAFE %	DON'T KNOW/ NOT STATED %
URBAN AREAS						
Women	18	38	42	27	15	2
15-24 years	15	36	49	33	16	—
25-44 years	20	43	37	24	12	1
45-64 years	20	36	41	26	15	2
65 years and over	11	26	55	29	26	8
Men	55	32	12	9	3	1
15-24 years	57	34	9	6	3	—
25-44 years	59	30	10	8	2	—
45-64 years	54	33	12	10	2	—
65 years and over	35	36	25	18	7	4
RURAL AREAS						
Women	37	33	28	19	9	2
15-24 years	30	41	29	23	6	—
25-44 years	42	32	25	16	9	—
45-64 years	39	31	29	18	11	—
65 years and over	27	33	34	22	11	—
Men	70	22	8	6	2	—
15-24 years	74	17	9	7	—	—
25-44 years	70	25	5	4	—	—
45-64 years	70	21	9	4	5	—
65 years and over	58	25	13	—	—	—

Source: General Social Survey, Statistics Canada, 1988.

violation as opposed to property violation, and in this regard, urban residents are at a greater psychological disadvantage. When comparing these results to actual victimization rates, it is clear that the relative security (Table 8.3) that young rural males feel, especially with regard to physical attack (Table 8.1), is somewhat unfounded. Similarly, the greater fear of theft or vandalism that rural people perceive (Table 8.3) is equally groundless when set against actual incidence (Table 8.1); urban people are much more susceptible to property crimes. In conclusion, the overall security which people feel in rural areas is, in general, not supported by actual victimization rates. Further, victimization studies do not support official crime rates which maintain a rather marked gap between rural and urban crime rates.

Family Violence and Rural Society

A distressingly neglected area of concern regarding crime and justice is the problem of family violence. While some recent North American research addresses the issue at an aggregate national level, very little substantive research exists on family violence in rural society, especially in Canada (Kennedy and Dutton, 1987). The reasons for this involve the traditional neglect which legislative and legal agents have exercised toward spouse and child abuse, and the persistent rural cultural traditions which divorce public issues from private troubles. Only recently have we become aware that family violence is endemic and that such violence warrants legislation and official intervention.

Linda McLeod's work for the Canadian Advisory Council on the Status of Women reveals the nature and extent of wife abuse in Canada, and explicates the social and psychological pressures which conspire to maintain conjugal violence. Although her work is primarily urban-based, McLeod (1980) makes reference to rural society and suggests that contrary to public perception, wife abuse does occur in small communities, although the problem remains hidden due to the difficulty in establishing transition homes for battered women in small towns. Some initiative has been taken in this regard by Oxford County in southwest Ontario which has recognized the need for rural programs for battered women and children and battering men. The recognition of the need for rural programs is presented as unique and, indeed, almost revolutionary in a Canadian context (Potgieter, 1988). Chalmers and Smith (1989), in assessing counteracting strategies for abused spouses in Canada, reveal the endangering potential of physical isolation for rural women. The authors stress the double-edged nature of social and physical isolation for rural women where private family troubles such as spouse and child abuse are culturally and physically easy to hide, and where support services for the abused are non-existent. An added dilemma for women on farms, on reserves, or in isolated communities is economic entrapment. When

Table 8.3 Crime of most concern, by urban/rural area, gender, and age group, Canada, 1987

CRIME OF MOST CONCERN					
AREA, GENDER, AGE GROUP	ATTACK OR THREAT OF ATTACK %	THEFT OF HOUSEHOLD OR PERSONAL BELONGINGS %	DELIBERATE DAMAGE TO HOUSEHOLD OR PERSONAL BELONGINGS %	SOMETHING ELSE %	NOT STATED %
URBAN AREAS					
Women	58	28	10	3	1
15–24 years	69	21	6	4	—
25–44 years	58	29	9	3	—
45–64 years	55	29	12	3	—
65 years and over	49	33	12	5	—
Men	31	44	19	5	1
15–24 years	36	40	20	4	—
25–44 years	34	41	19	5	1
45–64 years	26	51	18	5	—
65 years and over	25	48	21	5	—
RURAL AREAS					
Women	45	33	14	6	1
15–24 years	54	27	14	—	—
25–44 years	46	33	14	5	—
45–64 years	42	38	11	7	—
65 years and over	25	48	21	5	—
Men	24	45	21	9	2
15–24 years	28	43	22	6	—
25–44 years	23	45	22	9	—
45–64 years	23	49	17	9	—
65 years and over	15	40	23	14	—

Source: General Social Survey, Statistics Canada, 1988.

employment opportunities are limited, it becomes virtually impossible for abused women to become independent.

Kennedy and Dutton (1987) are the first in Canada to actually assess the extent of rural wife assault. Their research reveals a lower rate of wife assault in rural society (8.3%) than in urban society (12.8%). Although the rate of wife assaults is relatively low in rural societies, we can predict that if traditional and rural societies in Canada become increasingly characterized by economic crises, the incidence of family violence will increase. A limited amount of research has tried to document the increase in family violence (especially wife and child abuse) in rural areas, and has attempted to relate violence to increasing levels of stress resulting from unstable economic conditions (Howard, Cunningham, and Rechnitzer, 1978). However, the problem of wife assault and child abuse in rural areas is compounded by the distressing lack of support services for victims of family violence. It is equally distressing that the strong ethos divorcing the private and the public persists; this ethos coupled with society's overall neglect of internal family crime creates a rural environment that is no longer idyllic, but rather dangerous for relatively powerless people.

Criminological and legal research have been appallingly neglectful of family crime and justice. In this light, the importance of this final section on rural family violence cannot be stated strongly enough. It is important also to underscore the necessity of studying hidden violence in rural areas, considering that such areas will continue to suffer demographic, social, and economic disruptions as Canadian society attempts to exploit its natural resources in the absence of social and cultural considerations.

Summary

I have attempted in this chapter to present an overview of the issues central to crime in rural Canada. An overriding concern in this presentation is that Canada's rural communities are not homogeneous, and that the formal and informal systems of social control vary greatly from region to region. As a result, it is difficult to discuss crime as simply a reflection of a rural-urban cultural difference. Rather, rural crime must be seen in the contexts of economic development, cultural collision, and the changing nature of agriculture and fishing economies.

Our findings reveal that rural life in Canada is changing dramatically, and that the upheavals which all rural areas experience are accompanied by changes in crime committed and in the nature and extent of social control. The concern with victimization and family violence among rural residents is evidence that the rural fabric is undergoing a psychological as well as a structural transformation. In light of these changes, the necessity of conducting region- and culture-specific research on crime and justice in rural Canada cannot be emphasized strongly enough. If we persist in studying rural Canada as a homogeneous entity, we run the risk of reaffirming the legal status quo which is premised on one prevailing legal system for a diversity of peoples and economies, and which has been relatively unsuccessful and undemocratic in its approach to crime and justice, and neglectful of private violence.

CHAPTER NINE

OLDER RURAL CANADIANS

NORAH C. KEATING

Rural Canada was settled by young people who came to exploit its natural resources: land, minerals, fish, and timber. One hundred years later both the means of livelihood and the age structure of the rural population had changed dramatically. The exodus of younger people from farming left some farming communities with high proportions of elders. And migration of retired city dwellers to small communities meant that rural Canada has some of the largest groups of seniors in the country (Hodge, 1984).

There is probably as much folklore about being old in rural Canada as about almost any other aspect of aging. Rural Canada is considered to be both the best place to be old—and the worst. The assets of growing old in rural areas include having a supportive network of family and friends and being close to the land. The liabilities include poor housing and health care, lack of services, and great distances to travel in a harsh northern climate. The purpose of this chapter is to address some of these stereotypes by reviewing four facets of the lives of rural elders in Canada: work, independence, health, and family.

Norah C. Keating is Professor and Chair of the Department of Family Studies at the University of Alberta.

Being Old in Rural Canada

Determining who is a rural elder depends on how both 'old' and 'rural' are defined. Canadian definitions of old have developed in an urban milieu, associated with institutionalized rites of passage from work to retirement and eligibility for social security benefits such as Old Age Security. Many of these markers of old are not relevant to those living in rural areas who have traditionally been involved in primary industries with no established age of retirement. In rural areas, age may be a matter of how well-equipped one continues to be in coping with the environment (Adams, 1975). One of the tasks of future researchers in rural aging will be to develop definitions of old within a rural context. However, because of urban conventions and the predisposition of researchers to use age 65 as the beginning of old age, much of the discussion in this chapter will, by necessity, use these same indicators.

Although there is no consensus on the question of what is rural, three aspects are most common. Traditionally, rural has been determined by occupation. Until 1961, the general term rural referred to a population that derived the majority of its livelihood from agricultural production or related industries such as mining and fishing (Miller and Luloff, 1981). Since then, rural has been divided into farm and non-farm, an acknowledgement that the economic base of rural parts of the country is now broader than agricultural (J.M.Watkins and D.A.Watkins, 1984). Rural now includes one group defined by their occupation and another which is not, although some would still argue that the only truly rural elder is the retired farmer.

The second aspect of rural is population density. The current census definition of a rural area is one in which the population is less than 1,000 people with a population density of less than 400 per square kilometre (Statistics Canada, 1987a). The population density definition is useful but does not take into account distance from population centres. Seniors in small communities in the Northwest Territories do not experience rural life in the same way as those in 'cottage country' north of Toronto. Geographically remote communities may be culturally remote as well, bypassed by economic development and having forms of social life that are rare elsewhere (Stalwick, 1983). Geographic and cultural remoteness as well as low population density are important aspects of the experience of rural aging.

The third element of rural is ideology. Much described but little documented, the rural ideology is a set of values presumed to be held by rural dwellers. These include being conservative in religion, right-wing in politics, supportive of a strong nuclear family, economically frugal, hard-working, self-reliant, and valuing interdependence of family, friends and neighbours (Bilby and Benson, 1977). Relevant to the discussion of aging in rural Canada is the question of the variety in beliefs about rural life held by those who live there. As rural elders become more heterogeneous in their backgrounds, beliefs about rural life and experiences of aging in the rural environment are likely to change (Martin Matthews, 1988a). Thus it seems important to include rural ideologies in the definition of what is rural.

Although it is not possible to include all three facets of rural in a single definition, this chapter attempts to address the diversity of aging in rural Canada. Occupational, population density, and ideological issues are discussed when possible. Experiences of rural elders are compared to those of urban elders where appropriate. However, I have not taken the perspective that rural is a residual category of urban, nor that the only way to understand rural issues is to compare them with urban. Reliance on a population density continuum is insufficient to capture the heterogeneity of the rural population (Martin Matthews, 1988a).

Work and Retirement

Labour Force Participation

Among older rural workers, the occupational designation of rural as farm versus non-farm still has some utility, since most of the current cohort of older rural workers are in farming. Over 75% of older workers in Canada are in agriculture, service, and trade (Government of Canada, 1982). Farmers have the highest average age (49 years) of all occupational groups in Canada and farm men over 55 make up 65% of all farmers. Of older women involved in primary occupations, the largest proportion (65%) are in farm-support jobs including farm and nursery workers. Married women farmers tend to be placed in this category since they are more often designated as farm workers and their husbands as farmers (Lee, 1987). In contrast, less than 6% of men and 1% of women over 55 are involved in fishing, forestry and mining (Methot, 1987), occupations still done by younger workers.

Labour force attachment of older rural workers may be part of the rural ideology which includes a strong work ethic. Of Canadian workers over 65, the highest work attachment is among those who have no employer-sponsored pensions (McDonald and Wanner, 1989) such as farmers. Farmers over age 65 have dramatically higher labour force involvement than either urban or non-farm seniors. Self-employment allows them to continue working as long as they wish and are able (Mark, 1981). Labour force attachment of rural seniors may also be due to a lack of alternative means of support. Highest rates of employment are found among those who must support themselves, such as single women (Table 9.1).

It is not clear whether self-employment is the major variable explaining the difference in employment patterns of older rural and urban workers. There have been few studies comparing self-employed people in these settings. Nor have marital status, gender and other economic factors been fully explored. As well, many older workers may have high work commitment but be out of

Table 9.1 Labour force activity of workers over age 65 by gender and marital status, rural-urban, farm non-farm

	PARTICIPATION RATE*		
	TOTAL	MALE	FEMALE
URBAN			
Total 65 & over	8	13	5
Single	14	13	15
Married	10	14	4
Widowed & Divorced	5	8	4
RURAL			
Total 65 & over	14	22	6
Single	20	24	12
Married	16	23	5
Widowed & Divorced	8	15	6
FARM			
Total 65 & over	57	83	19
Single	65	75	25
Married	63	89	16
Widowed & Divorced	34	57	22
NON-FARM			
Total 65 & over	8	12	4
Single	12	12	11
Married	9	13	4
Widowed & Divorced	5	9	4

Source: Statistics Canada, Population Labour Force Activity, Census of Canada 1981, cat. no. 92 - 915, Table 1.

*Participation rate is total employed over total population in that age category.

the work force involuntarily by age 65 (Methot, 1987) because of inability to compete successfully for jobs due to age discrimination, rapid technological change, and distance from employment opportunities.

Retirement of Employees

Most urban workers are employees of large or small businesses. For them, retirement is often seen as a single event or rite of passage (McDonald and Wanner, 1989). Retirement of rural employees has been studied from the perspective of rural-urban differences in timing, symbolic importance, and influence of retirement on the rural culture.

Despite some evidence of stronger labour force attachment of rural seniors, especially farmers, there is no evidence of overall rural-urban differences in timing of retirement. Almost half of both rural and urban residents in a study based in Kitchener, Ontario, retired before they were 65; the majority of both groups said their retirement was voluntary (Brown and Martin Matthews, 1981). There has been some speculation that the event of retirement has little symbolic importance in the lives of retirees (McDonald and Wanner, 1989). In a study of 300 retired men and women living in southern Ontario, Martin Matthews *et al.* developed a life events scale in which respondents generated and then ranked the impact of life events including retirement. Of 34 life events, retirement ranked 28th, suggesting that it is not an important life event (Martin Matthews *et al.*, 1981).

Wage labour is now well established in most parts of rural Canada, ensuring that the majority of future rural retirees will be employees who will have a defined retirement event. However, wage labour is still a new phenomenon in some remote parts of Canada. The introduction of wage labour into the Arctic has only recently created retirement as a rite of passage (McClelland and Miles, 1987) and has changed the nature of retirement from a gradual process associated with biological aging to an abrupt event marked by the cessation of wages. Changes in the nature of work and retirement in the Arctic provide only one example of the potential impact on rural communities of this shift. Further research on the nature of rural retirement will help determine both its symbolic meaning and its effect on rural communities as they move away from an agricultural base.

Retirement of the Self-Employed

Farmers are the major group of self-employed workers in rural areas, although there are many others in such diverse occupations as equipment dealers, pharmacists, and restaurant owners. The investigation of retirement from self-employment has been almost entirely focused on farmers whose retirement is usually viewed as a lengthy process occurring over several years. In a study of older farmers in Alberta, Keating and Munro (1989) proposed a process of retirement which included a sequence of exit from farm work, livestock holdings, production management, marketing management, financial management, land holdings, and equipment holdings. The exit process began with reduction in work when the farmer was in his early fifties, and extended to his seventies or beyond before the final transfer of ownership.

Some process models of retirement from farming also include a focus on both the retiring and receiving generations. In a qualitative study of a farming community in northern Alberta, Selles and Keating (1989) found that partial retirement occurred when sons were young adults still living at home. During this stage, the son took on more fieldwork, was consulted on management decisions, and became 'interested and involved' with the father. Semi-retirement occurred when the son married, some property was transferred to him and he assumed management responsibility. The father assisted in some farm chores, worked at peak times of the year such as planting and was 'interested and involved with the son'. The final stage was complete retirement, seen often as forced and undesirable. During this final stage there is evidence of the rural ideology of negative value placed on enforced idleness.

The heterogeneity of work patterns of rural workers provides an opportunity for an expansion of the models of retirement. We have yet to determine the importance of the rural environment in determining patterns of work and retirement. Nor do we know if urban and rural retirement are similar if type of work is held constant. Although there is evidence that the timing, meaning and process of retirement are different for farmers than for those who are not self-employed, we have insufficient data to know whether other self-employed groups operate in the same manner. The cultural milieu of work and retirement such as the shift of native people toward wage economies deserves some special consideration.

Independence

The principle of independent living is one of the basic tenets of the rural ideology. Rural elders are assumed to place high value on independence but they live in an environment which makes it difficult to maintain that independence (Krout, 1988). Three major themes are evident in research on independence of seniors. First is the dimension of control over the near environment which includes having adequate housing and being able to carry out personal care tasks (McClelland and Miles, 1987). The second theme is that of being part of the community which includes living in one's own household and being integrated into the community (Kivett and Learner, 1980). The third aspect of independence is access to basic services (Havens, 1980).

Control over the Near Environment

When housing of rural elders is compared to that of urban elders, rural elders are seen to be badly served. Table 9.2 shows the age of housing of urban, rural farm, and rural non-farm residents of all ages. Regional differences reflect the settlement patterns in the country with people in the west living in newer houses. Rural-urban location also relates to age of housing. More urban than rural dwellers live in newer housing, with farmers living in the oldest housing. Farm elders are much more likely than non-farm or urban elders to live in houses built before 1920 (Stone and Fletcher, 1980).

The theme of the relative deprivation of the near environment of rural elders also includes evaluations of the adequacy of housing amenities. Rural seniors are less likely than urban seniors to have hot and cold running

Table 9.2 Period of construction of private dwellings, Canada and provinces: urban, rural non-farm, rural farm, 1981

LOCATION	PERCENTAGE OF HOMES BY PERIOD OF CONSTRUCTION			
	pre-1921	1921-45	1946-70	1971-81
CANADA				
Urban	9	13	47	31
Rural non-farm	15	12	34	40
Rural farm	32	16	30	22
NEWFOUNDLAND				
Urban	8	12	47	33
Rural non-farm	9	13	42	35
Rural farm	6	20	46	29
PRINCE EDWARD ISLAND				
Urban	20	15	36	29
Rural non-farm	27	12	23	39
Rural farm	55	13	17	15
NOVA SCOTIA				
Urban	19	16	37	28
Rural non-farm	25	11	30	34
Rural farm	59	10	16	14
NEW BRUNSWICK				
Urban	16	15	40	29
Rural non-farm	18	13	28	42
Rural farm	53	11	19	17
QUEBEC				
Urban	9	14	50	27
Rural non-farm	17	12	30	41
Rural farm	48	17	19	16
ONTARIO				
Urban	10	13	47	28
Rural non-farm	20	10	37	33
Rural farm	58	11	17	14
MANITOBA				
Urban	10	15	47	29
Rural non-farm	10	15	39	36
Rural farm	17	19	41	23
SASKATCHEWAN				
Urban	7	13	47	34
Rural non-farm	12	19	37	32
Rural farm	16	21	40	23
ALBERTA				
Urban	3	6	43	48
Rural non-farm	6	14	32	48
Rural farm	8	18	42	32
BRITISH COLUMBIA				
Urban	5	12	46	37
Rural non-farm	3	8	36	53
Rural farm	7	15	40	38

Source: Statistics Canada, Occupied Private Dwellings, 1981 Census of Canada, cat. no. 92-932, Table 7.

water, indoor toilet, indoor bath or shower, central heat, electricity, gas or electric stove and refrigerator (Chamberlain, 1976). Most people who are without one amenity are lacking in several. Among those without hot and cold running water, most have no central heat, live in houses less than 1,000 square feet in size, and cook with a wood stove (Chamberlain, 1976).

People in remote areas and those on reserves may be even less well served. Hohn (1986) states that in 1977 fewer than 40% of houses on rural and remote reserves had running water, sewage disposal, or indoor plumbing compared to 60% in all Canadian rural homes. A more recent survey in 1983 showed that 75% of elders on the Frog Lake Reserve in Alberta had no indoor plumbing and 92% were without telephones.

Objective findings on housing and housing amenities support the contention that rural elders face greater difficulties in meeting basic personal needs for adequate housing. Yet these findings tell us little about the relationship between quality of housing and perceived adequacy of that housing. One fruitful area of research might increase understanding of what objective aspects of housing are critical in influencing the ability of residents to have control. It seems unlikely that age of housing is an important indicator. The retired Ontario farm couple who have carefully restored great-grandfather's stone farmhouse would surely consider themselves greatly advantaged in terms of their housing environment. However, some housing amenities may be especially important for some groups of elders. An example is the tradition of three- and four-generation households among some Native families. Such traditions are not easily accommodated within the contemporary Canadian approach, which is to build small houses adequate for a three- or four-person family. Some flexibility in design of new housing could facilitate rather than hinder traditional approaches to generational living. Creative solutions to such special housing problems as these are essential if people are to remain in their own homes.

A second aspect of control over the near environment is an ability to care for personal needs, often subsumed under the category of activities of daily living (ADLs). Such activities include bathing, dressing, eating, and walking. There have been few studies of the ability of rural elders to perform activities of daily living, or of whether rural versus urban environments are likely to facilitate the ability of elders to manage daily tasks.

One of the few studies to directly address this question was conducted by Coward and Cutler (1988). Using data from the United States National Health Interview Survey, they examined residential differences in the degree to which activities of daily living are performed with difficulty. Four residential categories were used: central city, not central city, farm, non-farm. All respondents were over age 65. Residents of rural non-farm areas had the most difficulty in performing tasks; farm residents the least. The authors suggest that older farmers may also be more physically fit because of their active lifestyle. More systematic evaluation needs to be done of variations in rural elders' abilities to perform ADLs.

As with other aspects of independence, attitudes toward ADLs may be as important as actual abilities. Raiwet (1989) conducted extensive interviews with couples living in remote areas of the Peace River district of Alberta. She was interested in how these couples coped with the physical changes that accompany age. Many had chronic illnesses that were quite disabling by objective standards. Raiwet found that independence for these people was a matter of doing what they wanted to do. Most compensated for activities they could not do by increased use of technology, by relying on their spouse or other family members, or by changing their activities.

Although we now have adequate assessment tools to measure functional status of older people, we know much less about what Rowles (1988) has called the phenomenological perspective of rural elders. Rowles argues that in order to understand aging, we need to know about the ways in which individuals organize and create their worlds as well as about their objective circumstances. Control over the personal environment may be influenced as much by how people view their physical abilities as by their objective functional status.

Integration into the Community

Rural elders, like their urban counterparts, wish to remain in their own homes in their own communities. Studies in all parts of the country, in both rural and urban areas, confirm that this is the first choice in accommodation (Agbayewa and Michalski, 1984).

In a study of rural elders in Alberta, Keating and Brundin (1983) found that remaining at home was the first choice of rural retirees. In general, rural seniors choose to remain in their own homes even when they need more supportive care. This is one of the major dilemmas of maintaining independence. Despite overwhelming evidence of preferences to remain at home, problems of service delivery in rural areas threaten some seniors' independence.

Community involvement may be a more sensitive indicator of independence than community living. Scheidt (1984) analyzed levels of community integration of small town rural seniors and found four major patterns of integration into the community: fully engaged, partially engaged, disengaged, and frail. The majority of each group lived in their own homes. However, the groups were differentiated by the amount of activity and involvement with others. The fully engaged and partially engaged had contact with friends and relatives and were involved in community activities. The disengaged and frail groups had little social or community involvement and were isolated because of social and physical reasons. The latter two groups seem most at risk of losing their independence because of their isolation.

Access to Services

Ability to gain access to services is a critical element in independent living, and distance from services has been of great concern to practitioners and policy-makers. Hodge (1984) has developed a list of basic community services (bank, grocery store, doctor, church, post office, drug store, beauty shop/barber, restaurant, social clubs, variety store, department store, clothing store/shoe store) described by seniors in small communities as most important. Hodge says that these services are used extensively by seniors in small communities if they are available (present with some choice) and accessible (within walking distance). Clearly, accessibility is a different issue for farming communities and those in remote rural areas with few basic services in the local community. Of the nine towns studied, Hodge found that those with populations over 2,000 had greater availability of services than towns under 1,000 population and that 500 metres was a preferred upper limit for average walking distance to community resources. Small towns rather than villages appear to be the best locations for access to basic services for rural seniors.

An interesting contrast to Hodge's objective indices of availability and accessibility of services is Windley and Scheidt's (1988) study of the perceptual environment of rural elders. They found no differences in awareness of services or in perceived access to services among residents in towns of different sizes. Rather, any negative evaluation of the environment was based more on personality and personal attributes such as ability to walk comfortably, than on availability of services.

Findings from this study and those of Hodge suggest that both the objective and perceptual environment need to be evaluated in order to determine whether a community has adequate services. Windley and Scheidt also suggest that programs and services may need to be targeted to specific communities since one kind of intervention may not be appropriate in all communities. Concepts of what is a comfortable distance to services may be different for in-migrants from cities with high density services than for farmers who are used to driving long distances for basic services such as groceries.

Our knowledge of issues related to independence of rural elders is very uneven. The finding that seniors wish to remain in their own homes has been substantiated. Remaining at home appears to be one of the important symbols of independence. Yet since most seniors do remain in their own homes, there is little variance in this element of independence. In contrast, findings of the relatively poor quality of housing of rural seniors would suggest that many are at risk of not having a good-quality near environment. We have yet to determine which aspects of the physical environment might enhance a sense of control over the home environment. Further exploration of the perceived necessity of particular housing amenities may help identify subgroups of rural seniors who feel most disadvantaged by the lack of urban amenities.

The systematic mapping of community resources can provide a useful index of their availability. Combined with information on perceived availability, this information could be very useful both to town planners and to those who would try to be of assistance to rural seniors. Finally, it seems that we must pay more attention to how seniors define independence and the strategies they use to maintain that independence. Here, too, there is likely to be great variety among subgroups of rural seniors. While elderly farmers may remain in control through withholding transfer of the farm, Native elders may do so by providing accommodation in their homes to extended family members.

Health

As well as independence, good health is basic to a high quality of life for seniors. Yet rural elders are often seen as in poorer health than their urban counterparts and as under-served by health services.

Health Status

A major source of debate is whether rural seniors' health status is better or worse than that of those in urban areas. In a review of morbidity data on rural and urban seniors, Martin Matthews (1988a) argues that there are no significant differences in general health between the two groups. Results from provincial research projects across the country support her contention. Studies of health of seniors in Newfoundland and Labrador (Vivian, 1982), in Alberta (Thurston *et al.*, 1982) and in Ontario (Morton *et al.*, 1984) found no consistent differences in physical health status.

The majority of seniors in Canada (84% of males over 65 and 87% of females) have at least one chronic physical problem (Health and Welfare Canada, 1981). Of problems requiring hospitalization, most prevalent are disorders of the circulatory or respiratory systems, and cancers. Problems requiring hospitalization are similar for rural seniors (Senior Citizens Provincial Council, 1983). Of illnesses not requiring hospitalization, the most common among rural seniors is arthritis, with estimates that from 50% to 60% of seniors suffer from this ailment (Morton *et al.*, 1984; Thurston *et al.*, 1982; Vivian, 1982).

Despite high levels of chronic health problems, most older Canadians rate their health positively (Health and Welfare Canada, 1989). Studies in Alberta, Saskatchewan, and Newfoundland have found that 60% to 70% of seniors rate their current state of health as excellent or good. Similar proportions rate their health as the same or better than five years previously. Even those in institutional settings rate their health quite highly. Half of institutionalized respondents in studies in Alberta and Newfoundland said their health was excellent or good (Senior Citizens Provincial Council, 1983; Thurston *et al.*,

1982; Vivian, 1982). Some authors have maintained that rural seniors rate their health positively because they do not want to be seen as complainers or are more tolerant of disability (Lubben *et al.*, 1988).

The one area in which there is some indication of general health status differences between rural and urban seniors is in problems that are amenable to correction if health services are available and used. Rural seniors report more uncorrected problems with vision (Kivett, 1985), dental, hearing, and foot care problems (Thurston *et al.*, 1982).

The most consistent differences in health status of seniors are among Native seniors, most of whom live on reserves which are culturally and often geographically remote. Mortality data from Saskatchewan indicate that principal causes of death among Natives are similar to those of provincial seniors but mortality rates are higher (Gillis, 1987). Morbidity data show that Native seniors in northwestern Ontario are prone to nutritional deficiencies such as obesity, iron deficiency anemia, and vitamin deficiency (Young, 1987). Native seniors are the group most at risk of poor health among Canada's rural elders.

Morbidity data on rural elders suggests that, like urban elders, most have at least one chronic health problem. However, mortality data show that both groups are living longer. In the fifty years from 1930 to 1980, life expectancy of men at age 65 increased one year from 13 to 14 years. Life expectancy of women increased four years from 14 to 18 years (Senior Citizens Provincial Council, 1983). Thus seniors are living longer with chronic health problems.

From the state of research in the area, it is impossible to determine the nature or magnitude of rural-urban differences in health. Most studies are descriptive and there are no consistent definitions of urban or rural, nor consistent measures of health status. Krout (1988) suggests that a more fruitful pursuit would be that of asking a fundamental question: why and how rural versus urban residence interacts with health-related variables. Does living in the midst of a greater or lesser number of people affect an older person's health, and if so, why? Does a smaller population lead to a denser social network, which in turn leads to a greater sense of security and psychological satisfaction and thus acts as a buffer against physical illness? Does the 'more natural' physical environment positively affect health, or negatively affect it through higher risk of accidents, etc.? How much do limited opportunities for occupational mobility earlier in life in rural areas lead to lower incomes, lower nutritional levels, lower standard of living and thus lower levels of health? Do rural values of self-reliance lead to lesser likelihood of admitting to health problems, so that only objective measures of morbidity will lead to findings of differences between rural and urban groups?

Health Service Utilization

Canadian seniors are heavy users of health services. A typical pattern is that of

Alberta, where seniors use 33% of acute care hospital days and 83% of home care services, but comprise only 8% of the population (Alberta Senior Citizens Secretariat, 1986). Urban seniors account for much of this high service use, while rural seniors are presumed to be lower users because of unavailability of services. In the United States there is support for this presumption of low service use by rural seniors. Rural seniors are less likely to receive hospital treatment, or to visit physicians or dentists (Palmore, 1983). They also have a narrower range of health services with fewer health-care providers (Coward and Cutler, 1989).

Canadian data are more equivocal and conclusions about the level of service use must be considered in the context of the type of service, region of the country, and ethnicity. Several Canadian studies have suggested that the lack of physicians in rural areas accounts for the fact that rural seniors of all age categories make significantly fewer visits to a physician per year than do urban seniors (Peace River Health Unit, 1986; Shapiro and Roos, 1984). In contrast to physician availability, some areas of rural Canada are well served by hospital facilities (Shapiro and Roos, 1984) with higher numbers of hospital days per year for rural seniors of all age categories. Native elders also have high rates of hospitalization. Older Indians in Saskatchewan are almost three times as likely to be hospitalized than are other seniors (Gillis, 1987).

Higher hospital use among rural seniors is probably not due to poorer health status since rural residents have slightly better survival rates than urban elderly. Rather, rural poverty may make home treatment a less viable option and lead a physician to admit people to hospital more often than might otherwise happen. Travel distances and transportation problems during winter may also encourage in-hospital treatment. And finally, the greater availability of hospital beds in rural areas may encourage admissions (Shapiro and Roos, 1984).

Native elders are the most disadvantaged of rural seniors in terms of most health services. Although Native seniors living on reserves have the same health-care coverage as non-natives, Natives are deprived of good, responsive health care (Bienvenue and Havens, 1986; Hohn, 1986). There are virtually no nursing homes or auxiliary hospital beds on reserves and almost none exist that cater to the particular needs of older natives. Putting a Native relative in a nursing home is often seen as unthinkable by family members. Great distances to travel, lack of staff who speak Native languages, unfamiliar food, and lack of contact with families are some of the reasons for under-utilization of health services by Native elders.

Also disadvantaged in terms of health services are others who live in remote areas. Not only is there a lack of choice within any one service (Coward and Cutler, 1989), some services are simply unavailable. Services such as Meals on Wheels, mental health or drop-in centres are much less available to those in remote areas than to those in small communities. For example, the Northwest Territories provides few formal outreach services because it is difficult to attract health professionals to the north. With limited professional resources, the mandate has been to provide acute care and some public health services, with few resources for health promotion (O'Neil, 1987).

No general comment can be made about the adequacy of formal health services to rural seniors. While some services such as rural hospitals are available, physicians to staff those hospitals are often in demand. And there are great regional and ethnic differences in adequacy and appropriateness of health services. In remote areas, seniors use fewer traditional health services and have access to almost no preventive health services.

Health Service Needs

By many objective measures rural seniors are poorly served with health services. However, the variety of health needs in different parts of rural Canada means that there is no clear way to determine whether seniors have unmet health service needs. Perceived availability and appropriateness of services; culture and ethnicity; length of rural residence; and whether service needs are based on medical or health promotion philosophies, all affect whether services are seen as appropriate and available.

Perceived need for services by rural seniors does not always correspond closely to objective measures of service availability. In fact, seniors who are most remote from services often express low levels of need. This apparently stoic nature of rural elders may come not from being well-served by medical services but from attachment to place. For Peace River elders living in remote areas, staying in their own homes is paramount. The majority said that they would be unwilling to move to an institutional setting under any circumstances. There were no extended care facilities in that area and leaving the community was seen as too emotionally costly. In contrast, 84% of town elders said that if necessary they would move to an institution (Peace River Health Unit, 1986). Although remote seniors may be underestimating their needs, they may also be making a conscious choice to avoid institutional services.

Perceived need for services and service availability is influenced in other ways by rural beliefs. Rural elders have a different concept of distance than do urban dwellers. Three miles to the nearest neighbour and 200 to 900 miles for specialized medical treatment may be seen as close (Weinert and Long, 1987).

Other services may be appropriate and accepted in some rural communities but inappropriate in others. Meals on Wheels is considered an essential and very economical service in support of good nutritional health in many rural areas. However, O'Neil (1987: 25) states that Meals on Wheels is unavailable and may not be appropriate in most parts of the NWT. 'Many clients prefer country food which is usually shared. Where there are younger men who are involved in wage labour, often they do not have enough time to hunt to provide for all the needs in the community. Most often family or visitors prepare food for someone who is not able to prepare it themselves.' The authors felt that most families looked after their elderly. When this was not possible, a homemaker was seen as more beneficial since that person could prepare meals especially for the elder using her own community produce.

The majority of rural seniors see that services available in their communities meet or exceed their needs. Yet some communities are under-served by urban standards, while others are receiving services inappropriate to the rural culture in which they live. One group that warrants further study concerning appropriate type and level of services is remote seniors. Our knowledge of the variation in health status of rural seniors remains limited.

Family

A fundamental belief about rural Canada is that rural elders are embedded in an extended, supportive family, connected to one another through work and a feeling of closeness to the land. Rural families are presumed to be close-knit, private, and to 'take care of their own', including their elders (Cape, 1984).

Household Structure of Rural Seniors

Although in the past households of rural seniors were more extended (Arcury, 1984), most contemporary Canadian rural seniors live in nuclear households (Table 9.3). Farm elders are the most 'nuclear' of any group of seniors in Canada. In comparison to both non-farm and urban elders, farm seniors are most likely to live with their spouse and less likely to live alone. However, they are also most likely to live in an extended household, either with other relatives or non-kin.

These differences in household composition of farm and non-farm rural seniors are still based on the family traditions in agriculture. Elderly farm

Table 9.3 Population over age 65, Canada, 1986

	CANADA	URBAN	RURAL	RURAL NON-FARM	RURAL FARM
People over 65	10%	10%	9%	10%	6%
Living with spouse and/or unmarried children	61	58	68	67	78
Living alone	28	30	21	22	7
Living with other relatives	10	9	9	9	12
Living with non-relatives	2	2	2	2	7

Source: Selected Characteristics for Urban and Rural Areas, for Canada, Provinces and Territories, 1986 Census-100% data.

households are nuclear in part because few women remain on the farm homestead once they are widowed. In many farm operations, widowhood is the signal for the next generation to take on sole operation of the farm and to move into the 'big house'. Most farm widows subsequently move into the nearest town, leaving a lower proportion of nuclear families among farm than non-farm seniors and a higher proportion of singles in non-farm centres. The majority of farm elders living alone are never-married men.

The family structures of seniors in fishing communities are similar to those in farming. Two household structures predominated among retired fishermen in one Newfoundland community. Most (79%) lived in nuclear family households which included unmarried adults who usually lived with their parents. Only if they could not cope on their own, did older people move in with children. The second most common household structure was single men living alone (McCay, 1987). Both fishing and farming communities have a tradition of having high male-female sex ratios, resulting in large proportions of never-married men.

In both farming and fishing communities, most elders live in nuclear families, with higher proportions of unmarried children living with parents in more isolated communities. Elders may live with other relatives if they are unable to maintain their own households. In comparison to other rural areas, people living alone in farming and fishing communities are more likely to be never-married men rather than widowed women (McCay, 1987).

Family Networks

Examination of the structure of rural households has shown that few rural elders live in extended-family households. However, it does not address the question of whether rural elders have larger extended families living nearby than do urban elders, nor whether rural families are closer and more emotionally supportive (Wister, 1985).

Canadian seniors in general have large family networks. Approximately 80% of all seniors have children, siblings, and grandchildren (Connidis, 1989). Although there is some evidence that rural seniors have larger family networks than urban elders (Martin Matthews, 1988a), age, cohort, and marital status may account for more differences than place of residence. Those over 85 and those who have never married are likely to be without kin. The latter group may be less vulnerable as they age, since never-married seniors often compensate for lack of close kin by developing intimate relationships with friends and more distant kin (Connidis, 1989).

Availability of kin also depends greatly upon the type of rural resident. Long-term residents of rural areas are likely to have a relatively stable network size and close-kin membership (Wenger, 1986). In contrast, in-movers may have virtually no established kinship network nearby, while those who move to be close to one of their children will have a small local network. Perhaps because of the variation in availability of kin, rural-urban comparisons of network availability have been inconsistent. While urban elders in Saskatchewan are more likely than rural dwellers to have family members nearby (Grant and Rice, 1983), the opposite is true in some communities in Quebec (Corin, 1984).

Perhaps a more important difference between rural and urban seniors is that rural elders perceive themselves to be more conveniently situated to friends and family than do their urban counterparts (Scott and Roberto, 1987), regardless of actual distance. Rural elders are also more likely to stress the importance of their friends and neighbours, especially long-standing associations going back to early adulthood or childhood (Kivett, 1988a).

Despite the perception among rural elders that their social network is more accessible, studies of amount of contact with relatives and friends show few rural-urban differences. Most elderly Canadians see at least one of their children on a regular basis, with other relatives seen much less frequently (Connidis, 1989). Network membership of distant kin, neighbours, and friends is more fluid than that of close kin, although among these more distant groups, neighbours are seen most often (Wenger, 1986; Vivian, 1982). While some have argued that urban men and women have more contact with friends than their counterparts in rural areas (Keith and Nauta, 1988) others find that rural elderly have higher levels of contact with neighbours (Wenger, 1982).

Overall, rural Canadian seniors are as integrated into family and non-family networks as are urban seniors (Martin Matthews, 1988a). However, the amount of integration into a family network is dependent upon whether the elder is a recent immigrant or long-term resident (Harper, 1987).

Unlike the stereotype of the large extended household, rural seniors are most likely to live in nuclear households. However, as with their urban counterparts, most have a network of kin and friends which they perceive to be accessible. A fruitful avenue of investigation will be into the impact of 'rural type' on the variety of patterns of contact with kin and non-kin.

Family Support

One of the major areas of interest in social gerontology is family support, and how the nature of support changes over the history of the family. This emphasis arises from the expectation that with age, the older person will have increasingly asymmetrical relationships, typified by less receiving of affection and affirmation and increased direct aid (Black, 1985). The emphasis on the provision of direct aid has been seen as unfortunate since it creates the impression that all older people need help (Connidis, 1989). It also means that we know less about affection and affirmation aspects of support than we do about the giving of material or symbolic aid.

Support as Affirmation: The Parent-Child Relationship

Most rural and urban seniors have a high level of trust and positive regard for their children (Kivett, 1988b). However, sources of the quality of the relationship differ for urban and rural dwellers. Mercier *et al.* found that for rural parents, geographic proximity of the child was the best predictor of a high quality relationship from the perspective of the parent (Mercier *et al.*, 1988). Other predictors were high level of parental education, internal locus of control, and low filial expectations. For urban respondents, parents with a higher quality relationship were older, lived farther away and had higher internal locus of control. It seems that parental perceptions of high quality relationships occur when child obligations are low. Thus for rural seniors, relationships were best if the parents felt they had control over their lives; did not turn to the child in an emergency; and did not expect high levels of interaction, provided the child was available.

Rural seniors in households shared with children have lower morale and perceive relationships with children to be more strained than do those in independent households, perhaps because of the interdependence in such households. Those who have higher morale effectively reduce the affirmation obligations of children through high levels of community participation in clubs, organizations, or church (Kivett and Learner, 1980).

Adult children are expected to maintain the relationship with their parents because of feelings of obligation and a sense of long-term reciprocity. Among middle-aged children of Mennonite faith in rural Manitoba, Bond and Harvey (1987) found a strong sense of obligation with a 'rule-bound' approach to family life. Other North American studies have found that much parent-child contact in rural families is at prescribed times such as birthdays, family reunions, other family ceremonies and emergencies, suggesting that a sense of obligation plays a significant role in association (Kivett, 1988b).

These findings on the quality of the parent-child relationship illustrate how the relationship might vary considerably, depending upon the resources of the elderly parent. Because parent-child relationships are almost invariably asymmetrical, it seems that there should be more potential for high-quality relationships among same-generation peers including siblings, friends, and neighbours.

The Marital Relationship

Overall, older Canadians are highly satisfied with their marriages and place high value on emotional security, respect, and communication. As they grow older, couples become increasingly interdependent (Connidis, 1989). Interdependence is especially relevant to rural couples whose lives are based on a close partnership in work and family roles. Farming couples have symmetrical work roles in which both husbands and wives produce goods necessary for the survival of the business and the family (Vanek, 1980). An important source of personal satisfaction for farm wives is their husbands' acknowledgement that they have a farm-work as well as a family role (Keating, 1987). Throughout a long married life, couples work out the interrelationships between work and family roles, and women over 65 are most satisfied with their farm and family roles (Keating and Munro, 1988).

Non-farm couples are less likely to be bound together by joint work roles. However, during the post-retirement years they tend to move toward more role integration and less gender differentiation through decreasing the amount of household role segregation (Dorfman and Heckert, 1988). Husbands may be compensating for their lost work role by participating in household roles. Alternatively, couples may choose to share household tasks in order to spend more time together during retirement. Rural women's retirement satisfaction is related to the proportion of family decisions shared jointly with their spouses (Dorfman and Hill, 1986).

Although it seems as if the marriages of rural seniors are interdependent, these data do not provide a full picture of the relationship of husbands and wives. We still know relatively little about levels of intimacy in such marriages or conflict that may arise from the pressures of working together.

The Sibling Relationship

The sibling relationship appears to have great potential for positive affection. It is often the first intimate relationship among peers (Connidis, 1989). Of all close kinship ties, the sibling relationship may be the most free, since societal expectations are that it endure but need not be actively pursued. In a review of research on sibling relationships, McGhee (1985) found that sibling contact is not motivated by obligations to keep in touch but by geographic proximity, affectional closeness, and enjoyment. She found that bonds among sisters were closest, and that there are great positive benefits of associating with a sibling of the same sex who shares one's history, values, and interests.

Support as affirmation appears to be important to quality of life of rural elders. Depending upon the kinship relationship, affirmation is manifested somewhat differently. Paradoxically, relationships that are less intense such as sibling relationships have more potential for positive affection without obligation.

Support as Aid

Both young and old rural Canadians see a hierarchy of obligation to provide aid to elderly family members. C. Storm, T. Storm and Strike-Schurman (1985) explored perceived obligations to assist a frail old person with physical care, financial aid and psychological support among a group of women aged

18 to 85 in a small town in the Maritimes. Respondents in all age groups saw children as more obligated to provide aid than other family members. Next to children were siblings who in turn were more obligated than old friends.

Although the stereotypes of family support are that rural elders are cared for by their families more than urban elders, there are abundant data showing that the majority of long-term care needed by all older people is provided by family members (see Connidis, 1989 for a review of Canadian data). Data from rural Canada suggest that this pattern exists there as well. Almost all (75%) seniors who say they need help rely on children for that help. Few (5%) say they would never turn to children (Vivian, 1982). Help is more likely to be given by daughters to mothers than by sons to fathers (Kivett, 1988b). Perhaps only in remote rural communities do patterns of assistance differ. Studies of geographically remote (Peace River Health Unit, 1986) and culturally remote (Bond and Harvey, 1987; Scott and Kivett, 1980) communities show great emphasis on the provision of family care despite burdens or inconvenience.

The available information on family networks and family support of rural elderly suggests that most aid is provided in a family-based environment. Yet the provision of aid by family members, although intuitively appealing, is not without cost to caregivers and recipients. Rural spouse caregivers are likely to have more kin available for support (Martin Matthews, 1988a) but face personal caregiver costs similar to those of urban caregivers. These include high levels of caregiver stress, decrease in social network, lack of respite, risk to personal health, feelings of guilt and loss (Johnson and Johnson, 1983; Zarit, Reever and Bach-Peterson, 1980). A substantial proportion (37%) of rural residents providing day-to-day care to an ill relative use no relief services even though the majority (68%) say that caregiving affected their health and that caring for a relative meant that they could not go away for a vacation (Earle, 1984).

Although most support as aid is provided by rural families as it is in urban areas, the rural informal system may be less reliable (Martin Matthews, 1988a). Those in farming and remote communities have few formal services to fall back upon and must rely almost exclusively on family and friends, placing a strain on affective family relationships. Never-married seniors are another special group since they have mostly same-generation kin. As their network ages, there may be few family members able to provide reliable aid when needed. For seniors with financial or land resources, the ability to reciprocate help means that relationships can remain symmetrical. There seems to be little substitution of formal aid for informal aid except among those who are affluent enough and skilled enough to hire formal services as they need them. In general, those who are high users of formal services are also high users of informal help (Beland, 1986).

It appears that rural Canadian seniors' family structure and kinship interaction are similar to those of urban seniors. Some differences in structure and interaction among farm and non-farm elders have been found. However, with the decrease in the size of the farm population, these comparisons may be less fruitful than those between other types such as long-time residents and in-movers. Families who move to a rural area to be near a child may be vulnerable as they try to establish patterns of both affirmation and support during a crisis period such as bereavement. Ethnic differences in family patterns and expectations about care also need to continue to be studied as the cultural mosaic of Canadian elders changes. Finally, the question of whether lack of formal services puts pressure on family caregivers remains unresolved. It seems that when formal services are available they are used to maintain privacy and independence. However, seniors appear relatively unconcerned when formal services are not available. Family research in which caregivers and elders are both asked to comment on lack of formal services would address this question more completely.

Above all, this chapter serves to highlight the heterogeneity of the current cohort of rural seniors. The variety of experiences and living situations of rural seniors can only be expected to increase. The range of rural occupations is not as great as that of urban workers and the influence of agriculture will continue to decline as fewer people are involved in farming. Levels of health and independence will increase for many groups of rural seniors, although Native peoples and others in remote areas are at risk of poor health and dependence. While some rural seniors are well served with health and community services, others are isolated and have little access to basic amenities. Their stoic acceptance of this situation may disappear as future cohorts have higher expectations of service availability. Finally, rural families appear to operate much as do urban families to provide support and caring as necessary. The healthiest families appear to be those in which generational relationships can be symmetrical and intimacy at a distance maintained.

CHAPTER TEN

BEYOND 'ADD WOMEN AND STIR' IN CANADIAN RURAL SOCIETY

PAMELA SMITH

A Feminist Context

During the last two decades no field of intellectual endeavour has been untouched by the influence of the women's movement, nor by its call that Canadian women's contributions to all aspects of public and private life receive just recognition. The progress of feminist scholarship can be measured by the sheer volume of, for example, print material.

Fortunately, this crude, potentially misleading index is not the only obvious measure of growth. Other signs that feminist scholarship has come of age are just as evident in some of the following areas:

i) Reforms to legislation and regulations based on such scholarship: reform in the areas of taxation, child care and matrimonial property are all examples.

ii) In both the social sciences and the humanities feminist use of an increasingly complex, imaginative range of techniques and methodologies (Harding, 1987) on a widening and deepening variety of issues, without sacrificing inter-disciplinary co-operation which, in the first instance, fostered feminist scholarship.

iii) Independently conducted 'state of the art' reviews identifying clear

---

Pamela Smith is a member of the Sample Survey and Data Bank Unit at the University of Regina.

stages of development in feminist scholarship (such as Laurin-Frenette, 1981 and Eichler, 1985, as cited in McLaren, 1988).

iv) A clear understanding that diverse perspectives—as well as debate based on respect for them—are not merely healthy, but indispensable for continued growth.

All of these measures signal the progress of feminist scholarship. But if many disciplines have begun to move beyond the 'add women and stir approach' (McLaren, 1988: 5), the application of feminist perspectives has been uneven and almost invisible in some disciplines in Canada. Until the publication of McLaren (1988) for example, no text systematically illustrated the application of feminist perspectives to a wide range of issues addressed in Canadian sociology.

Feminism and Women in Agriculture

These observations apply equally to Canadian rural sociology. A considerable literature addressing the needs and interests of Canadian rural women has developed over the twenty years since the Royal Commission on the Status of Women (Canada, 1970). Much of the literature, however, has been prepared on shoestring budgets for specialized audiences. As a result, these works are often quite difficult—if not impossible—to locate, and very few of them have been collected and systematically reviewed.

While Canadian urban and rural women's interests and issues are often similar, those of concern to rural women frequently differ in magnitude, if not in kind.[1] A review focused on the development of feminist scholarship and its relationship to issues of concern to rural women in Canada would be an important project.

Such a review is overdue, but conducting it is not the purpose of this chapter.

Supplementing Current Typologies Representing Women's Contribution to Agriculture

The purpose of this chapter is to encourage work in this direction, by more narrowly focusing on the data and the concepts currently used to represent and describe Canadian women's various contributions to primary agriculture. Our overview focuses exclusively on two types of contributions made by women—through their on-farm and off-farm work—using data available from Statistics Canada. Domestic or household work is not included in the overview because no comparable national data are available concerning this type of contribution.

Proposing that the typology emerging from current literature is adequate only insofar as it represents some, but not all, of the ways Canadian women contribute to all spheres of private and public life in agricultural communities, the following section describes two ways in which the typology might be supplemented, and provides some data about both of these additional types of contribution, as well as data about contributions made through household work.

The resulting typology offers a set of concepts which may more accurately represent the historic and contemporary role women play in Canadian agricultural communities. Although the supplemented typology may be limited,[2] it is offered as a schematic representation to foster policy development and implementation by all women and men concerned about the future of Canadian agricultural communities and the quality of life in them.

Canadian Farm Women: Trends in Participation[3]

Patterns from 1921 to 1986

Throughout the last six decades, generation after generation of Canadian farm families has witnessed a steady decline in their numbers, accompanied by a constant growth in the size of farms. During the first half of this period—from 1921 until after World War Two—the number of women who were recorded by the census as actively 'working' in agriculture remained quite low and relatively constant[4] (Connelly, 1978).

Drawn from the general population census for Canada as a whole, Figure 10.1 shows how rapidly this apparent lack of involvement has changed in the decades following World War Two, as women have become increasingly involved in primary agriculture.[5]

In 1951, women represented only 4% of all Canadians reported as being employed in agriculture. But in the following decades, their participation

Figure 10.1 Employment in primary agriculture by sex, Canada, 1951–1986

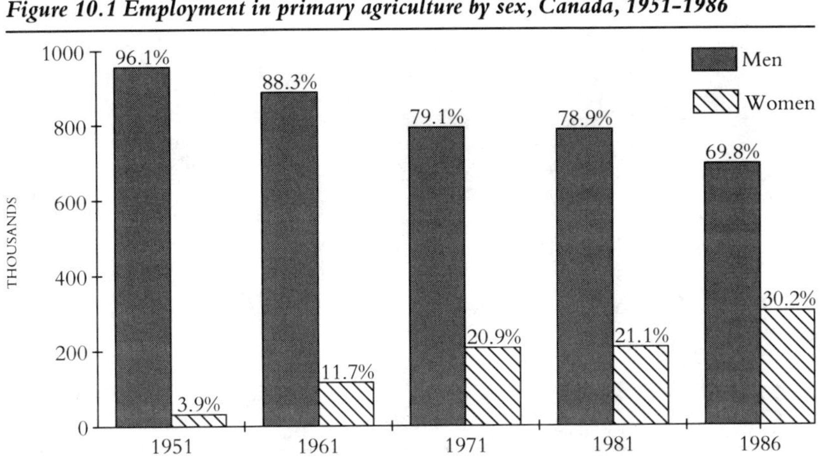

climbed sharply, reaching 12% in 1961 and almost doubling again to 21% by 1971. Remaining very stable at 21% between 1971 and 1981, women's share of the agricultural labour force increased again by 1986, so that almost one in every three persons (30%) working in the agriculture industry as a whole was a woman.

This is only the general pattern, however. To develop a more detailed picture of the situation of farm women, links of the agriculture and population censuses for 1971, 1981 and 1986 are used, and the discussion is restricted to women whose partners are described by the agriculture census as 'farm operators'. By 1986, there were roughly 236,000 of these women across Canada.

Trends in Farm Women's On-Farm and Off-Farm Work

Figure 10.2 shows that there have been remarkable shifts in the number of women who report either on- nor off-farm work in the last fifteen years. In

Figure 10.2 Occupation reported, women spouses in Canada, 1971, 1981, 1986

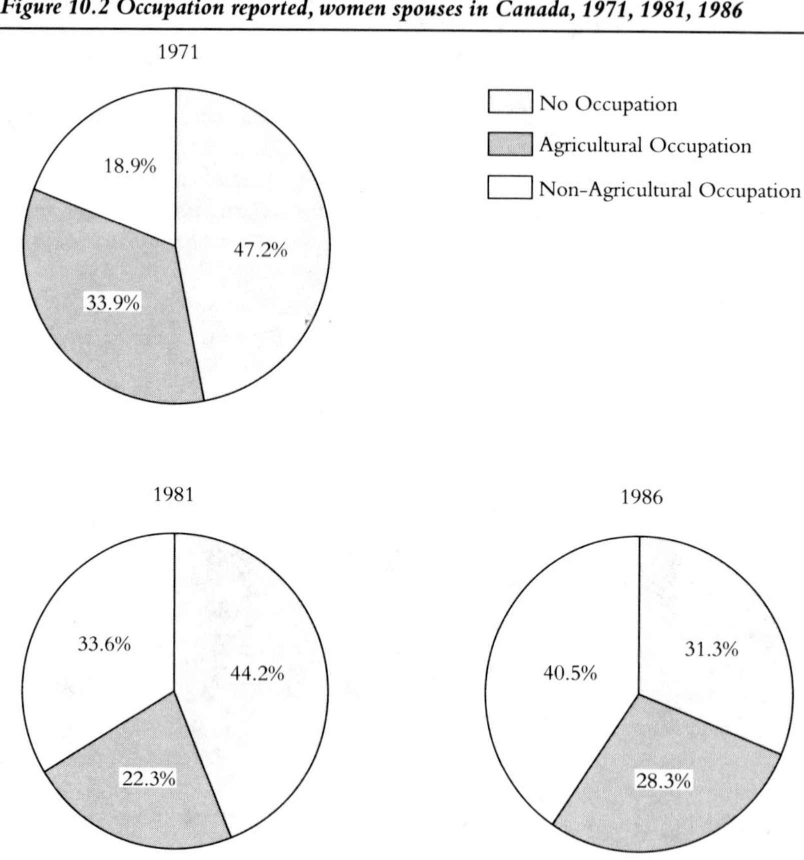

1971, almost half (47%) of farm women were reported as neither working on- nor off-farm. By 1981, this proportion decreased slightly to 44%; it dropped rapidly by 1986, when only 31% of all farm women across Canada were reported as not having 'worked' in either an agricultural or non-agricultural occupation.

Most of this change has been accounted for by the growth in women's off-farm employment, as shown in Figure 10.2. In 1971, fewer than 2 of every 10 farm women worked off the farm. This had climbed to 3 of every 10 by 1981 and grew again to 4 of every 10 in 1986.

Hours Per Week and Weeks Per Year

Over the last 15 years, there have also been increases in the number of hours per week and weeks per year worked by women either on or off the farm, as Figure 10.3 shows.

Canadian farm women whose main occupation was agricultural have increased both the hours worked per week (from 40 to 42) and weeks per year (from 42 to 44). Those farm women who worked off-farm have the same pattern of modest increase in average weekly hours worked (from 33 to 34), but the weeks they worked grew more sharply from 36 to 42, on average throughout the year.

Figure 10.4 provides some information relevant to a commonly asked question: 'Are there significant differences in the off-farm work participation among farm women across Canada?'

Off-farm work has increased among farm women in all provinces or regions (the four Atlantic provinces are combined).

But the rate of growth in off-farm work has been most pronounced in Quebec (220%) where only 10% of all farm women worked off-farm in 1971. By 1986, however, almost one in every three (32%) farm women in Quebec had off-farm employment as their main occupation.

Alberta had the next highest rate of growth (200%), followed by Saskatchewan (180%), and British Columbia (170%). Since the average rate of growth across Canada was 170%, Manitoba (160%), the Atlantic provinces (130%) and Ontario (120%) recorded below average rates of growth over the last 15 years.

But growth rates can be misleading. As Figure 10.4 shows, provinces with greatest rates of growth in off-farm work participation by farm women are generally those where it tended to be lower 15 years ago—Quebec (10%), Saskatchewan (17%), and Alberta (19%) in comparison to Ontario (25%), for example.

Trends in Off-Farm Occupations, by Region

Figure 10.5 shows the five main occupational groups in which women who

Figure 10.3 Agricultural and non-agricultural hours of women spouses, Canada, 1971–1986

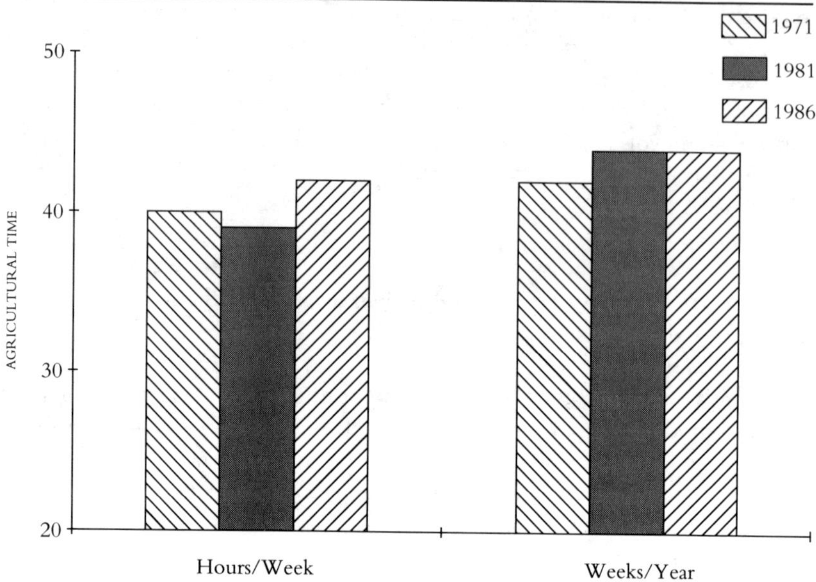

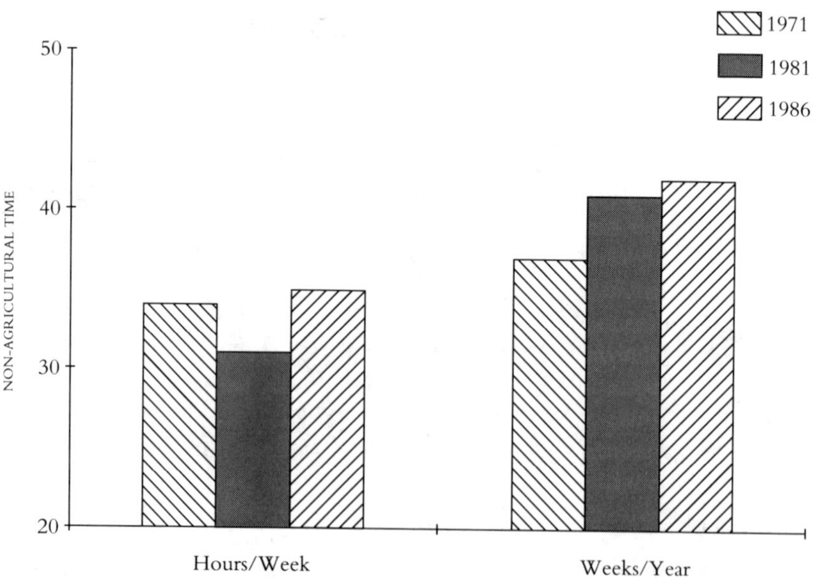

Figure 10.4 Per cent of women spouses reporting non-agricultural occupations, Canada and by province, 1971–1986

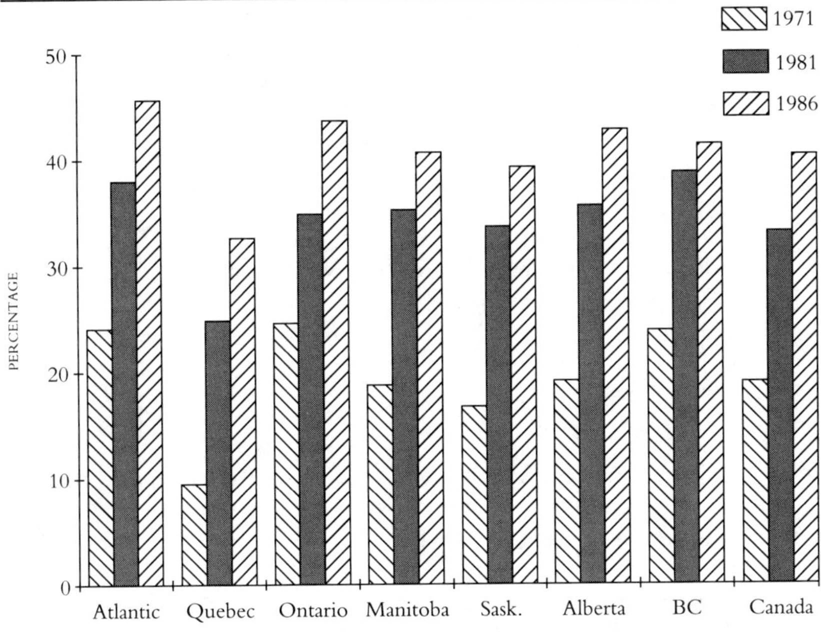

Figure 10.5 Occupational distribution of women spouses, Canada, 1971–1986

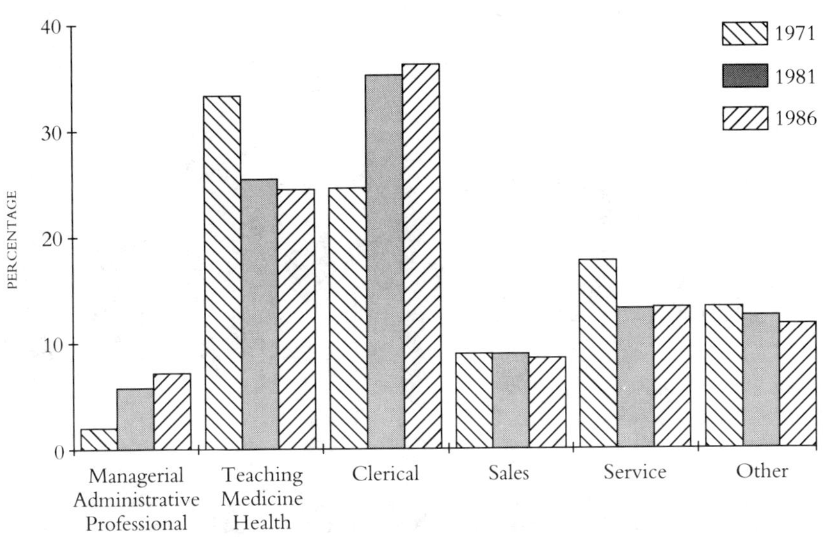

work off the farm are employed. The two most significant of these are teaching/medicine/health, as a single group, and clerical occupations.

Dramatic changes have occurred in the percentages of women employed in both groups over the last 15 years, across Canada as a whole. In 1971, roughly one in every three farm women who worked off-farm was employed in teaching/medicine/health, but by 1986 only a quarter of women working off the farm worked in these occupations. Most of the shift has been accounted for by a growth in employment in clerical occupations, which increased from 25% in 1971 to 36% by 1986.

Rates of decline in teaching/medicine/health were most pronounced in the Atlantic provinces (0.8), Ontario (0.9), Quebec (1.1) and Saskatchewan (1.1). Rates of growth in clerical occupations were strongest by far in Quebec (5.2), outstripping other provinces such as Alberta (2.4) and Saskatchewan (2.1) where growth in clerical employment was also relatively strong, as shown in Figure 10.6.

The Current Typology: an Overview

Many difficulties and dangers confront those attempting to delineate the ways in which women are involved in and contribute to productive work in the economy generally (Waring, 1988). These problems may be enhanced when

Figure 10.6 Per cent of women spouses in clerical occupations, Canada and by province, 1971–1986

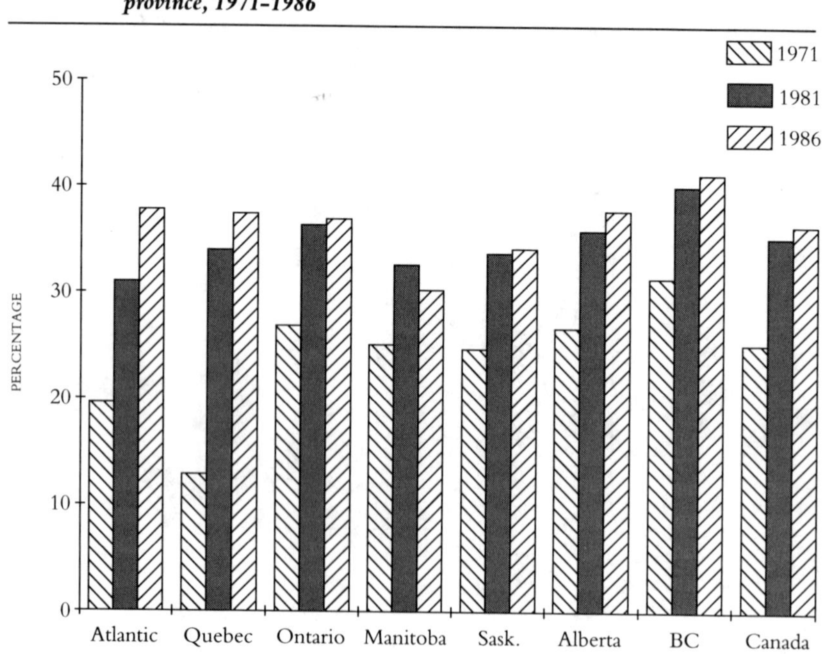

farm women's work is considered, given the intertwining of the family with agricultural enterprise (Ghorayshi, 1989).

Despite the evident indivisibility of the productive, reproductive, and consumption activities of farm family households, describing the ways in which women are involved in, support, and/or assist agriculture (Smith, 1987) is important. Farm women's work has been minimized so often and entirely ignored with such frequency that the challenge, while difficult, cannot be avoided. There is another, equally important reason to take up the challenge to recognize the contribution of women. If it is true that some farm women themselves tend to underestimate their work (Jones and Rosenfeld, 1981) or their own abilities (Ross, 1990), listing, describing, and classifying it may encourage them to value it more accurately.

And this challenge has been taken up in Canada[6] and elsewhere.[7] Many aspects of farm women's work have been identified, classified and, in most instances, quantified. Even though the terms used for classification may vary and the appropriate 'classification' of some activities may be disputed, a typology of farm women's work has emerged.

Early typologies developed to represent farm women's contributions to agriculture principally focused on their involvement in on-farm and off-farm work.[8] Contributions arising from women's work in farm households ordinarily were acknowledged; frequently, however, this type of contribution was not documented to the same extent as were contributions made to agriculture through on-farm and off-farm work.[9]

As it has emerged from the literature, therefore, the typology representing farm women's contribution to agriculture has three main classifications:

i) on-farm work;
ii) household or domestic work; and
iii) off-farm work.

Decision-Making

No national-level data are collected about decision-making, the fourth way in which women contribute to Canadian agriculture. To supplement other provincial or regional studies examining this type of contribution, Figure 10.7 has been prepared from a 1987 survey of four farming communities in Saskatchewan.

In most husband-wife farm households, women are involved with their partners in three different types of decision-making, on a joint or equal basis (Figure 10.7): major farm acquisition (64%), day-to-day farm (70%), and major household acquisition (78%) decisions.

Variations in these percentages seem attributable to the type of decision. Women in Saskatchewan are less likely to be involved alone in decisions on major farm acquisitions, as opposed to day-to-day farm decisions. Household

Figure 10.7 Contributors to three types of farm household decisions (four Saskatchewan communities)

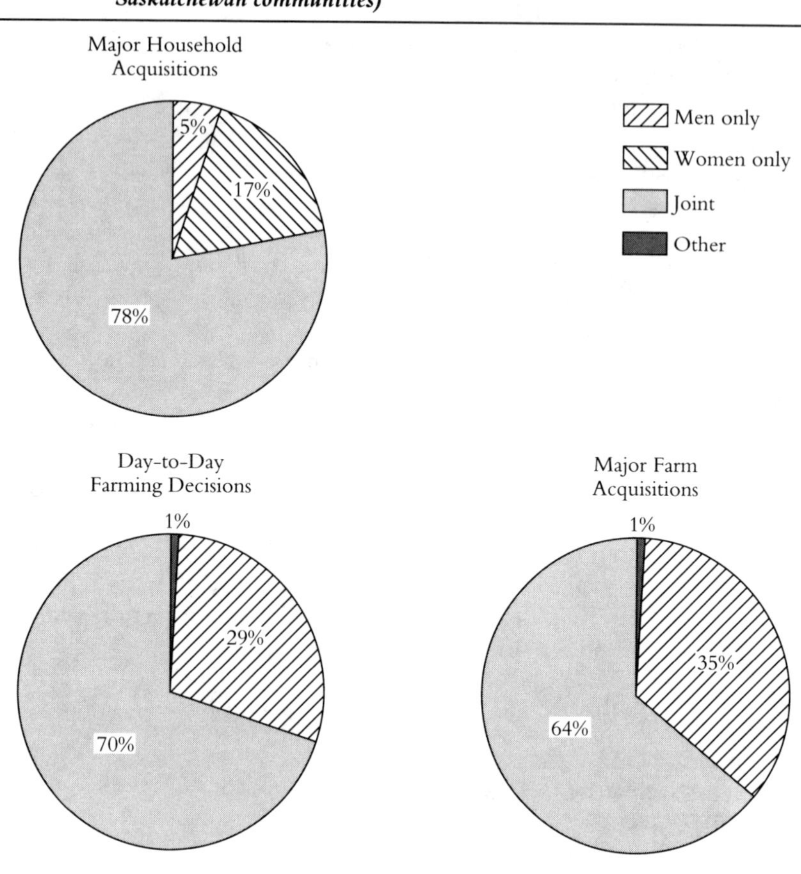

acquisition decisions are the only type which women undertake on their own (17%), without the involvement of their husbands.

On-Farm Work

The structure of the Population and Agricultural Censuses may underestimate the degree to which farm women (and men) are involved in work on their farms, since respondents are asked only to report their main occupations. The 1987 survey in four farming communities in Saskatchewan sought to overcome this by asking questions about each type of work (on-farm, off-farm, and household work).

It shows that three of every four farm women are involved in some capacity in on-farm work, working an average of 19 hours a week for 28 weeks a year (Figure 10.8).

Figure 10.8 Involvement of men and women in on-farm work (four Saskatchewan communities)

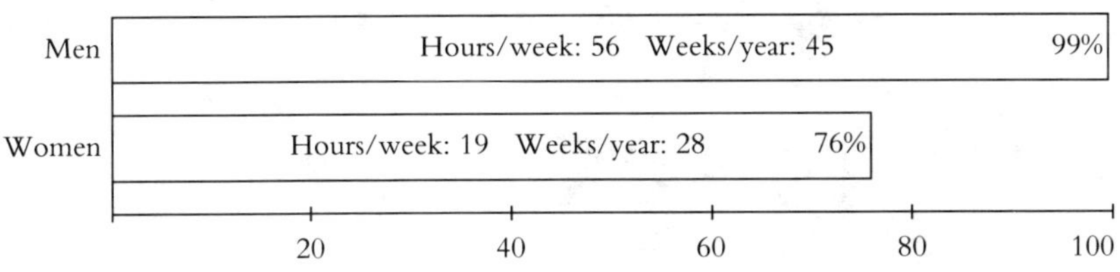

Women are much more likely to be involved in some specific types of farm work (Figure 10.9)—getting supplies (66%), farm bookkeeping (51%), and tending livestock (44%)—than in others, such as driving machinery (35%), delivering meals to the fields (35%), and repairing machinery (11%). These results are consistent with other studies which report a tendency for some types of farm work to be gender- (and, perhaps, age-) specific.

Household Work

Work in and around the home is another type of contribution which cannot be assessed using the census, since information about household work is not collected by Statistics Canada for either farm or urban households.

The 1987 survey on farm families in four Saskatchewan communities shows virtually every woman is involved in certain household tasks, and is less likely to be involved in others. These tasks are exclusively women's work in many—but by no means all—farm households (Figure 10.10).

For example, almost all women did dishes (98%), prepared meals (98%), cleaned house (94%), and washed/ironed clothing (96%) in the week prior to the survey, but some of their husbands assisted with this work (dishes, 38%; meals, 36%; housecleaning, 21%; and washing/ironing, 9%).

Husbands in households with children are more likely to assist: Figure 10.9 shows that 52% of the women and 38% of their husbands were involved in caring for children, and that 31% of women and 14% of their husbands helped children with homework.

As well, husbands in households with children contribute proportionally greater hours to either the care of children or helping with homework than they do to other household tasks, such as doing dishes or housecleaning (Figure 10.11).

Figure 10.9 Men and women and farming tasks (four Saskatchewan communities)

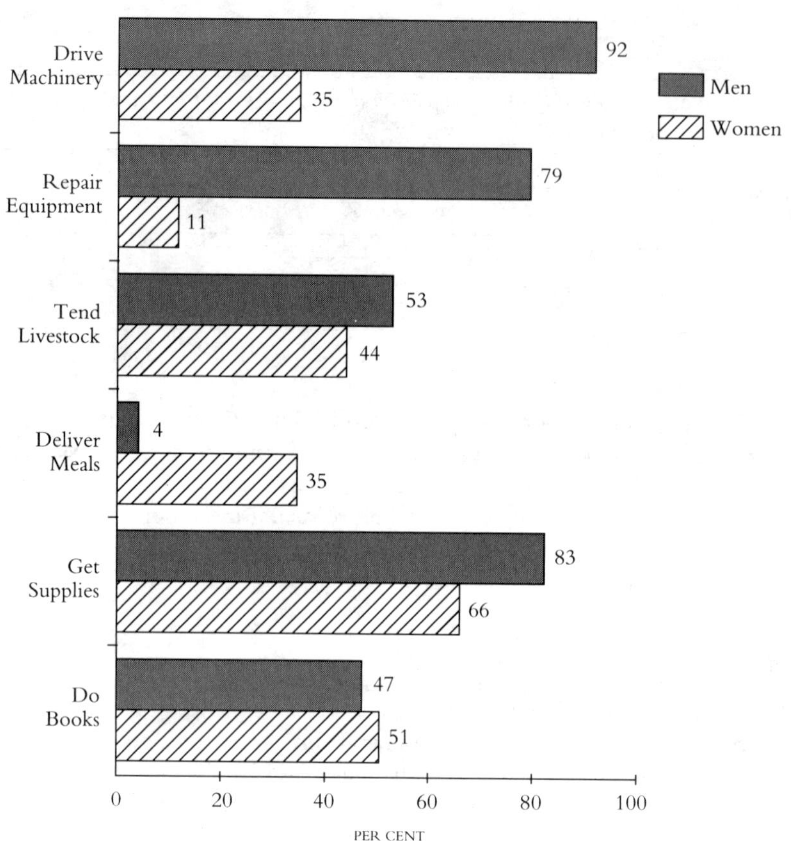

Volunteer Work

Greatest 'parity' between women and men is found in the fifth way in which women contribute to Canadian agriculture—through volunteer work (Figure 10.10). Slightly more than half (55%) of the farm women in the 1987 survey of farm families in four Saskatchewan communities were involved in some sort of volunteer work, as were 44% of their husbands. It is, however, noteworthy that women contribute more hours (2 hours on average) to volunteer work than do their husbands (1.6 hours on average—Figure 10.11).

Summary and Conclusion

Women are an increasingly important part of the total agricultural labour

Figure 10.10 Men and women and household tasks (four Saskatchewan communities)

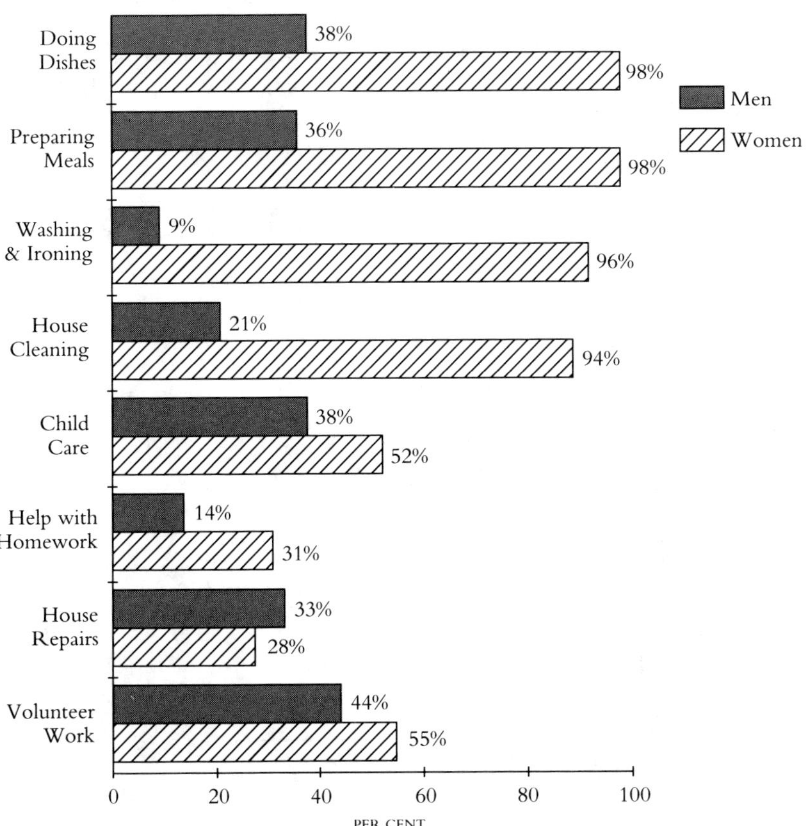

force in Canada—almost one in every three persons employed in primary agriculture in 1986 was a woman.

Farm women are now more likely to report working off or on the farm than was the case about two decades ago, in 1971. In 1986, 41% worked off-farm, 28% had an on-farm occupation, and 31%—down from 47% in 1971—reported neither off- nor on-farm work.

Regardless of whether their main occupation was agricultural or non-agricultural, farm women in 1986 worked more hours per week and weeks per year than they did in 1971.

When they worked off the farm in 1986, farm women were more likely to work in clerical occupations (36%), followed by teaching/medicine/health occupations (25%). This is almost a precise reversal of the distributions in 1971.

All trends summarized here apply generally for all provinces in Canada, and for all farms, regardless of the type of commodity in which they specialize or their level of gross sales.

A survey of farm households in four Saskatchewan communities shows that three of every four farm women were involved in farm-related work, and that they were more likely to tend livestock, get supplies or keep farm accounts, in comparison to three other tasks (driving machinery, delivering meals to fields, and repairing machinery).

Figure 10.11 Men's and women's average hours per week: farm household tasks (four Saskatchewan communities)

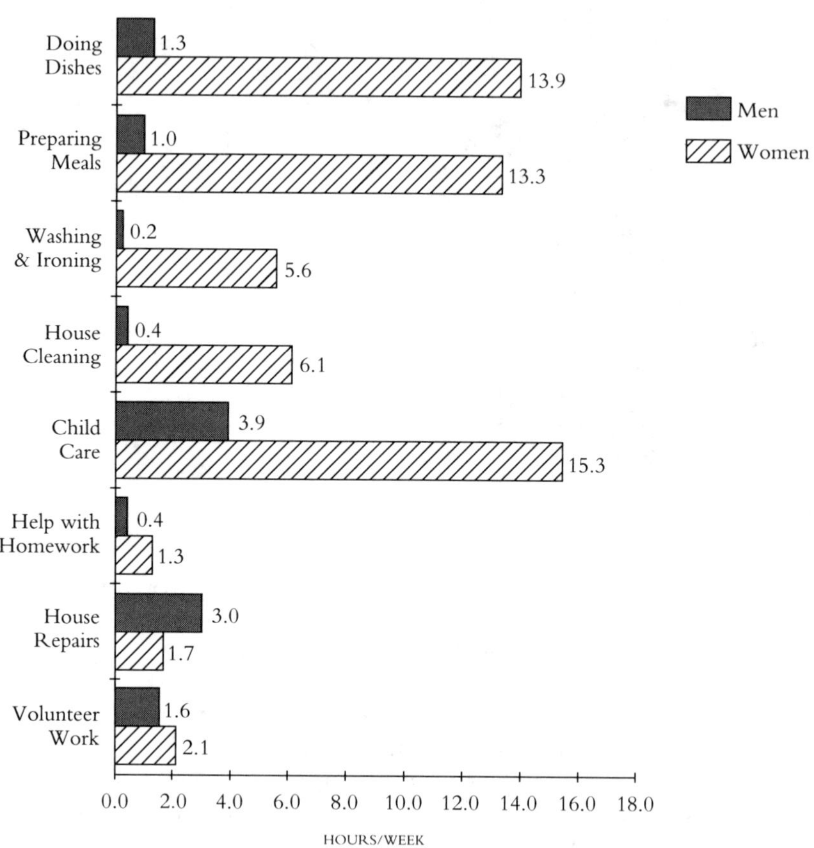

The same tendency to 'sex-specialization' for household tasks was evident in this regionally-specific survey. Roughly one of every three farm men contributed to three household tasks in which all women work. Interestingly, however, in households in which there were children farm men seem much more likely either to care for children or help with homework than other men were to be involved in other household tasks.

The single household/community activity in which women and men are almost equally likely to be involved is volunteer work—55% of farm women and 44% of farm men contribute to their communities and, perhaps, to agriculture more generally, through this type of work.

Findings available concerning farm women's contribution to Canadian agriculture available from Statistics Canada, as reported in our overview, or about Saskatchewan women's contributions, as noted in the preceding section, suggest several conclusions.

Women are an integral part of Canadian agriculture, and their contributions to this industry take several forms. Two types of contributions—on-farm work and off-farm work—have been widely acknowledged in recent years. A third form of contribution, which women make almost exclusively in most households, takes the form of domestic work. The fourth and fifth ways in which women contribute are through their involvement in decision-making, on the one hand, and volunteer work, on the other.

If rural sociology is to move beyond the 'add women and stir' approach, it will be necessary to adopt both methodologies and data collection techniques infused fully with 'an awareness of sex as a social variable' (Eichler and Lapointe, 1985: 6).

Notes

[1]Several factors contribute to such differences. Canada's rural population and communities are dispersed, diverse, and subject to extreme climates. Their access to urban centres as well as the services and amenities typical of them, is widely variable. Although agricultural exports continue to play an important role in Canada's balance of trade and significant concentrations of population and inhabited land mass are devoted to agricultural production, rural populations and communities cannot be confused with their agricultural counterparts. In many parts of Canada, rural and 'purely' agricultural communities are clearly distinguishable, and their circumstances and needs are quite different.

[2]In particular, the size of the 'sample' of Saskatchewan farm families, its doubtful representativeness and its specialized geographic location should prohibit any assumptions about the universal applicability of findings based on it and reported later in this text.

[3]Parts of this section are drawn from Smith (1989).

[4]Those interested in one critique of the reliability of census estimates may wish to consult Waring (1988). Somewhat different assessments of the difficulties associated with 'counting women into agriculture' are provided in Smith (1987) and Villani (1990).

[5]Family farm agriculture is a 'subpart' of the industry 'primary agriculture' and the two should be carefully distinguished. The classification used by Statistics Canada to report primary agriculture includes many more individuals than those who are involved in family farming. For the most part, these others may be women and men employed by farm families who do not themselves own farm property. For a useful, if sadly under-acknowledged, discussion of women who work on farms as 'pure' wage labourers, see Lee (1987).

[6]Some Canadian studies include Berry, 1986; Dion, 1983; Ghorayshi, 1989; Ireland, 1983; Keating, Dougherty and Munro, 1987; Kohl, 1976 and 1978; Koski, 1982; Reimer, 1980; Ross, 1990; Taylor, 1976; Williamson, 1981; Women for the Survival of Agriculture, 1985.

[7]Selected American and British studies are Boulding, 1980; Bokemeier and Garkovich, 1987; Buttel and Gillespie, 1984; Gasson, 1981; Haney, 1983; Hill, 1981; Jones and Rosenfeld, 1981; Meiners and Olson, 1987; Rosenfeld, 1986; Ross, 1985; Sachs, 1983; Salant, 1983; Whatmore, 1988; Wilkening, 1981.

[8]For an attempt to schematically represent some of the early typologies, please see Smith (1987: 196, Figure 5).

[9]There are several possible explanations for the relatively greater emphasis given on-farm and off-farm work in comparison to household or domestic work. One, domestic work is common to all households, farm and non-farm alike, even if there is reason—and some evidence—to believe it is greater in terms of hours in farm households. Two, courts have typically not looked to domestic labour as a form of contribution to household operation, until recently. Three, another, principal, explanation is undoubtedly that data concerning household or domestic work are not routinely collected at the national level.

SECTION FOUR

RURAL ENVIRONMENTAL ISSUES

The two chapters in this section deal with topics not generally included in Sociology textbooks. A long-standing problem in Canada as well as other countries, and one receiving increasing attention in recent years, is the degradation and depletion of our nonrenewable resources and the future sustainability of agriculture and other rural enterprises.

These two chapters emphasize the deleterious effects of past and present agricultural practices on the supply and quality of Canada's soil and water resources, food quality, and other related environmental issues. Gertler examines the problem from a more general environmental perspective, discussing the desirability and bases of many of the current farming practices and technologies. These practices and technologies are supported by policies, programs, and economic, social, and cultural beliefs as means of maintaining or increasing the production of food, although their advisability is questionable when the adverse side effects on the quality of food, soil and water, health and the degradation and depletion of the soil resources are considered.

Gertler examines the potential viability and benefits of organic and other non-traditional methods of farming as alternatives to reliance on fertilizers, herbicides, insecticides and other chemical inputs, as well as some of the economic, institutional, social, and cultural factors that inhibit the acceptance and utilization of these alternative methods.

Environmental problems created by the widespread use of chemical farm inputs and other farming practices are also discussed in the chapter by Anderson. He outlines the major types of soil formations in Canada and their effects on farming practices and types of farm production, as well as the reciprocal effects of farm practices and types of production on the quality of land and water resources. In addition to the loss of farm land to erosion and other types of depletion and to the encroachment of urban uses, the loss of wildlife habitat to farm uses is also examined.

CHAPTER ELEVEN

THE SOCIAL ECONOMY OF AGRICULTURAL SUSTAINABILITY

MICHAEL E. GERTLER

Definitions of sustainable agriculture usually include socio-economic criteria, such as farm sector viability and adequate production of safe and nutritious food, along with ecological criteria, such as resource conservation and protection of environmental quality (MacRae *et al.*, 1990; AIC, 1991).[1] Such multifaceted specification of agricultural sustainability links technical decisions about production methods to social, economic, and ecological criteria. This would appear to be a step in the right direction—towards a more holistic framework for designing and evaluating production and consumption systems. In practice, however, sustainable agriculture means different things to different groups.

Those who feel comfortable with a market-determined resource management regime embrace the economic viability criteria and maintain that, with minor alterations in economic incentives, the present technical and social organization of agriculture can yield optimal resource-use solutions. Those whose first concern is ecological emphasize redesign of farming systems to minimize environmental threats and to guarantee integrity of the resource base in perpetuity. For partisans of this perspective, short-term profitability is less critical than long-term, system viability. Moreover, this group can point

Michael Gertler is Assistant Professor of Sociology at the University of Saskatchewan.

to micro-level data suggesting that individual farmers can make a living pursuing alternative farming systems (Lockeretz *et al.*, 1981: 546), as well as macro-level data suggesting that farmers collectively would benefit economically under a scenario in which alternative low-input systems were widely adopted and production was somewhat reduced (Taylor and Frohberg, 1977). There is a tendency among people in this latter camp, as well, to assume that moving towards more ecologically sound farming systems would necessarily involve moderate-sized, family-labour farms (Buttel *et al.*, 1986: 59).

Competing and even contradictory visions of agricultural development are subsumed under the rubric of sustainability. The debate also suffers from a dearth of systematic analysis of contradictions between economic systems on the one hand, and ecological *and* social objectives on the other. Rarely is there more than superficial analysis of the broader socio-political parameters of sustainable development (Redclift, 1987; Batie, 1989). Social and cultural dimensions are typically neglected or dealt with at a very general level. Seldom are structural, institutional, and organizational barriers to sustainability examined with enough specificity to reveal how unsustainable resource management regimes become entrenched. [2]

Agricultural Sustainability in the Canadian Context

Agricultural development in North America has been linked to significant environmental problems. Soil resources have been degraded through erosion, compaction, salinization, and organic matter depletion (Manning, 1988). Water resources have been damaged by inorganic fertilizers, livestock wastes, and pesticides (Buttel and Swanson, 1986). Wildlife habitat has been destroyed. There is concern, as well, about the effects of agro-industrial practices on the health and well-being of consumers, agricultural labour, and livestock (Manning, 1988; Madden, 1988).

The environmental issues confronting agriculture are related to dilemmas challenging other resource-based industries. With the exception of indigenous, subsistence economies, conservation has not been a major criterion in the development of any industry based on renewable resources. The fishing and forest industries have earned notoriety for the exhaustion of stocks and the degradation of productive ecosystems (Cameron, 1990; Nikiforuk and Struzik, 1989; Kennedy, 1990). Whether the resources are privately owned, rented, leased from governments, or accessed via international agreements, resource users have been slow to adopt sustainable modes of operation. The state has also been slow to regulate resource management. Concern for the short-term viability of firms—and for the survival of governments—has usually overridden other considerations of sustainable development, including the long-term viability of industries and communities and the long-term sustainability of production. In the context of commercial capitalist development, one should perhaps be asking if it is reasonable to expect agriculture to hold to standards which have not normally been imposed elsewhere?

Farmers must find ways to achieve competitive returns on capital if they are to bid for land, buy inputs, and borrow money. Volatile commodity markets, shrinking margins, high debt loads, and high interest rates likewise help to focus their attention on short-term survival rather than long-term sustainability (Buttel and Swanson, 1986). When commodity prices are profitable, expected returns are capitalized into the price of land. Paradoxically, higher land prices then become a further motivation to adopt cropping schemes and management practices that maximize cash flow and minimize risk of crop loss (Buttel and Swanson, 1986: 35). The typical result is heavier use of agrochemical inputs and shorter crop rotations featuring the one or two commodities that provide highest returns. Few can afford to implement resource management strategies internalizing erosion and water pollution costs that others may treat as externalities. Beyond immediate economic pressures, a dominant ideology that equates productivity and efficiency with low labour costs and high returns on capital, creates a chilly climate for those who would question the wisdom of current practices.

Local ecology must be considered when discussing agricultural resource management. Ecological and economic possibilities differ from region to region and from commodity to commodity. What works in Pennsylvania or Brittany will not necessarily work in Nova Scotia or Alberta. Much of Canadian agriculture is practised under conditions that approach agronomic limits of growing season and moisture availability. This means that farmers have limited flexibility in adopting practices that might increase sustainability. On the Prairies, for example, short growing seasons and lack of moisture limit options for including nitrogen-fixing legumes in crop rotations.

With the exception of a few urbanized areas, Canada is sparsely populated. In many areas, the population base is not adequate to support a diversified farming economy along the lines of, say, New England. Arrangements that have facilitated alternative farming programs—direct marketing of specialty food products, for example—are not a strong prospect for most Canadian agriculturalists. Distance from markets and lack of access to processing and handling facilities also limit production options. The small domestic market means, as well, that much production is destined for export. In the context of competitive international markets, the promotion of sustainable resource management practices, whether through voluntary compliance or by government regulation, becomes more problematic.

Geography, demographics, and culture all shape the political context of resource management debates. The Canadian population is increasingly urban with little direct experience on the land. Though they may be alarmed by reports of resource destruction or toxic residues, few urbanites understand the exigencies of agricultural production in a northern climate. Rural populations, meanwhile, are preoccupied with wresting a living from a difficult environment. They often resist regulatory constraints on resource use. In addition, as indigenous scholars have observed, profound alienation from nature is typical among Canadians from all walks of life.

The public—whether urban or rural—is concerned about many agricultural practices. A 1989 poll found 57% of Canadians were 'very concerned' and 26% were 'somewhat concerned' about pesticide use while 47% were 'very concerned' and 33% were 'somewhat concerned' about soil depletion (Campbell *et al.*, 1990: 313). About three out of four said they favoured greater restrictions on farm chemical use (Campbell *et al.*, 1990: 314). The demand for organically grown produce and livestock products has grown markedly in the last decade, although it still represents only a small percentage of the total market. Groups lobbying for humane treatment of farm animals enjoy increasing support as do those campaigning against the routine use of antibiotics in animal feeds, against hormone implants for beef cattle, and against the use of bovine somatotropin (i.e., bovine growth hormone) for dairy cattle.

Despite public fears, pesticide use has increased. In 1970, 2% of improved land in farms was sprayed with insecticides and, in 1980, just under 4% was treated. In 1985, 10% of improved land, some 4.6 million hectares, was sprayed for control of insects or disease (Statistics Canada, 1989: 108). Herbicide use has likewise increased. In 1970, 20% of the improved land was sprayed. By 1980, this had expanded to 34%. In 1985, one-half of the improved land in farms or almost 23 million hectares were sprayed with herbicides (Statistics Canada, 1987: 6; Statistics Canada, 1989: 106). Inorganic fertilizer use has also increased. In 1970, only 16% of improved land was fertilized. In 1980, 40% was treated. By 1985, some 4 million metric tonnes of commercial fertilizers were applied to 23 million hectares, or just over one-half of the total improved land in farms (Statistics Canada, 1987: 6; Statistics Canada, 1989: 102, 104). Farming without fertilizer may be unsustainable in the absence of other strategies for maintaining soil fertility. There is little doubt, however, that wider and more intensive use of pesticides and inorganic fertilizers constitutes an ecological burden and potential environmental health hazard.

Resource management problems associated with farming persist despite increased awareness of environmental issues, and despite improvements in technology and the scientific knowledge base. At least part of the explanation can be found in the way that agriculture has been reorganized over the past half century. Many of the technological and managerial innovations that have increased yields and labour productivity have also contributed to the environmental cost of farming.

Structural Change and the Prospects for Sustainable Agriculture

The socio-economic context of agricultural resource management includes the changing structure and organization of the farm sector, of agro-industries, and of international markets. Agro-industrial firms have the power to reshape the farm sector and to influence farming practices (Gertler, 1991). The implementation of sustainable practices in the farm sector is thus partially dependent on the degree to which sustainability becomes a central criterion in other segments of the agro-food industry. Given the global character of commodity markets and industrial input production, the prospects for sustainable agriculture in Canada are also closely tied to advances made internationally. The links come via technologies and standards as well as through trade and competition. Some European countries have introduced sweeping regulatory reforms designed to improve agricultural sustainability (cf. Drake, 1989; Weinberg, 1990). The close integration of the Canadian and United States economies may mean, however, that it would be difficult to introduce subsidies, taxes, or regulations that depart substantially from those of our larger neighbour.

The structure of farming includes such characteristics as the number, size, and legal organization of farm firms; land tenure arrangements; the distribution of assets, income, and debts; levels of capitalization and mechanization; levels of specialization; and the involvement of farm household members in farm and off-farm work. The structural transformation of farming since the 1940s has involved increased scale, mechanization, and capital intensity together with related agronomic practices such as increased enterprise and regional specialization, separation of crop and livestock production, and intensification of production through greater use of purchased inputs (van Es, 1983; Buttel and Swanson, 1986; Fulton *et al.*, 1989). Where increased size of operations involves purchase of large, specialized equipment, the tendency towards specialization and monocultures is reinforced. Producers specialize in particular commodities and expand their operations in order to distribute fixed costs over a larger acreage (Buttel and Gertler, 1982; Buttel and Swanson, 1986).

Farmers have adopted many technologies and practices that reduce the environmental risks associated with particular procedures or cropping programs. Examples include using sprayers designed to reduce pesticide drift, avoiding fall application of nitrogen fertilizers, and landscaping to intercept run-off from animal housing. Resource-conserving practices are not all equally susceptible to adoption, however. Farmers will be most likely to implement techniques that are compatible with time-tested strategies for economic advancement. That is, they will tend to adopt only those practices that fit within an overall program of expansion, specialization, and replacement of labour with machinery and agrochemical inputs (Buttel and Swanson, 1986).

In this context, selective adoption of resource-conserving techniques may lead to structural reorganization of farming operations along lines that increase the overall environmental impact of commodity production. At the same time it becomes more difficult to implement more sustainable strategies, such as longer crop rotations, reduced pesticide use, or recycling of barnyard wastes. A prime example is the adoption of minimum tillage techniques to reduce soil erosion and to save energy. Paradoxically, the use of no-till and minimum tillage equipment is frequently associated with farming programs that involve bigger fields, heavier and faster machinery, greater use of agrochemicals, and specialized, continuous production of row-crops or cereal grains (Buttel *et al.*, 1990). Each of these adds to the environmental risk or environmental burden created by farming.

Research examining the association between farm operator, farm household, and farm firm characteristics, on the one hand, and propensity to adopt conservation practices, on the other, yields somewhat inconclusive results. Unexplained variance is high no matter how many causal variables are incorporated (Swanson *et al.*, 1986; Lockeretz, 1990). Smaller farmers may have certain advantages in implementing certain labour- or management-intensive alternative farming strategies but farm size, measured by gross sales, land area, or net worth, has been shown to be positively correlated with the adoption of soil conservation practices—particularly no-till and reduced tillage equipment (Buttel *et al.*, 1990). One important finding is that implementation of conservation practices lags well behind awareness of resource management problems. Many farm operators are aware of the problem, accept a degree of social responsibility for resource preservation, manifest favourable attitudes towards conservation, and are knowledgeable about conservation practices applicable to their farms. Yet they still employ practices that degrade land and water resources (Swanson *et al.*, 1986: 110-11).

Tenancy has been found in some studies to be negatively associated with soil conservation practices such as crop rotations, contour planting, strip cropping, cover cropping, and manuring, or implementation of measures such as grass waterways, terraces, sediment retention basins, and windbreaks. Other studies find little or no difference between practices used on owned and rented land (Buttel *et al.*, 1990: 160). Perhaps the pressures to simplify cropping systems are more significant than any incentives for conservation that might be associated with ownership, particularly where land is heavily mortgaged. Perceived security of tenure is low even with ostensible ownership.

With the tighter integration of the farm sector into commodity systems that include input suppliers, processors, and distributors, the structure of agro-industries becomes relevant for agricultural resource management. This includes the size, number, location, and control of agribusiness firms, as well as direct or contract integration with farming operations. It also includes links between agricultural suppliers and other industries, e.g., petrochemical and pharmaceutical firms, and links between food processors and food retailers.

Where farmers produce crops or livestock under contract for a processor, the contract may stipulate certain inputs, practices, and standards. Contracts under which tomatoes, sweet corn, and cucumbers are grown for processing frequently stipulate pesticide use (Gertler, 1991). Farmers must apply the product themselves or allow the processor to spray. This precludes alternative practices even where these might be effective in achieving desired levels of pest control. Related examples can be cited in the livestock industry. Where pigs are grown under contract to an integrating firm that is a feed supplier, or meat processor, or both, the farmer has little control over feed formulation. Raising livestock on an alternative regime becomes a non-option as long as the producer is under contract. Lack of a contract may mean loss of market outlet and loss of operating credit (Perreault, 1982).

Integration of the seed industry as part of multinational pharmaceutical and petrochemical conglomerates also has implications for the design of farming systems and for the locus of control over production (Gertler, 1987). A disproportionate share of biotechnological research goes into development of seed varieties resistant to particular herbicides. The companies involved hope to market a package of complementary products—proprietary herbicides and patented herbicide-tolerant seed varieties (Kloppenberg, 1988).

More fundamentally, the increasing preponderance of private research means that scientific effort is not applied to other potentially fruitful projects that might facilitate reduced use of agrochemicals (Buttel and Gertler, 1982). Sustainable agriculture is management-intensive, requires locally specific strategies, and tends to minimize the use of conventional commercial inputs. These characteristics render it less compatible with classical formulae for exploitation of commercial potential in the development of farm technologies. Sustainable agriculture therefore implies an expanding role for public sector research. Meanwhile, however, state funding is being reduced and agribusiness corporations are pressing for reorientation of remaining public agency research in a supportive role, bolstering their own commercially oriented projects (Buttel *et al.*, 1986; Kloppenberg and Buttel, 1987).

Public Policy and the Prospects for Sustainable Agriculture

The structure and orientation of Canadian agriculture have been shaped by state intervention starting with settlement policies and continuing to the present (Rosaasen *et al.*, 1990). Relatively few of these interventions were primarily construed as agricultural resource management policies. Most were either economic policies for the sector, or general economic policies designed primarily to support economic development in other sectors. Exceptions include the Prairie Farm Rehabilitation Administration, initiated in response to massive soil erosion and attendant social dislocation in the 1930s, and numerous smaller federal and provincial initiatives to study and protect soil resources. Unfortunately, programs and policies have inadvertently rewarded or supported resource management practices that lead to degradation of soils and off-site damage to water resources. While this is not too surprising given the constraints under which the Canadian state must operate, it suggests that implementation of a more sustainable agriculture would require substantial reformulation of policies, programs, and regulations affecting the agricultural sector.

A number of agricultural and general economic policies stand out as deficient in this respect. On the Prairies, the quota delivery system of the Canadian Wheat Board has encouraged specialization in grain production, excessive use of summer fallow, and the cultivation of marginal land (Rosaasen *et al.*, 1990: 373). Grain transportation subsidies under the Western Grain Transportation Act have also rewarded Prairie farmers who specialized in cereal grain production, rather than implementing a more diversified crop and livestock production regime (Rosaasen *et al.*, 1990: 376). Commodity subsidization policies encourage expansion and specialization in that they reward increased production of supported crops and reduce risks associated with simplified cropping programs (Buttel and Gertler, 1982: 108).

Marketing boards, as quasi-governmental agencies, are often unresponsive to the needs of producers attempting to market certified organic products (MacRae *et al.*, 1990: 80). Government livestock regulations may require the use of certain pesticides, while grading standards emphasize cosmetic as opposed to other qualities (MacRae *et al.*, 1990: 80). At the same time tax and credit policies have encouraged expansion, intensification, mechanization, and specialization (Buttel and Gertler, 1982). Credit agencies may make agrochemical use—evidence that the producer is following recommended practices—a condition for loans (MacRae *et al.*, 1990: 80). Monetary policies that include high real interest rates lead farmers to shorten their planning horizon and to concentrate on maximizing returns in the short run. Money made in farming can then be more profitably invested in bonds or treasury bills (Van Kooten, 1987: 161).

Towards a Political Sociology of Alternative Agriculture

Political support for an ecologically rational agriculture comes from many quarters: the broad environmental movement, soil conservation groups, farmers involved in organic production, scientists, and consumers interested in food quality and related rural development issues. Mainstream farm and agricultural organizations have played a relatively minor role in these debates though their communications organs have, at least until recently, typically aligned with the agrochemical industry to discredit and denigrate the potential of any alternative approach to farming.[3]

Agriculture is coming under scrutiny as part of a broader 'greening' of public consciousness. Numerous groups are focusing on the environmental problems of industrial society—resource depletion and degradation, pollution, habitat destruction, and so on. While this movement is not uniquely focused on agriculture, farming and agribusiness are often singled out for special attention. Farming enjoys a special status as an industry and occupation. What is being produced is of intimate concern. The production process is also culturally 'loaded' in that it involves human use of nature to produce food. Beyond this, agriculture occupies a special ideological position as a sector in which household-based enterprise remains numerically dominant. This status helps in mobilizing public support for subsidies, exemptions from labour statutes, and minimal environmental regulation. The political price, however, is public interest not lavished on other industries. This interest, as already suggested, includes soil and water conservation, the safety of food, the occupational health and safety of farm workers, and, lately, the treatment of farm animals.

Farmers who have taken steps to improve the environmental sustainability of their farm operations can be classified into two main groups: conventional operators who have made marginal adjustments in cropping programs and techniques in order to reduce adverse environmental impacts, and farmers who have implemented alternative, organic, biological, biodynamic, ecological, or sustainable farming systems. Farmers belonging to the first category are relatively numerous. They are frequently involved in soil conservation organizations and programs but do not necessarily embrace many of the assumptions and broader objectives of the sustainable agriculture movement.

A much smaller group of farmers has implemented alternative farming programs that may make their production certifiable as 'organic'. Such programs involve numerous prescribed and proscribed practices. Synthetic pesticides and inorganic fertilizers are avoided. Crop rotations with leguminous species, alternative cultivation practices, and other organic means are used to maintain soil fertility and to control weeds and pests. Where livestock is kept, barnyard manures are carefully recycled to the land and animals are raised without routine recourse to antibiotics and other conventional medication.[4]

According to one recent estimate, there are approximately 4,000 farms in Canada that are operating under, or in transition to, such alternative systems (Thorne, 1990: 27). The popularity of this option has recently increased among several groups of farmers. Producers in Eastern Canada are benefiting from rising consumer demand for organic produce. Grain farmers in Western Canada are finding that depressed commodity prices hardly justify the cost of commercial fertilizers and pesticides. Both routes lead to greater interest in organic and other sustainable, low-input strategies.

The adherents of alternative farming programs are diverse in terms of scale, origins, and approach. Their operations range in size from modest, market garden or dairy operations, to very large commercial farms. Many of these farmers formerly used conventional inputs and techniques. However, due to personal or livestock health problems, soil or water management problems, economic exigencies or opportunities, and/or social or religious convictions, they have switched to alternative strategies for maintaining soil productivity and controlling pests (Lockeretz and Wernick, 1979; MacRae *et al.*, 1990). There are also families who have more recently entered farming with a counterculture agenda that may include, along with organic farming, ideals of self-reliance and locally-based economy.

Resistance to large-scale substantive environmental and social reforms in agriculture has long shaped debates over agriculture development in North America and abroad. High yielding seeds, inorganic fertilizers, pesticides, mechanization, and cheap credit raised yields and transformed farming in industrialized countries in the decades following World War II. A version of this same package of technical interventions and agricultural policies has been promoted as the solution to Third World agricultural development problems. This Green Revolution has been underwritten by Western governments and foundations as an alternative to more sweeping social reforms, such as land redistribution, and in place of efforts to increase the productivity of low-input farming systems by building on the local knowledge base (Griffin, 1974; Pearse, 1980).

At least until recently, those who questioned the resource efficiency, ecological wisdom, or social equity of this Green Revolution strategy at home or abroad, risked being labelled a kook or a subversive. If you worked in the public bureaucracies responsible for agricultural research, education, or extension—not to mention in the direct employ of agribusiness or the agricultural media—your career was at stake. Practitioners of alternative farming strategies have likewise had to contend with the vehement opposition of most agricultural scientists, institutions, and organizations. Until recently, only those willing to adopt practices viewed as irrational by the agricultural establishment, could join the ranks of alternative agriculturalists.

In the absence of adequate research or extension support, 'conversion' to an organic program involved something of a leap of faith. Organic producers have been very dependent on their own resources, on networking among experienced practitioners, and on information published in the alternative agricultural press. Limited assistance and encouragement has also come from a small number of researchers and popularizers who have operated on the fringes of established agricultural science, and from the purveyors of organic soil amendments who provided advice in much the same manner as sales staff for agrochemical products. Whether one was zealous to start with, the experience of dealing with unsupportive neighbours, extension agents, and loan officers, not to mention a mostly hysterically negative farm press, would soon foster a certain siege mentality. In effect, one had to be part zealot—or at least a tenacious heretic—to survive as an organic farmer.

The social philosophies and personal politics of producers who have made relatively marginal changes in their cropping programs reflect the range of ideologies present in the rural population. The alignments of producers who, by one or another path, have come to implement programs that represent a substantial departure from conventional practices, likewise reflect a broad ideological spectrum. It is hard to generalize about the political orientation of the alternative farming movement which bears the marks of the hostile environment in which it grew and also reflects aspects of the socio-political reality of rural North America. This includes the influence of various strains of agrarian fundamentalism, the commercial and private property orientations of most farmers, and the economic survival pressures confronting family farms. The net effect of external constraints and internal tendencies seems to have been a movement whose central tendency falls towards individualistic survival strategies. This is not to ignore individuals in the alternative farming movement who are participants in various types of organizations and alliances, both local and international. As their numbers increase, so do opportunities for collaboration and affiliation with other groups involved in environmental and social reform efforts.

The political economy of the alternative agriculture movement is tied up with the issue of certification. Discussion of standards for organic products, and lobbying to secure appropriate government certification standards, has taken up a considerable share of the energies of the movement. Certification is of interest mainly, however, to the minority of environmentally concerned farmers who have undertaken to adopt the full 'organic' or 'biological' program. While there are historical and political as well agronomic reasons for going the whole distance in dispensing with conventional methods of fertility maintenance and pest control, the 'purist' posture of the organic producer has frequently been reinforced by economic realities. Especially where market gardening is concerned, valorization of the extra labour and management effort involved in organic production has hinged on marketing one's produce at a premium.

The need to qualify for certification introduces certain rigidities. One must operate under a restrictive code of acceptable practices and one is less free to experiment with intermediate approaches. While there is some evidence that ecological approaches work best where there is a complete break with agrochemical use, it is also possible that intermediate solutions—such as meaningful reductions in chemical use under an integrated pest control program emphasizing preventive measures and biological control agents—may be more widely adoptable. Wide adoption of intermediate types of husbandry might do much more for soil and water conservation, and for food safety, than the purist regimes practised by a relatively small minority of producers willing and able to do so. It is hard to judge, however, whether the purist position adopted by many advocates of sustainable agriculture has hastened or retarded a general movement in the direction of more environmentally rational practices.

Interests opposed to the reorientation of agriculture have tried to convince farmers and consumers that conventional agricultural practices are environmentally sound while alternative practices are costly, unreliable, and far from environmentally benign (Wernick and Lockeretz, 1977; Buttel *et al.*, 1986).

Their resistance is not merely based on misunderstanding or serious doubts about the potential of alternative practices. They recognize that in its more radical versions, sustainable agriculture implies a direct challenge to conventional socio-economic and scientific reasoning (Beus and Dunlap, 1990). The ecological critique carries with it an implied rejection of reductionist science and calls into question the assumptions and rationality of neo-classical economics (Batie, 1989). It also challenges the logic of 'value-free' development (Molotoch and Logan, 1984).

The movement for a sustainable agriculture therefore presents a direct challenge to mainstream agricultural science, to agribusiness, and to farmers operating in a conventional mode. It is also seen as a threat by some groups, usually thought of as outside agriculture, who nevertheless perceive an interest in the debate over alternative development trajectories. These include the petrochemical, pharmaceutical, and nuclear industries, as well as some scientific and professional organizations (Council on Scientific Affairs, AMA, 1991).

Given the powerful players opposed to any major reorientation of agriculture, one must be cautious in predicting significant change. Recently, however, the situation has become more complex due to the unprecedented mobilization of public opinion around environmental issues, the increasing organizational resources of the alternative agricultural movement, and the prolonged crisis gripping many parts of the Canadian farm sector. Thus, the stage may now be set for significant changes in attitudes and policies in both the public and private sectors.[5]

In belated response to consumer concerns, major food processors, manufacturers, and retailers are feeling their way towards providing products certified free of pesticide residues (Thorne, 1990). This response is tentative and somewhat contorted. While consumer interest in chemical-free and organically grown foods presents an important commercial opportunity, it also presents a dilemma. Any response to this demand constitutes a partial endorsement of claims that conventionally produced and processed products are, in some sense, inferior (Thorne, 1990). While grocery retailers may have no fundamental problem with offering shoppers another option, grocery manufacturers have prospered under a regime that called for cheap inputs, standardization, extensive processing, elaborate packaging, and heavy use of preservatives to allow long-distance shipping and to extend shelf life. This may put grocery manufacturers into a contradictory position with respect to promotion of their own product lines, as well as into conflict with the increasingly powerful retail sector.

When discussing the potential for reforms leading to agricultural sustainability, it is important to consider the impact of the feminist movement and its links to environmentalism (Shiva, 1989). Women, as organizers of household production and consumption activities, have been in the forefront of consumer advocacy for food and water free of industrial pollutants. The gender division of labour and decision-making on most farms, including many organic operations, has been traditional and patriarchal (Vail, 1982). Anecdotal evidence would suggest, nevertheless, that women farmers have often promoted an alternative environmental and occupational safety agenda in farm management. The influence of women as researchers, politicians, and managers in public and private sector organizations remains limited to date, but as it expands, there is reason to expect that ecological concerns will emerge as more central elements in decision-making.

The Social Economy of Sustainability

Whether in the guise of conversion to some comprehensive program like organic farming or in the form of more minor modifications to conventional farming practices, the adoption of resource-conserving farming practices involves a logic that goes beyond typical profit optimization and risk management strategies (MacRae *et al.*, 1990: 78-9). The culture of agriculture seems to matter. Values, meaning some sort of socially constructed framework for evaluating the desirability of behaviourial alternatives in production and other aspects of living, would seem to account for some of the choices made by alternative practitioners (Van Kooten, 1987). Perhaps such values account for a portion of the large unexplained residual that surfaces when empirically-oriented researchers attempt to quantify the social and structural factors that contribute to conservation behaviours (Lockeretz, 1990).

Culture and values are, of course, social products that reflect, among other things, the dominant structures of production and reproduction within which people live and work. Without retreating to any form of deterministic essentialism, we can take account of the constraints which socio-political institutions and economic structures place on the development of a culture of sustainability. It takes a 'total institution' of the order of Amish society, Hutterite colonies, or the organic farming movement to sustain people in orientations to production and consumption that represent anything like a significant departure from mainstream conventionality (Van Kooten, 1987).

Viewed through this optic, the issue of sustainable development becomes one of providing conditions in which it is socially, as well as economically and technically, possible to move towards a sustainable model of food production and consumption. The preceding discussion of the implications of agro-industrial structure and of state policies, as well as of the importance of the environmental and consumer movements, should make it plain that such solutions will not be forthcoming via changes initiated at the farm or rural community levels alone. This should not, however, prevent discussion of prerequisites for sustainable development of local resources or of social and institutional innovations that may be necessary ingredients for a sustainable agriculture.

The ecological, economic, and social sustainability of farming systems may require consideration of alternative approaches to assembling, managing, and transferring farm resources. Sustainable agriculture requires farmers with a long planning horizon, security of tenure, and a on-going interest in the land and local communities. Security of access to land may be achieved in a number of ways but it is plain that refinancing the farm every generation is fraught with insecurity and inimical to establishment of a sustainable production regime. Again, the necessary reforms are institutional as much as technical. Acceptable alternatives to classical models of private ownership need to be developed and supported (Buttel, 1983). Land banking, community ownership, community land trusts, communal and co-operative ownership, long-term leases with rights of succession and provisions for encouraging stewardship, are all institutional options which are drastically underdeveloped in the Canadian context.

Similarly, arrangements for pooling labour, management effort, finances, and land have received little state support and have been attempted only by a few. In Manitoba, Saskatchewan, and Alberta, Hutterite colonies operate diversified and economically successful farms using the pooled labour of ten to fifteen families. Evidence from studies of machinery co-operatives and co-operative farms in Saskatchewan suggest that multi-household operations involving three to ten families are likewise able to manage diversified, mixed farming operations while achieving important economies in machinery (Gertler and Murphy, 1987: 256). Such group operations also have greater resources with which to implement conservation practices or experiment in alternative cropping systems.

Rural agricultural communities have changed dramatically in the last several decades. Community of a local and regional nature remains important, however, in fostering sustainable management of resources. There is a reciprocal relationship involved. Sustainable management of renewable resources is necessary to preserve the economic base of rural communities. On the other hand, sustainable management of resources is more probable where there are functioning rural communities with confidence in the future, capacity to plan and implement democratically generated strategies, and frameworks for sharing in the risks and rewards of development (Fuller *et al.*, 1990).

Conclusions

While the characteristics of individual farmers and particular farm operations affect propensity to adopt resource-conserving practices, neither seems to explain a large fraction of the variation. Personal philosophies, the characteristics of local resources, the economics of particular commodity subsectors, and the culture of the local agricultural community may, in the last analysis, be at least as important (Lockeretz, 1990: 522). At the same time, strong pressures emanating from the structural reorganization of farming and the global restructuring of agribusiness, tend to override many influences emanating from the individual, from the particular farm firm, or from the immediate local context. Agricultural policies, and those which provide the general business environment, are also key factors in the development of particular resource management regimes. Policies directly encourage or discourage certain practices and, likewise, indirectly affect husbandry choices through their impact on farm structure (Buttel and Gertler, 1982; Buttel and Swanson, 1986).

The social ecology of sustainable agriculture involves both social institutions and natural ecosystems. Agricultural land should be viewed as a multi-purpose resource. Food should be viewed as a joint product with preventive health care, watershed protection, historical landscape preservation, and rural development (Drake, 1989: 120). Because of complex interdependencies, sustainable development requires a qualitative reorientation of research and development effort, including adoption of a more holistic world view, a longer time horizon, and an adaptive approach to dealing with circumstances that are evolving and not wholly predictable (Franklin, 1990).

Sustainable farm economies and sustainable production practices are interdependent but neither can go far if not linked to a broader project of sustainable rural redevelopment. This will require institutional frameworks for mobilizing the capacities of social actors at all levels. The project must include those heretofore marginalized from decision-making but must also involve the regulatory and supportive capacities of governments. Grassroots movements are much more likely to be sustainable and to achieve their objectives where organizational resources are not monopolized by those disinterested in reform.

Notes

[1]Agriculture Canada provides the following definition:
'Sustainable agriculture systems are those that are economically viable, and meet society's needs for safe and nutritious food while conserving natural resources and the quality of the environment for future generations' (AIC, 1991: 5).
Researchers affiliated with Ecological Agriculture Projects at Macdonald College adopt a broader definition:
'Sustainable agriculture is both a philosophy and a system of farming. It is rooted in a set of values that reflects an awareness of both ecological and social realities and a commitment to respond appropriately to that awareness. It emphasizes design and management procedures that work with natural resource processes to conserve all resources and minimize waste and environmental damage, while maintaining or improving farm profitability. This is accomplished by taking into account nutrient and water cycles, energy flows, beneficial soil organisms, natural pest controls, and the humane treatment of animals. Such systems also aim to ensure the well-being of rural communities, and to produce food that is nutritious and uncontaminated with products that might harm human and livestock health' (MacRae *et al.*, 1990: 76).

[2]Resource management regime, in the sense that I am using the term, is shorthand for the prevailing technical, economic, and cultural system under which nature is appropriated for human purposes. With reference to farming, it would include such things as cropping programs and soil management strategies; the level of technical and industrial development; policies, programs, and regulations; the criteria used in evaluating investments and projects; as well as the values and attitudes of direct and indirect users. Regime, in this sense, includes all parameters impinging on resource management.

[3]The National Farmers Union has been something of an exception. At least since the late 1980s, its newspaper has regularly featured articles supportive of the sustainable agriculture movement.

[4]It could be argued that practices associated with recent inititiatives to develop Regenerative, Resource-Efficient, and Low-Input Sustainable Agriculture (LISA) systems constitute a middle ground between the purist, organic, position and conventional farming with a few modifications to reduce environmental impact. However, the extent to which such intermediate approaches will be adopted remains in question.

[5]Even a partial list of the producer organizations involved in education, research, certification, marketing, and lobbying is fairly impressive: Organic Crop Improvement Association (OCIS), which has chapters in several provinces, Canadian Organic Growers (COG), Mouvement pour l'Agriculture Biologique (MAB) in Quebec, Ecological Farmers Association of Ontario, Sustainable Agriculture Movement of Manitoba, Sustainable Agriculture Association (SAA), Peace River Organic Producers Association, Similkameen Okanagan Organic Producers Association, Canadian Organic Producers Marketing Co-operative, Ltd, Saskatchewan Organic Industry Development Council, Parkland Organic Producers Co-op, Organic Producers Association of Manitoba Co-op Ltd, Ontario Bio-Organic Farmers Co-op Inc. In addition, there are at least a half dozen journals and newsletters published in Canada, supplementing the many now available from the United States (Cushion, 1991).

CHAPTER TWELVE

AGRICULTURE, SOILS, AND THE ENVIRONMENT

DARWIN W. ANDERSON

Canada is a large country with a limited area of land where soils and climate are suitable for agriculture. Only about 7% or 67 million hectares (670,000 square kilometres) of Canada's land area is suitable for farming, with an additional 6% considered suitable for grazing (McKeague, 1975). This land occurs in the southern parts of Canada, mostly in the Maritime provinces, the St Lawrence Lowlands of Quebec and Ontario, the prairie provinces and in the lower mainland of British Columbia (Figure 12.1). About 22 million hectares or 2.4% of Canada's land is considered to be prime agricultural land, with only slight limitations for farming. The total fresh water resources of Canada are equally vast, but the water is mainly in northern regions, distant from agriculture and industry. Agriculture, particularly in the semi-arid regions of the prairies, is often limited by inadequate water supply, or low quality water. Pollutants from pesticides or nutrients from fertilizers are a serious concern to water quality and the aquatic environment in many areas.

This chapter describes the soil resources of Canada, briefly outlines the development of agriculture, and reports on the present quality of soil and water in relation to agricultural activities.

Darwin Anderson is Professor and Head of the Department of Soil Science and Director of the Saskatchewan Institute of Pedology.

Figure 12.1 Current and potential agricultural lands, Canada

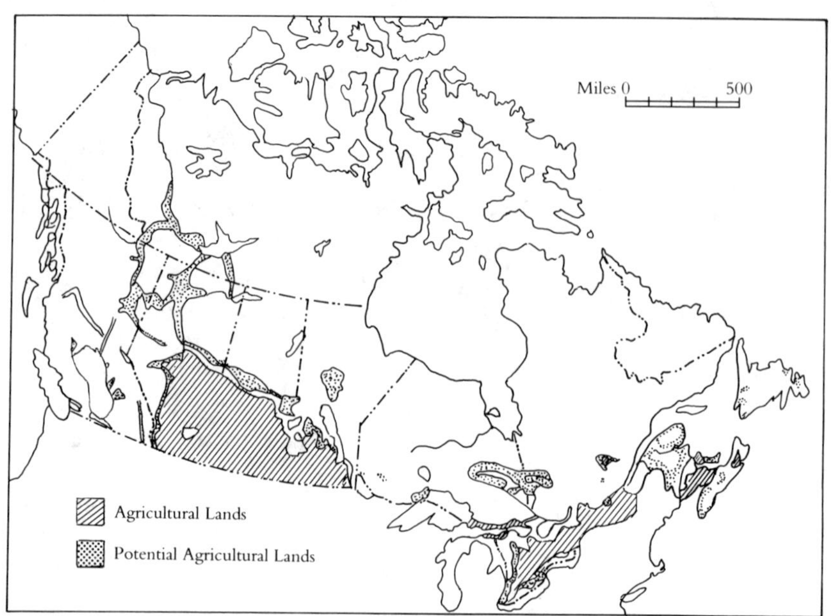

Source: McKeague, 1975

What is a Soil?

Soils, in comparison to plants and animals, are probably the least understood component of the natural world with which agriculture is concerned. The features that distinguish different types of soils and geological materials occur below ground, and are readily apparent mainly to people trained in soil science. The joint action of plants, micro-organisms, and animals interacting with mineral materials, along with the kind of climate, degree of wetness or drainage, nature of the original geological material, and the time period for soil formation all influence the character of a soil. Distinctive layers or soil horizons that make up the soil profile result from the action of different kinds of processes over time.

Differences in soils result mostly from differences in vegetation and the interacting elements of the climate. Grassland soils occur mainly in semi-arid to sub-humid climates where the amount of water entering the soil is limited, and a large proportion of the vegetative residues are added below ground as roots. The build-up of organic matter in the upper part of the soil forms the dark horizon of grassland soils. The loss of soluble components by water moving right through the soil is minimal under dry climates. Therefore, grassland soils are well supplied with mineral elements such as calcium, magnesium and potassium, and are generally not acidic. Grassland soils contain a large reserve of nutrient elements such as nitrogen, sulphur, phosphorus, and many other trace elements in association with organic matter.

Forest soils occur in more moist areas where the amount of water entering and moving right through the soil is greater than in grasslands (Anderson, 1987). Trees add a much higher proportion of their residues to the soil surface with annual leaf fall causing a layer of organic matter to build up on the surface. Acidic, organic materials produced by decomposition in the organic layer move downwards with percolating water, promoting the solubilization of mineral elements and their leaching from the soil. Consequently, most soils of forest regions are acidic, have low concentrations of nutrients such as potassium, phosphorus and others, and have only a minimal store of nitrogen and sulphur in the organic matter.

It is important that conditions that are toxic or harmful to plants not occur in soil. Soil acidity may be a consequence of natural processes of strong leaching, the addition of acid-forming materials in precipitation, and the process by which the ammonium present in most nitrogen fertilizers is oxidized to nitrate. Strong acidity is harmful, mainly because of increased solubility of elements such as aluminum and manganese that are toxic to plants. At the other extreme, in semi-arid regions, the amount of water moving through the soil may not be adequate to remove ions that have been made soluble by weathering, and toxic levels of salts may accumulate, forming saline soils.

Man-made or xenobiotic chemicals may also accumulate in soils and water, both from industrial sources and from the improper use of pesticides and fertilizers in agriculture. The chemicals sometimes move right through the soil to contaminate ground water. Soil and water pollution from these sources may be site-specific and related to industrial activity, but non-point pollution from the inappropriate use of pesticides and fertilizers occurs as well. In areas with intensive agriculture contamination of ground water by agricultural chemicals is a serious concern.

Soils and Soil Degradation in Canada's Regions

Atlantic Provinces

The soils of the Atlantic provinces have developed under forest vegetation and a cool, moist climate (Beke and Hilchey, 1977). Sandy glacial till over bedrock ranges in thickness from one or two metres to five metres or more, and is the most common parent material. The till is quite stony, strongly compacted and of low porosity, particularly in the subsoil. Podzolic soils are general and are, by nature, acidic and of low fertility. Roots are usually not able to penetrate strongly compacted layers, nor does water move easily through such layers. The best agricultural soils occur on the flood plains of rivers in areas such as the Annapolis and St John River valleys. The uplift of the land surface that resulted from the retreat of the glaciers thousands of years ago has resulted in the exposure of large areas of marine sediments along the Bay of Fundy and the Gulf of St Lawrence. The marine deposits, still influenced by tidal action, form large areas of salt marsh. These tidal marshes have wet soils that require dyking, drainage and reclamation for agricultural use. Some of these wet soils become more acidic after drainage because of the oxidation of sulphur minerals to form acidity.

Agriculture in the Atlantic region developed in the eighteenth century as subsistence farming for societies based mainly on fishing and forestry. As early as the late 1800s food for export was being produced. Farms were mainly small, based on dairying and livestock but producing apples and potatoes for export. Crop rotations included forage crops, some small grains for livestock feed, and potatoes. Potatoes were grown in Prince Edward Island, and in New Brunswick west of the St John River. Fruit orchards developed mainly in the Annapolis Valley of Nova Scotia. Agriculture of this kind had minimal negative impacts on soil or water, because fields were small, most were under cover of vegetation except for short periods when cash crops were grown, and manure from livestock was spread on the land. This is not to say that there were not problems in agriculture, as discussed by Taylor (1942). Farms often were developed on land cleared by lumbering, sometimes on land not at all suited to farming, and with people not skilled in farming. Many of these farms were not successful and were abandoned after a few years or decades.

After World War II, there was a move to fewer but larger farms, and a trend to people living on farms but not using the land. The remaining farms utilized larger fields, often for intensive production with large machinery, and substantial inputs of agricultural chemicals (MacRae, 1986). Potato farming is a good example. Today's potato farmers supply large processing plants and grow many acres of potatoes, often on the same fields year after year. Potato monoculture is efficient in terms of labour, but has resulted in increased possibility of disease, extensive use of pesticides to control pests, higher rates of fertilizing, and an increase in soil erosion. Water erosion may be particularly severe in the late winter as snow melts from fields not protected by vegetative cover (MacRae, 1986). Cover-cropping with an annual crop such as rye, which is seeded following the potato harvest, helps to control erosion but does little to build up organic matter in the soil and improve soil quality. Farms where high rates of nitrogen fertilizers are used appear to have more acidic soils than do those with rotations that require less fertilizer (Coote *et al.*, 1981). The possibility of nitrogen from fertilizer (as well as pesticides) leaking from the soil to contaminate ground water is being assessed by Agriculture Canada scientists at Charlottetown. Large amounts of fungicides and insecticides are also applied to potatoes (Frank *et al.*, 1982). In other parts of the

Atlantic region, much more corn is grown than in previous times, with negative impacts.

The use of large, heavy machines compacts the soil, particularly wet soils during the potato harvest. Compaction reduces the pore space in soils and makes it difficult for roots to grow. In New Brunswick the bulk density of soil (a measure of compaction) increases with the number of years that the land has been cropped to potatoes (Saini and Grant, 1980). Compaction appears to be at least partly responsible for reduced yields in fields cropped to potatoes for long periods. The glacial till soils of the Atlantic region have high stone contents. Stones are considered a nuisance, particularly to the mechanical harvesting of potatoes. Stones, however, appear to be beneficial to potato yield in concentrations up to 12%, by covering the soil to keep soil temperature lower and the soils more moist. Stone removal increases the susceptibility of soils to erosion, in that small stones on the surface absorb much of the energy from heavy rain and lessen the dislodgement of soil particles (Saini and Grant, 1980).

Central Canada

The Great Lakes/St Lawrence Lowlands of Ontario and Quebec form a large and important agricultural region, producing about 42% of Canada's net farm income. Gray Brown Luvisol and Melanic Brunisol soils occur in areas where rich, deciduous forests once grew, mostly on gently rolling lands with loam to clay loam glacial till (Mathews and Baril, 1960). These soils, despite their occurrence in forest regions, are not strongly acidic because of the presence of carbonate minerals in the parent material, and the biocycling of alkaline elements by the deciduous forests. The mixing of mineral soil and the leaf litter by earthworms formed humus-rich, well-structured surface horizons. These soils are among the most productive in Canada. Sandier soils occupy about one-quarter of the region, on glacial outwash and deltaic plains. Near the Canadian Shield in the northern part of this region, more acidic podzol soils are dominant above sandy materials. Clayey and silty soils occur on level plains formed in glacial lakes, in both southwestern Ontario and along the St Lawrence and Ottawa rivers. Most clayey soils are poorly drained and require drainage for farming. The agricultural capability of lands in this region is best on the level landscapes with good soils and the mild climate in southwestern Ontario, as well as along the St Lawrence Valley. The soils in northern regions near the Canadian Shield and the Laurentians, and in the southern part of Quebec adjacent to the Appalachians are less suited to agriculture.

Farming has been carried out in this area since before European colonization. Many of the native Indian nations were essentially agricultural, producing crops that included maize, beans, and squash. Agriculture developed from the time of European settlement, mainly as comparatively small farms that included a variety of crops as well as livestock and dairy production. The good land of southwestern Ontario, combined with the most favourable climate in Canada, resulted in efficient mixed farms, specialized operations such as fruit-growing in the Niagara Peninsula, vegetable production on deep organic soils, and tobacco on sandy soils.

Starting in about 1950 there has been a move to larger and more specialized farms, with an increase of 40% in the volume of production in the 1960 to 1984 period (MacRae, 1986). The area of improved farmland in Ontario remained relatively constant at about 5.3 million hectares from 1921 until 1951, but declined to 4.3 million hectares by 1976. The greatest absolute loss occurred in the 1961-1976 period (McCuaig and Manning, 1982). The reduction in farmland had been even greater in Quebec with a decrease from a pre-1951 area of 3.6 million hectares to 2.2 million hectares today. About one-quarter of Quebec's farmland was taken out of agriculture in the 1961-1976 period. Despite the large area of prime farmland lost to urban expansion in the Montreal to Quebec City corridor, the largest area removed from agriculture was on the fringe of the farming regions (Bursa, 1975). These lands occur adjacent to the forest region, and are not well suited to large-scale, mechanized farming.

The transformation in agriculture and land use that occurred in this region can be illustrated by considering the Saugeen River Valley, an area of 5,261 square kilometres in the agricultural heartland to the east of Lake Huron in southern Ontario (McCuaig and Manning, 1982). The area of farmland decreased from 518,000 to 425,000 hectares over the 1951 to 1976 period, a loss of 8.9%. The number of farms decreased from 8,358 to 5,681, with a related increase in average farm size from 62 to 77 hectares. The trend to increased mechanization is illustrated by the number of tractors, with an average 0.69 tractors per farm in 1951 (many farms evidently used horses for power) to two tractors per farm in 1976. The area of tame hay and mixed grains remained relatively constant, maize (corn for grain and ensilage) increased from about 3,000 to 42,000 hectares, while oats decreased from 40,000 to about 5,000 hectares. Oats were required for feeding draft horses, and are planted in rotation with other grains and forage, requiring little fertilizer or herbicides. Oats are seeded in rows about 15 centimetres apart and soon cover the ground and reduce the possibility for water erosion. Corn, on the other hand, is usually grown on the same land year after year with the application of high rates of fertilizers and herbicides. Corn is a row crop, planted in rows about 90 centimetres apart, generally with tillage between the rows to control weeds during the early growing season. Water erosion can occur even in fields with a tall stand of corn. Corn grown on the same land year after year (continuous corn) is made possible by the intensive use of herbicides, particularly atrazine. Atrazine controls the growth of a broad spectrum of plants, and restricts the choice of crops that can be grown in subsequent years, making continuous corn the most practical cropping strategy. The area planted to either corn or beans without forage crops in the rotation increased substantially between 1957 and 1977 in Ontario (Ketcheson, 1980). In the Saugeen Valley more specialty crops such as tree fruits, beans, and tobacco were produced in 1976 than in 1951 (McCuaig and Manning, 1982).

Nearly 90% of the land lost from agriculture was not converted to urban uses, but reverted to forest and scrub in areas with soils of low agricultural capability. About 3% was converted to urban development, with use of land for recreation, quarries, and a nuclear power plant accounting for the remaining few per cent. Those changes contrast with losses of land in the Niagara Peninsula and near large urban centres such as Toronto and Montreal where urbanization has accounted for virtually all the land lost from agriculture. Changes in the Saugeen Valley, however, are typical of a general situation on the fringe of agriculture where low quality land, not well suited to large-scale operations, moves from small farms to non-farm uses such as forestry, recreation, or rural residences.

Serious problems of soil deterioration have resulted from the intensification of agriculture. The shift from small grains and forage in rotation to continuous corn has had negative impacts on soil organic matter, erosion, the degree of compaction of soils, and water quality (Ketcheson, 1980). Soils under continuous corn have lower organic matter content and fewer stable aggregates than soils in corn-oats-hay rotation. Stable aggregates make soils easier to till and reduce susceptibility to erosion and compaction. Corn yields are generally less where corn is grown every year rather than in rotation. Similar findings have been reported for Quebec where continuous corn was compared to cereal-hay rotations on podzol soils (Martel and MacKenzie, 1980). Soils under continuous corn have fewer earthworms than soils in hayfields, and lack the system of pores that results from the movement of earthworms through the soil.

Some of the negative impacts of growing corn every year can be remedied by restricting or replacing tillage with herbicides to control weeds. Conservation or zero-tillage has the advantage of reduced erosion and crop yields that are at least equivalent to those of conventionally tilled fields. Negative impacts of zero-tillage centre mainly on the high inputs of herbicides required, both from an economic perspective (Ketcheson and Stonehouse, 1983) and in relation to the contamination of surface and ground waters (Hallberg, 1987). Another alternative to tilled row crops and attendant high rates of erosion is the use of solid-seeded cover crops planted between the rows of the main crop, a practice known as intercropping. Vegetative cover to limit erosion is particularly important in the winter following the growing of a row crop, when a thin layer of thawed soil can be lost easily from mainly frozen soils (Wall *et al.*, 1988). Intercropping red clover with corn reduces soil erosion without significantly reducing the yield of the corn crop (Wall *et al.*, 1991).

The Prairie Provinces and the Peace River Area of British Columbia

The agricultural lands of the prairie provinces and the Peace River Valley of British Columbia are among the most extensive agricultural regions in the world, with 500,000 square kilometres where agriculture is the main land use. This region stretches from the American border to the agricultural frontier at the margin of the boreal forest. The climate of the prairies and adjacent forest land is cool to cold, semi-arid to sub-humid. The driest region has an annual precipitation of 300 to 350 millimetres and a marked water deficit, in that potential evapotranspiration is much greater than precipitation. The natural vegetation in the driest area was mid-grass prairie, and Brown soils predominate (Figure 12.2). Dark Brown soils occur in the slightly more moist area, forming a broad band that surrounds the area of Brown soils. Black or Chernozemic soils occur in the sub-humid northern grasslands and adjacent aspen parkland. These sub-humid regions receive up to 500 millimetres of precipitation, and are considerably more moist than the dry prairie to the south because of reduced evapotranspiration and cooler temperatures. Gray or Gray Luvisol soils that formed under forest vegetation are used for farming in the northern part of the farming area in Saskatchewan, in the foothills region of Alberta, and in the Peace River Valley.

Figure 12.2 The soil zones of the prairie provinces

Loam to clay-loam textured soils that have developed on glacial till are common over the entire region. The mixing of minerals from a variety of sources into the till resulted in naturally fertile soils. The areas of silty to clayey soils that occur on the large nearly level plains of the Red River Valley in Manitoba, the Regina, Indian Head and Rosetown plains in Saskatchewan and large parts of central Alberta are former glacial lakes. These clayey soils are among the best agricultural lands of the region, combining fertility with high moisture storage capacities. Localized areas with sandy to gravelly soils occur, and are of low capability for cultivated agriculture as well as being susceptible to wind and water erosion.

Grassland soils have large amounts of organic matter and associated nutrients in their natural condition. The content of organic matter in a soil is an equilibrium level that depends upon the relative amounts of inputs (primarily from plant residues added to the soil and root exudates), and outputs or the amount of organic matter and added residues that are decomposed by micro-organisms to release nutrients for the next crop. When cultivated, the fertility of former grassland soils relates mainly to the release of the large store of nutrients stored in the organic matter. Gray soils have low organic matter content, and are more acidic than the soils of the grasslands, resulting in generally lower capability for agriculture.

The Prairie Region and Agriculture

Palliser, exploring the prairie region between 1857 and 1860, concluded that vast areas, particularly the valleys of the Red and North Saskatchewan rivers, had potential for agriculture, but that the dry regions of the southwest did not. The dry regions, termed the Palliser Triangle, include much of the land within the Brown and Dark Brown soil zones of Saskatchewan and Alberta. Hind (1859), another explorer, described the prairie region as a fertile belt stretching across the British territory from the Lake of the Woods to the Rocky Mountains, and recommended settlement. People continue to view the prairies differently today. Agriculturists consider the prairies to be a bread-basket for the world, whereas others describe the prairies as 'one of the most disturbed ecosystems in the world' (Gauthier and Henry, 1989).

The period following the construction of the Canadian Pacific Railway across the prairie region in the early 1880s until about 1910 was a time of intense railroad building and related settlement. The area of cultivated land increased from two million hectares in 1901, to 13 million hectares by 1913 (MacEwan, 1986). Settlers were able to obtain open Crown land in exchange for cultivating a minimum area of land and establishing a farm. Land was made available to settlers based on location, with little consideration of the land's capability for farming. Methods that were suitable for farming in the humid regions of eastern Canada or Europe were brought to the prairies with devastating results. Ploughing and harrowing to prepare seedbeds left the soil bare and easily eroded, and led to the serious soil erosion of the 1920s and 1930s.

Prairie soils contain reserves of nutrients in their organic matter, and are quite productive when first cultivated. Inappropriate farming methods, deteriorating soil, and drought combined with the economic depression of the 1930s to result in serious problems for the region. Many farms in the driest regions were abandoned (estimated at 10,000 farmers) and farmers moved north to new farms in the more moist forest regions (MacEwan, 1986). Interestingly, the total number of farms in Saskatchewan did not decrease in the 1930s, perhaps because the severe depression limited economic opportunities away from the farm.

The climate of the prairie region was generally moist between 1940 and 1980. The favourable climate, plus improving yields that resulted from increased use of herbicides and fertilizers, improved crop varieties, and farming methods that are better adapted to semi-arid climates resulted in four decades of expanding agriculture and increasing yields (Ridley and Hedlin, 1980). Farms became larger and more specialized, and increasingly vulnerable to changes in prices for both inputs and the grains that were produced.

Problems of deteriorating soil quality continued, however, and were most evident in areas with a large proportion of the land in summerfallow. Summerfallowing has the objective of storing two years' precipitation in the soil for use by crops grown during the second year. Weeds usually are controlled on the idle land by cultivation, resulting in bare soil and increased susceptibility to wind and water erosion. Several studies have indicated the negative effects of summerfallowing on soil organic matter content and fertility. The proportion of land in summerfallow is greatest in the semi-arid Brown and Dark Brown soil zones where about 45% of the land is in summerfallow each year. The area of summerfallow is less in the more moist Black and Gray soil zones.

At the University of Manitoba, an experiment with clayey Black soils found that soil organic matter content was lowest in soils under wheat-summerfallow rotation, about 50% higher in soils summerfallowed every third or fourth year, and highest under continuous wheat (Ridley and Hedlin, 1968). Similar negative effects from summerfallowing have been reported for Dark Brown soils at Lethbridge, Alberta (Dormaar and Pittman, 1980), and for Gray soils in the more moist forest region of Alberta (McGill *et al.*, 1986). Reductions in soil organic matter content resulted in a reduced supply of nutrients from organic matter, and soils that are more difficult to till, as well as increased susceptibility to erosion, particularly wind erosion.

Moderate to severe wind erosion affects an estimated 6.4 million hectares of land in the prairie region, mostly in the drier parts with a large area of summerfallowed land and frequent high winds. Wind erosion, however, can occur even in the more moist regions, particularly where fields are cultivated intensively for crops such as potatoes and canola.

Water erosion is a serious problem in the prairie region, particularly on hilly and sloping land in the more moist Black and Gray soil zones. Moderate to severe erosion occurs on an estimated 5 million hectares (Table 12.1). The combined cost of wind and water erosion to farmers in the prairie region is an estimated $275 million per year (Dumanski, 1986).

Table 12.1 Estimates of area and annual on-farm economic impact of land affected by erosion and compaction

EXTENT OF LAND AFFECTED			ECONOMIC IMPACT[a] (MILLION $)	
REGION	AREA (MILLION HA)	PORTION OF IMPROVED LAND[b] (%)	LOW ESTIMATE	HIGH ESTIMATE
MODERATE AND SEVERE WATER EROSION[c]				
BC	0.02	3.5	17	24
Prairies	4.64	12.4	155	197
Ontario	0.85	18.8	68	157
Quebec	0.20	8.5	5	17
Atlantic	0.10	17.2	21	29
Canada	5.84	12.7	266	424
MODERATE AND SEVERE WIND EROSION[d]				
BC	<0.01	<0.1	2	2
Prairies	6.31	16.6	213	271
Ontario	0.04	0.9	1	8
Quebec	0.01	0.4	2	2
Atlantic	<0.01	<0.1	<1	<1
Canada	6.36	13.8	218	283
SEVERE RISK OF SOIL COMPACTION[e]				
BC	0.02	3.5	6	12
Prairies[e]	-	-	-	-
Ontario	0.45	10.0	21	71
Quebec	0.36	15.3	30	99
Atlantic	0.10	17.2	6	18
Canada	0.93	2.0	63	200

[a]Calculations are based on inferred yield losses and compensating inputs using current prices.
[b]Calculations based on improved land areas as reported in 1981 census; BC values are exclusive of Peace River area.
[c]These classes represent erosion losses in excess of 10 tonnes per hectare per year, as calculated by the Universal Soil Loss Equation and Wind Erosion Equation, respectively.
[d]This represents an expected-yield reduction of at least 10% for named crop.
[e]Compaction appears to have no significant economic impact in the Prairies.

Source: Extracted from Dumanski *et al.*, 1986. *Journal of Soil and Water Conservation* 41,4: 204-10.

In a recent study at the University of Saskatchewan (Verity and Anderson, 1990), adding back as little as five centimetres of topsoil to severely eroded knolls was found to increase wheat yields by nearly 50%. Equivalent yields could not be obtained by adding chemical fertilizer without topsoil. Many fields in the prairies have lost five centimetres or more of topsoil since farming began, indicating that erosion has seriously decreased yield potential.

Conservation-oriented farming practices can do much to maintain or improve the quality of the soil. Stubble-mulch tillage reduces erosion by maintaining a protective cover of straw and stubble on the soil, and has been shown to maintain organic matter in prairie soils. Experimental plots on Brown soils at the Swift Current Research Station in Saskatchewan actually had slight increases in soil organic matter where continuous cropping (no summerfallow) was practised, with adequate fertilization to produce good crops (Biederbeck *et al.*, 1984). A study of crop rotations on the clayey Black soils at the Indian Head Experimental Farm showed that soils that were summerfallowed every second year had lowest organic matter content, with slightly more organic matter in soils summerfallowed every third year (Greer, 1989). Highest organic matter content occurred in soils cropped continuously to wheat with fertilizers added, or in six-year rotation with three years of forage crops and wheat. A wheat-wheat-clover rotation also had good yields, and was the best money-maker when input costs were high and wheat prices low (Zentner *et al.*, 1988). Results from a long-term experiment at Lethbridge, Alberta, show that obtaining top yields with adequate fertilizer application, particularly nitrogen fertilizers, will do much to maintain soil organic matter levels, and build up the fraction that is most important to nutrient supply (Janzen, 1987).

The positive effects of growing grass and legumes in rotation can be illustrated by findings for Gray soils at Breton, Alberta. Soil organic matter was 3% in soils with forages in rotation, compared to 2.2% in wheat-summerfallow (McGill *et al.*, 1986). The soils of the Breton study were moderately acidic when the experiment began, and have become more acidic because of the addition of even moderate amounts on nitrogen fertilizer for a long time. Soil acidity is a natural feature of strongly leached soils. Soils can be made more acidic by applications of nitrogen fertilizers, and by inputs of acidic precipitation.

Many farmers in the prairies are practising improved soil conservation, even in difficult economic times. Farmers in the drier areas, where summerfallow makes good economic sense by reducing the risk of crop failure, maintain a protective cover of crop residues on summerfallow fields. The frequency of tillage is reduced, residue-conserving tillage implements are used, and herbicides rather than cultivation may be used to control weeds. The proportion of summerfallow land in the more moist regions across the prairies has decreased in recent years. Other farmers have planted forage crops on highly erodible, sandy or hilly land. Government-supported conservation programs encourage and assist farmers to improve soil conservation by taking erodible land out of cultivation, planting tree shelterbelts, obtaining soil-conserving tillage implements, or replacing tillage with herbicides for weed control.

Despite these positive developments, a deterioration of the soil resources is still a problem in the prairie region. Many farmers cannot afford to put conservation measures in place, or purchase the farm machinery that permits them to control weeds and seed their crops with minimal tillage. Summerfallow, which reduces the need for fertilizers and herbicides, looks like a better alternative when crop prices are low. The serious droughts and high winds of the late 1980s resulted in soil erosion, even where farmers were using recommended practices. Reduced incomes to farmers, mainly because of low prices in international grain markets, often limit their ability to adopt new, soil-conserving production methods.

Agricultural Lands of British Columbia

The most important agricultural lands in British Columbia occur in the lower mainland, mainly along the Lower Fraser Valley, in the southern part of Vancouver Island, and in the southern interior (Farstad and Rowles, 1960). These areas do not have particularly good agricultural soils, but the mild climate results in these lands being some of the most important in Canada. Horticultural and orchard crops are produced, and dairy farming is prevalent in much of the Lower Fraser Valley. The semi-arid but mild Okanagan Valley is part of the southern interior region, and has substantial areas of irrigated orchards that produce apples, pears, peaches, cherries and other fruits. Dairy and livestock farming are more common in the northern part of the Okanagan, and in many other interior valleys. Cattle ranching in much of the dry interior region utilizes grasslands and open forest for summer grazing, with hay produced under irrigation in the limited areas of the flood plains along rivers.

British Columbia has about 950,000 hectares of improved farmland, including 377,000 hectares in the Peace River Valley that are used mainly for grain farming. The areas most strongly affected by losses of land to urban expansion are comparatively small, with slightly more than 100,000 hectares in each of the Lower Mainland-Vancouver Island areas, and in the Okanagan Valley. Soil degradation affects these lands as well. Organic or peat soils have high potential for producing horticultural crops but gradually decompose or subside with continued use, and productivity is reduced. Water erosion is a problem where row crops and berry fruits are produced on sloping land. Contamination of ground water by agriculture is a serious problem in parts of the Lower Fraser Valley.

Intensive Agriculture: Effects on Ground and Surface Water

Since farming began, agriculture has led inevitably to negative impacts on surface and ground waters, but modern agriculture's reliance on pesticides and fertilizers has intensified the effects (Dance and Hynes, 1980). Application rates for chemical fertilizers and pesticides are substantially higher in intensively farmed and more humid regions of Ontario, Quebec, the Atlantic provinces, and the lower mainland in British Columbia than in the prairie region (Bird and Rapport, 1986). Eighty per cent of the herbicides used in Canada, however, are applied to the large areas that are farmed in the prairie region.

The severity and nature of the effects of agriculture on surface waters can be illustrated by comparing two adjacent watersheds, both with farms, but with significantly different land use patterns (Dance and Hynes, 1980). The area drained by the west branch of the Cangagique Creek in Ontario has mainly dairy farms, and about 56% of the land is planted to corn and small grains, with little forest land. Manure is spread on frozen soils in winter and there is substantial run-off from barnyards. Much of the land along the creek is pasture. The east branch has a similar number of livestock, but five times more land is in forests, including forests along the stream bank. The waters of the west branch have about twice the load of suspended sediment due to the erosion of cultivated land along the creek, and more eroding stream banks. The waters of the west branch have more coliform bacteria, a higher requirement for oxygen to decompose organic inputs, more phosphorus and nitrogen; the creek dries up in summer. The east branch has less spring run-off but keeps flowing over the summer with cooler water. There are fewer species of insects in the west branch, and those present are mainly those that can tolerate barnyard run-off, higher water temperatures, and intermittent flow. More kinds of insects are present in the east branch, particularly species that require cool water, and others that feed on the input of leaves from the streambank forests. The fish population was not evaluated, but other studies have shown that pollution from feed lots results in a loss of species, and a decline in the abundance of the species remaining.

Phosphorus is a nutrient that promotes the growth of algae in lakes (eutrophication), when its concentration increases above natural levels. About 70% of the 3,000 tonnes of phosphorus that enter the Great Lakes from Canada comes from agriculture (McEwen and Miller, 1986). Most of the phosphorus moves in association with sediment from eroded farm land. Another 20% of the phosphorus moving to the Lakes originates from livestock activities such as feedlots, and 10% comes from natural sources and streambank erosion. A plan to reduce phosphorus loading in Lake Erie includes the following elements: agricultural practices such as conservation tillage, crop rotation, and wise use of fertilizers; structural measures such as grassed waterways and vegetated strips along streams; and better management of wastes from livestock, particularly manures from feed lots (Wall *et al.*, 1989).

Agricultural inputs of nitrogen to the waters of the Great Lakes has also been evaluated (Neilsen *et al.*, 1982). Nitrogen in concentrations above the level thought to be the critical threshold value at which eutrophication begins were present in 88% of the run-off samples from agricultural land. The amount of soluble nitrogen or nitrate in water leaving a watershed was strongly related to the amount of nitrogen applied as fertilizer or as manure to fields, the percentage of the watershed that was cultivated in corn and other row crops, and the area of tile-drained farmland. Reducing the loss of nitrogen from corn fields by better fertilizer management, assuring that run-off from livestock manures does not enter streams, and reducing run-off from crop fields are recommended as methods to reduce nitrogen inputs to surface water from agriculture.

Tobacco and potato fields with porous, sandy soils can lose large amounts of the nitrogen that has been added as chemical fertilizer, because of the leaching of nitrogen below the root zone. Losses of nitrogen were lower from a soy bean field that received less fertilizer. Nitrogen for the soy bean crop was supplied by fixation from the atmosphere by *Rhizobia* bacteria that live on the roots of the legume crop (Cameron *et al.*, 1978).

Inputs of nutrients to lakes in the prairie region were probably high prior to settlement, but have increased in recent decades because of contributions from municipal sources and agriculture (Bird and Rapport, 1986). Run-off from unfertilized, summerfallow fields in the Brown soil zone of Saskatchewan raised nitrogen and phosphorus concentrations above the level at which algae growth occurs in surface waters (Nicholaichuk and Read, 1978). Nutrient losses, however, were considered to be of little agronomic significance in that losses were minimal compared with crop requirements. Summerfallowing land enhances the conversion of organic nitrogen to soluble nitrate, making the nitrogen susceptible to losses by leaching. Nitrates have been measured at two to three metres depth in Brown soils a decade or two after breaking from the prairie sod (Doughty *et al.*, 1954). Accumulations of nitrate in the deep subsoil have been measured under both wheat-summerfallow rotations, and wheat-hay-summerfallow rotations, indicating that nitrates can leach below the root zone even when recommended practices such as the wheat-hay rotation are used. High nitrate concentrations were measured at depth in sandy, Black soils and attributed to the leaching of nitrate from summerfallow fields (Hedlin, 1971). Nitrate concentrations in water wells that were high enough to present a health risk, however, were associated with ground water under farmsteads where animal and, occasionally, human wastes had been managed poorly. Many wells in Saskatchewan have nitrate concentrations above the drinking water standard of less than 10 milligrams of nitrogen per litre (10 parts per million) of water (Hogg and Henry, 1990).

Wells with highest nitrate concentrations had shallow water tables and were located mainly in farmsteads where animal manures appeared to be substantial contributors of nitrogen.

In southwestern British Columbia, much of the water in the sandy to gravelly Abbotsford aquifer has been contaminated with nitrates and pesticides. The most probable source is considered to be manure wastes that are produced by large poultry farms, which are not carefully stored, and applied to land in large amounts (Kohut *et al.*, 1989). Contamination of ground water is a common problem with intensive livestock farms.

The contribution of pesticides to ground and surface waters is another concern being evaluated by several studies. In Ontario the insecticide aldicarb, which has been used for the control of the Colorado potato beetle, has been detected at concentrations that are of concern in water under potato fields with permeable soils and shallow ground water (Beck and Scafe, 1989). Similarly, two of 56 wells tested in New Brunswick had significant concentrations of aldicarb (Sexsmith, 1989). Atrazine, commonly used for weed control in corn, was found at concentrations of 0.3 to 72 parts per billion (ppb) in ground water under corn grown on sandy soils in Ontario (Beck and Scafe, 1989). The Canadian standard for safe drinking water is less than 2 ppb of atrazine. Atrazine and a harmful breakdown product were present at concentrations greater than 2 ppb in the ground water of a corn field with both sandy and clayey soils (Masse *et al.*, 1989). These and other results indicate a situation in Canada that is similar to that reported after an extensive survey of thousands of wells in the United States by the Environmental Protection Agency. The survey found detectable levels of pesticides and nitrates in only a small proportion of the wells, but an incidence of contamination that indicates a problem requiring attention in order to minimize or avoid harmful and long-term impacts of agriculture on the aquatic environment.

Loss of Agricultural Land to Non-Agricultural Uses

The expansion of cities onto prime agricultural land results in the irreversible loss of the land from agriculture. Losses are all the more acute because many Canadian cities are located on good agricultural land. It has been estimated, for example, that 37% of Canada's Class 1 agricultural land is visible from the top of Toronto's CN Tower on a clear day (if that were to occur!). There were 62,200 hectares of land converted to urban uses between 1966 and 1971, and another 87,100 hectares between 1971 and 1976 (Warren and Rump, 1981). Despite legislation and other initiatives to limit land conversion, 98,000 hectares were built on between 1976 and 1981, and an additional 55,200 hectares between 1981 and 1986 (Warren *et al.*, 1989). The Toronto region accounted for 23.2% of the land lost, but Montreal, Edmonton, Calgary and the St Catharines-Niagara area also had high rates of conversion. Prime agricultural land made up 58% of the area lost to urban expansion between

1966 and 1986 (Table 12.2), an area of 1,750 square kilometres. Replacing the production from prime land with equivalent production from lower quality land on the agricultural frontier would require almost twice the land area (Warren *et al.*, 1989).

Conversion of rural land to urban uses has been particularly high in Quebec, where urban development used up 50,590 hectares of land between 1966 and 1986, much of it prime land in the Montreal to Quebec City corridor. In 1978 the Quebec government passed the Provincial Act to Preserve Agricultural Land, restricting the non-agricultural development of land within designated agricultural regions. Three thousand hectares of land owned by speculators within designated agricultural regions returned to agricultural production following passage of the Bill (MacRae, 1986).

The climate of Ontario's Niagara region is well suited for producing tender fruits such as peaches and grapes. The substantial area of land that has been removed from agriculture in Niagara cannot be replaced by development on the agricultural frontier. Strong American competition in the fruit and wine industries resulting from the Free Trade Agreement may result in another period of high losses of orchard land in the Niagara region, and in British Columbia.

Table 12.2 Total rural land and prime agricultural land converted to urban use, 1966 to 1986

	RURAL LAND CONVERTED		
PROVINCE	TOTAL (HECTARES)	PRIME LAND (HECTARES)	% PRIME LAND
British Columbia	45,330	9,360	21
Alberta	51,691	31,429	61
Saskatchewan	10,613	6,918	65
Manitoba	13,046	11,447	88
Ontario	105,952	83,040	78
Quebec	50,587	24,912	49
New Brunswick	10,848	2,425	22
Nova Scotia	8,043	3,047	38
Prince Edward Island	2,280	2,197	96
Newfoundland	3,050	15	<1

Source: Warren *et al.*, 1989.

Winnipeg is an urban centre located on good agricultural land (Warren, 1982). Between 1970 and 1977, as much land was transferred from improved agriculture to unimproved pasture and rangeland as was converted to urban uses (Figure 12.3). Conversion to pasture mainly represents land purchased by

Figure 12.3 Changes in land use in the Winnipeg urban-centred study area between 1971 and 1977

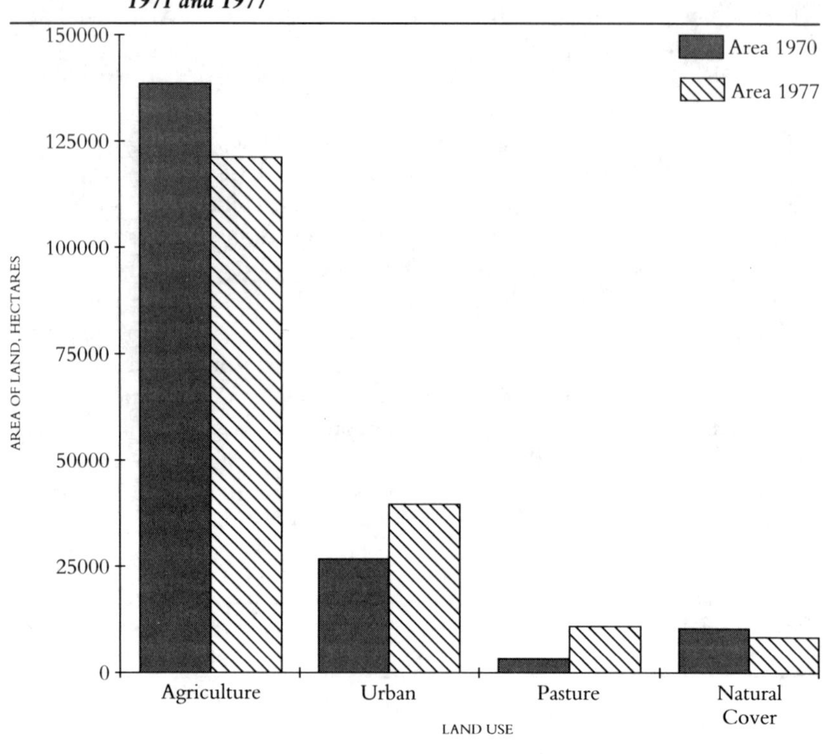

Source: Warren, 1982

speculators and held in anticipation of future urban development. This is one reason why it often appears that cities are developing on unused land. Land adjacent to cities may not be farmed because of ownership by non-farmers, or other pressures such as high taxes because of 'urban' improvements, or odours from livestock operations that make agricultural use impractical. Only about 4% of the land in British Columbia is suitable for agriculture (MacRae, 1986). This land is mainly in the lower mainland (Fraser Valley), parts of Vancouver Island, and in the Okanagan Valley. These areas have the strongest pressure for urban development, and are partly responsible for the introduction of the Land Commission Act in 1973. The Land Commission has the power to designate land as agricultural land and restrict non-agricultural use (Bursa, 1975). The Land Commission has had mixed success, but there is little doubt that it has been a factor in limiting the loss of good agricultural land to urban uses.

Rates of conversion of farm land to urban uses are higher during periods of prosperity, with much less conversion during slow economic periods when cities and industry are not expanding. Small urban centres have high rates of land conversion in relation to population increase. Centres between 25,000 and 50,000 population used up 242 hectares per 1,000 increase in population, compared to only 53 hectares for cities with more than 500,000 population (Warren *et al.*, 1989).

The area of improved farmland in the prairie region has increased in recent decades despite major losses of land to cities, particularly to Edmonton and Calgary, and to strip-mining for lignite coal in central Alberta and southern Saskatchewan. Much of the additional land is on the northern fringe of agriculture, where former forest land is now being farmed. These lands have a low capability for agriculture, and a short, cool growing season. Some low quality land that was left unploughed within farmed areas because of steep slopes, sandy soil, stoniness or other problems, has been broken in recent years. Some of this land presents an almost immediate soil erosion problem, and may be returned to permanent vegetative cover by the government-funded programs of the National Soil Conservation Program.

Lands with hummocky to hilly topography and a large number of undrained sloughs or potholes are critical breeding grounds for much of North America's waterfowl (Lynch-Stewart, 1983). Potholes have been drained and developed as farmland since agriculture began, but dry years and economic pressure to increase grain production have resulted in a continuing decline in the area of wetlands. Good crops may be grown on drained wetlands in dry years, but during wet springs they are often flooded, and not seeded. Current efforts as part of the National Soil Conservation Program and the North American Waterfowl Management Plan are to integrate good soil conservation with the retention of prime waterfowl nesting habitat, the prairie potholes. Potholes often occur in areas with saline soils. The impact on local hydrology and soil salinity of draining and clearing wetlands of their natural vegetation of groundwater-nourished species such as willow and poplar remains largely unknown. Increased salinity can be expected if drainage (or removing the natural vegetation) upsets the established equilibrium between soil salinity, salinity of the ground water, and the depth to the water table.

Summary

Canada is a vast country with plenty of fresh water but only a small proportion of land that is well suited to agriculture, and grave concerns for water quality and quantity in those agricultural areas. The soils of Canada are under pressure on two fronts. Soil quality is declining in many areas, due mainly to decreases in organic matter content, loss of topsoil by erosion, soil compaction, increased soil acidity, and salinity. A second concern is the loss of prime agricultural land to urban and industrial uses, with a probable loss of more than 2,000 square kilometres since the 1950s.

Contamination of ground and surface waters by leakage of nutrients from heavily fertilized fields and intensive livestock operations, by soil eroded from farmland, and by chemicals applied as pesticides is an additional concern. The problems are of a local nature, and most serious in intensively farmed areas such as Central Canada and the lower mainland of British Columbia, but occur to some degree in nearly all agricultural areas.

Simple solutions to bring about remedial action and long-term sustainability are not easily found. The nature of the solutions must be as varied as the agriculture and land of Canada, but do have common elements. The first solution must involve a change in our attitudes about agriculture. Agriculture has been regarded as an industry with the objectives of feeding the populace as cheaply as possible, and being competitive in world markets. Historically, there have been only minor concerns about using up the soil resource, the deterioration of adjacent environments such as water, the serious loss of natural habitats for wildlife, and the quality of life in rural areas (Rowe, 1990). The new vision of agriculture must consider an agriculture that exploits neither land (soil, water, flora, and fauna) nor people (Berry, 1981). Included in this vision is the wise use of land, with farming the prime use of well-suited soils with good climate, probably requiring government intervention to protect these lands (Federal-Provincial Committee on Agricultural Sustainability, 1990). Alternate uses such as woodlots or grassland are best on fragile, low-capability lands and on strategic areas such as the land along waterways. The new vision must look to the resilience of natural ecosystems, and develop agro-ecosystems that have diversity and a high degree of internal cycling of nutrients as provided by crop rotations, and reduced dependency on external solutions and inputs. The goal of sustainability must include economic viability for rural Canada, and may involve structural change and financial incentives that have conservation as the goal. The development of such an agriculture will lead eventually and almost incidentally, to the provision of safe, plentiful, and nutritious food without drawing down soil and water resources. Solutions of this kind will involve more people in rural Canada, working with resources and within systems that are both local and enduring.

SECTION FIVE

SOCIAL, ECONOMIC, AND POLITICAL IMPLICATIONS

In Chapter Thirteen Bronson examines the Free Trade Agreement (FTA) with the US and its implications for rural industries in general and agriculture in particular. Some economists supported the FTA by using Ricardo's idea of production and export of commodities on the principle of 'comparative advantage'. Some farm groups supported the FTA hoping to attain free access to the large US market for their exports. But, according to Bronson, some agricultural industrial sectors, such as vegetables and fruit, will suffer, and if the Canadian Dairy Commission loses its ability to regulate supply, the dairy industry will be devastated. Bronson looks at the impact that the FTA will have on the agricultural sector in the context of the Capitalist World Economy Model and concludes that the general impact of the FTA will be negative for the Canadian economy in general, and working class wages in particular. According to Bronson, the corporate sector in Canada and abroad will try to appropriate as much as possible from workers to increase their profits. Workers will be asked to pay the price of creating a competitive economy and increasing productivity by accepting lower wages, working as part-timers, giving control of their work process to capitalists, and accepting the use of labour-saving technological changes. Bronson, however, is optimistic that workers will unite to meet this challenge.

Bolaria's paper examines the structural forces for the production and reproduction of farm labour, their work conditions, and health risks. A fair amount of work by rural sociologists has considered the living and working conditions of farm labour in general and migrant farm labour in particular. Very little research, however, has been conducted on the relationship between citizenship, gender, race, and class of farm labourers and their living and working conditions. According to this chapter there are different kinds of farmworkers (citizen workers, landed immigrants, migrant workers, and criminalized labour) engaged in capitalist agricultural production. These workers are exploited because of their citizenship and legal status, their class race, and gender, and the contractual constraints under which they work. Unless we understand the nature of capitalistic agricultural production, immigration policies, the role of the Canadian state, and the power of agribusinesses, we cannot understand the situation of farm labour in Canada. Bolaria then focuses on the working conditions and health risks of farm labour, pointing out that farmworkers are not covered under Workers' Compensation Board regulations. Farm labour is subjected to various health risks, and farming is the third most dangerous industry in North America. As farm labourers are primarily from lower class, marginalized, non-unionized, non-white, migrant, and/or criminalized labour, they do not have much economic, social and political clout. The probability is that they will continue to live under poor working conditions and experience various health risks.

The third paper in this section, by Shields, looks at the capitalist state and farm labour policy. This chapter poses the question 'Why have paid agricultural labourers been the most legally and socially dispossessed workers in

North America?' According to Shields, you can only answer this question if you consider the state policy of promoting 'cheap food' in Canada. He looks at the interaction between farmworkers, farmers and the agribusiness sector. Farmers are not independent, and are squeezed between the demands of the farm labour force and the power of agribusiness. The state policy is to maintain low prices for food in Canada and help the agribusiness sector to make a profit. The state policy also provides for cheap contract labour from Third World countries which further depresses the wage demands of the Canadian farm labour force. Farm labour is vulnerable, not organized, racialized, and the super-exploited part of the general labour force. Most of the farm labour in Canada is contract labour, non-white, or belongs to an ethnic minority (from Quebec). They are vulnerable because of their class, race, ethnicity and gender. Thus the Canadian state, farmers, and agribusiness do not have to treat them like an industrial labour force.

CHAPTER THIRTEEN

THE FREE TRADE AGREEMENT: IMPLICATIONS FOR RURAL INDUSTRIES

HAROLD E. BRONSON

Before the signing of the Canada-US Free Trade Agreement (FTA) in January 1989, the general argument put forward in its support from an agricultural perspective had been summarized by Elmer Menzie, the chairperson of the Department of Agricultural Economics at the University of Guelph. In trading relationships, he advised, 'the status quo is no longer a viable option'. Similarly assuming a need for major adjustments was Robert Sequin, the head economist in the Ontario Ministry of Agriculture and Food. He concluded that 'we will have to specialize in what we do best and eliminate production in areas where we are weak' (Bertin, 1986).

That perspective reflects the close relationship between the current pro-FTA arguments and those which became prevalent in the early nineteenth century. Formalized in a mathematical model by David Ricardo (1963: 71-2), that model assumed that in trade between two countries, each should confine itself to producing and trading the product in which it had a 'comparative advantage'.[1] Each would then share in the extra wealth produced. Reflecting the free market ideology of Adam Smith, the model depended on competition to ensure that there would be no price fixing on either side.

Harold Bronson is a Community Educator and recently retired from the Department of Economics and Political Science at the University of Saskatchewan.

In addition to that unrealistic assumption, Ricardo neglected differences in national power and influence by referring to trade between Britain, a dominant imperial power, and Portugal, a weaker and more dependent colonizer. Analyzing that relationship, Harry Magdoff emphasized 'Portugal's inability to hold on to its overseas empire without the protection of the British navy' (1971: 1-17). Britain used that dominant power to enforce a series of treaties which applied the Ricardian model. The commodities were Portuguese wine and British wool products.

Portugal was forced to reduce restrictions on the entry of the British cloth, and to concentrate on wine production for sale to Britain at greatly reduced tariff rates. The resulting sales of both commodities were advantageous to Britain, causing a Portuguese trade deficit which that country could only balance with gold and silver acquired from its colonies (Warnock, 1988: 75-6). Magdoff explained how this source of money supported Britain in its growth as a world banker and colonizer (1971: 12). That exercise of power included the imposition of trade barriers against colonized India with respect to its sales of textiles which could have undersold the British product.

Despite the greater complexities of present world trade, there are parallels to this early model. Supporters of free trade still insist that each country should concentrate on production and export of commodities in which they seem to have a comparative advantage. They see the Canada-US FTA as a first step towards global free trade. Gold is still part of the balancing money flows.

The exercise of dominant economic power continues. Globally, increasingly concentrated corporate structures are expanding that power. Those who approve of the trends insist that they are 'beyond the power of national governments' (Lipsey, 1986). Or as international corporate leader Maurice Strong has observed, 'the multinationals will be performing more and more of the functions of government....Of course governments play a role... through incentives and support. But the real actors are the private sector corporations' (Johnston, 1990).[2]

The related growth of impoverishment and indebtedness in the Third World indicates that this global system is an expanded form of the old colonialism. Imperialist nations are still involved. A major example is the conspicuous financial and military support for the corporate agenda provided by the US.

In Canada, US influence has been both economic and political, as post-FTA agricultural experience demonstrates. To assess the magnitude of that and its consequences, we can benefit by comparing pre-FTA promises and prospects with post-FTA trends.

Free Trade Expectations for Rural Canada

In agriculture as in other sectors, the primary objective expressed by proponents of the FTA was free access to the large US market. That hope was most evident among beef, pork and canola producers. Their vision was probably summarized accurately by Fred Mitchell, the President of Intercontinental Packers and of the Canadian Meat Council: 'I get excited about the 235 million Americans just a truck-ride away from many Canadian factories' (Mitchell, 1985). Some grain farmers expressed the hope that expansion of the livestock industry would be enough to add significantly to their sales. Saskatchewan trade officials predicted an approximate increase of 30% in livestock and red meat sales (Herman, 1988).

A federal government promotional brochure told farmers that:

> The Agreement does not affect the right of federal and provincial governments to protect and stabilize farm incomes. The existence of farm marketing boards for grains, dairy, poultry and egg industries, as well as Canada's right to establish new boards, will not be affected by free trade. (External Affairs, 1987: 9)

A Saskatchewan government booklet subsequently supported these promises. It included promises that 'The Canadian Wheat Board will continue to be the sole exporter of western Canadian wheat, oats, and barley [and that] Canada's system of supply management for poultry, eggs and dairy' would be unaffected (Trade and Investment Saskatchewan, 1988: 20).

Such assurances, whether private or from government, usually include little or no reference to the intricacies of the Agreement, or to possible weaknesses. Opponents, however, see complexities and hazards in the agreement, especially when they contemplate recent experience in Canada-US trade relationships. A legal analysis by retired judge Marjorie Bowker (1988: 50-5) pointed out that the Agreement's chapter on agriculture was 'by far the longest [and incorporated] many rules and definitions from outside documents'. Therefore, 'to fully comprehend the meaning of the FTA provisions on agriculture, it would be necessary to master these voluminous documents which are outside the FTA and which could only be grasped (if at all) by top-level international trade experts.'

Referring to FTA Article 711 on abolishing export subsidies, Bowker (1988: 53) concluded that Canadian beef exports would be one of the areas affected. Also, in Article 706, she noted that Canada is required 'to import chicken, turkey and egg products from the US up to a certain percentage of our domestic production', while an annex 'defines what these products include'.

Other critics expect that the US will insist on definitions and interpretations which will help to solve its numerous trade problems, and which will give priority to the interests of its corporations. A number of the anticipated responses in relation to agriculture appear below. The contributors to that list are obviously apprehensive about the FTA's effects on all major sectors of Canadian agriculture.[3]

> FREE TRADE FACTS
> *Agriculture:*
>
> – the US will be able to increase imports of food products, and Canada will

eliminate all tariffs within ten years, but agriculture and the food industry in Canada can never compete on an equal footing with their US competitors because of a shorter growing season, lower population density, greater transportation distances, and higher energy costs.
– the removal of all tariffs will mean the collapse of the vegetable and fruit industry in Canada and the increase in import quotas threaten the poultry and egg industries.
– other agricultural programs and subsidies are subject to negotiations with the Americans, including crop insurance and the PFRA.
– transportation subsidies under the Western Grain Transportation Act are eliminated for all agricultural products going to the US through west coast ports.
– marketing boards have been put in a vulnerable position. The Canadian Wheat Board could be stripped of its control over import licensing for wheat, barley, oats, and their products. The agreement pledges that both governments will work to eliminate import barriers. The US government has long viewed supply management marketing boards as import barriers. So while marketing boards will continue to exist, they will not function as before.
– beef, veal, and pork are freely traded now so the Mulroney-Reagan deal will not provide guaranteed access to the US market. And the agreement does not prevent the US industry from seeking countervailing duties on the export of beef from Canada.
– the dairy industry will be devastated as the Canadian Dairy Commission loses its ability to regulate supply.
– the end of two-price wheat.
– since there are no tariffs on imports of farm machinery from the US, machinery costs will not change.
– the deal does nothing to end the international grain price war. The free trade deal acknowledges the right of the US to continue subsidizing grain sales to Canada's customers.

(*Briarpatch*, March 1988).

Vindication of those concerns began before the FTA was signed, when the government moved as expected to bring about 'the end of two-price wheat' (Masse, 1988). The two-price system had involved government support for the domestic price of wheat to compensate farmers partially for declining export prices. Carol Masse reported an estimate that elimination of the program would cost grain farmers $433 million annually. She concluded that 'As compensation, the Canadian government will pay only $227 million, just once. Why end this program at a time of disaster? To accommodate the FTA.'

That concept of adjustment to the FTA and to US objectives had already been anticipated in the 'Capitalist World Economy Model' outlined by Basran and Hay (1988: 49). It identified Canada as 'a semi-peripheral society... [which]...has fallen under the economic and cultural influence of the US as a core society', and is thereby exploited. Assuming that the US government's financial and military power operates as a promoter and defender of corporate global interests we would be led to expect that power to affirm Canada's semi-peripheral status, including imposition of detrimental trade procedures. The validity of that hypothesis can be tested further by considering relevant trends after the signing of the FTA.

Post-FTA Developments

In the early post-FTA period, debate continued as to the impact and significance of the Agreement. Supporters discounted immediate setbacks as necessary competitive adjustments, perhaps not all attributable to the FTA. Opponents regarded adverse developments as merely beginnings of free trade pressures which would move Canada from a semi-peripheral to a peripheral status. As we shall see, early losses justified some of the fears concerning agriculture. Before examining these specific developments, it will be useful to consider some more general tendencies.

Some General Trends

One of the most negative developments was the Bank of Canada's high interest rate policy. This raised the value of the Canadian dollar. Although this may have had a restrictive effect on price increases for imported farm machinery and other farm inputs, it made Canadian exports more expensive to foreign buyers. It also added further to farm debt costs.

The fact that a higher Canadian dollar helps US exports to Canada, and makes Canadian exports more costly, is a reason to suspect that Washington may have promoted Canada's high-interest policy as part of the FTA implementation process. Canada's trade balance 'slipped into the red' in October 1989—the first such deficit in 13½ years. The traditional trade surplus had declined by $2.5 billion since the FTA was signed. Statistics Canada attributed that decline to slower growth in the US, to the higher Canadian dollar, and to a falling demand for Canadian car exports (Drohan, 1989). A major decline in Canada's food trade surplus was also a factor. Liberal trade critic Lloyd Axworthy attributed that decline to the high-interest policy, and he insisted that Canada informally accepted that policy when the FTA was signed (Wilson, 1989).

Farmers were affected by another general result of the FTA—a loss of jobs and a greater proportion of low-wage employment. Farm families are increasingly involved in these trends as they are driven to seek wage income which might help to prevent foreclosure or bankruptcy. A loss of 72,000 jobs was directly attributable to the FTA in its first year, according to a Pro-Canada Network estimate. About three times that number were lost indirectly through plant closures and cutbacks (Howard, 1990). Furthermore, the consumer price reductions promised by FTA promoters had failed to materialize (Kidd, 1989).

These employment-wage effects and price effects obviously make conditions worse for farm communities. As well, reduced urban wage incomes cause reductions in the sales of more expensive foods, including dairy products and meats. FTA supporters promise that there will be long-run net gains. Opponents expect even greater losses. To the extent that we can use established historical criteria to examine current facts and trends pertaining to agriculture, we improve our ability to assess these contending positions.

The FTA and the Grain Industry

One of the concerns listed above is the possibility that the Canadian Wheat Board could lose its licensing power over exports of grain and grain products. Soon after the Agreement was signed, Ottawa removed oats from the board's jurisdiction, while denying that this was a threat to its survival. However, the Prairie Pools saw the move as 'a definite threat to the board' (Dryden, 23 February 1989). By June 1990, the threat had developed further. The Canadian Millers Association warned that the board would have to lower its prices on domestic sales by nearly one dollar a bushel, or lose sales to wheat imported from Minneapolis (Wilson, 1990).

Those developments supported a warning given by Art Macklin of the National Farmers Union (NFU) from his perspective as a member of the Wheat Board Advisory Committee. He concluded that under the FTA, 'The American grain multinationals hope to see the Board undermined and eventually destroyed' (Pugh, 1990). As an indication of that process, the initial Wheat Board payments announced in May 1990 represented an estimated $452 million reduction in revenues to the grain farmers.

Their money problems were already severe. As reported by University of Saskatchewan agricultural economist Julia Taylor, the growers in that province were not receiving enough income to make a living and pay their debts.[4] 'The financial difficulties are not just restricted to small and large farms.' 'The hardships are across the board' (Zakreski, 1990).

The low prices for grains are not attributable to an over-supply relative to world needs. Grain shortages, hunger, and malnutrition are widespread, especially in Third World countries which lack the necessary buying power or domestic agricultural development. The main exporting countries have been competing for sales by using government subsidies to lower export prices while paying farmers more than the world market can offer.

In a study focused on the leading grain exporters, the Organization for Economic Co-operation and Development (OECD) calculated that the cost of each farm job saved by subsidies amounted to $20,000 in the European Community (EC) and the US, and almost $100,000 in Canada. The report also estimated that without subsidies, farm output would drop in Japan, the EC, Canada, and to a lesser extent the US, while rising in Australia and New Zealand (Reuter, 1990).

Canadian trade specialist Phil Stone criticized several aspects of that OECD report (Wilson, 1990). He noted that the OECD definition of Canadian subsidies was not always consistent with Canada's definition. Comparisons with European, American and Japanese farm subsidies were unfair because theirs 'are programmed support levels guaranteed by legislation', while Canadian subsidies are 'ad hoc and in reaction to others'. Furthermore, Stone pointed out that the period of comparison, 1986-88, was misleading because in those years, drought and US subsidy competition had forced Canadian subsidies to 'historic highs'.

The US had been operating through its Economic Enhancement Program (EEP), which has subsidized the sale of grain through private companies since 1985, giving farmers a guaranteed price. Saskatchewan Wheat Pool President Garf Stevenson observed that the EEP, in its first five years of operation, had raised the US world market share from 29% to 40% (Braden, 1990).

What would happen if this and other types of grain subsidies were eliminated? The OECD and other critics give little consideration to this question. Evidently, world selling prices would rise sharply as some formerly subsidized producers were forced out of operation. The reduced grain output would eventually bring higher prices that would further damage the economies of debt-burdened food importers. The underdeveloped countries, where hunger is already prevalent, would suffer most.

Severe problems could emerge even in the European Community. With a major reduction in farm subsidies, and a resulting elimination of many producers. These countries would face the prospect of grain shortages or huge import costs in the event of poor crops in other major production areas. World prices would rise more sharply, making food purchases even more difficult for the poorer countries. As an indication of the EC's determination to avoid such problems, its executive announced plans to spend over $3 billion (US) through 1990-95 to maintain and expand its farming communities (*Western Producer*, 10 May 1990).

The main beneficiary of subsidy elimination or reduction would be the US. Its production costs are likely to remain among the lowest as long as its farmers are avoiding most of the long overdue soil rebuilding expenditures, and while the climate survives global environmental damage. According to farm analyst Russell Mitchell, if repetitions of the 1988 drought did not occur, US agriculture would benefit greatly from a world move to eliminate subsidies. In the long run, however, US taxpayers would still have to face the cost of soil rebuilding. Both there and in Canada, the loss of the original organic matter in the grain fields is now estimated at 50% to 60% (Sheppard, 1990).

Public financial support also seems necessary in other food production areas. In Canadian fruit and vegetable growing, for example, even before the FTA there was severe competitive pressure from production 'in California, Mexico and other low wage countries' (Shields, 1988). By 1990, BC apple growers had production costs which almost tripled the five cents a pound attainable in the world market (CBC, 1990). Agribusiness can thus exert more pressure against the farm workforce as these people struggle to organize and to avoid discrimination on the basis of sex and ethnic origin. In general, such conditions indicate little possibility that the major food exporters will initiate major subsidy reductions.

An Expanding Imperialism

While the US has been calling for more free trade, a study by the General Agreement on Tariffs and Trade (GATT) has shown that that country has 'a growing arsenal of subsidies, import quotas and fees to protect its producers' (Lewington, 1989). The study identified 64 'voluntary' agreements to reduce US imports, with 80% of those measures having been initiated since 1984. This contradictory approach is a reminder of the British attitude regarding trade relations with Portugal and India. Like Ricardo's Britain, the US favours free trade from which its businesses can profit, but it applies trade restrictions when needed to achieve the same result. Like Portugal, Canada is continuing as a primary victim of this economic imperialism, despite the FTA.

The US-backed corporate-financial élite has large accumulations of money requiring investment. The working people do not have sufficient incomes to buy the present and potential output of goods and services. So the rulers encourage them to borrow, not only to support buying, but also to provide interest income for the lenders. Governments are also persuaded to borrow so that they can provide service and subsidies without equivalent tax increases. The major investors even attain tax reductions.

As elsewhere, US government borrowing relies partly on foreign investors, who are encouraged by high interest rates to buy national securities. They are also offered tax incentives and subsidies to invest in the service and industrial sectors, which they often do through takeovers. Where US-based corporations invest abroad, they are encouraged to repatriate the proceeds. Thus the borrowing government welcomes operations which bring funds into the country, while resisting outflows such as caused by expenditures for imports. Since Canada also seeks net money inflows, a direct conflict of interest exists.

In both countries it was hoped that rural industries would be able to expand their exports and reduce their imports. In that contradictory situation, as in the Ricardian example, the predominant economy has the power to make its interests prevail. The international corporate agenda also endorses that outcome as a means of ensuring effectiveness for the North American trading bloc while it is in contention with the European and East Asian blocs.

As in the past, this process reflects corporate class interests working in opposition to working class interests. The workers are therefore pressured to accept lower incomes as a means of improving the competitiveness of their economy. These corporate objectives help to explain why a 1990 Canadian Senate report stated that Americans were becoming 'more aggressive in harassing Canadian exporters' (Drohan, 1990). The Senate Foreign Affairs

Committee pointed out that the expected lessening of US 'harassing actions [under the FTA] does not appear to be happening'. In agriculture, the Canadian meat industry provided a clear example.

The FTA and the Meat Industry

The Senate committee identified increased US inspections of meat shipments from Canada as an initial example of increasing trade restrictions. In August 1989, the US International Trade Commission ruled in favour of a demand by the US pork industry for increased tariffs on Canadian pork. The result was a 4% increase in the cost of those exports. Since about 25% of Canadian pork production had been going to the US, the ruling created a severe problem for the industry despite some extra sales to the Soviet Union and Japan.

As with grains, these extra sales led to subsidy battles. The US National Pork Producers Council complained that its members were at a disadvantage because of European and Canadian subsidies. Council spokesperson Karen Coble argued that 'those subsidies which Canada has been proven to have, make it tough for our industry to compete' (Canadian Press, 1990).

In Saskatchewan, 'tripartite' stabilization payments by the Pork Producers Marketing Board were criticized by the US Department of Commerce as subsidies.[5] The US responded with 'countervail' duties as high as $30 a hog in 1989 (*Western Producer*, 1990).

These US protectionist policies in the meat trade extended into non-tariff 'harassment', as indicated by a 1990 inspection controversy. Inspection fees on border shipments of Canadian meats rose from $100 (US) to $700 in some cases. Responding to exporters' complaints, Canada's grains and oilseeds minister Charles Mayer stated that 'Americans should know that they run a sizeable trade surplus with us in agricultural products, to the tune of $1 billion per year. . . . We expect that to be recognized. . .' (Greenshields, 1990).

US restrictions have also raised problems for Canadian meat packers. Intercontinental Packers of Saskatoon, which had regarded the FTA as an expansion opportunity, was forced by US restrictions to discontinue its shipments there, and to lay off workers as its hog slaughter declined by 50% (Goulding, 1990). Meanwhile, the former giant of Canadian meat packing, Canada Packers, was planning a sellout to British interests because the industry was 'competing heavily' in raw meats, and also in poultry and oilseeds. The oilseed business had been made 'particularly difficult in Canada as a result of American and European competition' (Bertin, 1990).

The Canadian cattle industry also began to lobby for more protection because 1989 had been a year of record beef imports into Canada. The amount was 260 million pounds, up 4% over 1988. Most cattlemen had favoured the FTA, but were finding that under US rules, 'the Canadian border is more open than the American border' (Wilson, 1990).

Corporate Objectives and Policies

In each trading sector, the FTA's emphasis on freedom of transborder investment flows has been an important factor. An example was the major new investment by Cargill Grain of Minneapolis in the Western Canadian farm economy. Already, in 1988, its world sales of $43 billion (US) made it the world's tenth largest corporation. After the FTA, it added meat packing to its extensive Canadian branch plant operations in grains, oilseeds, and farm supplies. The meat plant was built at High River, Alberta—helped by $4 million in subsidies from the Alberta government. The capacity of that 'state-of-the-art' facility was a threat to competitors, including Gainers and Burns Foods (Powell, 1990).

Cargill also reached an agreement with Saskatchewan to build a $435 million fertilizer plant at Belle Plaine. The opposition expressed concern about this 'joint venture' and its impact on the environment and on existing plants, which already had enough capacity to meet market demands (Burton, 1990). Later, some US senators revealed that Cargill was investing only a controlling $65 million at Belle Plaine, and that the remainder of the $435 million was covered by the government's $64 million in equity and $306 million in loan guarantees (Sproat, 1990).

These government support programs show how corporate bargaining power has been enhanced under the FTA. In Manitoba, Cargill 'walked away' from investment in a hog slaughtering plant because of what it called the uncertainty of attaining 'more secure and privileged access' to the US market. The apparent problem was US countervailing duties against Canadian hogs. Presumably, if the Manitoba government had emulated Alberta and Saskatchewan by providing enough funding to overcome Cargill's concerns, the company would have proceeded with the plant in that province (Drohan, 1990).

Meanwhile, another form of corporate pressure on governments was put by McCain Foods (New Brunswick), which had always opposed the FTA. It complained that as tariffs are phased out on US dairy and poultry products, the Canadian supply management systems in those sectors will put processors at an increasing disadvantage in competing with US imports. It concluded that if such companies are to survive in Canada, the FTA must be terminated, or at least modified to accommodate supply management (Drohan, 1990).

A similar warning about the threat to supply management was issued by the chairperson of the National Farmers Union regional dairy commission in Ontario. His analysis showed that an apparent extension of the FTA into the GATT negotiations of early 1990 was causing pressure on processors and retailers to demand cheaper and lower wages. These demands, he concluded, 'would lead to the demise of the family farm and the redundance of domestic processing and retailing industries' (Visser, 1990).

Such developments are reminders that an assessment of the FTA's impact on Canadian policies and institutions requires consideration of the pressures which the corporate élite can apply to governments. Since the US has a population and an economy ten times greater than Canada's, the pressures from south of the border are proportionally stronger. In 1988, 22 of the world's 50 largest corporations had their headquarters in the US (*Fortune*, 1989). Increasingly, these firms and their ruling billionaire families have been shifting productive facilities to lower wage countries. Facilitation of these shifts is a major reason for corporate insistence on free international movement of capital.

Financial Sector Involvement

One result of this external investment drive is a smaller inflow of profits to the US. As noted above, Washington has tried to compensate for the outflow and external retention of money by encouraging the sale of US dollars and bonds to foreigners. The central bank has kept interest rates high enough to support that objective. One result has been the movement of the country from a net creditor position to being one of the world's largest net debtors. It has become 'a haven for capital' (MacEwan, 1990: 87).

US indebtedness increased further as foreigners repatriated some of their dividends and interest. So there was more emphasis on improving cash inflow from merchandise exports, including farm products. A major obstacle was the slower growth rate in the European Community and the Third World during the 1980s. This tended to reduce the American export-import ratio still further (MacEwan, 1990: 94-5), and thereby created more resistance to imports from Canada.

To obtain more money inflow from repatriated profits, the US moved to liberalize trade in services (including banks, tourism, telecommunications, insurance, transportation, and construction). It was 'particularly keen to remove restrictions that keep US banks out of some countries' (Zaracostas, 1990). Canada has already reduced those restrictions considerably under the FTA. The number of banks and trust companies covered by the Canada Deposit Insurance Corporation rose to more than 150 by early 1990. Foreign banks had 57 Canadian subsidiaries.

Some farmers might have hoped that such increased competition in loan offerings might reduce interest rates. But this would be neglecting the extra costs involved in establishing and maintaining the new competitors. Furthermore, in view of the failure record of banking in the US, and the increasing failure rate already seen in Canada, farmers as taxpayers or as borrowers must expect to pay some of the 'bail-out' costs and to suffer from more relentless foreclosure procedures.[6]

Another source of jeopardy which includes farmers appeared in the entry of 'insurance services' from the US. By 1990, up to $500 million worth of 'insurance protection' had been sold in Canada by businesses 'with questionable pasts and unsavoury connections'. These were mainly firms which had 'left a trail of woe behind them south of the border' (Francis, 1990).

These examples reflect the enduring characteristics of the free market and its competitive struggles, which are now expanding through corporate-dominated international structures. This extension of Smith-Ricardian ideology continues to promote the concept that the competitive struggle is a natural process which will maximize long-run benefits by ensuring the survival of the fittest.

Surveying the scientific criticisms of this supposedly natural evolutionary process, MacEwan concludes that there is 'nothing natural about the structure of the labour supply in various countries. Whether or not low-wage labour is readily available in a particular country for the production of goods for the US market is a consequence of substantial political and social conflict' (MacEwan, 1990: 92).

An Extension of Class Struggle

A few of the market's supporters recognize the problems facing those who suffer in the competitive struggle. As expressed by *The Economist* the world will become 'a safer, quieter, prettier place [if] prices reflect the full social, and not just private, cost of energy-burning or car-driving or waste-dumping' (1990). Evidently realizing that social costs are not being covered, these analysts went on to admit the existence of an ' "under class" of bag ladies and unemployed youngsters', even in the US and Western Europe. But they failed to consider the expansion of this under class as international corporate oligarchies gain even greater power. Increasingly beyond national regulation, these entities make the development of genuine democracy even more difficult.

As a defender of these new global forces, Frank Feather (1990) expressed the hope that they will stop being greedy, and will initiate equalization policies to help the underdeveloped countries. Criticizing that assumption, Heather Menzies indicated the failure of the model to 'address the reality that foreign aid spending is collapsing away from the equalization principle' (Menzies, 1990).

Some obvious elements of that collapse appeared when the US began negotiations with Mexico for that country's inclusion in a North American free trade bloc. The Canadian Labour Congress pointed out an obvious concern in the prospect of 'pressure coming from the US and from Mexico for Canada to push down private and social wages' (Scotton, 1990). That process would involve setting up a border zone in Mexico where cheap labour would be used to produce components for 'US-made goods, which when shipped to Canada, would place Canadian manufacturers at a disadvantage' (Scotton, 1990).

Would the Canada-US FTA preclude duty-free entry of such products? Would Canada gain more access to the Mexican market if the FTA were extended there? Since Ottawa began by merely 'monitoring' the talks, Carleton trade expert Michael Hart concluded that 'The benefits to Canada depend very much on the decisions taken in Mexico City and Washington' (Scotton, 1990).

Indicating how those decisions would affect agricultural industries, Brewster Kneen noted that agribusiness has access to a 'large reserve of cheap labour in Mexico', and to large numbers of illegal immigrants in the US. By taking advantage of these conditions, he warned, the industry 'has gained virtually total control over agricultural inputs as well as. . .the processing and distribution of food' (Kneen, 1989: 50-1).

Even if Canadian marketing boards survive the FTA, this control by agribusiness over input and output pricing transfers most of the farmers' revenues into corporate coffers. As the boards are eliminated under the FTA, the financial position of farmers must deteriorate even more rapidly. Some will become tenants of large corporate landowners. Others will be forced into the exploitation of urban wage systems. There they will continue to find that the wealth they produce is largely confiscated by the exploiting class through profits, interest and rent.

A Challenge for Democracy

The ruling class, using international communications technology to facilitate trade and investment, is establishing greater centralized domination and further reducing peripheral control and viability. Referring to this growth of centralized control, sociologist R.T. Schaefer reported an estimate that by the year 2000, 'a few hundred corporations will account for more than half the value of goods and services produced in the entire world' (1989: 422). Since these super-corporations are mainly controlled by a family or a small group with dominant shareholdings, they constitute a developing, highly undemocratic global oligarchy of unprecedented magnitude and power.

The neo-colonial and class pressures to be expected from these rulers are indicated by a Wood Gundy 'study' which reported that Canadian manufacturers have 'lost the edge they once enjoyed over their US competitors' because increases in the Canadian dollar value and in Canadian wage rates 'outstripped the growth of manufacturing productivity' (Rusk, 1990). However there are at least ten generally recognized causes of slow productivity growth, only three of which are related to labour (Kolko, 1988: 22). As Magdoff and Sweezy have shown, a major cause is excess capacity caused by 'competitive' investment and by inadequate consumer buying power. These factors cause corporations to divert more funds to speculation and takeovers—to ' "making money" as distinct from "making goods" ' (Kolko,

1988: 21). Under these conditions, Canadian branch plants are especially susceptible to cutbacks and closures.

Such developments were anticipated by J.B. Foster in his application of Marxist analysis to recent corporate activity (1986: 62-3). He found accuracy in Sweezy's conclusion that the expanding corporate system would produce larger profits at the expense of weaker firms and by 'a general reduction in the level of real wages'. Similarly, André Ascrow's examination of current colonialism showed that the major corporate contenders will proceed with the 'subjugation and oppression' of weaker countries. They will thus be fulfilling Lenin's prediction that the system must bring about 'the negation of democracy in general, of all democracy' (1983: 213-14). Ascrow therefore concluded that success in the workers' struggle for widespread democracy requires 'elimination of capitalist relations of production' (1983: 216).

To those who insist that global consolidation of capitalist production is inevitable, computer specialist Theodor Sterling has pointed out that this is ignoring net technological advances (Sterling, 1990). There are 'many examples' showing that computers can provide 'the automatic, fast, reliable and efficient allocation of resources that central planning requires' (Sterling, 1990). It thus appears that the corporate oligarchies and the new pro-market leaders in Eastern Europe are rejecting national planning just when new computer technology can facilitate and democratize that planning.

It should thus be easier for rural and urban workers to organize a genuinely democratic alternative to the 'free market' expansion of corporate rule. To replace that rule, workers' democracies will need constitutional guarantees enabling them to initiate referendum and recall procedures to ensure that elected administrators perform responsibly. Administrative positions should also have constitutionally established rotation periods and appropriately restricted remuneration to prevent the development of oligarchies and privileged leadership cults.

With these 'Four Rs' of democracy firmly entrenched, the élitist rule which now prevails in dictatorships, 'capitalist democracies', and most 'socialist' regimes can be replaced by a genuinely democratic, classless society which will develop trade and other international relationships for mutual benefit rather than for competitive advantages leading to core-periphery exploitation.

We must expect that any exploiting class will ruthlessly oppose these changes. But as shown by the struggle in Canada against the FTA and the subsequent privations, rural and urban workers are greatly improving their ability to unite and to organize effectively.[7]

Summary and Conclusions

The imperial structures which have pursued advantageous free trade for more than two centuries have now developed a more international perspective based on technological advances in production and communication. Unprecedented concentrations of corporate economic power are working to eliminate government regulatory restrictions while retaining the financial and military support of the nation state. For rural and urban workers everywhere, this growing concentration of supra-national control has magnified the still unsolved problem of establishing workers' democracies as an alternative to corporate oligarchies.

The inadequacy of democracy in Canada was re-emphasized in 1988 when the pro-FTA government was re-elected with a majority of seats from a minority of votes. There is also no reliable method for the people to initiate a new election during the government's five-year term.

Defenders of the FTA often argue that even five years is insufficient for the development of its full benefits. Opponents see evidence that the initial adversities are likely to increase. Both sides agree, however, that the trend to free trade is part of a developing international corporate relationship which will require workers to become more competitive, domestically and internationally. That means lower real incomes and more arduous working conditions.

Throughout this new environment, the problem of growing debt is pervasive. Canadian farmers and urban workers recognize this from painful experience. Yet they are subjected to the same pressures that are felt by the indebted Third World. From the IMF to the local banks, the advice comes that they should accept further financial constraints in order to become more competitive.

This obvious exploitation of workers is developing into a new dimension of class struggle as their resistance grows. A fully acceptable alternative system has not yet been established by either revolutionary or reform movements. The Marxist concept of workers' democracy is still elusive. But the experience gained through past failures, combined with the new dangers evident in corporate internationalism, must inspire renewed efforts.

This progress has become evident already in the farmer-labour political mobilization which opposed the FTA, and which is continuing against the subsequent economic, fiscal and monetary adversities. New communication technologies can be helpful if constructively applied to political organization and to large-scale economic planning. These new and rapidly developing material conditions, when understood and utilized, can provide a basis for democratic and humanitarian societies in the twenty-first century, in sharp contrast to the destructive competition which emerged from the eighteenth century as reflected in free trade ideology.

Notes

[1]Ricardo's 'comparative advantage' model assumed that England might have an 'absolute disadvantage' in the wine production by requiring the labour of 120 men to

produce a given quantity in a year, while Portugal needed only 80 men for the same output. England might also have an absolute disadvantage ratio of 100 to 90 in cloth production. However, that lower ratio would mean a 'comparative advantage' in cloth. Thus if England concentrated on cloth, and Portugal on wine, there would be an addition to total product which could be shared as extra income. That assumption of fair distribution is an obvious defect in the model. Also, there remains the question of how the labour force could move and attain full employment.

[2]Maurice Strong, head of several corporate organizations, including The World Economic Forum Council based in Geneva, contended that 'our technological civilization has produced a single global community. . .corporations are, in fact, the principal instruments of globalization precisely because they are not circumscribed by borders and territories and limitations of jurisdiction' (Johnston, Spring, 1990).

[3]The *Briarpatch* listing was 'compiled from material supplied by the Pro-Canada Network, Steve Dorey, the National Farmers Union, the National Action Committee on the Status of Women, and John Warnock' (*Briarpatch*, March 1988: 16).

[4]Taylor defined an adequate farm income as $15,000 a year for living expenses after meeting operating costs and debt principal payments (Zakreski, 7 April 1990).

[5]'Tripartism' refers to equal funding by Ottawa, the provinces, and the farmers. 'Tripartite' payments are available on a national basis for enrolled cattle and hog producers and are made when the national market price falls below a predetermined support price. This provided 2,100 Saskatchewan pork producers with $23.4 million in May 1990 (Zakreski, 8 May 1990).

[6]By early 1990, cost estimates ranged from $300 to $500 billion for the bailout of more than 700 insolvent or collapsed savings and loan companies in the US (Mackenzie, 12 April 1990). More than 2,500 US financial institutions disappeared during the 1980s (Jorgensen, 7 May 1990).

[7]As one example of organized resistance by the oppressed, the Pro-Canada Network distributed a pamphlet opposing the FTA during the 1988 election campaign. It accompanied 20 daily papers and three rural papers, and represented 37 exploited groups. It undermined the government's re-election hopes to the extent that an 'alliance' of 150 corporations responded with massive pro-government advertising, estimated to have cost $6 million. In 1990, the Pro-Canada Network renewed its cross-country campaign by working with organized farm and labour groups to conduct a popular vote against Ottawa's proposed Goods and Services Tax.

CHAPTER FOURTEEN

FARM LABOUR, WORK CONDITIONS, AND HEALTH RISKS

B. SINGH BOLARIA

In capitalist societies there is often a pool of unused labour power, an industrial reserve army. These societies also face scarcity of labour, in either absolute or relative terms, the former due to the exhaustion of the indigenous labour supply and the latter due to the unwillingness of the workers to work in certain sectors. These are the sectors where, because of low pay, arduous work, irregular employment, unsafe and unhealthy work environment, workers with other options are unwilling to work. Employers in these sectors have not always been able to procure and retain labour under the normal operations of the capitalist labour market mechanisms. Agriculture is one such sector.

The demand for wage labour in agriculture is influenced by a number of factors, including type of agriculture, level of capitalization and mechanization, and the availability of unpaid family labour. In the absence of family labour and where agricultural production is still heavily labour-intensive, the survival of the small-scale production units and the profit margins of the larger units depend upon the availability of a pool of low-cost labour. This labour pool is primarily composed of workers who have been shut out of other labour market opportunities, workers-without-options, mostly racial

B. Singh Bolaria is a Professor and former Head of the Department of Sociology at the University of Saskatchewan.

minority transient workers who follow the harvest or picking seasons in agriculture. This national migrant labour force is supplemented by 'foreign' workers composed of recently arrived immigrants, migrant seasonal workers, and undocumented workers. Together these workers constitute a vulnerable, powerless, and super-exploited segment of the labour force. They labour under conditions where the agricultural production process and work conditions contribute to numerous health risks for them and their families. This chapter explores the linkages between agricultural production, work conditions, and health risks faced by farm labour.

Labour Market Inequalities and Differential Opportunity Structures

The Canadian labour market is characterized by occupational, gender, and racial stratification and segmentation (Royal Commission, 1984). Foreign workers entering the stratified and segmented labour market frequently end up in or are specifically brought in to fill positions where there is a shortage of Canadian labour or where Canadian workers are unwilling to work. Often non-market sanctions have been required to procure and retain domestic and foreign labour in lower strata. This has taken the form of un-free labour, and other workers with tenuous legal-political status (non-citizen workers) have been an important source supplementing the domestic workforce (citizen workers) in agriculture. This distinction between citizen and non-citizen workers, free and unfree labour, helps to explain the various processes involved in the production and reproduction of the low-cost, powerless, super-exploited segment of the labour force.

Citizen Workers

Included in the category of citizen worker are native-born and naturalized citizens. Citizen workers enjoy, in the formal sense, all legal and political rights and can circulate in the labour market freely. These workers constitute 'free wage labour'—free to sell their labour power to the highest bidder, freedom of physical mobility, and free of any political-legal compulsion or coercion to sell their labour power to a particular employer.

This, however, does not mean that the worker is free in the absolute sense. Without independent means of support (separated from the means of production, landless, propertyless) a vast majority of people earn their living by selling their labour power. Thus, workers are compelled by economic necessity to enter the labour market to sell their labour power in exchange for wages to buy necessities to reproduce themselves and their work capacity (Satzewich, 1989).

Some workers face other constraints to circulating freely in the labour market because of social ascriptive factors, such as race and gender. Being shut out of better opportunities, these workers end up in lower strata and are incorporated into the labour market in a subordinate status. Certain groups, whether Canadian citizens or not, continue to be socially defined as foreigners. These are members of various racial minority communities who are often treated as alien labour (Sakala, 1987). The characteristics of the workers become associated with characteristics of the jobs. Certain jobs become identified as 'Mexican work', 'Chinese work', or 'East Indian work'.

Economic deprivations, differential opportunity structures in the labour market, and social and cultural isolation contribute to their vulnerability and push them into low-paying, arduous and seasonal work.

Non-Citizen Workers

Foreign workers can be broadly classified as composed of landed immigrant settler labour, migrant contract labour and transient workers, and illegal or undocumented workers. It is the immigration laws and regulations which determine the admissibility criteria and the legal-political status of foreign labour, that is, whether the workers are immigrants or migrants.

Landed Immigrants: Probationary Citizens. Landed immigrants are those workers who have 'lawful permission to come into Canada to establish permanent residence'. A permanent resident is 'a person who has been granted landing, has not become a Canadian citizen or has not lost his permanent resident status' (Canada, Employment and Immigration, 1984: 100). Landed immigrants are entitled to seek employment and enjoy many legal rights. They are not, however, citizens. They are entitled to apply for citizenship after a three-year residency in this country. It is precisely this 'probationary period' which is dealt with in this chapter.

During the probationary period these workers occupy tenuous legal-political status. For instance, in the Canadian context, the new Immigration Act has given the state the powers to impose many restrictions on permanent residents, such as the power to impose almost any type of 'terms and conditions' for six months on new arrivals (Act S.14); the power to photograph and fingerprint permanent residents (Act S.115[1][n]); the right to refuse re-entry unless he or she has obtained a 'returning resident permit' (Act S.25). Some of these provisions were found in the Chinese Immigration Act in the 1920s and 1930s. However, the current regulations apply to all permanent residents (The Law Union of Ontario, 1981: 47).

Permanent residents can also be deported on the basis of somewhat vague grounds, such as simply being accused by a police or immigration officer that he or she is likely to commit an indictable offence (Act S.27[1][a] and 19 [1][d]). Failure to willingly support themselves or their dependents also constitutes grounds for deportation (Act S.27[1][f]).

Many of these clauses have been seriously questioned by the Canadian Civil Liberties Association, which has told the government that they are 'concerned about rendering permanent residents. . .deportable on the basis of "reasonable grounds to believe" (they) are likely to engage in criminal activity'. The Association is of the opinion that 'this country owes such persons something more precise than an exercise in prophecy. The removal of such people from this country on the basis of anticipated anti-social conduct should require at the very least, certain proved anti-social acts' (Canadian Civil Liberties Association, 1977: 13).

The implications of these clauses in the legislation are quite serious for the legal-political rights of landed immigrants. Immigrants would be reluctant to engage in union activities and complain about working conditions lest they be considered subversive. Participation in 'undesirable' activities may also put into jeopardy approval of the citizenship application. In any event, the important point is that the existence of these clauses is likely to be intimidating for the arrivals, particularly the unskilled, uneducated, racial minority workers.

Migrant Labour: Unfree Labour Force. Another source of additional labour is the workers who enter Canada under the Non-Immigrant Employment Authorization Program. An employment authorization is 'a document issued by an immigration officer whereby the person to whom it is issued is authorized to engage or continue employment in Canada' (Canada, Employment and Immigration, 1984: 100).

At a broader level, non-immigrant employment authorization regulations were introduced in 1973 to allow admission of non-immigrants for employment. Since the implementation of this program, thousands of workers have come to Canada to work.

The data on immigrant and non-immigrant workers for 1973-88 are reported in Table 14.1. It is evident that a large number of work authorizations are issued to import migrant labour to this country.

Temporary work authorizations are given only if the immigration office is satisfied that no Canadian citizen or permanent resident is available for the job. This means that, in most cases, jobs will be either menial and low-paying, such as domestic worker or farmworker, or highly skilled and specialized. Also the work authorization is specific to the job and for a specified time period (The Law Union of Ontario, 1981: 113-14). It is crucial to note that these workers have been allowed to enter Canada even when there is high unemployment in this country. Canada continues to import migrant contract workers to supplement the labour force in agricultural and service sectors (Bolaria, 1984; Bolaria and Li, 1988).

In addition to their temporary status in this country as migrant workers, these workers have other constraints imposed by restrictive state-administered contractual obligations which 'tie' them to a particular job. Therefore, the compliance and the vulnerability of migrant labour is achieved through the control of political boundaries, immigration laws, and contractual obligations.

Table 14.1 Landed immigrant workers and non-immigrant work authorizations, 1973 to 1988

YEAR	IMMIGRANT WORKERS	NON-IMMIGRANT WORK AUTHORIZATIONS
1973	92,228	83,912
1974	106,083	86,183
1975	81,189	96,045
1976	61,461	91,103
1977	47,625	89,120
1978	35,080	63,320
1979	47,939	94,420
1980	63,403	108,871
1981	56,978	126,583
1982	55,482	125,901
1983	37,119	130,717
1984	38,500	143,979
1985	38,459	177,165
1986	48,200	205,747
1987	76,712	231,576
1988	76,350	267,076

Source: Figures for immigrant and non-immigrant workers for 1978-1984, Employment and Immigration, *Immigration Statistics*, 1984: 53, 87. Figures for non-immigrant workers for 1973-1977 made available through Employment and Immigration Canada. Figures for immigrant workers for 1973-1976, Department of Manpower and Immigration; and for 1977, Employment and Immigration Canada. For 1985-1988, Employment and Immigration immigration statistics. Employment Authorizations for 1985-1988 include 'short-term' and 'long-term' authorizations. Short-term: persons who were in Canada in any particular year and whose duration of stay did not exceed one year. Long-term: persons who were in Canada in any particular year and whose duration of stay was one year or more.

Criminalized Unfree Labour. In addition to landed immigrants and migrant workers, in many countries illegal or undocumented workers now contribute a significant part of the labour force. Illegals are aliens without citizenship. These workers officially do not exist. Illegal status and threat of deportation assures compliance, docility, and cheap labour. These workers are in a weaker position than any other form of labour.

Estimates of illegal workers vary considerably. One estimate placed the number of illegal workers in Canada at about 200,000 (*Globe and Mail*, 4 March 1983). The majority of these persons were visitors who had overstayed their permissible entry period, worked without authorization, or had violated some aspects of the Immigration Act (Canada, Employment and Immigration, 1983).

The discussion is summarized in Figure 14.1. I am quite aware of the considerable differentiation within each category of workers; nevertheless, it is crucial to make the distinction between citizen and non-citizen and free and unfree labour. This is significant because in Canada a large number of workers are being imported as non-immigrant transitory workforce without any prospects of permanent settlement and citizenship. A proportion of this labour force is specifically recruited under state administered contracts as unfree labour to work in areas of labour scarcity, including agricultural labour.

Figure 14.1 Labour market inequalities and differential opportunities

CITIZEN WORKERS	NON-CITIZEN WORKERS		
	Immigrant Labour	Migrant Labour	Illegal Labour
-Canadian-born labour	-Landed immigrants not yet naturalized	-Non-immigrant contractural labour on work authorizations and other programs	-Criminalized labour
-Naturalized (citizens) foreign-born labour	-probationary citizens		
FREE LABOUR		UNFREE LABOUR	

LOW ———— Degree of Subordination, Powerlessness and Exploitation ———— HIGH

Farm Labour: a Low-Wage and Powerless Workforce

Historically, family labour and rural wage workers have been an important part of the workforce in agricultural production. Over the years, changes in the agriculture sector, mechanization, capitalization, non-farm job opportunities, and a decline in the rural population have led to the depletion of the traditional supply of agricultural labour, and alternative sources of labour have had to be found. As Parr (1985: 92) states:

> By the twentieth century, the capital requirements in agriculture had grown relatively, and as the alternatives to farm work became more attractive and numerous, smallholders' and farmers' sons and daughters were in part drawn, in part driven to leave the countryside. Their places on the farm as wage labourers were taken up by others who were often migrants, and almost always landless.

Because of the nature of agricultural work—low pay, seasonality, arduous labour, unhealthy work environment—this sector has often faced scarcity of labour supply. A supply of labour has been often secured through various joint federal-provincial programs which have provided for transportation of workers from one part of the country to the other (e.g., bussing workers from the Maritimes and Quebec to Ontario) during the harvest season. Assistance and preference is given to those immigrants who intend to become farmworkers (Parr, 1985; Satzewich, 1989).

Foreign workers have been a permanent structural necessity in agriculture precisely because the employers have difficulty in attracting and retaining workers. In almost all cases this labour pool is composed of racial and ethnic minority workers. For instance, in the beginning of this century, when farmers in British Columbia faced a shortage of labour and a consequent increase in labour costs, they petitioned the government for more immigrant labour. As a consequence, 10,000 Japanese and 5,000 East Indians were allowed to enter Canada to supplement the agricultural labour force (Sharma, 1982; BC Human Rights Commission, 1983). Presently farm workforces in British Columbia are mainly composed of East Indians, Chinese, Native Indians, francophones, and migrant youth (Sharma, 1982; Sharma, 1983; BC Human Rights Commission, 1983). There has been a succession from one labour pool to another equally vulnerable labour force consisting primarily of racial minorities or recently arrived immigrants. The agricultural sector in the United States and Canada makes extensive use of the low-cost labour provided by racial or ethnic minorities (Burawoy, 1976; Waitzkin, 1983; Sharma, 1982; Sharma, 1983; BC Human Rights Commission, 1983).

The agricultural labour force is supplemented by migrant labour under the Non-Immigrant Work Authorization Program (initiated in 1973) and the Seasonal Agricultural Workers' Program (initiated in 1966). These workers provide a valuable labour force for many producers and 'meet identifiable shortfalls in the available supply of Canadian workers for the harvesting of fresh fruit and vegetable crops and the processing of these same commodities' (Canada Employment and Immigration Commission, 1981: 2). Ontario continues to be the primary destination for temporary farmworkers (Canada, Immigration Statistics, 1980-84). In recent years, about half of the agriculture labour in Ontario has been composed of migrants from other provinces, off-shore immigrants, and exchange students (Parr, 1985: 103).

Long before the introduction of non-immigrant work authorizations, foreign workers had been admitted to meet the seasonal labour demand in agriculture. This program, initiated in 1966, helped to create a versatile labour pool for farmers harvesting highly perishable fruit and vegetable crops. In light of the experience with the Caribbean countries, a similar bilateral agreement was signed with Mexico in 1974. In 1976 the Caribbean program was extended to include the eastern Caribbean islands.

Table 14.2 shows the number of non-immigrant work authorizations issued in agriculture between 1973 and 1988. With the exception of 1981, when 16,479 migrants were in Canada on work authorizations, the number of temporary immigrants in agriculture ranged between about eight and eleven thousand, while the number of landed immigrants destined for agriculture ranged between one and three thousand. A large proportion of these temporary workers are Caribbean Blacks or Mexicans.

Table 14.2 Non-immigrant work authorizations in agriculture and landed immigrants destined for agriculture, 1973 to 1988

YEAR	NON-IMMIGRANT WORK AUTHORIZATIONS IN AGRICULTURE[a]	LANDED IMMIGRANTS DESTINED FOR AGRICULTURE[b]
1973	9,208	3,079
1974	10,408	2,637
1975	9,841	1,511
1976	8,937	1,162
1977	8,149	1,215
1978	8,260	937
1979	8,738	1,597
1980	8,773	2,462
1981	16,479	2,931
1982	9,229	2,187
1983	8,290	1,419
1984	8,067	1,170
1985	7,962	1,050
1986	7,896	1,330
1987	8,976	1,817
1988	11,194	2,017

Source: [a]Figures for 1973-79 computed from data made available through Employment and Immigration Canada, Saskatchewan Regional Office; 1980-87, Immigration Statistics, Employment and Immigration Canada. Figures for 1980, 1981, 1985-1988 are based on the sum total of work authorizations in agriculture issued to 'long-term' and 'short-term' visitors. The former refers to visitors remaining in Canada for more than one year, whereas the latter to those of one year or less. For 1982 and 1984, no such distinction was made in published reports.

[b]Immigration Statistics 1973-87, Employment and Immigration Canada.

These workers enter the country under state-administered contractual arrangements and are not free to circulate in the labour market; that is, they are not free to sell their labour power in the open market. They are imported for specific jobs; immigration regulations and contractual obligations assure their physical immobility and subordinate status. For example, one of the contractual obligations in the case of seasonal agricultural labour requires that these workers 'not work for any person without the prior approval of the employer, the Government's agent and the Canada Employment and Immigration Commission' (The Law Union of Ontario, 1981; Task Force on Immigration Practices and Procedures, 1981). An unofficial 'grace' period may be allowed for changing jobs. This is a discretionary practice and 'its availability and length are nowhere specifically set forth or guaranteed, adding to the employee's uncertain position' (Task Force on Immigration Practices and Procedures, 1981: 26).

Migrant workers on employment authorizations 'accept' interpersonal subordination and low wages because alternative job opportunities are blocked. Their tenuous legal status (legal-political coercion) in this country and vulnerable work arrangements produce docility, compliance and obedience. Many workers are afraid that they might be deported if they complain about their working conditions (Task Force on Domestic Workers, 1981). In the case of domestics who are admitted under similar arrangements as the agricultural workers, Arnopoulos reports that immigration authorities are quite aware of the necessity to restrict employment opportunities to assure that the employees continue to work as domestics. Arnopoulos (1979: 25) notes: 'Senior immigration officials say privately that this policy of employment authorization was introduced because women will work as live-in domestics only if they have no choice.' For example, landed immigrants admitted for employment in household service occupations invariably leave these jobs soon after their entry in Canada (Task Force on Immigration Practices and Procedures, 1981).

Thus from the point of view of the labour-importing countries and employers, migrant labour because of their juridical weakness are 'ideal' workers. They are imported when needed, and sent back home when the work is done. The national state through control of borders assures a flexible labour force and with each rotation a renewed and healthy pool of workers is imported to do the arduous back-breaking work. As Berger and Mohr (1975: 137-8) state:

> migrant workers fill a labour shortage in a specifically convenient way. . .a labour reserve, which can be laid off during recessions and brought in when the economy is expanding. If a large part of the labour reserve is made up of migrant workers they can be 'imported' when needed and 'exported' (sent home) when made temporarily redundant.

These migrants in the words of Berger and Mohr (1975: 64) are immortal: 'immortal because continually interchangeable. They are not born; they are not brought up; they do not age; they do not get tired; they do not die. They have a single function—to work.' Access to off-shore workers assures an almost infinite supply of labour. The workers on non-immigrant work authorizations may be characterized as a 'bonded forced-rotational' system of labour procurement (Bohning, 1974; North, 1980).

In addition to contractual migrant labour, illegal (criminalized) workers are an additional source of farm labour. These workers face consistent intimidation and harassment by both the employers and the state agencies. Their 'criminal' status and the corresponding ever-present threat of deportation places them in a defenceless position conducive to super-exploitation. As Sassen-Koob (1980: 70) states: 'Border enforcement is a mechanism facilitating the extraction of surplus labour by assigning criminal status to a segment of the working class—the illegal immigrants.' This point is also emphasized by Kreckel: 'Being officially criminalized, no open strategies of defence are available to them. The cheapness of their labour is their only "asset" ' (Kreckel, 1989: 543).

Thus, agricultural wage labour is primarily composed of indigenous transient workers-without-options, recently arrived immigrants, migrant, and illegal workers. Because of low wages, often the labour of the whole family is required to earn subsistence wages. Women, children, and very old adult members of the family work in fields to earn subsistence. Employers, consequently, exploit the labour of the whole family. As a large segment of the agricultural labour force is composed of racial minorities, racial discrimination and prejudice makes them even more vulnerable. Being defined as 'undesirable immigrants'—socially stigmatized—these workers can be subjected to working conditions which are not socially acceptable for other labour, conditions associated with work at the bottom of the labour market. As Portes and Borocz (1989: 621) state: 'Manual labour migrants arriving in contexts in which their kind are unwelcomed or discriminated against tend to be channelled toward the lower tier of the receiving labour market.' Workers in the lower tier and secondary sector 'are often hired according to racial, ethnic or gender markers indicative of their labour market vulnerability, rather than according to their skills. In particular, immigrants in a tenuous legal status are frequently preferred for such jobs' (Portes and Borocz, 1989: 621).

Additionally, farmworkers lack any union organization and are not protected under labour relations legislation, Workers' Compensation Board regulations, and health and safety regulations which may be available to workers in other sectors. This, combined with the factors discussed earlier, render these workers a powerless, subordinate segment of the labour force.

The interest of the employers lies in procuring not only low-cost labour, but also labour that can be consumed under specific conditions. These conditions have to do with the organization and the control of the production process. The institutionalization of this control varies with the nature of the production process. In the case of low-cost labour, management's control rests primarily on the powerlessness of the workers (Sassen-Koob, 1980). Foreign workers because of their tenuous political and legal status and its associated powerlessness assume special significance for the employers. As Sassen-Koob (1980: 27) states: 'Immigrant workers can then be seen as one basic factor in the reproduction of low-wage, powerless labour supply, and not simply as a quantitative addition to cheap workers.' The transient and temporary workforce lacks bargaining power (The Law Union of Ontario, 1981: 115) and employers in this country have access to this 'captive and powerless labour force' (Economic Council of Canada, 1978: 126).

Agricultural labour is in many respects a sub-proletarianized, marginalized, and subordinate segment of the working class. The marginal working class, Leggett (1968: 14) writes, 'refers to a sub-community of workers who belong to a subordinate ethnic or racial group which is unusually proletarianized and highly segregated'. Oppenheimer (1974: 10) defines sub-proletarian labour as 'unskilled, physically exhausting and uncomfortable (as in a hot kitchen, stoop labour) work utilizing a minimum of machinery. . .unionization tends not to exist, hence there is a low level of job, wage and safety protection. . .'.

To be subordinated means to be 'disadvantaged with regard to the labour market or labour process in comparison with another group of workers' (Barrera, 1979: 39). While labour market segmentation exists by race, class, gender, and occupation, Oppenheimer argues that there is an equally serious segmentation of the working class due to the existence at the bottom of the blue collar life of a permanent group of 'sub-proletarians' whose working conditions are so markedly different from that of even many unskilled manual workers. Oppenheimer (1974: 7-8) also states that in the Western world this 'sub-proletariat correlated closely with the populations that are dark-skinned, and that the work engaged in by the sub-proletariat is regarded by that particular society at that particular moment as the least desirable, the "dirtiest" '. Agricultural 'dirty' work in many countries is now performed by 'dark-skinned' foreign workers (Martin, 1985).

Ironically, while these sub-proletarianized, marginalized, subordinated, and powerless workers are indispensable for the production of fruit, vegetables and other food commodities which are essential for a nation's health and nutrition, they themselves suffer from a vast range of work-related health risks.

Work Conditions and Health Risks

During the past few decades there have been tremendous changes in agricultural production processes. The capitalization and mechanization of the agricultural sector are accompanied by improved methods of cultivation, intensive farming, and increased use of chemicals, all contributing to increased production and efficiency in agriculture. Agricultural production is also increasingly dependent upon hired, seasonal, and migrant labour (Coye, 1985). This structural transformation of agricultural production has mixed blessings. For instance, while the use of chemicals has substantially contributed to an increase in agricultural production, it also poses numerous health risks for farmers and farmworkers; when some of these chemicals end up in the food chain, the health of the whole population is threatened. While the structural transformation of agricultural production has produced a number of other social and economic contradictions (Bolaria, Dickinson, Wotherspoon, 1991) the focus here is on the health effects of agricultural production.

Numerous studies indicate that farmworkers and their families have poor health status, which is reflected in such indicators as life expectancy and mortality (Rust, 1990; Coye, 1985; Sakala, 1987). A number of factors contribute to this ill health: chemicals, intensification of farm work, ramshackle housing, low wages, non-existent sanitation facilities, and long hours of arduous labour.

In any discussion of the health risks in agricultural production, the chemical industry occupies a central place. There has been a tremendous increase in use of chemicals in agriculture (Bird and Rapport, 1986). While these chemicals control pests such as insects and weeds, they also pose environmental hazards. As Bird and Rapport (1986: 174) state: 'some of these pesticides are known to be highly persistent, mobile and bio-accumulative and have already been associated with adverse ecological or human health effects'. The human cost of the use of agricultural chemicals has been severe. It is estimated that each year they are responsible for 10,000 deaths and the acute poisoning of 400,000 people in the Third World (Rogers *et al.*, 1988: 284). These health hazards are not confined to the Third World. Agricultural workers in Canada and the United States face extensive chemical exposure and associated health risks (Matsqui, Abbotsford Community Services, 1982; Strigini, 1982; Stubbs *et al.*, 1984; Barthel, 1981). The 1982 survey of 270 farmworkers by the Matsqui, Abbotsford Community Services revealed that they are exposed to dangerous pesticides:

– 8 out of 10 farmworkers regularly suffer from direct contact with pesticides and a majority (55%) have been directly sprayed;
– 8 out of 10 farmworkers have had to work immediately after a spraying;
– over a quarter have had their living quarters sprayed with pesticides;
– 7 out of 10 farmworkers became physically ill after a direct spraying, yet only 3% received medical help provided by their employers;
– almost one-fifth frequently breathe pesticide fumes while working.

Many of the workers spend long hours in the fields and therefore have prolonged periods of exposure to pesticides. As many of the pesticides are carcinogenic, farmworkers suffer from many ill effects of exposure to spraying. The Matsqui study revealed that 90% of the workers had experienced one or more symptoms of pesticide spraying (Matsqui, Abbotsford Community Services, 1982). For instance,

– 44% suffered skin rashes;
– 47% suffered itching;
– 50% reported headaches;
– 35% experienced dizziness;
– 17% suffered from gastro-intestinal problems;
– almost 60% of the children working in the fields experienced the same sorts of symptoms;
– almost half reported various central nervous system disorders;
– 1 out of 5 had missed work due to work-related health problems.

The majority of the workers did not speak the English language and many of them did not receive information or instructions on health hazards of pesticides. A vast majority (over 80%) ate their lunches in the sprayed field areas. One writer has commented that 'the living and working conditions of Canadian farm labourers (especially in BC's Fraser Valley) bear a closer resemblance to those of Third World peasants than to those of the average Canadian worker (Labonté, 1982-83: 6). Also, the pesticide safety regulations are either non-existent or not enforced. There is continued use of pesticides that have never been adequately tested for safety and cases of severe pesticide poisoning and death are not uncommon. Labonté describes one of these cases.

> One of these involved a twenty-year-old man who, after two hospital admissions within a month for poisonings, was re-admitted in a life-threatening comatose state that persisted for six days. It was caused by the ingestion of the extremely lethal organophosphate, methamidophos (tradename Monitor), and the highly toxic fungicide, donoseb (tradename Top-Killer). The medical health officer investigating the case, according to a story in the October 9 Vancouver *Sun*, 'is leaning towards the theory that behavioural changes caused by gradual exposure to toxic pesticides may be the only mystery of why Deol (the farmworker) consumed the chemical'. Deol died four weeks later, never regaining consciousness, a day after the BC Medical Association joined the Canadian Farmworkers Union and other organizations in calling for better regulatory safeguards. (Labonté, 1982-83: 6-7)

Studies of farmworkers in the United States also pointed to the grim health status of farmworkers. Their life expectancy is 20% less than the average American and the infant mortality among their children is 60% above the national average (US Congress, 1972). Other evidence from the US indicates that 'Farmworkers have an injury rate due to toxic chemicals almost three times as high as injuries of all types for workers in other industries', and 'Farmworkers lost twice as many hours due to pesticide-related illnesses than hours lost by manufacturing workers due to all causes' (BC Human Rights Commission, 1983: 22). Migrant workers in the United States have a life expectancy of only forty-nine years. Eitzen and Zinn (1989: 456) state that 'this low rate is a consequence of living in poverty or near poverty and, most significant, the exposure to herbicides and pesticides sprayed on the fields where they work.'

Farmworkers' direct exposures to chemicals have quite serious health consequences. For instance, Temik, a pesticide used to control potato bugs, is associated with a higher number of miscarriages for pregnant women and increased rates of stomach cancer (Freudenberg, 1989). Other chemicals are associated with cancer, sterility, and other ill effects (Chase *et al.*, 1973; Epstein, 1979; Freudenberg, 1989; Kahn, 1976; Milvay and Wharton, 1980).

In the face of all the ill effects of pesticides, the 'agrichem' business continues to flourish and use of many pesticides continues without their having been properly tested and in some cases when they are known to be carcinogenic (Goff and Reasons, 1986; BC Human Rights Commission, 1983).

The deplorable working conditions of both domestic transient farm labour and migrant imported workers are well documented (Sanderson, 1974; Labonté, 1980, 1982; Sandborn, 1983; Canada, Department of Manpower and Immigration, 1973; Report of the Special Committee on Visible Minorities in Canadian Society, 1984; Sharma, 1982; Kelly, 1983; BC Human Rights Commission, 1983). Workers and their families are often exposed to harmful substances on the farms. There is inadequate or non-enforcement of the Health Act regulations concerning physical danger, occupational diseases, pesticides, and a high risk of injury. Farmworkers are also not fully and adequately protected by minimum wage legislation, working hours, and overtime wages (Report of the Special Committee on Visible Minorities in Canadian Society, 1984). Both the living and working conditions of farm labour contribute to their ill health. In 1973 a federal task force report on seasonal migrant farmworkers uncovered instances of 'child labour, sick, pregnant, and otherwise unfit adults working in the fields; and of entire families working with only the head of the family being paid' (Sanderson, 1974: 405). The task force was 'shocked, alarmed, and sickened' at the working conditions, wage levels, malnutrition, non-existent health facilities, and people living in 'indescribable squalor' (Canada, Department of Manpower and Immigration, 1973: 17; Sanderson, 1974).

The task force uncovered many cases of violations of the Immigration Act, the Child Labour Act, human rights, and minimum sanitation standards. The employers, of course, benefit from family labour and are 'delighted' to have foreign workers with large families (Canada, Manpower and Immigration, 1973).

The working and living conditions of farmworkers in British Columbia are similar to the conditions which minority workers face in Ontario. Farmworkers in British Columbia receive low wages, face exploitation due to the labour contracting system, work long hours, receive no overtime pay or benefits, work in unhealthy conditions, lack toilet or drinking water facilities on many farms, live in crowded and dangerous shacks, and are exposed to chemicals and pesticides in the field (Sharma, 1982; Canadian Farmworkers Union, 1980; Labonté, 1980, 1982-83; Kelly, 1983).

The entire family works and 'lives' in the fields. Families live in crowded, unhealthy and unsanitary accommodations—lacking proper wash-up facilities and clean drinking water. Often there are no toilet or drinking water facilities on the farm for the workers (Sharma, 1982). In some cases workers have to pay high rents for 'housing accommodations' provided by the farmers. These 'accommodations' are usually small, overcrowded and unhealthy firetraps without in-unit bathrooms or running water (Sharma, 1982: 13). A survey of 270 farmworkers in 1982 revealed that a large proportion of the accommodations (about 80%) had no proper wash-up facilities and 44% had no access at all to shower facilities (Matsqui, Abbotsford Community Services, 1982).

Mothers are forced to work to support their families, and daycare facilities are lacking. Incidents of children's deaths by drowning—in a bucket of drinking water in the shacks, or in unfenced ponds—have been reported (Sharma, 1982; Sharma, 1983). The Coroner's Jury which, in August 1980, investigated the death of a child who rolled off a bunk and drowned in a water bucket, recommended that immediate steps be taken to establish standards for farm labour housing. The irony is, however, that existing standards, established in 1946, are not being enforced (BC Human Rights Commission, 1983).

Both British Columbia (Canada) and the State of Washington (US) during the past few years offered illustrations of the continuous health risks and mortality faced by children.

– In 1988, Binh Thanh Hoang, 9, is left alone in a parked car on a Matsqui, BC, farm where his mother is picking raspberries. He is killed when the car rolls down an embankment.
– That September, Joel Campos, 14, is cutting vines in a hops field in Moxee, Washington. He falls asleep in a furrow and is crushed to death by a truck.
– Dina Pedro, 7, drowns in an uncovered and unfenced tank of pesticide on a Saanich, BC, farm.
– A child under 10 is killed crossing a road to work in a Washington asparagus field.
– Gurjit Pejatta, 8, his brother, Sumin, 9, and Boota Bassi, 10, all drown in a pond in Aldergrove, BC, in 1980. The parents are picking berries on a nearby farm. A few miles further up the Fraser Valley, an infant, Sukhdeep Madhar, rolls off a cot in a farmworker cabin and drowns in a bucket of water (MacQueen, 1990: B1).

Farmworkers are not covered under the Workers' Compensation Board (WCB) regulations. The BC government in May 1982 had decided to protect farmworkers through such measures as WCB inspection of farms, safety standards, and pesticide control. However, the government reversed its plan in March 1983 to extend WCB regulations regarding health and safety to farm labour. This decision came during a Coroner's Jury inquest into the pesticide poisoning death of a farmworker. The Jury ruled that the death was 'preventable homicide' (18 March 1983; Pynn, 1983; Koch, 1983). The extension of the WCB regulations to farmworkers was opposed by the BC Federation of Agriculture on the grounds that it would be costly, unrealistic, and impractical (Victoria *Times-Colonist*, 12 March 1983). Failure of legal protection in this case greatly affects racial minority workers.

As noted above, agricultural workers fare badly in regard to general living conditions. Unsanitary, unsafe, and overcrowded accommodations combined with long hours of arduous work tend to produce ill health. Insecure and depressing working conditions; social and environmental deprivations; racial subordination; long-distance migrations and uprooting from stable traditional cultures and disruption of stable community ties, all contribute toward psychological distress and mental disorders (Doyal and Pennell, 1979; Eyer, 1984; Waldron *et al.*, 1982). Kuo and Tsai (1986: 133) state:

> an excessive amount of social stress among immigrants—resulting from social isolation, cultural conflicts, poor social integration and assimilation, role changes and identity crisis, low socioeconomic status, racial discrimination—has led to a high prevalence of ill health and psychological impairment among them.

It should be noted that the health hazards in the fields vary according to the type of farming. In addition to exposure to various chemicals, farmers and farmworkers have excessive exposure to commercial solvents, sunlight, and heat. Those who work with animals are at risk of bacterial and viral infections (George, 1976). Prairie farmers and farmworkers suffer from serious lung diseases, particularly those who handle wet or mouldy grains and hay. The most common lung diseases are Farmer's Lung due to inhalation of mouldy grain dust; grain dust asthma; and Silo Filler's Lung. Respiratory problems are likely to be higher among farmers and farmworkers who handle wet and mouldy grains or hay. These episodes are even higher among those who work with inadequate equipment for drying and storing grains and hay. Small and less profitable farms are likely to have inadequate equipment. It is also on these farms that wives and other family members who assist in farm work, and whose labour is essential to survival of the small farm units, are exposed to health hazards. Therefore, under these circumstances the incidence of respiratory and other symptoms associated with handling of mouldy and wet grains and hay are likely to be higher among the family members (George, 1976).

Chronic back injury is the most common occupational disease among farmworkers who work with short hoes. As Waitzkin (1983: 15) states, 'The short hoe's human toll is crippling back disease for thousands of farmworkers; the main injuries are slipped discs and degenerative arthritis of the spine.' Waitzkin (1983: 15) further states that 'these problems occur in younger workers who do stoop labour, and their physical effects are irreversible. Since migrant workers most often lack educational opportunities and frequently know little English, farmworkers' back usually means permanent economic disability.' Yet this is a preventable disease. Migrant workers are an easily replaceable workforce. A reserve army of migrants is available to replace workers who are crippled by back injuries or who resist conditions of their work. As Waitzkin (1983: 15) states: 'powerlessness resulted from lack of organization; individual farmworkers had no alternative to the crippling effects of the short hoe, because resistance meant loss of work.'

Farming in North America is the third most dangerous industry (Reasons *et al.*, 1981), and perhaps least protected in regard to acceptable labour standards. The intensification of farm work in association with farm machinery has increased the likelihood of being killed on the job (Sandborn, 1986; Ontario Task Force Report, 1985).

Summary and Conclusions

This chapter has discussed the linkages between agricultural production, work conditions, and health risks faced by farmworkers. Numerous studies indicate that agricultural production processes and work conditions contribute to health risks for farm labour. Both the living and working conditions of farm labour are 'dangerous to their health'. Unsafe and unsanitary living conditions and exposure to dangerous pesticides and other health hazards all contribute to their excessive physical health problems, injuries, and premature deaths. These living conditions are also damaging to workers' psychological health. Insecure and depressing working conditions, social isolation and racial subordination, all contribute to psychological stress. The health hazards vary according to the type of farming. For instance, those who work with animals are at risk of bacterial and viral infections. Other farmworkers suffer from serious lung diseases and chronic back injuries. Farmworkers are inadequately protected by labour relations legislation and health and safety regulations.

As a segment of the agricultural labour force is composed of racial minority and immigrant and migrant workers, mostly from the Third World, the higher accident and illness rates among them are often attributed to 'accident proneness' due to their cultural background and their inability to function in an industrial setting. However, evidence suggests that 'immigrants and indigenous workers tend to fall into separate categories with immigrant workers consistently filling the most dangerous jobs (Lee and Wrench, 1980: 563). Their job-related accidents have 'less to do with immigrants themselves than the tasks they perform and the environment in which they find themselves. The reasons are technical, rather than psychological or cultural' (Lee and Wrench, 1980: 563). For instance, the health problems of farmworkers have essentially nothing to do with their inability to function in an industrial setting: it has to do with their engaging in unprotected manual labour.

The lack of protection provided to farmworkers under the labour relations legislation and health and safety regulations might seem surprising at first glance, even if only because good health and physical fitness are important to maintain high worker productivity and a stable labour force. As Marx wrote, 'When capitalist production lengthens the hours of work, it shortens the lives of the workers.' However, employers' concern about workers' health depends upon the reproduction costs, availability and replaceability of the workforce. When labour is plentiful and can be easily replaced, employers will be less concerned about the health of the workers (Schatzkin, 1978). Access to offshore workers assures an almost infinite supply of labour. Workers who become ill are 'sent home' and can be easily replaced by healthy workers at little or no cost to the employers or the state. Health screening tests assure the supply of physically fit immigrant labour.

In conclusion, it is argued that the greater exploitation of farm labour and their health status is to be understood in the context of objective vulnerability of this labour force and agricultural production. The health, health care, and safety of the worker is to be analyzed in the context of class relations and the organization of the labour process.

CHAPTER FIFTEEN

THE CAPITALIST STATE AND FARM LABOUR POLICY

JOHN SHIELDS

This chapter examines the political economy of social class relations at the point of primary agricultural production — on the farm. Analysts of labour movements in North America have centred their attention upon the rather straightforward class antagonism that exists between urban capital and the industrial working class. But the position of the farmworker in modern capitalism is particularly intriguing since it is more complex. The pattern of class interests and struggles in the agricultural sector takes on at least a three tiered form, with paid farm labour on the bottom, agribusiness on top, and the farmer sandwiched in between. In the first part of the twentieth century, independent agricultural commodity producers were the major force behind mass protest movements and political change in Canada. In the class struggle of farmers, however, the role of paid farm labour has tended to be neglected.

Consider the place of the rural proletariat in the agrarian class structure. A central question is why paid agricultural labourers have been the most legally and socially dispossessed workers in North America. In order to begin to answer this question it is necessary to document not only the estrangement which has developed between the class interests of farm labourers and

John Shields is an Assistant Professor at Ryerson Polytechnical Institute in Toronto. All views expressed herein are the author's, although he would like to thank Hawley Neuert for critically reviewing this text.

farmers, and the subordinate position both of these classes occupy in relation to agribusiness, but also the state's role in sustaining this exploitative relationship. The key to comprehending the state's role, we argue, lies in the Canadian government's long-term policy of promoting 'cheap food'.

While the discussion which follows is applicable to Canadian agriculture as a whole, it highlights developments in the fruit, vegetable and tobacco farm sectors of British Columbia and Ontario. The province of British Columbia registers, per capita, the greatest use of farm labour and is where the strongest efforts to unionize farmworkers have occurred, while Ontario houses the largest number of farms in Canada. By focusing on these sectors we can begin to gain some insight about why farm labour has been systematically discriminated against by the state, about the place farmers have come to occupy in this relation of class forces, and about the nature of the farmers' class struggle. Finally, we explore how agribusiness is linked to the farmer, and what interests it has with regard to farm labourers.

The Class Makeup of the Fruit, Vegetable and Tobacco Industry in British Columbia and Ontario

The Farmworkers

The single largest component of the Canadian workforce until the 1940s was located in the agricultural sector. Most of this sector was composed of 'farm operators whose ownership of land set them apart from traditional definitions of the working class', no matter that many of them have endured, in a material sense, conditions that paralleled those of the urban working class (Thompson and Seager, 1978: 153). Employment in farming has steadily decreased since the Second World War, constituting less than 4% of the Canadian labour force today. Furthermore, working in agriculture has undergone a structural change, with hired labour making up a greater share of the total. By 1983 wage labour made up 30% of the total hours of agricultural employment, whereas in 1961 it rested at only 18% (McEwan and Howard, 1989: 733).

The paid agricultural labourer can be said to be part of the working class. However, this rural proletariat has differed from its urban counterpart in a number of ways. The nature of the work has tended to be seasonal, transitory, low-paying, and dependent on 'marginal' domestic and/or immigrant workers. Moreover, in the industrial sector of the economy, wage/salary employment makes up over 90% of the workforce, while in the agricultural sector paid labour, even though it is becoming increasingly significant, constitutes only a minority fraction of labour performed.

The paid agricultural labourer has been relatively untouched by unionization efforts. Historically the labour movement and the political left have tended to view this group as unorganizable because the workers have been isolated on farms, and have largely seasonal employment patterns which necessitate that they have numerous employers in a year. The few attempts which have been made to organize such workers have occurred where their agricultural work has the character of industrial occupations (Thompson and Seager, 1978: 153).

For example, during the 1930s in southern Alberta the Beet Workers' Industrial Union was an active if short-lived force. This labour-intensive occupation, like the factory, provided a forum for close activity among workers, making organizing an easier task (Thompson and Seager, 1978: 153). In the United States the best known agricultural labourers' organization has been the United Farm Workers Union (UFWU), established in the early 1960s in California and most successful among the West Coast grape workers. Many of these workers were employed for ten months of the year, and their skills were relatively high. Consequently, stability in this labour force was closer to that in the industrial workforce than in those groups harvesting other crops (Hurd, 1974: 52).

Agricultural labour in an advanced capitalist country has been described as 'a form of labour directly dependent on the conditions of structural unemployment and its resulting social migration' (Beveridge and Condé, 1982: 319). The fact is that farmworkers are part of the working poor. The term 'super-exploitation' has been applied to their situation. Theoretically, the term refers to the reduction of wages to a level which falls below the necessary level for the production and reproduction of labour power (Dixon *et al.*, 1983: 11). Many members of the family or extended family unit must labour in the fields, including women, old people, and very young children, so that when their financial resources are pooled a meagre existence is possible.

Canada like most other countries has experienced a trend toward the concentration of land and capital by larger agricultural producers. The traditional farming unit which relied upon unpaid family labour is giving way to what might best be termed commercial family farming—a farming operation increasingly dependent upon employed labour, intensive capital investment, and the logic of the market. Commercial family farming is reflective of the long-term trend toward reduction in the number of farms and the increase in farm size.

A brief survey of some agricultural employment data is revealing. In British Columbia the trend toward the use of paid labour on the farm is most pronounced. In 1977, for instance, 47.6% of the agricultural labour force was waged (Select Standing Committee on Agriculture, 1979c: 22). Pynn estimates that there are about 16,000 full- and part-time farmworkers in BC (1983b: B8), most of them engaged on a seasonal basis in the cultivation and harvesting of fruit and vegetable crops in the Fraser and Okanagan valleys. Roughly 90% of paid farm labourers are new immigrants to BC, the majority being East Indians from the Punjab (Labonté, 1982b: 9), with some immigrants of Chinese origin. Some 60% of this total are women. In the Okanagan the great bulk of the seasonally hired labour force is drawn from a migratory group of young people mostly of Quebecois background (Bolaria and Li, 1985: 158).

In BC about half of farms report using at least some paid labour. The conclusion of the Select Committee on Agriculture is revealing: 'Paid workers in BC's primary agriculture are more significant to the agricultural workforce than in any other region of Canada. Primary agriculture is, therefore, relying less on farm families to produce food' (1979c: 26, 151).

Ontario farmers also utilized an above average amount of paid agricultural labour. In 1986 farmworkers constituted 40% of the labour force with about 41% of farms using this labour. Nearly 60,000 farmworkers, about half the Canadian total, were employed in the province in 1986, two-thirds of them seasonal employees. About 3,000 of these were migrant workers from Quebec and the Maritimes, and over 5,000 were 'guest workers' from the Caribbean and Mexico. The bulk of the seasonal wage labour force is found in fruit, vegetable, and tobacco operations. Ethnically, Ontario's farmworkers are considerably more diverse in their backgrounds than is the case in BC, with no one group predominating. Government employment agencies like the Canada Farm Labour Pool are responsible for nearly 33% of farmworker placements but the vast majority of recruitment is through personal contacts between farmers and local people, especially housewives and students (Ontario Task Force on Hours of Work and Overtime, 1987a: 18-21, 33-4).

According to Labonté, paid workers in BC earn an average of between $1.30 to $2.50 an hour. For six months of the year about 4,000 farmworkers, or 25% of the paid labour force, are housed in what can only be described as subhuman living accommodations (1982b: 10). In Ontario wage rates tend to be significantly below the industrial minimum wage, and living conditions are equally bleak. The common practice in harvesting pay is based on a piece-rate system. Farmers argue that the piece-rate system helps to increase productivity at harvest time when crops must be picked quickly before they perish. This of course necessitates that farmworkers labour exceptionally long hours, 10- to 12-hour days not being uncommon. Additionally, the piece-rate system frees the farmer from the necessity of supervision (Jhappan, 1983: 56).

The introduction of compulsory industrial-level minimum wages into agriculture would lead to the elimination of child labourers, a major source of seasonal farm labour, because of their low efficiency. Former federal Agriculture Minister Eugene Whelan noted the threat this would pose in these words: 'You can just imagine what it would cost for food in Canada without them; that's always been a part of farming' (Neilson and Christie, 1975: 351).

The exploitation of farmworkers has been further enhanced in BC through a labour contract system. Quite often farmworkers are hired through a third-party labour contractor. The contractor generally provides the labourer with transportation to and from the work site. The farmer pays the contractor who, in turn, pays the farmworker, minus a service charge of anywhere between 25% to 40% of the 'normal' wage. Bolaria and Li note that this contract system reinforces the depression of agricultural wages because contractors bid competitively with each other for jobs (1985: 159).

The utilization of a 'guest worker' program in Ontario is also of significance. Offshore migrant labour is used because of its dependability and due to labour shortages in highly skilled jobs necessary in such work as tobacco production. Interestingly, these migrant workers enjoy conditions and benefits more favourable than most domestically based agricultural labourers. This is due in large measure to the actions of Caribbean governments which demand that there be formal written contracts between farmers and guest workers. Moreover, these governments have supplied liaison officers who hear workers' complaints and act to represent their interests if a dispute arises with an employer. Contracts stipulate that the work term is to be no less than six weeks but no limit is set upon the hours in a day to be worked.

> The Ontario industrial minimum wage rate is required [$5 an hour] and must be paid for at least 40 hours each week whether or not work is done. The employer also provides adequate living accommodation and meals (or facilities for the workers to prepare their own meals). In addition, the employer pays most of the cost of return air transportation from the worker's home country to Canada and is responsible for transportation to and from the airport in Ontario. In return, the workers are expected to work diligently and safely and to maintain their living quarters in a clean condition. (Ontario Task Force on Hours of Work and Overtime, 1987a: 35-6)

Off-shore workers are particularly desired by many farmers because of their stability and productivity. Domestic farm labour has displayed a very high rate of turnover. One Ontario survey, for instance, found a 40% quit rate (Ontario Task Force on Hours of Work and Overtime, 1987a: 36). Thus, the reward for farmers in meeting improved pay and working conditions is a guarantee of a virtual inexhaustible supply of dependable labour (Neilson and Christie, 1975: 332).

Organizing farmworkers has been a difficult task. Linguistic, cultural, and ethnic barriers and divisions have often made organizing nearly impossible. The additional fact that sizeable numbers of workers are dependent upon on-site housing means that a 'feudal style of employer-employee relationship' can develop, frustrating unionization efforts (Jhappan, 1983: 49). Further, there often exists an over-supply of labour. This has been encouraged by the government's support of the importation of temporary foreign labour, which has traditionally served to hamper organizing attempts, especially since off-shore workers are not legally entitled to be organized. In BC, farmworkers were not covered under the Labour Relations Act until 1975. The Act provides protection from 'intimidation, dismissal or much worse if their employer dislikes their attempts to unionize' (Labonté, 1982: 11). In Ontario farmworkers are still excluded from Labour Relations Act protections and confront the full force of employer opposition.

Given the nature of farm work, success in organizing this segment of the proletariat will necessitate a departure from the traditional union organizational mould. Community unionism is a more appropriate model. This means that a farmworkers' union can not simply concern itself with standard industrial relations questions but must extend its interests to matters affecting workers beyond their labouring hours, such as housing, health, education, and the like. In short, the union must be actively engaged in working to improve the workers' total community. Moreover, because of the relatively weak position of farmworkers, the union must also enlist the support of outside, community-based groups to aid it in its struggle, through such activities as lobbying government and even orchestrating consumer boycotts which can become a major industrial weapon in the union's arsenal (Neilson and Christie, 1975: 344).

Farmworkers operate 'from a weak power base' and like other 'vulnerable' groups such as students, welfare recipients, and indigenous minorities, they have begun to react collectively in response to their marginal situations (Fields, 1982: 95). Farm labourers in BC and Ontario have been no exception to this, and in recent years have launched organizational drives. In the case of BC the ethnic homogeneity of much of this paid labour force in the Fraser Valley has proven to be a great strength in this pursuit, whereas in Ontario the heterogeneous ethnic makeup of the farm labour force has worked to frustrate organizing.

In March 1979, farmworker organizing began in BC with the establishment of the Farmworker Organizing Committee. In April 1980, the committee had re-formed itself into the Canadian Farmworkers' Union (CFU). Raj Chouhan, former president of the CFU, placed the union's membership at 1,200 or about 10% of the workforce in the early 1980s (Pynn, 1983: B8). Many of the traditional difficulties associated with organizing a seasonal workforce were overcome in BC because the union established itself in the East Indian community. As Ron Labonté observed: 'The simultaneous membership of BC farmworkers in two communities—an oppressed labour force and an oppressed ethnic in an alien land—has helped the CFU grow rapidly in one province' (1982: 11). The CFU in BC has concerned itself with the broader issues of farmworkers' lives and has consequently enjoyed some success in establishing community unionism. This was a strategy borrowed from the UFWU in California, which has emphasized its role as a Chicano union to entrench itself within this community (Hurd, 1974: 64-5).

The utility of this two-pronged strategy in no way lessens the importance of class in this setting. As E.P. Thompson has argued, class is a historical phenomenon, which is often as much a cultural as an economic and political process (Palmer, 1981: 70). Thus, East Indian farmworkers are potentially able to heighten their sense of class consciousness by visualizing their objective condition of exploitation through the prism of culture. In contrast, in the case of Ontario, the lack of a common cultural glue allowed the ethnic factor to be played against a common class interest.

In Ontario the CFU launched an organizational drive in the spring of 1981. They centred their efforts on the tobacco farms in the southwestern part of the province. This sector was chosen because the tobacco farms were among the most prosperous in the country, the work tended to be more highly skilled than required for many other crops, and the harvest period was the longest— conditions, in short, came closest to replicating those found in industrial settings. The CFU, however, quickly ran into formidable barriers, namely ethnic divisions which were played upon by hostile farmers and legislative exclusion from the protections of the Ontario Labour Relations Act (Beveridge and Condé, 1982: 321, 323). In May 1983 the CFU was forced to concede defeat and close down its Ontario office (Stultz, 1987: 295). Organizing agricultural workers in Ontario has been in virtual hibernation since.

The formation of the CFU in British Columbia, however, gave the farmworkers a force which had never existed before. It has struck for and won farm contracts, fought to ensure that farmworkers are not cheated by government, farmers, or labour contractors, and struggled at the political level to change discriminatory labour laws which exclude them from coverage. These include in BC the Payment of Wages Act, child labour laws, workers' compensation, maternity protection laws and others (Glavin, 1980: 19).

Since 1983 union membership in the CFU has fallen off and, while it has begun to recover, it still rested in 1988 at only a quarter of its early 1980s membership numbers (BC Ministry of Labour and Consumer Services, 1988: 41). The decline can be accounted for by the generalized legislative attack on organized labour which began in BC in late 1983. While all unions in the province have experienced declines in membership, the smallest unions, such as the CFU, have faced the brunt of the attack (see Shields, 1989). What is amazing is that such a small union with extremely limited resources has been able to survive at all to carry on its struggle in this hostile legislative environment.

The Farmers

Historically, farming has been a major component of the Canadian economy and Ontario has housed one of the most significant segments of this economy. In 1982, for instance, primary agriculture production generated $3 1/3 billion worth of value, making it the single most important natural resource in the province; only Saskatchewan produced more wealth from farming (Dyck, 1986: 263-4). Over the years agriculture's importance to the creation of Ontario's wealth has declined relative to other industries, such as manufacturing and services. Today the farm population of Ontario represents less than 4%

of the labour force. But while the number of farms has decreased dramatically, farm efficiency has risen significantly. Between 1941 and 1975 the physical volume of agricultural production more than doubled (Rea, 1985: 134). Still, most of the value of agriculture to Ontario's economy comes in the form of value added to the product once it leaves the farm gate. In fact the agrifood industry, defined here as only food processors, produces about 7% of the province's GDP, making it the second most important industry after automotive manufacturing (Skogstad, 1990: 59, 87).

While farming in most of the settled areas of Canada formed a major segment of the labour force earlier in the century, this is not so for British Columbia. In 1941 it constituted 13.1%; by 1961 this figure had fallen to only 4% (Robin, 1978: 32) and by 1984 it was only 2.8% of the BC labour force (BC Ministry of Agriculture and Food, 1985: calculated from Table 4:6). And yet agriculture has been important to the economy of the province. While only a very small percentage of British Columbia's land mass is suitable for agriculture, it is among the richest and most productive areas in the country. In fact, if agriculture is viewed in a larger context to include the 'food industry' in general (farming, food processing, wholesaling, and retailing) it ranks second in the BC economy (behind the wood industry) and generates about 22% of the province's economic activity (Warnock, 1986: 150).

BC farmers were remarkably untouched by the waves of farmer protest and populism that swept other parts of the Canadian countryside in the early twentieth century. In part this was due to the mixed nature of BC farming; it differed from the wheat monoculture of the prairies, which served to galvanize a sustained protest and unity (see Macpherson, 1977). Furthermore, the BC farmer was relatively wealthy and carried a considerably smaller debt load than his prairie counterpart, due in part to the nature of the crops and the favourable climatic conditions which prevented crop failure. Even the Great Depression had a 'relatively' mild effect on these farmers (Robin, 1968: 342). In addition, the gentlemen farmers from Great Britain who settled in the Okanagan and southern Vancouver Island (Hutchison, 1965: 291) were hardly a fertile base for a populist movement.

Farmers in Ontario, by contrast, were swept up in populist fervour and abandoned, if only briefly, their support for the old two-party system. In 1919 the United Farmers of Ontario (UFO) took over the reins of government with the aid of the Independent Labour Party (ILP). The goals of the UFO were political and social reform, along with the aim of the promotion of Christian rural values. Internal divisions with the UFO, along with conflicts with the ILP over such matters as the eight-hour day, brought the defeat of the government in the subsequent provincial election in 1923 (Dyck, 1986: 279-80). Once again the diversified nature of farming, dependence on local rather than export markets, and the relative prosperity of Ontario farmers worked to unglue radical populist tendencies in the countryside and reinforced more traditional political values and the belief in the 'free market'.

In Canada, the farmer has traditionally operated as an independent capitalist-producer, owning his own land and farm equipment, and providing the labour to run the farm almost exclusively out of his own family unit. In social class terms, the farmer is part of the petite bourgeoisie.

In 1984, the average net worth of the Canadian farmer (total assets minus debt) stood at $417,851, which was nearly ten times the net worth of the average family in Canada. In order to earn a living, the farmer must invest nearly half a million dollars (Fisher, 1986: 26). Farmers today, with their extensive use of farm machinery and wage labour, find themselves in a position of greater isolation and independence from other farmers. The farmer no longer plays the simple role of 'independent producer' but has become a boss over labour. Increasingly, farmers perceive themselves as farmer-businessmen operating in the farm industry. Productivity and efficiency have become the key words in agriculture today and this orientation has transformed traditional agrarian values. What distinguishes the family farm from the industrial farm is that labour is primarily carried out by wage workers (Pfeffer, 1983: 38). If we accept this depiction, then we must conclude that farming in BC and Ontario is becoming increasingly industrial. This new status cannot but affect the farmer's political consciousness (Mitchell, 1975: 15, 26).

The equation of the farmer with capital must, however, be tempered. Clearly, farmers occupy an intermediate class location between labour and agribusiness. But this middle position does not mean they are 'independent' commodity producers. Wallace Clement seriously questions whether farmers in North America were ever a class that warranted this label. He notes that they have never been 'independent' in any true sense of the word, as large-scale capital has been. Farmers do enjoy one key freedom, freedom from wage labour. But, aside from this, capital has dominated them to a considerable extent. Farmers retain the individual ownership of their farming operations but the real economic control remains with capital; 'in other words, the dependent commodity producer becomes an extension of capitalism' (Clement, 1983: 227, 242).

Several years ago there was a good deal of speculation that farming operations would be taken over by large corporations (for instance see Burbach and Flynn, 1980). And while there has, over time, been a increase in the size of farms, corporate farming has never become the dominant mode of agricultural production. Corporate farms represent only the tiniest fraction of total farm operations in Canada. The fact is that in most instances it is not profitable enough for agribusiness to own farms directly; there is simply far too much risk in farming and far too little return on investment for the capital expenditure. However, agribusiness can integrate itself into farming in another way, namely through production contract arrangements with farmers. In short, food processors sign contracts with independent producers which commit the farmers to sell all their produce to the said processors for an agreed upon price. In this way processors are able to secure, well in advance, crops for their plants while the farmer is still left with most of the risks of farming. This contract system is especially dominant in Ontario among vegetable growers (Ontario Ministry of Agriculture and Food, 1972: 56). The system firmly integrates the producers of crops into corporate agriculture.

During the first part of this century, farmers directed their 'political demands to the marketing side of agriculture rather than the "cost of production" side'. This was in part due to the more visibly exploitative dealings with farmers which these agencies had because of their powerful abilities to affect price and marketing conditions (Mitchell, 1975: 14). The changing nature of agriculture today has shifted this focus. Because contemporary North American farmers are caught in a cost-price squeeze, their concern is no longer so heavily with the prices crops will yield, but also with increasing input costs. The decision of whether or not to harvest is based, after all, on two basic factors, the market price of the crop and the cost of harvesting the crop. At each of these levels the grower has made attempts to control costs and prices. On the one hand, we have witnessed the growth of co-operative selling agencies and marketing boards (discussed below). On the cost side, while the prices of farm machinery and other goods and services from the capitalist sector have largely been beyond the control of farmers, their own labour costs have not. The importance of keeping down labour costs increases as farmers' ability to spend more on the other capital investments increases and profit rises as a result (Weiner, 1978: 182).

This is evident when one considers the increase in the use of paid agricultural labour in the production of labour-intensive crops such as fruits, vegetables and tobacco. In the case of BC, wages represent the rapidly rising second largest component of farm operating expenses. In 1977, wages accounted for 14.9% of operating expenses but by 1983-84 they came to represent 19.7%. Only interest on debt in 1983-84 cost the farmer more—20.6% (BC Ministry of Agriculture and Food, 1977 and 1984b: 10, 17). And in BC's fruit and vegetable production wages are estimated to comprise up to 60% of farm costs (BC Ministry of Agriculture and Food, 1984a: 1). In Ontario, as well, wages are the third most costly operating expense, comprising 14.9% of the total in 1988 (Ontario Ministry of Agriculture and Food, 1989: viii). In the labour-intensive Ontario fruit, vegetable, and tobacco farms, labour costs made up a significantly larger segment of total farm costs. By comparison, for Canadian farmers as a whole, wages in 1980 ranked as the fifth major cost and absorbed only 8.8% of farm expenses (Agriculture Canada, 1981: 17). However, between 1981 and 1987 wages were an increasingly significant factor of production, increasing by 30% between these dates; only the cost of pesticides increased more (Statistics Canada, 1989: 9-15).

Furthermore, there is a very strong economic interest on the part of farmers to retain control over production. An organized agricultural labour force would, of course, threaten this. Moreover, enhancement of state protective legislation for farmworkers could add significant costs to the farmers' production bill. For instance, increased legislative control over farmworker health and safety would mean not only extra expenditures for safety education and the provision of protective equipment, but could lead to production disruption as well. Workers would have to leave the fields during pesticide spraying; it could be days after spraying before workers could 'safely' re-enter the fields and continue their labour. Some pesticides may have to be discontinued because they are too dangerous. Such eventualities would place worker health and safety in a more prominent position, at the cost of certain production requirements. In a sector as sensitive as agriculture, where even short-term delays can often mean the difference between success and disaster, such considerations become extremely important. It is, of course, neither in the interests of farmers nor agribusiness to see such legislation enacted.

Marketing boards and co-operatives constitute a major part of the growers' selling strategy. Both of these institutions are controlled by producers themselves, with no attempt to draw representation from other sectors of the industry (Select Standing Committee on Agriculture, 1979d: 36). Marketing boards and co-operatives serve essentially as central selling agencies but in fact pose no real threat to the corporate-controlled food industry. They even provide the service of 'guaranteeing the processing firms a steady supply of the basic food product'. These agencies provide farmers 'with a better chance to obtain a reasonable price'. The fact is, however, that they are selling in 'a highly concentrated market, with only a few major buyers' (Warnock, 1978: 261-2). In Ontario, for instance, over 80% of its farmers rely upon provincial food, beverage, and tobacco industries to purchase their products. The lack of farmer clout in the market was a stimulant to the creation of marketing boards in the first place. The farmers' reliance on a few key buyers has established a clear system of dependency, one which seems to have infected the farmers' own ideology. The prevailing attitude among agricultural producers is that their well-being is inseparably linked to the health of the agribusiness industry, an attitude which has operated 'to undermine the development of a "we/them" attitude which could foster a general farm organizational development'. In fact the reality in Ontario has been more of a fragmentation between different commodity producers, with each of these groups linking their interests with the industries that buy their products (Skogstad, 1990: 62).

The power of marketing boards is further compromised by the fact that most food products have such low tariffs that they are subject to intense competition from US farmers and low-wage countries, which serves to undermine the position of domestic growers. When we couple this with the fact that chain supermarkets often 'use fresh non-processed foods as loss leaders', we can understand that such circumstances do not place marketing boards or co-operatives in a position to set prices (Warnock, 1978: 263).

The attempt by some producers, such as the Okanagan fruit growers, to move into processing, with the establishment of Sun-Rype Ltd., has netted the growers some financial gain. Such moves are, on the other hand, far from a formidable threat to agribusiness. They have in fact tended to develop in instances where there was a lack of an industrial purchaser for the farm product. These developments, however, do reinforce and make concrete the position of the growers as farmer-businessmen.

Agribusiness

There has been a virtual revolution since World War II in how North American food is produced, distributed, and eaten. The chain supermarket has replaced the small independent grocery store as the prime supplier of consumer food needs; hosts of new food items crowd grocery store shelves; and food in general undergoes a far greater level of processing, packaging, and handling than before. This development has dramatically altered in the manner in which the consumer food dollar is divided. Between 1949 and 1977 the farmers' share of the retail food dollar has fallen from 60% to 38% (Warnock 1976: 53; Agriculture Canada, 1977: 8). While prices have risen along with this distribution change, the fact is that the farmers' return per pound of product has dropped relatively. It is only through an increase in the size and efficiency of the farm that the producer has been able to maintain his position. It is agribusiness which has grown and reaped the lion's share of the benefits of this process.

The agribusiness industry can be divided into two broad categories: first, the farm supply sector which provides farmers with the goods and services necessary to run their operations, and secondly, the food, beverage and tobacco industry, which purchases the farmers' products and then processes, packages, and markets them (Mitchell, 1975: 100-1). The fruit and vegetable processing industry in Canada has become increasingly dominated by about seven large and predominately American-based conglomerate firms (Warnock, 1978).

While discussing the food industry in national terms may be appropriate when looking at Ontario, since the conglomerates all tend to be active in this large provincial market, it can be misleading in understanding the operation of the food system in other parts of the country. The fact is that many of the food and beverage industries enjoy no national market but rather are organized on a regional basis. Consequently the region often becomes a much more useful unit of analysis. If we adopt this perspective, concentration becomes much higher than national figures would lead us to suppose (Warnock, 1976: 69). In British Columbia the vegetable and fruit processing industry has been primarily concentrated into four leading firms, namely York Farms Ltd, Fraser Valley Frosted Foods Ltd, Empress Foods Ltd (Canada Safeway) and Sun-Rype Ltd. Together their sales constituted 59.7% of the BC total between 1972 and 1976, and 81.4% of the industry's profits. The profit figure is, in fact, an understatement of the dominance of the three leading private firms, since Sun-Rype, as a co-operative, makes no profit (Select Standing Committee on Agriculture, 1979a: 114).

Canada Safeway, a subsidiary of Safeway Ltd of America, controls the retail grocery market in BC ('Safeway Canada', 1973: 10). And recently it has strengthened its hold on the western market by its purchase of Woodward's Food Floors (*Globe and Mail*, 24 December 1986). In BC all the other supermarkets, especially Overwaitea and Super-Valu, closely watch the prices that Safeway sets and attempt to establish their prices accordingly (Select Standing Committee on Agriculture, 1979b: 160). Clearly Safeway is the trendsetter in the retail trade. The chain supermarkets are, in most cases, vertically integrated into the food wholesaling and processing functions. In Ontario there are a few more actors in the grocery retailing market but in 1988 five major chains nevertheless controlled over 66% of the market (Ontario Ministry of Agriculture and Food, 1989: 21). The tobacco industry complements this general pattern, having long been monopolized by a few giant corporations.

Of course, at the farm supply level, the market is a highly monopolized sector. In terms of farm machinery sales, the market has been dominated by a few companies, namely International Harvester, John Deere, Massey-Ferguson, and Ford Motor Co. (Warnock, 1975: 39). Herbicides, insecticides, and fungicides 'are produced and sold by the agricultural departments of huge foreign chemical corporations which dominate Canada': Uniroyal, I.C.I., Sherwin-Williams, Allied Chemical Corporation, and Dow Chemical ('Safeway Canada', 1973: 16).

It is not difficult to reach the conclusion that agribusiness in Canada is increasingly becoming ever more concentrated. Also, it is clear that there is a good deal of vertical integration in the industry, especially between the retail and wholesale levels. This increasing monopolization of the industry has by and large meant market domination by foreign, primarily American, multinationals.

The Government Policy of Cheap Food

While the federal and provincial governments both play important and active roles with respect to Canadian agriculture policy, in the British Columbia and Ontario cases their general policy on agriculture does not significantly diverge or conflict (Skogstad, 1990: 70). In the prairies, the role of provincial governments would no doubt have to be clearly distinguished from that of the federal since, at important junctures of these provinces' histories, agrarian populist movements formed provincial governments. The prairies, unlike BC or Ontario, have a long-established history of conflict with the central authorities over agrarian policy, so in the case of the latter provinces it is possible to address the question in broader terms.

Merle Weiner observed that industrial and agrarian class conflict in America displayed many similarities, but possessed a striking difference. While both conflicts involved militant and often violent struggles, on the industrial front the end result was generally a 'shifting in the balance of formal power in favour of the workers involved'. Urban industrial labour was able to win a place for itself in the system, recognized both by capital and the state as a force which needed to be bargained with, and accommodated with important reforms, including organizing and striking rights as well as a host of other protective legislation. In the agrarian sector, however, farmworkers' struggles for such rights were on the whole a failure. Weiner maintains that no one factor prevented agricultural labour from winning victories comparable to the industrial working class. The explanation was instead to be found in the nature of relationships between the agricultural sector, the state, and the non-agricultural sectors.

> The roots of the repression of agricultural labour can be located in a systemic commitment to maintaining a continual supply of cheap food. A supply of cheap food allows lower costs in the reproduction of labour power, thereby benefiting capital as a whole. The lower the cost of food, the lower the possible wages that labour may subsist on. Because cheap agricultural labour was an important precondition for cheap food. . .it is evident that the struggle to keep farm labour cheap and unorganized had a logic which appealed to more than the individual agricultural entrepreneur or even to agricultural capital as a whole. Capitalist accumulation was based, in part, on the assumption of cheap agricultural labour.

Further, the smaller the portion of industrial wages allotted to food payments, the more would be left over to buy consumer goods, thereby expanding capitalist markets (Weiner, 1978: 181-2).

Weiner notes that while in the industrial sector, state institutions have been actively involved in the mediation of labour disputes and construction of 'compromise' solutions (the state is at least theoretically concerned about the interests of both capital and labour), in the agricultural sphere the actions of the state 'have been almost uniformly to the direct benefit of agricultural capital'. Thus agricultural labour in the United States has been systematically excluded from protective labour legislation. Such protection would facilitate organization, and therefore empower these workers to win direct wage increases. In addition, similar legislation would require employers to contribute funds to such programs as Workers' Compensation and therefore increase the farmworkers' 'social wage'. All of this, of course, increases the cost of paid labour to the agricultural employer. This did not mean that the state was acting as an instrument of one faction of capital, namely agricultural capital, but rather that such action benefited all factions of capital by helping to minimize food prices (1978: 182-3).

Systematic discrimination against farmworkers, in relation to the rights and protections which workers in other sectors enjoy, provides evidence of a cheap food policy in Canada as well. However, this kind of discriminatory treatment must not be attributed solely to the inherent difference between industrial labour's and farm labour's relationship to the state and capital. Contrary to Weiner's argument, while agricultural workers' class struggle may indeed display many similarities to that in the industrial sector, the factor sharply distinguishing them is the intensity of the class struggle. The agricultural wage labourer is in an extremely vulnerable and weak position, so the level of struggle in this sector is much weaker than in the industrial. The policy of cheap food has been made possible in part because of the weakness of resistance by agricultural labour.

The case of Western Europe is instructive. There the rural proletariat organized itself into powerful trade unions at the turn of the century and has, for the most part, been successful at winning inclusion in protective legislation awarded other workers and attaining wages in line with the industrial average. Farmers in Europe have also tended to be more successful than those in North America in organizing and pressing government to protect their interests. The end result is that the European states have not followed a cheap food policy; they have been driven away from such a strategy by the struggle of class forces in the agricultural sector. Prices for food products in the European Economic Community are 30% to 80% in excess of world prices (Warnock, 1987: 139).

Having qualified Weiner's analysis, we should still recognize its value in pointing us in the right direction. To enable certain corporate interests to generate high profits and for 'core' workers to earn relatively high wages, there must exist segments of the economy that experience instability in profits and low wages. Capitalism, even in its advanced manifestations, is an unplanned system which necessitates this unevenness (Friedman, 1978: 105). This type of relationship between differing sectors of the economy was well recognized by the prominent Canadian political economist, Vernon C. Fowke. He argued that from Canada's conception, agriculture has deliberately been used as the basis for economic empire building. Agriculture has been the tool used to make money for other economic activities—agribusiness, other industrial sectors, railways, banks, and the like. If government aid has been given to the farming sector it has been done, Fowke maintained, 'because of what agriculture was expected to do for other dominant economic interests' and not because of what it might do for agriculture (1978: 3, 272). Fowke's concerns were directed toward the exploitation of the farmer, but his analysis applies equally well to the position of the farmworker. The state's 'cheap food' strategy is, consequently, an important consideration when examining the position of the agricultural sector.

Canadian food prices have been low; in fact, in terms of proportion of income spent on the food bill, Canadians spend the second lowest in the world. This is about 18% of personal disposable income, with only the Americans occupying a more favourable position. This figure has remained relatively stable for a good number of years (Agriculture Canada, 1981: 52). Canadian agricultural tariffs have played an important role in this. They have been considerably lower than those in most other countries, which has made it very attractive for cheap foreign fresh and processed agricultural products to enter the Canadian market and compete with domestic goods. The Free Trade Agreement with the US will lower these barriers even further.

Government creation of producer-controlled marketing boards, which have only in small measure improved the position of the farmer, reflect the farmers' own struggle to organize in response to their class position. Thus, while farmers would agree with past government policy which has acted to subdue paid farm labour, they have done so for different motivations. The cheap food policy has been one over which farmers as a class have been in conflict with capital and the state. Farmers have politically reacted to counter this policy with pressure for such measures as marketing boards. By the 1920s farmers came together (in wheat pools on the prairies, and in co-operatives for fruit growers in BC) in an attempt to increase their bargaining power. Improvement of their economic standing in relation to that of other sectors of the economy has been a persistent goal of Canadian agricultural producers throughout the twentieth century. Up until 1945 they were largely unsuccessful in this goal.

In tracing Canadian government agricultural policy, E.L. Menzie has concluded that in the years up to and through the Second World War the state pursued the goal of low food prices, by following a policy which kept the costs low at the farm gate. After 1945 this policy was modified—there came to be a greater concern for price and income security for the farmer. This was expressed, in part, through the creation of marketing boards, for a more solid and stable economic base for farmers was felt necessary to ensure reasonable supplies of foodstuffs at relatively stable prices for consumers. The objective, however, was to achieve greater economic security for the farmer by increasing the productivity of farms, not by increasing food product prices automatically. Since 1945 there has been a tremendous 'rationalization' of farming, illustrated in part by the increasing size of the average farm unit. By the 1970s, Canadian farmers' incomes were equal to or greater than those in most non-farm occupations. So to a degree, both farmers' concerns for greater economic returns, and government's and consumers' goals of secure and reasonably priced food supplies, have been maintained (1980: 17-19). The 'cheap food' strategy remains a mainstay of Canadian agricultural policy.

The Farm Labour Question and State Policy

Canadian governments have a long history of involvement in the farm labour market. This is due to the frequent shortages and lack of stability of farm labour. Agricultural reports of over 100 years ago indicated that labour scarcity was a major factor in limiting production (Carroll, n.d.: i). In the early period, farmworkers moved out of farm labour to become farmers themselves and, in later years, to take up more highly paid industrial work in the cities. Additionally there was always the need to move workers from areas of high unemployment to locations in need of seasonal labour. The state, through numerous policies, has attempted to create cheap pools of agricultural wage labour.

Private railways in 1896 were perhaps the first to attempt to address the problem of the farm labour shortage on the prairies by sponsoring the movement of seasonal labour from Eastern Canada. During both World Wars the federal government became actively involved in recruiting farm labourers. Farm workers were legally limited in the time they could be employed outside agriculture, to help ensure that there were adequate supplies of labour during peak demand periods. Farm labourers were even given special exemptions from military service if they continued to work on the farm (Smit *et al.*, 1984: 18-19).

Immigration became the main plank in state farm labour policy in the immediate post-World War II period. In 1946-47, 4,527 Polish army veterans were recruited to do farm work in Canada. They had to sign an agreement to remain in farming for a period of two years. This experiment paved the way for subsequent groups of immigrants. For instance, displaced workers from prison camps in Germany and Austria and farm families wishing to emigrate from Holland were recruited into farm labour (Haythorne, 1960: 79-80). Canadian government policy explicitly gave preference to immigrants who indicated their willingness to become farmworkers. Between 1946 and 1953 more than 25,000 immigrants came to Canada under agreements which locked them into paid farm work for periods of one to two years (Canadian Department of Labour, 1960: 13). Immigration was the key in this period to solving the problem of finding sources of cheap farm labour.

Early in the century governments also became active in establishing employment offices designed to facilitate farm placements. In Ontario for instance there are Canada Employment Centres, Canada Employment Centres for Students, and Canada Farm Labour Pools (CFLP). In 1986 the CFLP made 26,300 local placements and 4,940 workers were placed directly on farms to work for a period of time (Ontario Task Force on Hours of Work and Overtime, 1987a: 34). These farm labour programs are designed 'to assist the economic and social forces in the labour market to adjust quickly with a minimum of time and effort' (Haythorne, 1960: 78). In short, the state assists in the movement of low-waged workers to labour-starved farmers.

Of course the most important way in which the state ensures a wage-poor rural proletariat is through discriminatory legislation. The stated rationale for regulating the workplace is to provide 'a minimum safety net for individuals with little bargaining power'. Such legislation provides a way by which the weakest sections of our population can enjoy working conditions which meet acceptable community standards (Ontario Task Force on Hours of Work and Overtime, 1987b: 9). Yet farmworkers in Ontario are excluded from the Labour Relations Act, and in both Ontario and BC they are exempt from many sections of the Employment Standards Act (including such things as the industrial minimum wage, overtime pay, vacations and vacation pay, public holiday pay and overtime regulations), and while farmworkers can claim compensation for injury on the job they do not have the right to safety committees or the right to refuse unsafe work (Stulty, 1987: 293). In fact since the first substantial piece of labour legislation, the Factories Act of 1884, agriculture has been exempted. The question naturally arises as to why farmworkers, who face so many disadvantages, are excluded from such legislation.

The exemption of farmworkers from such legislative coverage has been defended on two basic grounds. First, if the labour relations regime that operates in the factories was put into place on the farms labour costs would rise, causing harm to farmers and consumers (Beatty, 1987: 90). Labour standards in agriculture in the US, farmers argue, are even weaker than those now in Canada; to make our regulations stronger would place Canadians at a decided competitive disadvantage. Further, because of the variability of weather and the perishability of crops, restrictions on hours of work and such regulations that might disrupt the labour process should not be applicable in agriculture (Ontario Task Force on Hours of Work and Overtime, 1987a: 57, 49). All of these factors would significantly increase farm costs. The second argument for the exclusion of farmworkers is that such a system of laws 'would substantially interfere with, and ultimately jeopardize, the existence of the family farm' (Beatty, 1987: 90).

Including farmworkers under the umbrella of protective labour legislation would indeed raise costs to farmers. Consider the exclusion of farmworkers from the right to overtime pay premiums, for instance. Agriculture has the highest average hours of weekly work of all industries; in Ontario, agriculture averages a work week of nearly 42 hours compared to the industrial average of under 37 hours. Extra overtime pay would thus have a significant impact on the farmers' wage bill (Ontario Task Force on Hours of Work and Overtime, 1987b: 23). In terms of the threat posed to the traditional family farm due to state over-regulation, it would seem that the forces of the marketplace have already served to thoroughly transform the old style farm into a commercial venture. The state has clearly stepped in, ignoring its own rationale for protective legislation, in order to keep farm wages low and thus help reduce the overall cost of food for consumers.

Conclusion

State policy is, of course, not simply a direct reflection of the dominant class interest but is tempered by class struggle. Historically, the lack of legislative protections for farm labourers was, in large measure, a product of farmworkers' inability to launch and sustain effective class resistance in Canada. In BC the rural proletariat was able to begin to unionize and intensify its class struggle. This resulted in some success, as in 1983 they were able to win partial protection under Workers' Compensation legislation (Shields, 1988). Unionization was facilitated in BC by the reinforcement of the relatively homogeneous ethnic composition of the labour force. Improved organizational strength cannot, however, disguise the group's comparative weakness *vis-à-vis* other class forces. In Ontario, ethnic diversity coupled with other difficulties has helped to maintain a divided and weak rural proletariat. The Western European experience, however, demonstrates that the active organization and struggle of farm labourers do not make legislative exclusion inevitable.

Larger factors at work in the agricultural industry must also be considered. The increasing concentration of capital in agribusiness has largely eliminated traditional relationships between locally owned processors, wholesalers, and retailers, and has placed growers in the position of having to sell in a highly concentrated market. If domestic costs begin to become prohibitive, multinationals have greater flexibility; that is, they can shift production to, and be supplied by, foreign countries that can produce at lower costs. This places increased economic pressures on growers and small processors, wholesalers and retailers to keep the costs of production low at the source of production. Further, the state must take these factors into consideration and ensure the competitive position of the growers if it does not wish to lose domestic investment and employment in the agricultural industry.

Farmers who depend on wage labourers for their operations are engaged in a system of class relations that differs significantly from the 'simple worker-capitalist dichotomy of Marxist class struggle', for in this situation we have at least three classes: at the top, agribusiness which controls the processing and marketing of the finished product; next, the growers who are obliged to sell the bulk of their unprocessed product to agribusiness; and on the bottom the farmworkers who have contracts with the farmers to cultivate and harvest their crops (Thompson and Seager, 1978: 158). While the farmer acts as the direct employer of farm labour, the farmer in turn is tied into a dependent relationship with agribusiness.

For the small commercial family farm to stay afloat, the *sine qua non* is a cheap and servile labour force. The farmer is squeezed by retailers, wholesalers, canners, and the banks (Glavin, 1980: 19). Larger 'industrial' farms are in a similar position. With the highest percentage of paid agricultural labour in Canada concentrated in the fruit, vegetable, and tobacco agricultural sector, labour costs are necessarily a major factor of production. The 'necessity' of a cheap and easily dominated agricultural labour force to these farmers is thus quite clear.

The prosperity of farmers is therefore 'rather precariously balanced on the backs of the labouring class' (Thompson and Seager, 1978: 174). Not surprisingly, the farmer would not want to be the first to upset this relationship. Moreover, a strongly organized agricultural labour force poses a direct threat to the interests of farmers since it could 'wield an incredible amount of power at harvest time'. This reflects, in part, the crucial difference between the non-agricultural and agricultural enterprise, since the latter is based on the perishability of crops. Any delay in harvest can mean great cost to the farmer. Growers, as a result, have battled hard against agricultural worker organizations and interests since they realize the potential power of a strongly organized union. For instance, Okanagan Valley Socred MLA Bill Ritchie argued that a farm labourers' union would spell disaster to the farming industry. Ed Pratt, the leader of the BC Coast Vegetable Marketing Board, insisted that agriculture be declared an essential service and that strikes be banned while crops were in the fields. The BC Federation of Agriculture (BCFA) reiterated the position of Pratt and insisted that the piece-work system be maintained in agriculture (Glavin, 1980: 19). The BCFA adopted a resolution at its 1982 annual convention that the Ministry of Labour be petitioned 'to have the food industry declared an "essential service" ' (1982: B7). In Ontario farmers have echoed similar concerns and demands (Neilson and Christie, 1975: 342).

The growers possess a formidable ideological weapon to wield against farmworker organizations: they claim that such developments threaten 'to deny the very staff of life to the nation' (Weiner, 1978: 185-6). This claim serves to disguise the extent to which the farmers now view themselves as small businessmen, and subscribe to a corporate/business ideology, which is quite incompatible with any imaginable farmworker/labour ideology (Reasons *et al.*, 1981: 104).

Agribusiness may be subdivided into a number of segments whose boundaries crosscut in numerous directions. The service and supply sector has an interest in farmers remaining profitable and spending as little on wages as necessary, since the more profit farmers net the more they have to spend on their goods and services.

At the processing, wholesaling, and retailing end there is again an interest for both big and small, but especially for small, agricapital to keep produce costs low. It is in the larger interests of the capitalist class to promote a 'cheap food policy'. It is clear that both agribusiness and the growers have a common interest in defeating or retarding the class struggle of farmworkers. Agribusiness and capital in general wish to keep food as cheap as possible and maintain 'full' control of the production process. It is true that the grower may have conflicting interests with agribusiness because of its increasing levels of concentration, which leads to an unequal bargaining relationship between growers and agricapitalists. The grower is also discomfited by aspects of the 'cheap food policy' (notably commodity price levels and external competition) which capital in general supports. But with respect to paid farm labour, growers and agricapitalists are in agreement.

Even on the prairies, where class-based populist movements were strongest, the class position of farmers did not bring them to criticize capitalism fundamentally. As members of the petite bourgeoisie, their antagonisms were directed toward the 'bigness of industry. . .rather than its ownership and control' (Drache, 1978: 19). Their opposition was directed against the 'most advanced manifestations' of capitalism (monopolies) rather than at capitalism itself. Such a position did not make alliances between labour and farmer easy and, in provinces such as Ontario, Manitoba and Nova Scotia, when worker demands for the eight-hour day impinged on the interests of farmers as employers, these alliances collapsed.

CHAPTER SIXTEEN

THE FUTURE OF RURAL CANADA IN AN INDUSTRIAL SOCIETY

DAVID A. HAY AND G. S. BASRAN

We need to know where we are going in order to understand where we are.

–Otis Dudley Duncan

The preceding chapters have presented selective perspectives on the changes that have substantially transformed the structure and functioning of the rural sector of Canadian society. What are the probable future directions and alternative developments for rural Canada?

The movement toward the post-industrial information society has resulted in the ascendence of tertiary service activities and the diminishing relative importance of the primary extractive industries. As a result farming is of declining importance to the national economy and, as indicated previously, of lessening importance to the rural sector. In this context it is necessary to recognize, as argued by Swanson (1989: 14), that 'the old axiom that farm well-being. . .determines rural well-being. . .is no longer useful'.

However, as indicated by Warner (1974: 307-9), the passing of the dominance of agriculture—either in numbers or ideology—does not mean the demise of rural society or of the agrarian sector. The rural or agrarian society has not disappeared—nor is it likely to—but it has changed in fundamental ways in relation to romanticized nostalgic images of the 'sacred' rural environment and the family farm. Warner maintains that it is unrealistic to treat rural and urban societies as separate and alternative social entities. He believes that this reification of rural and urban as distinctive social systems is less and less tenable as the transformation in Canadian society continues.

Consequently, he maintains that rural society can best be understood as part of the larger society. This implies that Rural Sociologists should go beyond comparing the characteristics and relative size of the rural and urban populations. Rural Sociologists should also go beyond documenting the relative flows of people from one area to the other, and do more than examine the connections between rural communities and organizations and those in urban centres. Rather, they must examine how the fundamental structure and processes of the larger society differentially involve, represent, and affect rural people.

It follows that a much wider than localistic analysis is essential for comprehending the transformation of rural society. Such analysis, according to Warner, cannot focus solely on rural society but must examine the web of social and economic organization in national and increasingly global perspectives with special emphasis on the implications for rural society.

Warner suggests that important insights into rural life may be gained by examining whether the transformations affect rural society in the same ways they affect the urban or national societies. Swanson (1989: 15) for example indicates that an examination of rural problems reveals marked similarities to those of inner cities. Both populations according to Swanson were being left behind in the economic expansions of the 1980s, and for many of the same reasons.

> Each of these geographic areas has similar problems with education and health services and, increasingly, in areas of social pathologies—particularly violent crimes and crimes against property. (Swanson, 1989: 15)

Olsen (1968: 277) has indicated that 'the development of contemporary "modernized" societies has involved four basic evolutionary trends or processes: industrialization, urbanization, bureaucratization, and centralization'. The latter two processes are of particular importance in reference to the present discussion. For instance, conventional approaches to providing a quality education for the declining rural population, as discussed by Randhawa, have resulted in the consolidation of schools in the larger rural centres and the subsequent closure of schools in the smaller centres or open countryside.

Similar trends resulting from centralization and bureaucratization are also evident in relation to rural hospitals, rail lines, elevators, governmental services, and rural services and businesses, which are being displaced from smaller centres in favour of sites in larger towns and urban centres. Accompanying this trend has been the virtual disappearance of the local entrepreneur; the main streets of small towns are increasingly characterized by the same businesses and activities as urban streets: chain stores, branch offices, franchises, and parking meters.

Warner (1974) and Warren (1956) indicate that the decisions and actions of consequence in society are increasingly concentrated with corporate or public boards which are generally located in urban centres at varying distances from the locality of concern. Accompanying this decline in the relative power of the rural population has been their increasing specialization and differentiation. The rural population's increased heterogeneity and dispersion reduce their shared interests and, according to Warner (1974: 310), further contribute to their inability to be involved and represented in the decisions affecting rural life. As a consequence,

> [r]ural society may increasingly take on characteristics like those of an 'inconspicuous minority group'. Thus it will have attributes different from those dominant in numbers, power, and resources; be neglected and underrepresented in decisions and actions affecting it; and be vulnerable to exploitation. (Warner, 1974: 309)

In addition to the displacement of people out of farming, fishing, mining and other rural industries because of technological advancement, exhaustion of resources, and/or relocation of industrial activities, developments in communication and transportation have also had significant effects on the rural population and their trade centres. The once 'isolated' rural populations are now subjected to the same messages as the urban population with a resulting expansion and reshaping of their expectations and wants. Developments in transportation have enabled rural consumers to travel with relative ease to larger, more distant centres to satisfy their changing demands. These developments have resulted in a spatial explosion of the boundaries of the rural community in comparison to the smaller, close-knit, relatively self-sufficient team-haul communities which were established on the basis of the previously available transportation technologies.

Successive developments in rural areas have 'transformed cohesive rural communities into components of spatially extended social and economic networks'. At the beginning of the century, rural residents tended to satisfy the majority of social and economic needs at one trade centre or its immediately surrounding area. Now the rural residents or family may travel to one centre to go to school, other centres for shopping and work, and still other centres to satisfy other needs, such as health care or recreation. The resulting 'new rural networks are sometimes referred to as "the extended city" ' (Fuller *et al.*, 1990: 15).

These developments, according to Coughenour and Busch (1978: 223),

> may have laid to rest that pattern of social life associated with the isolated, homogenous rural community. Those who have been unable or unwilling to adapt to life in modern communities, as well as some who have adapted, are often

dissatisfied and feel alienated. Apologists for an imagined rural utopia have been dismayed, and some foresee the eclipse of rural society.

Rural society continues to exist in our modern industrialized and urbanized Canadian society, but it is more differentiated and functionally interdependent with the larger society than was the rural society of the past (Coughenour and Busch, 1978: 223).

It is still a viable and continuing topic of concern to sociologists, policy makers, rural populations, and other audiences. As Diaz and Gingrich have indicated, strong interpersonal and inter-familial networks continue to flourish in many rural communities. Residents of rural communities should continue to work together to strengthen the intra-community ties and relationships weakened by the diverse directions extended-city networks.

Most rural people and farmers in particular subscribe to rugged individualism and the free enterprise system. The petit-bourgeois status of farmers lends itself to this ideological position. Moreover, farmers are not a homogeneous group. Land tenure, income, type of commodity production, region of residence, and general socio-economic status determine the political ideology, values, attitudes, and behaviour of the farm population. As a result, the development of provincial and/or national organizations to represent the farmers' interests has been an elusive objective.

Present and future developments of concern to rural populations must be seriously pursued if this declining but still important segment of the Canadian population is to comprehend and effectively deal with the future. Some of the initiatives in this respect may involve the bringing together of the diverse segments of the rural population lest they become the 'voiceless minority' suggested by Warner.

Warner (1974: 311) has indicated that rural issues tended to be approached on an individualistic or localistic basis. For example, the introduction of new productive technologies (farm, fishing, etc.) has typically been through individual adoption of the new practices. Similarly, problems at the community level have been pursued through localistic initiatives and self-help programs without due recognition of the 'extended-city' networks, or the larger regional, national, or international interdependencies. New initiatives may involve regional or multi-community developments and programs rather than attempting to deal with these problems primarily at a local community level.

It may be unrealistic to expect that every small rural trade centre can support the full or wide range of services and institutions possible in the team-haul community B.C. (before cars). The concept of community might well be expanded to a wider geographical area circumscribed by a comfortable one-day automobile trip. If the rural population were to consider everything within this larger regional radius as their community and to co-operate in the location and delivery of services, the problematic availability and quality of rural services might be alleviated.

It is also necessary to recognize, as indicated by Fuller *et al.* (1990: 8), that rural Canada is a diverse patchwork of farming, fishing, mining, forestry, tourism, energy, retirement and rural manufacturing regions. 'While rural Canada as a whole is diversified, each region has become increasingly specialized in a particular activity.' It may therefore be necessary to develop specific programs to fit the unique characteristics of each region, rather than one overall plan for all regions.

Eldridge (1963: 13) emphasizes that in addition to considering the natural and technological resources it is important to consider the human component: the abilities, attitudes, values, and knowledge of the people. Local developments and initiatives may involve a number of value and other conflicts. Rural people valuing the benefits of patronizing more distant centres, may jeopardize the viability of their local community, services and businesses.

The development of more optimistic attitudes to overcome the frustration and defeatism experienced by rural people must also be considered (Eldridge, 1963: 3). The maintenance or potential rejuvenation of the local community may also require the development or emergence of leadership to replace the leadership potential lost in the migration of the younger, better educated, and more energetic segment of the rural population to urban centres. There is no one pat solution for every group or community. Potential solutions or developments as indicated by Eldridge (1963: 1) may be dependent on the nature or manner in which the problem is posed.

For example, defining the problem as a lack of jobs or opportunities to retain people in the community implies the need to create more jobs through the diversification of the economic base in 'single enterprise communities'. On the other hand, defining the problem as too many people for the available jobs and opportunities implies out-migration. People go where the jobs are (Eldridge, 1963: 2).

If local people and planners are to better comprehend and deal with the problems resulting from the transformation of rural areas, they must have adequate information. Increased recognition of the problems of rural areas on the part of policy-makers, scholars and other interested parties is essential. For example, Crown and Heady (1972: 171) indicate that the amount of research devoted to rural social problems is relatively low in comparison to other areas:

> In 1967, only 1.4 per cent of all professional man-years spent on Canadian agriculture was devoted to the study of sociology, in comparison to 89.2 per cent devoted to studying the developments which tend to create problems for rural people.

More recent information on this relationship was not available but we believe that the relative investment and expenditures have not changed to any great extent, and in fact the situation may have worsened since 1967.

The problems presently confronting rural areas are the result of technological, demographic, and a multiplicity of other planned and unplanned changes. The solution to these problems also involves change. The essence of every problem is change. If nothing ever changed there would never be a new problem, nor could current problems ever be solved.

The prospect of a future without change is relatively unattractive. For without it we could not solve the present problems and it would also deprive us of any potential benefits or progress. Not all change may be considered progress; more often than not it may hurt some people while benefiting others. But rural people and areas cannot simply be dismissed as the price of technological progress in rural industries, transportation, and communication.

If we are striving toward an improvement of the present situation it cannot be achieved by *status quo*-ism; we must have change. The challenge of the future is to contend effectively with change and the problems it engenders. We believe that the potential solutions to these problems and planning for the future developments should include the local people, their experiences and their aspirations for the future. This should encompass the people to be affected in all stages of the process from the definition of the problem, the development of the objectives, and the implementation of the program. In this manner we believe that more realistic plans based on the peoples' experiences and resources can be developed and implemented. We also believe that these programs will be more readily accepted by the people affected. That is, people can make a difference and should be active participants and not just passive recipients.

Rural people and areas have survived and surmounted other challenges, such as harsh conditions during the initial periods of settlement and the Depression of the 1930s. We believe that rural people still have the power and ability to rally around their trade centres and businesses to keep their communities alive. Although the survival of rural trade centres may be dependent on the presence of particular institutions and services, or combinations thereof, a critical component according to the Hall Commission (1979) is that it 'is the people and their spirit' along with their identification with the centre that determines the viability of the community.

Chapter One

Amin, S., G. Arrighi, A.G. Frank and I. Wallerstein
1982 *Dynamics of Global Crisis*. New York: Monthly Review.
Brandt, Willy
1983 *Common Crisis North-South: Co-operation For World Recovery*. London: Pan Books Ltd.
Buttel, F.H. and Howard Newby
1980 *The Rural Sociology of the Advanced Societies: Critical Perspectives*. Totowa, NJ: Allanheld, Osmun & Co. Publishers.
Canada 70 Team
1969 *The Prairie Provinces: Alienation and Anger*. Toronto: McClelland and Stewart.
Conway, John F.
1984 'Western Alienation: A Legacy of Confederation' in J. Fry, *Contradictions in Canadian Society*. Toronto: John Wiley and Sons Canada Ltd.
———
1983 *The West: The History of a Region in Confederation*. Toronto: James Lorimer and Co., Publishers.
Denis, Wilfred
1982 'Capital and Agriculture: A Review of Marxist Problematics' in *Studies in Political Economy: A Socialist Review*. Ottawa: Carleton University Graphics.
Drache, D.
1977 'Staple-ization: A Theory of Canadian Capitalist Development' in Craig Heron (ed.), *Imperialism, Nationalism, and Canada*. Toronto: New Hogtown Press and Between the Lines.
Fowke, Vernon C.
1957 *The National Policy and the Wheat Economy*. Toronto: University of Toronto Press.
Frank, A.G.
1967 *Capitalism and Underdevelopment in Latin America: Historical Studies of Chile and Brazil*. New York: Monthly Review.
Friedland, W.H.
1991 'Shaping the New Political Economy of Advanced Capitalist Agriculture' in W.H. Friedland *et al.* (eds), *Toward a New Political Economy of Agriculture*. Boulder, CO: Westview Press.
Fry, J.A.
1979 *Economy, Class and Social Reality: Issues in Contemporary Canadian Society*. Toronto: Butterworths Canada Ltd.

Goodman, David and Michael Redcliff

1985 'Capitalism, Petty Commodity Production and the Farm Enterprise'. *Sociologia Ruralis* 25, 3/4.

Globe and Mail

1990 'Farmers Hit by Bad News'. 12 July.

———

1987 ' "Cheap Food Policy" Cited in Farm Crisis' (Rudy Platiel). 13 June.

———

1987 'Why Not a World Food Cartel to Avert a Crisis For Farmers?' (Lawrence Kerr). 4 June.

———

1987 'The Farmers Take'. 22 April.

Grabb, Edward G.

1984 *Social Inequality: Classical and Contemporary Theorists*. Toronto: Holt, Rinehart and Winston of Canada, Ltd.

Green, Gary

1987 'The Political Economy of Flue-Cured Tobacco Production'. *Rural Sociology* 52, 2: 221-41.

Hansen, P. and Alicja Muszynski

1990 'Crisis in Rural Life and Crisis in Thinking: Directions For Critical Research'. *Canadian Review of Sociology and Anthropology*, 27, 1: 1-22.

Heron, Craig (ed.)

1977 *Imperialism, Nationalism and Canada*. Toronto: New Hogtown Press and Between the Lines.

Hiller, Harry H.

1986 *Canadian Society: A Macroanalysis*. Scarborough, Ont.: Prentice-Hall Canada Inc.

Howard, M. and J. King (eds)

1975 *The Political Economy of Marx*. Harlow (UK): Longman.

Innis, Harold A.

1956 *Essays in Canadian Economic History*. Toronto: University of Toronto Press.

Knuttila, K. Murray and James N. McCrorie

1980 'National Policy and Prairie Agrarian Development: A Reassessment'. *Canadian Review of Sociology and Anthropology* 17, 3: 263-72.

Lianos, Theodore P.

1984 'Concentration and Centralization of Capital in Agriculture' in *Studies in Political Economy: A Socialist Review*. Ottawa: Carleton University Graphics.

Lipset, Seymour M.

1968 *Agrarian Socialism: The Co-operative Commonwealth Federation in Saskatchewan: A Study in Political Sociology*. New York: Doubleday & Co, Inc.

McCreary, G.L. and W.H. Furtan

1988 'Income Distribution and Agricultural Policies' in G.S. Basran and D.A. Hay (eds), *The Political Economy of Agriculture in Western Canada*. Toronto: Garamond Press: 57-72.

McMichael, P. and F.H. Buttel

1990 'New Directions in the Political Economy of Agriculture'. *Sociological Perspectives* 33, 1.

Macpherson, C.B.
1962 *Democracy in Alberta: Social Credit and the Party System*. Toronto: University of Toronto Press.
Mandel, Eli and David Taras
1987 *A Passion for Identity: An Introduction to Canadian Studies*. Toronto: Methuen Publications.
Mann, S.A. and J.M. Dickinson
1980 'State and Agriculture in Two Eras of American Capitalism' in F.H. Buttel and H. Newby (eds), *The Rural Sociology of the Advanced Societies: Critical Perspectives*. Totowa, NJ: Allanheld, Osmun & Co. Publishers.
Matthews, Ralph
1983 *The Creation of Regional Dependency*. Toronto: University of Toronto Press.
Miliband, Ralph
1977 *Marxism and Politics*. Oxford, England: Oxford University Press.
Mills, C. Wright
1962 *The Marxists*. Harmondsworth: Penguin Books, Ltd.
Mitchell, Don
1975 *The Politics of Food*. Toronto: James Lorimer and Co., Publishers.
Mooney, P.
1982 'Labour Time, Production Time and Capitalist Development in Agriculture'. *Sociologia Ruralis* 27, 3/4: 279-91.
Moore, Steve and Debi Wells
1975 *Imperialism and the National Question in Canada*. Toronto: Better Read Graphics.
Murdock, Steve H., Don E. Albrecht, Rita R. Hamm, F. Larry Leistritz, and Arlen G. Leholm
1986 'The Farm Crisis in the Great Plains: Implications For Theory and Policy Development'. *Rural Sociology* 51, 4: 406-35.
Ossenberg, Richard J.
1971 *Canadian Society: Pluralism, Change and Conflict*. Scarborough, Ont.: Prentice-Hall of Canada, Ltd.
Panitch, Leo
1977 'The Role and Nature of the Canadian State' in Craig Heron (ed.), *Imperialism, Nationalism, and Canada*. Toronto: New Hogtown Press and Between the Lines.
Poulantzas, Nicos
1974 *Political Power and Social Class*. London: New Left Books.
Pratt, Larry and John Richards
1979 *Prairie Capitalism: Power and Influence in the New West*. Toronto: McClelland and Stewart, Ltd.
Research Division of Saskatchewan Wheat Pool
1970 'Direction for Canadian Agriculture in the Seventies'. Task Force Digest. Saskatchewan.
Sills, David L. (ed.)
1968 'Rural Society' in *International Encyclopedia of the Social Sciences*. New York: The Macmillan Company and The Free Press.

Skogstad, Grace
1980 'Agrarian Protest in Alberta'. *Canadian Review of Sociology and Anthropology* 17, 1: 263-72.

Smiley, Donald V.
1963 *The Rowell/Sirois Report: Book I.* Toronto: McClelland and Stewart, Ltd.

Star Phoenix, Saskatoon
1987 'Census Finds Fewer Young Farmers' (Vern Greenshields). 4 June.

———
1987 'Saskatchewan Farmers Pay Most Interest' (Ray Guay). 5 June.

———
1987 'Farmers' Problems Stump Legislators' (Marvin Lipton). 6 May.

Stirling, R. and J. Conway
1988 'Fractions Among Prairie Farmers' in G.S. Basran and D.A. Hay (eds), *The Political Economy of Agriculture in Western Canada.* Toronto: Garamond Press: 73-86.

Whyte, D.R.
1979 'Farm Production and Capital Integration in Canadian Agriculture' (unpublished paper).

World Bank
1989 *World Development Report: Financial Systems and Development; World Development Indicators.* New York: Oxford University Press.

Chapter Two

Burke, Mary Ann
1988 'Loss of Prime Agricultural Land: The Example of Southern Ontario'. *Canadian Social Trends* 9 (September): 33-4.

Davis, Arthur K.
1971 'Canadian Society and History as Hinterland Versus Metropolis', in Richard J. Ossenberg (ed.), *Canadian Society: Pluralism, Change and Conflict.* Scarborough, Ont.: Prentice-Hall of Canada, Ltd: 6-32.

Dominion Bureau of Statistics
1936 1931 Census of Canada, Vol. I. Ottawa: Minister of Trade and Commerce.

———
1950 1941 Census of Canada, Vol. I. General Review and Summary Tables. Ottawa: Minister of Trade and Commerce.

———
1953 1951 Census of Canada, Vol. II. General Characteristics. Ottawa: Minister of Trade and Commerce.

———
1963a 1961 Census of Canada, Vol. I. Population, Marital Status by Age Group. Catalogue 92-522. Ottawa: Minister of Trade and Commerce.

———
1963b 1961 Census of Canada. Population, Urban and Rural Distribution. Catalogue 92-536. Ottawa: Minister of Trade and Commerce.

Dumas, Jean
1987 Report on the Demographic Situation in Canada 1986. Catalogue 91-209E. Ottawa: Minister of Supply and Services.

Fowke, Vernon C.
1957 *The National Policy and the Wheat Economy*. Toronto: University of Toronto Press.

———

1978 *Canadian Agricultural Policy: The Historical Pattern*. Toronto: University of Toronto Press.

Hall Commission
1977 *Grain and Rail in Western Canada*, Vol. 1. Ottawa: Minister of Supply and Services.

Kohl, Seena B.
1976 *Working Together: Women and Family in Southwestern Saskatchewan*. Toronto: Holt, Rinehart and Winston.

McCrorie, James N.
1971 'Change and Paradox in Agrarian Social Movements: The Case of Saskatchewan', in Richard J. Ossenberg (ed.), *Canadian Society: Pluralism, Change, and Conflict*. Scarborough, Ont.: Prentice-Hall of Canada, Ltd: 36-51.

McSkimmings, Judie
1990 'The Farm Community'. *Canadian Social Trends* 16 (Spring): 20-3.

Rainey, Kenneth D. and Karen G. Rainey
1978 'Rural Government and Local Public Services', Chapter 8 in Thomas R. Ford (ed.), *Rural U.S.A. Persistence and Change*. Ames: Iowa State University Press: 126-44.

Statistics Canada
1973 1971 Census of Canada, Vol. I. Population, Age Groups. Catalogue 92-715. Ottawa: Minister of Industry, Trade and Commerce.

———

1978 1976 Census of Canada. Population: Geographic Distributions Urban and Rural Distribution. Catalogue 92-807. Ottawa: Minister of Supply and Services.

———

1980 Canada's Cities. Catalogue 98-803E. Ottawa: Minister of Supply and Services.

———

1982 1981 Census of Canada, Vol. I. Population, Age, Sex and Marital Status. Catalogue 92-901. Ottawa: Minister of Supply and Services.

———

1984a Canada's Changing Population Distribution. Catalogue 99-931. Ottawa: Minister of Supply and Services.

———

1984b Urban Growth in Canada. Catalogue 99-942. Ottawa: Minister of Supply and Services.

———

1986 'Canada in the 21st Century'. *Canadian Social Trends* (Summer): 3-5.

———

1987 *The Daily*. Catalogue 11-001E. 3 June.

———

1988 1986 Census of Canada. Urban and Rural Areas, Canada, Provinces and Territories, Part 1. Catalogue 94-127. Ottawa: Minister of Supply and Services.

———

1989 Canada Yearbook 1990. Catalogue 11-402E. Ottawa: Minister of Regional Industrial Expansion.

Whyte, Donald R.

1970 'Rural Canada in Transition', in M. Tremblay and W.J. Anderson (eds), *Rural Canada in Transition*. Ottawa: Agricultural Economic Research Council of Canada: 1-99.

Wilson, Barry

1981 *Beyond the Harvest*. Saskatoon: Western Producer Prairie Books.

Chapter Three

Agriculture Canada

1982 Incomes of Farm Taxfilers. Ottawa: Minister of Supply and Services.

Arguellos, O.

1981 'Estrategias de Sobrevivencia: Un Concepto en Busca de Contenido'. *Demografia y Economia* 15, 2.

Baker, Harold

1980 'Rural Development Issues: A Summary'. Saskatoon: Division of Extension and Community Relations, University of Saskatchewan, No. 429.

Bell, Colin and Howard Newby

1971 *Community Studies. An Introduction to the Sociology of the Local Community*. London: Allen and Unwin.

Bollman, Ray and Pamela Smith

1987 'The Changing Role of Off Farm Income in Canada', Proceedings of the Canadian Agricultural Outlook Conference, Ottawa: Agriculture Canada: 155-66.

Boyd, Hugh

1938 *New Breaking: An Outline of Cooperation Among the Western Farmers of Canada*. Toronto: J.M. Dent.

Conway, John

1983 *The West: The History of a Region in a Confederation*. Toronto: James Lorimer and Co., Publishers.

Cox, Kevin

1981 'Capitalism and Conflict Around the Communal Living Space' in Michael Dear and Allen Scott (eds), *Urbanization and Urban Planning in Capitalist Society*, New York: Methuen Publications.

Dasgupta, S.

1984 'Modernization and Rural Community Organization: Changing Community Structure on Prince Edward Island'. *International Review of Modern Sociology* 14.

Derek, Gregory and John Urry

1985 *Social Relations and Spatial Structures*. London: Macmillan.

Diaz, H.P. and P. Gingrich

1989 'Survival Strategies in Saskatchewan', paper presented at the annual meeting of the Canadian Association for Rural Studies, Université Laval, Quebec City.

Fowke, Vernon C.

1957 *The National Policy and the Wheat Economy*. Toronto: University of Toronto Press.

Friesen, Gerald
1987 *The Canadian Prairies: A History*. Toronto: University of Toronto Press.
Gallagher, John
1983 *To Kill the Crowd*. Moose Jaw: Challenge.
Gasson, R.
1986 'Part Time Farming: Strategy for Survival?'. *Sociologia Ruralis* 26, 3: 40.
Hale, S.
1990 *Controversies in Sociology: A Canadian Introduction*. Mississauga, Ont.: Copp Clark Pitman.
Hall Commission
1977 *Grain and Rail in Western Canada*. Ottawa: Minister of Supply and Services.
Jackson, John
1980 'Locale and the National Political Economy: An Alternative Perspective for Community Studies'. Montreal: unpublished manuscript, Concordia University.
Mitchell, Don
1975 *The Politics of Food*. Toronto: James Lorimer and Co., Publishers.
Olsen, L. and A. Brown
1975 'A Study of the Growth of Selected Service Centers in Saskatchewan'. Saskatoon: University of Saskatchewan, Research Report 75-03.
Redclift, M.
1986 'Survival Strategies in Rural Europe: Continuity and Change'. *Sociologia Ruralis* 26, 3: 40.
Redfield, Robert
1947 'The Folk Society'. *American Journal of Sociology* 52.
Smith, P.
1987 'Changes in Off Farm Work and Off Farm Income in Saskatchewan', paper presented to the Agricultural Outlook Conference, Ottawa.
Voisey, Paul
1988 *Vulcan: The Making of a Prairie Community*. Toronto: University of Toronto Press.

Chapter Four

Abell, Helen C.
1966 'The social consequences of the modernization of agriculture' in M.A. Tremblay and W.J. Anderson (eds), *Rural Canada in Transition*. Ottawa: The Agricultural Economics Research Council of Canada.
Barber, C.L.
1971 *Report of the Royal Commission on Farm Machinery*. Ottawa: Information Canada.
Bollman, Ray D. and Pamela Smith
1988 'Integration of Canadian farm and off-farm markets and the off-farm work of farm women, men, and children' in G.S. Basran and D.A. Hay (eds), *The Political Economy of Agriculture in Western Canada*. Toronto: Garamond Press: 185-202.
Bowles, Roy T.
1982 *Little Communities and Big Industries*. Toronto: Butterworths Canada Ltd.

Connelly, M. Patricia and Martha MacDonald
1983 'Women's work: domestic and wage labour in a Nova Scotia community'. *Studies in Political Economy* 10 (Winter): 45-72.
Denison, Merrill
1949 *Harvest Triumphant: the Story of Massey-Harris*. New York: Dodd, Mead, and Company.
Flora, Cornelia Butler and Jan L. Flora
1988 'Characteristics of entrepreneurial communities in a time of crisis'. *Rural Development News* 12, 2 (April): 1-4.
Friedland, William H., A. Barton, and R.J. Thomas
1981 *Manufacturing Green Gold: Capital, Labor and Technology in the Lettuce Industry*. New York: Cambridge University Press.
Gough, Joseph
1988 'Fisheries History'. *The Canadian Encyclopedia*. Edmonton: Hurtig: 781-4.
Hayter, Roger
1987 'Technology and the Canadian forest-product industries'. Background Study 54, Ottawa: The Science Council of Canada.
Hedley, Max J.
1976 'Independent commodity production and the dynamics of tradition'. *The Canadian Review of Sociology and Anthropology* 13, 4: 413-21.
Hodge, Gerald and Mohammad A. Qadeer
1983 *Towns and Villages in Canada: the Importance of Being Unimportant*. Toronto: Butterworths Canada Ltd.
Kloppenburg, Jack Ralph, Jr
1988 *First the Seed: the Politics of Plant Biotechnology, 1492-2000*. New York: Cambridge University Press.
MacFarlane, David L.
1972 'Farm electrification'. *Encyclopedia Canadiana*. Toronto: Grolier Ltd.
Marchak, Patricia
1983 *Green Gold: the Forest Industry in British Columbia*. Vancouver: University of British Columbia Press.
Melody, William H.
1988 'Satellite Communications'. *The Canadian Encyclopedia*. Edmonton: Hurtig: 1941-2.
Mitchell, Don
1975 *The Politics of Food*. Toronto: James Lorimer and Co., Publishers.
Patching, T.H.
1988 'Mining work force'. *The Canadian Encyclopedia*. Edmonton: Hurtig: 1363.
Reimer, Bill
1984 'Farm mechanization: the impact on labour at the level of the farm household'. *The Canadian Journal of Sociology* 9, 4 (Fall): 429-43.
Rosenberg, Nathan
1982 *Inside the Black Box: Technology and Economics*. New York: Cambridge University Press.
Savoie, Donald J.
1986 *Regional Economic Development*. Toronto: University of Toronto Press.
Selby, John
1977 'The myth of local control in Ontario' in Richard A. Carlton, Louise A.

Colley, and Neil J. MacKinnon, *Education, Change, and Society: a Sociology of Canadian Education*. Agincourt, Ont.: Gage Educational Publishing Ltd.

Smucker, Joseph
1980 *Industrialization in Canada*. Scarborough, Ont.: Prentice-Hall Canada Inc.

Chapter Five

Bennett, Terry and David L. Anderson
1988 *An Inter-sectoral Study of Canada's Resource Industries*. Kingston, Ont.: Queen's University, Centre for Resource Studies.

Bowles, Roy T.
1981 *Social Impact Assessment in Small Communities: An Integrative Review of Selected Literature*. Toronto: Butterworths Canada Ltd.

Bowles, Roy T. (ed.)
1982 *Little Communities and Big Industries: Studies in the Social Impact of Canadian Resource Extraction*. Toronto: Butterworths Canada Ltd.

Bowles, Roy T. and Cynthia Johnston
1987 'Communities in a nonmetropolitan region: An Ontario case'. *The Rural Sociologist* 7: 421-33.

Bradbury, John H.
1980 'Instant resource towns in British Columbia: 1965-1972'. *Plan Canada* 20: 19-38.

———
1984a 'The impact of industrial cycles in the mining sector: the case of the Quebec-Labrador region in Canada'. *International Journal of Urban and Regional Research* 8: 311-33.

———
1984b 'Declining Single-Industry Communities in Quebec-Labrador, 1979-1983'. *Journal of Canadian Studies* 19: 125-39.

———
1985a 'Housing policy and home ownership in mining towns: Quebec, Canada'. *International Journal of Urban and Regional Research* 9: 1-13.

———
1985b 'International movements and crises in resource oriented companies: the case of INCO in the nickel sector'. *Economic Geography* 61: 121-43.

——— and Isabelle St-Martin
1983 'Winding Down in a Quebec Mining Town: A Case Study of Schefferville'. *Canadian Geographer* 27: 128-44.

Bradwin, Edmund
1972 *The Bunkhouse Man: A Study of Work and Pay in the Camps of Canada 1903-1914*. Toronto: University of Toronto Press (originally published 1928).

Budgen, Mark
1983 'Tumbler Ridge: planning the physical and social development of a new community'. *Habitat* 26: 8-12.

Canada, Task Force on Mining Communities
1982 Report of the Task Force on Mining Communities, established by Federal, Provincial and Territorial Ministers with responsibility for Mining (Ottawa: September, 1982).

Depape, Denis

1984 'Alternatives to single project mining communities: a critical assessment' in Margo J. Wojciechowski (ed.) *Mining Communities: Hard Lessons for the Future*. Kingston, Ont. Queen's University, Centre for Resource Studies: 83-95.

Detomasi, Don D. and John W. Gartrell (eds)

1984 *Resource Communities: A Decade of Disruption*. Boulder, CO: Westview Press.

Gill, Alison M.

1987 'New resource communities: the challenge of meeting the needs of Canada's modern frontierpersons'. *Environments* 18: 21-34.

———

1990 'Friendship formation in a new coal-mining town: planning implications'. *Sociology and Social Research* 74: 103-6.

——— and Geoffrey C. Smith

1985 'Residents' evaluative structures of northern Manitoba mining communities'. *The Canadian Geographer* 29: 17-29.

Goltz, Eileen

1974 'Espanola: the history of a pulp and paper town'. *Laurentian University Review* 6: 73-104.

Hawley, A. H. and S. M. Mazie

1981 *Nonmetropolitan America in Transition*. Chapel Hill: University of North Carolina Press.

Hobart, Charles W.

1982 'Impact of Commuting Employment on Coppermine in the Northwest Territories' in R. T. Bowles (ed.), *Little Communities and Big Industries*. Toronto: Butterworths Canada Ltd: 182-98.

———

1984 'Impact of resource development projects on indigenous people' in D. D. Detomasi and J. W. Gartrell (eds), *Resource Communities: A Decade of Disruption*. Boulder, CO: Westview Press: 111-24.

Hodge, Gerald and Mohammad A. Qadeer

1983 *Towns and Villages in Canada: The Importance of Being Unimportant*. Toronto: Butterworths Canada Ltd.

Humphries, G.

1958 'Schefferville Quebec: a new pioneering town'. *The Geographical Review* 48: 151-67.

Institute for Research on Public Policy

1986 *Towns, Wheels or Wings?: For Resource Development*. Victoria, BC: The Western Research Program of the Institute for Research on Public Policy.

Institute for Local Government, Queen's University

1953 *Single-Enterprise Communities in Canada*. A report to the Central Mortgage and Housing Corporation. Kingston: Queen's University.

Knight, Rolf

1975 *Work Camps and Company Towns in Canada and the U.S.: an Annotated Bibliography*. Vancouver, BC: New Star Books.

Lucas, Rex A.

1971 *Minetown, Milltown, Railtown: Life in Canadian Communities of Single Industry*. Toronto: University of Toronto Press.

McCann, L. D.

1978 'The changing internal structure of Canadian resource towns'. *Plan Canada* 18: 46-59.

———

1980 'Canadian resource towns: a heartland-hinterland perspective' in R. E. Preston and L. H. Russwurm (eds), *Essays on Canadian Urban Processes and Form II*. Waterloo, Ont.: University of Waterloo, Department of Geography: 213-67.

McGrath, Susan

1987 'A retrospective assessment of the local governance model of resource community development'. *Impact Assessment Bulletin* 5: 9-31.

Marchak, Patricia

1983 *Green Gold: The Forest Industry in British Columbia*. Vancouver: University of British Columbia Press.

Matthews, Geoffrey J. and Robert Morrow, Jr

1985 *Canada and The World: An Atlas Resource*. Toronto: Prentice-Hall Canada Inc.

Matthiason, John S.

1970 *Resident Perceptions of the Quality of Life in Resource Frontier Communities*. Winnipeg: Center for Settlement Studies, University of Manitoba.

Morrison, George R.

1989 *Espanola on the Spanish*. Espanola, Ont.: Oliver Graphics.

Paget, Gary and Brian Walisser

1984 'The development of mining communities in British Columbia: Resilience Through Local Government' in Margo J. Wojciechowski (ed.) *Mining Communities: Hard Lessons for the Future*. Kingston, Ont: Queen's University, Centre for Resource Studies: 96-150.

Riffel, J. A.

1975 *Quality of Life in Resource Towns*. Ottawa: Ministry of State, Urban Affairs Canada.

Robinson, Ira M.

1962 *New Industrial Towns on Canada's Resource Frontier*. Chicago: University of Chicago, Department of Geography Research Paper No. 73.

———

1984 'New resource towns on Canada's frontier: selected contemporary issues' in D. D. Detomasi and J. W. Gartrell (eds), *Resource Communities: A Decade of Disruption*. Boulder, CO: Westview Press.

Robson, Robert

1988 'The decline of resource towns'. Presented at the Canadian Urban and Housing Studies Conference, Institute of Urban Studies, University of Winnipeg, Winnipeg, Manitoba, 18-20 February.

Ross, W. Gillies

1957 'Knob Lake on Canada's New Frontier'. *Canadian Geographical Journal* 54: 239-45.

Sarrinen, Oiva W.

1986 'Single Sector Communities in Northern Ontario: Historical Perspectives' in G. A. Stelter and A. F. J. Artibise (eds) *Power and Place*. Vancouver: University of British Columbia Press: 219-64.

Shea, Wes
1984 'New Resource Communities: Dilemmas in Social Development'. *Social Development Issues* 1 & 2: 144-55.
Statistics Canada
1989 *Labour Force Annual Averages: 1981-1988.* (Catalogue 71-529).
Storey, Keith and Mark Shrimpton
1988 '"Fly-in" mining and northern development policy: the impacts of long-distance commuting in the Canadian mining sector'. *Impact Assessment Bulletin* 6: 127-36.
———
1989 *Long Distance Commuting in the Canadian Mining Industry*. Kingston, Ont.: Queen's University, Centre for Resource Studies. Working Paper No. 43.
Stelter, Gilbert A.
1974 'Community development in Toronto's commercial empire: the industrial towns of the nickel belt: 1883-1931'. *Laurentian University Review* 6: 3-53.
——— and Alan F. J. Artibise
1978 'Canadian resource towns in historical perspective'. *Plan Canada* 18: 7-16.

Chapter Six

Breton, Yvan, Marie Giasson, Jean-Marc Darveau, and Daniel Roy
1988 *Pêcheries et municipalisation Old Fort-Blanc Sablon: une vision anthropologique*. Québec: Université Laval.
Canada
1983a *Navigating Troubled Waters. Report of the Task Force on Atlantic Fisheries*. Ottawa: Supply and Services Canada.
———
1983b Canadian Fisheries Annual Statistical Review 1981. Ottawa: Department of Fisheries and Oceans.
———
1990 Leslie Harris and Northern Cod Review Panel. Independent Review of the State of the Northern Cod Stock. Ottawa: Communications Directorate: Department of Fisheries and Oceans.
Clement, Wallace
1986 *The Struggle to Organize: Resistance in Canada's Fishery*. Toronto: McClelland and Stewart.
Davis, Anthony
forth-coming *Dire Straits: The Dilemmas of a Fishery. The Case of Digby Neck and the Islands*. St John's: Institute of Social and Economic Research.
——— and Victor Thiessen
1988 'Public policy and social control in the fisheries'. *Canadian Public Policy* 14: 66-77.
Firestone, Melvin M.
1967 *Brothers and Rivals: Patrilocality in Savage Cove*. St John's: Institute of Social and Economic Research.
MacDonald, Martha and M. Patricia Connelly
1989 'Class and gender in fishing communities in Nova Scotia'. *Studies in Political Economy* 30: 61-85.

Nadel-Klein, Jane and Dona Lee Davis (eds)
1988 *To Work and to Weep: Women in Fishing Economies*. St John's: Institute of Social and Economic Research.
Neis, Barbara
1988 'From cod block to fish food: the crisis and restructuring in the Newfoundland fishing industry, 1968-1986'. PhD dissertation, University of Toronto.
Ommer, Rosemary E.
1989 'The truck system in Gaspé, 1822-77'. *Acadiensis* 19, 1: 91-114.
———
1981 'All the fish of the post: resource property rights and development in a nineteenth century inshore fishery'. *Acadiensis* 10: 107-23.
Porter, Marilyn
1987 'Peripheral women: towards a feminist analysis of the Atlantic region'. *Studies in Political Economy* 23: 41-72.
Sinclair, Peter R.
1985 *From Traps to Draggers: Domestic Commodity Production in Northwest Newfoundland, 1850-1982*. St John's: Institute of Social and Economic Research.
———
1986 'Theoretical Issues in the Sociology of Fisheries'. *Proceedings of the Exploratory Workshop in Fisheries Sociology*. Woods Hole Oceanographic Institute: Technical Report, WO-86-34: 31-40.
———
1987 *State Intervention and the Newfoundland Fisheries: Essays on Fisheries Policy and Social Structure*. Aldershot: Gower Avebury.
——— and Lawrence F. Felt
1990 'Home sweet home: dimensions and determinants of life satisfaction in a peripheral region'. Presented to the Atlantic Sociology and Anthropology Association, Saint John, NB, 22-24 March.
Stiles, R. Geoffrey
1979 'Labor recruitment and the family crew in Newfoundland'. R.R. Andersen (ed.), *North Atlantic Maritime Cultures*. The Hague: Mouton: 189-208.

Chapter Seven

Barker, R.A., and P.W. Gump
1964 *Big School, Small School: High School Size and Student Behaviour*. Stanford, CA: Stanford University Press.
Boyer, E.L.
1963 *High School*. New York: Harper & Row.
Burns, O.E., Gilbert Taylor, and John Miller
1984 'School closure policy development and implementation'. *The Canadian Administrator* 23, 7: 1-6.
Carlsen, W.S., and F. Dunn
1981 'Small rural schools: A portrait'. *High School Journal* 64: 299-309.
Dunn, F.
1977 'Choosing smallness: An examination of the small school experience in rural

America' in J. P. Sher (ed.), *Education in Rural America*. Boulder, CO: Westview Press.

Goodlad, J.I.
1984 *A Place Called School*. New York: McGraw-Hill.

Haller, Emil J. and David H. Monk
1988 'New reforms, old reforms and the consolidation of small rural schools'. *Educational Administration Quarterly* 24: 470-83.

Hamilton, S.F.
1983 'The social side of schooling: Ecological studies of classrooms and schools'. *Elementary School Journal* 83: 313-34.

Hanson, N.W.
1964 'Economy of scale as a cost factor in financing public schools'. *National Tax Journal* 17: 92-5.

Hind, Ian W.
1979 'Some economic aspects of the provision of educational services to rural areas'. Paper presented to the National Conference on New Directions in Rural Education, Perth, Western Australia. ERIC Document Reproduction Service No. ED 216 822.

Kay, S.
1981 'Public school organization and community development in rural areas'. Frankfort: Kentucky State University. ERIC Document Reproduction Service No. 201 433.

Lucas, Barry. G.
1982 'A rural perspective: School closure and community protest'. *McGill Journal of Education* 27: 251-62.

Marshall, David G.
1985 'Closing small schools or when is small too small?'. *Education Canada* 3: 11-16.

Peshkin, Alan
1978 *Growing Up American: Schooling and the Survival of Community*. Chicago: University of Chicago Press.

Randhawa, B.S.
1991 'Inequities in educational opportunities and life chances' in T. Wotherspoon (ed.), *Hitting the Books: The Politics of Educational Retrenchment*. Toronto: Garamond Press: 137-58.

——— and Julian O. Michayluk
1975 'Learning environment as a function of locale, grade, and sex'. *American Educational Research Journal* 12: 265-85.

Saskatchewan Education
1981 *Rural Education: Options for the 80's*. Regina: Saskatchewan Education.

Scharf, Murray P.
1974 *A Report on the Declining Rural Population and the Implications for Rural Education*. Regina: Saskatchewan School Trustees Association.

Sher, Jonathan P.
1981 *Rural Education in Urbanized Nations: Issues and Innovations*. An OECD/CERI report. Boulder, CO: Westview Press.

——— and Rachel P. Tompkins
1976 *Economy, Efficiency, and Equality: The Myths of Rural School and District Consolidation*. Washington, DC: The National Institute of Education, US Department of Health, Education, and Welfare.

Statistics Canada

1978 Population: Demographic Characteristics. Catalogue 92-823. Ottawa: Minister of Supply and Services Canada.

———

1979 Population: Demographic Perspectives. Catalogue 98-802. Ottawa: Minister of Supply and Services Canada.

———

1984 Urban Growth in Canada, Census 1981. Catalogue 99-942. Ottawa: Minister of Supply and Services Canada.

———

1987 Population: Population and Dwelling Counts—Provinces and Territories. Tables, Catalogue 92-109 to 92-120. Ottawa: Minister of Supply and Services Canada.

———

1988 Profiles: Urban and Rural Areas, Canada, Provinces and Territories. Part I, Canada 1986. Catalogue 94-129. Ottawa: Minister of Supply and Services Canada.

Chapter Eight

Boggs, Sarah L.

1971 'Formal and Informal Crime Control: An Exploratory Study of Urban, Suburban, and Rural Orientations'. *The Sociological Quarterly* 12: 319-27.

Carter, Keith A. and Lionel J. Beaulieu

1984 *Rural Crime in Florida: A Victimization Study of the Rural NonFarm Population in Florida.* University of Florida: Institute of Food and Agricultural Sciences.

Chambliss, William and Robert Seidman

1971 *Law, Order, and Power.* Reading, MA: Addison-Wesley.

Chalmers, Lee and Pamela Smith

1987 'Wife Battering: Psychological, Social and Physical Isolation and Counteracting Strategies' in K. Storrie (ed.), *Women: Isolation and Bonding.* Toronto: Methuen Publications.

Clark, S.D.

1978 *The New Urban Poor.* Toronto: McGraw-Hill Ryerson.

Cruikshank, Julie

1981 'Matrifocal Families in the Canadian North' in K. Ishwaran (ed.), *The Canadian Family.* Toronto: Holt, Rinehart and Winston.

Currie, Elliot

1986 *Confronting Crime: An American Challenge.* New York: Pantheon Books.

Fischer, Claude S.

1980 'The Spread of Violent Crime from City to Countryside, 1955 to 1975'. *Rural Sociology* 45: 416-34.

Hagan, John

1977 'Criminal Justice in Rural and Urban Communities: A Study of the Bureaucratization of Justice'. *Social Forces* 55: 597-612.

Howard, John, David Cunningham, and Peter Rechnitzer

1978 *Rusting Out, Burning Out, Bowing Out.* Agincourt, Ont.: Gage Publishing Ltd.

Kennedy, Leslie W. and Donald G. Dutton
1987 'The Incidence of Wife Assault in Alberta'. *Canadian Journal of Behavioural Science* 21: 40-54.

Kennedy, Leslie W. and Harvey Krahn
1984 'Rural-Urban Origin and Fear of Crime: The Case for "Rural Baggage" '. *Rural Sociology* 49: 247-60.

Kueneman, Rod, Rick Linden and Rick Kosmick
1986 *A Study of Manitoba's Northern and Rural Juvenile Courts*. Ottawa: Ministry of the Solicitor General of Canada.

LaPrairie, Carol Pitcher
1983 'Native Juveniles in Court: Some Preliminary Observations' in Thomas Fleming and L. A. Visano (eds) *Deviant Designations: Crime, Law, and Deviance in Canada*. Toronto: Butterworths Canada Ltd.

Lee, Gary R.
1982 'Residential Location and Fear of Crime Among the Elderly'. *Rural Sociology* 47: 655-69.

Linden, Rick and Candice Minch
1985 *Rural Crime Prevention in Canada*. Ottawa: Ministry of Solicitor General of Canada.

McLeod, Linda
1980 *Wife Battering in Canada: The Vicious Circle*. Ottawa: Minister of Supply and Services.

Potgieter, Rod
1988 'A Comprehensive, Centrally Co-ordinated, Cost-Effective Family Violence Counselling Program for Small Communities'. *Canadian Journal of Community Mental Health* 7: 137-45.

Royal Canadian Mounted Police
1984 Public Satisfaction Questionnaire: Dauphin Sub-Division, RCMP 'D' Division, Winnipeg.

———
1981 Police Services Community Project, 'D' Division. Ottawa: Crime Prevention Centre RCMP Headquarters.

Smith, Brent L. and C. Ronald Huff
1982 'Crime in the Country: The Vulnerability and Victimization of Rural Citizens'. *Journal of Criminal Justice* 10: 271-82.

Turk, Austin
1976 *Criminality and the Legal Order*. Chicago: Rand McNally.

Wright, Kevin N.
1981 *Crime and Criminal Justice in a Declining Economy*. Cambridge, MA: Oelgeschlager, Gunn, and Hain.

Chapter Nine

Adams, D.
1975 'Who Are the Rural Aged?' in R.C. Atchley (ed.) *Rural Environments and Aging*. Washington: Gerontological Society of America: 11-21.

Agbayewa, M.O., and B. Michalski
1984 'Accommodation Preference in the Senior Years'. *Canadian Journal of Public Health* 75: 176-9.
Alberta Senior Citizens Secretariat
1986 *Older Albertans 1986*. Alberta Senior Citizens Secretariat, Edmonton, Alberta.
Arcury, T.
1984 'Household Composition and Economic Change in a Rural Community, 1900-1980: Testing Two Models'. *American Ethnologist* 11: 677-98.
Beland, F.
1986 'Patterns of Health and Social Service Utilization'. Paper presented to the Annual Meeting of the Canadian Association on Gerontology, Quebec City, Quebec.
Bienvenue, R., and B. Havens
1986 'Structural Inequalities, Informal Networks: A Comparison of Native and Non-native Elderly'. *Canadian Journal on Aging* 5, 4: 241-8.
Bilby, R.W., and R. Benson
1977 'Public Perceptions of Rural County Social Service Agencies'. *Journal of Sociology and Social Welfare* 47: 1033-54.
Black, M.
1985 'Health and Social Support of Older Adults in the Community'. *Canadian Journal on Aging* 4, 4: 213-26.
Bond, J. and C. Harvey
1987 'Familial Support of the Elderly in a Rural Mennonite Community'. *Canadian Journal on Aging* 6, 1: 7-17.
Brown, K.H., and A. Martin Matthews
1981 'Changes in the Welfare of the Recently Retired: Rural-Urban Comparisons'. Paper presented to the Annual Meeting of the Rural Sociological Society, Guelph, Ontario, August.
Cape, E.
1984 'The Distaff Side of Retiring to the Country'. Paper presented to the Annual Meeting of the Canadian Sociology and Anthropology Association, Guelph, Ontario, June.
Chamberlain, S.
1976 'Study of the Housing and Health Care Needs of the Elderly Persons of North Frontenac'. Ottawa: School of Social Work, Carleton University.
Connidis, I.
1989 *Family Ties and Aging*. Toronto: Butterworths Canada Ltd.
Corin, E.
1984 'Manières de Vivre, Manières de Dire: Réseau Social et Sociabilité Quotidienne des Personnes au Québec'. *Questions de Culture* 6: 157-86.
Coward, R.T. and S.J. Cutler
1989 'Informal and Formal Health Care Systems for the Rural Elderly'. *Health Services Research* 23, 6: 785-806.

———
1988 'The Concept of a Continuum of Residence: Comparing Activities of Daily Living Among the Elderly'. *Journal of Rural Studies* 4, 2: 159-68.

Dorfman, L. and A. Heckert

1988 'Egalitarianism in Retired Rural Couples: Household Tasks, Decision-making and Leisure Activities'. *Family Relations* 37: 73-8.

——— and E. Hill

1986 'Rural Housewives and Retirement: Joint Decision-making Matters'. *Family Relations* 35: 507-14.

Earle, V.

1984 'Report of a Study to Develop a Comprehensive Proposal for a Pilot Caregiver Relief Program'. Durham Region Community Care Association, Durham, Ontario.

Gillis, D.

1987 'Indicators of Health among Elderly Native Canadians'. Paper presented to the Annual Meeting of the Canadian Association on Gerontology, Calgary, Alberta.

Government of Canada

1982 *Canadian Governmental Report on Aging*. Ottawa: Minister of Supply and Services, Cat. No. H21-89/1982E.

Grant, P.R. and B. Rice

1983 'Transportation Problems of the Rural Elderly'. *Canadian Journal on Aging* 2: 107-24.

Harper, S.

1987 'The Kinship Network of the Rural Aged: A Comparison of the Indigenous Elderly and the Retired Immigrant'. *Aging and Society* 7: 303-27.

Havens, B.

1980 'Differentiation of Unmet Needs Using Analysis by Age/Sex Cohorts' in V. Marshall (ed.) *Aging in Canada: Social Perspectives*. Don Mills, Ont.: Fitzhenry and Whiteside: 215-21.

Health and Welfare Canada

1989 *Active Health Report on Seniors*. Ottawa: Minister of Supply and Services.

———

1981 *The Health of Canadians:A Report of the Canada Health Survey*. Ottawa: Minister of Supply and Services.

Hodge, G.

1984 *Shelter and Services for the Small Town Elderly: The Role of Assisted Housing*. Ottawa: Canada Mortgage and Housing Corporation.

Hohn, N.

1986 *Issues Affecting Older Natives in Alberta*. Edmonton, Alberta: Alberta Senior Citizens Secretariat.

Johnson, C. and F. Johnson

1983 'A Micro-Analysis of Senility: The Responses of the Family and the Health Professionals'. *Culture, Medicine and Psychiatry* 7: 77-96.

Keating, N.

1987 'Reducing Stress of Farm Men and Women'. *Family Relations* 36: 358-63.

——— and G. Brundin

1983 'Factors in Consideration of Moving by Older Rural Men'. *Canadian Home Economics Journal* 33, 3: 137-40.

——— and B. Munro
1989 'Transferring the Family Farm: Process and Implications'. *Family Relations* 38: 215-18.

———
1988 'Farm Women, Farm Work'. *Sex Roles* 19, 3/4: 155-68.

Keith, P. and A. Nauta
1988 'Old and Single in the City and in the Country: Activities of the Unmarried'. *Family Relations* 37: 79-83.

Kivett, V.R.
1988a 'Aging in a Rural Place: The Elusive Source of Well-Being'. *Journal of Rural Studies* 4, 2: 125-32.

———
1988b 'Older Rural Fathers and Sons: Patterns of Association and Helping'. *Family Relations* 37: 62-7.

———
1985 'Aging in Rural Society: Non-Kin Community Relations and Participation' in R. Coward and G. Lee (eds) *The Elderly in Rural Society*. New York: Springer: 171-91.

——— and R. Learner
1980 'Situational Influences on the Morale of Older Rural Adults in Child Shared Households'. Paper presented to the Annual Meeting of the Gerontological Society, San Diego, California, November.

Krout, J.A.
1988 'The Elderly in Rural Environments'. *Journal of Rural Studies* 4, 2: 103-14.

Lee, J.
1987 'Women as Non-family Farmworkers' in Canadian Advisory Council on the Status of Women (eds) *Growing Strong: Women in Agriculture*. Ottawa: Canadian Advisory Council on the Status of Women: 91-122.

Lubben, J.P. Weiler, I. Chi, and F. DeJong
1988 'Health Promotion for the Rural Elderly'. *The Journal of Rural Health* 4, 3: 85-96.

Martin Matthews, A.
1988a 'Aging in Rural Canada' in E. Rathbone-McCuan and B. Havens (eds) *North American Elders: United States and Canadian Perspectives*. Westport, CT: Greenwood: 143-60.

———
1988b 'Variations in the Conceptualization and Measurement of Rurality: Conflicting Findings on the Elderly Widowed'. *Journal of Rural Studies* 4, 2: 141-50.

———, K. Brown, C. Davis, and M. Denton
1982 'A Crisis Assessment Technique for the Evaluation of Life Events: Transition to Retirement as an Example'. *Canadian Journal on Aging* 1, 3/4: 28-39.

McCay, B.
1987 'Old People and Social Relations in a Newfoundland "Outport"' in H. Strange and M. Teitelbaum (eds) *Aging and Cultural Diversity*. South Hadley, MA: Bergen and Garvey: 61-87.

McClelland, N. and C. Miles
1987 1985/1986 Assessment Project: Aged, Disabled and Chronically Ill. Yellowknife, NWT: Department of Social Services and Health, Government of the Northwest Territories.
McDonald, L. and R. Wanner
1989 *Retirement in Canada.* Toronto: Butterworths Canada Ltd.
McGhee, J.
1985 'The Effects of Siblings on the Life Satisfaction of the Rural Elderly'. *Journal of Marriage and the Family* 47: 85-91.
Mercier, J., L. Paulson, and E. Morris
1988 'Rural and Urban Elderly: Differences in the Quality of the Parent-Child Relationship'. *Family Relations* 37: 68-72.
Methot, S.
1987 'Employment Patterns of Elderly Canadians'. *Canadian Social Trends* (Autumn): 7-11.
Miller, M.K., and A.E. Luloff
1981 'Who is Rural? A Typological Approach to the Examination of Rurality'. *Rural Sociology* 46: 608-25.
Morton, M., S. Polowin, C. Murphy, and A. McDonald
1984 'Survey of Needs of Seniors in the Township of Rideau'. Rideau, Ont.: Township of Rideau Senior Citizens' Service Centre.
O'Neil, J.
1987 'Health Care in a Central Canadian Arctic Community: Continuities and Change' in D. Coburn, C. D'Arcy, G. Torrance and P. New (eds) *Health and Canadian Society: Sociological Perspectives.* Don Mills, Ont.: Fitzhenry and Whiteside: 141-58.
Palmore, E.
1983 'Health Care Needs of the Rural Elderly'. *International Journal of Aging and Human Development* 18, 1: 39-45.
Peace River Health Unit
1986 *A New Beginning. A Review of the Needs of Seniors in the Peace River Health Unit.* Peace River, Alberta.
Raiwet, C.
1989 'As Long as we Have Our Health: The Experience of Age-Related Physical Change for Rural Elderly Couples'. MSc thesis. University of Alberta, Edmonton, Alberta.
Rowles, G.D.
1988 'What's Rural about Rural Aging? An Appalachian Perspective'. *Journal of Rural Studies* 4, 2: 115-24.
Scheidt, R.J.
1984 'A Taxonomy of Well-Being for Small-Town Elderly: A Case for Rural Diversity'. *The Gerontologist* 24, 1: 84-90.
Scott, J., and V. Kivet
1980 'The Widowed, Black, Older Adult in the Rural South: Implications for Policy'. *Family Relations* 29, 1: 83-90.
Scott, J.P., and K. Roberto
1987 'Informal Supports of Older Adults: A Rural-Urban Comparison'. *Family Relations* 36: 444-9.

Selles, R. and N. Keating

1989 'La Transmission des Fermes par les Albertain âges d'origine Hollandaise' in R. Santerre and D. Meintel (eds) *Veiller au Quebec, en Afrique et Ailleurs*. Laval: University of Laval Press.

Senior Citizens Provincial Council

1983 *Profile '83. The Senior Population in Saskatchewan* (Volumes 1-4). Regina, Saskatchewan.

Shapiro, E. and L. Roos

1984 'Using Health Care: Rural/Urban Differences Among the Manitoba Elderly'. *The Gerontologist* 24, 3: 270-4.

Stalwick, H.

1983 'Canadian Perspectives on Aging in Remote Areas: A Challenge for Socio-medical Services'. Paper presented to the International Expert Group Meeting on Aging in Remote Areas, Limoges, France.

Statistics Canada

1987a Census/recensement Canada 1986 Reference dictionary. Catalogue 99-101E. Ottawa: Minister of Supply and Services.

———

1987b The Nation: Age, Sex and Marital Status. Catalogue 93-101. Ottawa: Minister of Supply and Services.

———

1984 Occupied Private Dwellings, 1981 Census. Catalogue 92-932, Table 7. Ottawa: Minister of Supply and Services.

———

1982 Population: Population by Marital Status and Sex. 1981 Census. Catalogue 92-901, Table 7. Ottawa: Minister of Supply and Services.

Stone, L.O., and S. Fletcher

1980 *A Profile of Canada's Older Population*. Montreal: The Institute for Research on Public Policy.

Storm, C., T. Storm, and J. Strike-Schurman

1985 'Obligations for Care: Beliefs in a Small Canadian Town'. *Canadian Journal on Aging* 4, 2: 75-85.

Thurston, N.E., D.E. Larsen, A.W. Redemaker, and J.C. Kerr

1982 'Health Status of the Rural Elderly: A Picture of Health'. Paper presented to the Annual Meeting of the Canadian Association on Gerontology, Winnipeg, Manitoba.

Vanek, J.

1980 'Work, Leisure, and Family Roles: Farm Households in the United States, 1920-1955'. *Journal of Family History* 5: 422-31.

Vivian, J.B.

1982 *Home Support Services Survey Project*. St John's, Newfoundland: Newfoundland Department of Social Services.

Watkins, J.M., and D.A. Watkins

1984 *Social Policy and the Rural Setting*. New York: Springer.

Weinert, C., and K. Long

1987 'Understanding the Health Care Needs of Rural Families'. *Family Relations* 36: 450-5.

Wenger, C.
1982 'Aging in Rural Communities: Family Contacts and Community Integration'. *Aging and Society* 2, 2: 211-29.
———
1986 'A Longitudinal Study of Changes and Adaptation in the Support Networks of Welsh Elderly Over 75'. *Journal of Cross Cultural Gerontology* 1, 3: 277-304.
Whyte, D.R.
1968 'Rural Canada in Transition' in M. A. Tremblay and W.J. Anderson (eds) *Rural Canada in Transition*. Ottawa: Agricultural Economics Research Council: 1-99.
Windley, P.G., and R. Scheidt
1988 'Rural Small Towns: An Environmental Context for Aging'. *Journal of Rural Studies* 4, 2: 151-8.
Wister, A.
1985 'Living Arrangement Choices Among the Elderly'. *Canadian Journal on Aging* 4, 3: 127-44.
Young, T.
1987 'The Health of Indians in Northwestern Ontario: A Historical Perspective' in D. Coburn, C. D'Arcy, G. Torrance and P. New (eds) *Health and Canadian Society: Sociological Perspectives*. Don Mills, Ont.: Fitzhenry and Whiteside: 109-25.
Zarit, S., K. Reever, and K J. Bach-Peterson
1980 'Relatives of the Impaired Elderly: Correlates of Feelings of Burden'. *The Gerontologist* 20: 649-55.

Chapter Ten

Berry, Ruth
1986 'Labour allocation of farm women'. Paper presented to the Canadian Rural Studies Association annual meeting, Winnipeg.
Bokemeier, Janet, Carolyn Sachs and Verna Keith
1983 'Labour force participation of metropolitan and farm women: a comparative study'. *Rural Sociology* 48, 2: 515-39.
——— and Lorraine Garkovitch
1987 'Assessing the influence of farm women's self-identity on task allocation and decision-making'. *Rural Sociology* 52, 1: 13-36.
Boulding, Elise
1980 'The labour of US farm women: a knowledge gap'. *Sociology of Work and Occupations* 7, 3: 261-90.
Brannen, Julia and Gail Wilson (eds)
1987 *Give And Take In Families: Studies In Resource Distribution*. London: Allen & Unwin.
Buttel, Fred and Gilbert Gillespie
1984 'Sexual division of farm household labour'. *Rural Sociology* 49, 2: 183-209.
Canada
1970 *Royal Commission on the Status of Women Report*. Ottawa: Queen's Printer.
Council on Rural Development Canada
1979 *Rural Women: Their Work, Their Needs and Their Role in Rural Development*. Ottawa: Supply and Services Canada (catalogue no. RE 41-5/1979).

Connelly, Patricia

1978 *Last Hired, First Fired: Women and the Canadian Work Force*. Toronto: The Women's Press.

Davis, Fay and Laurie Few

1989 *Legal, economic and social concerns of Saskatchewan farm women*. Saskatoon: Women's Legal Education and Action Fund (LEAF), Saskatchewan Branch.

Dion, Suzanne

1983 *Les femmes dans l'agriculture au Québec*. Longueuil, Quebec: Les éditions La Terre de chez nous.

Eichler, Margrit

1985 'And the work never ends: feminist contributions'. *Canadian Journal of Sociology and Anthropology* 22, 5: 619-44.

——— and Jeanne Lapointe

1985 *On the Treatment of the Sexes in Research*. Ottawa: Social Sciences and Humanities Research Council of Canada and Supply and Services Canada.

Gasson, Ruth

1981 'Roles of women on farms: a pilot study'. *Journal of Agricultural Economics* 32, 1: 11-20.

Ghorayshi, Parveen

1989 'The indispensable nature of wives' work for the farm family enterprise'. *Canadian Review of Sociology and Anthropology* 26, 4: 571-95.

Harding, Sandra (ed.)

1987 *Feminism and Methodology*. Bloomington: Indiana University Press.

Hill, Frances

1981 'Farm women: challenge to scholarship'. *Rural Sociologist* 1: 370-82.

Huffman, Wallace, and Mark Lange

1989 'Off-farm work decisions of husbands and wives: joint decision-making'. *Review of Economics and Statistics* 71, 3: 471-80.

Ireland, Gisele

1983 *The Farmer Takes a Wife*. Chesley, Ont.: Concerned Farm Women.

Jones, Calvin and Rachel Rosenfeld

1981 'American Farm Women: Findings From A National Survey'. Chicago: National Opinion Research Centre Report No. 130.

Kalbacher, Judith Z.

1982 'Women farmers in America'. Bulletin ERS-679. Washington: US Department of Agriculture. Economic Research Service.

Keating, Norah

1987 'The work of farm women'. *First Reading* (a publication of the Edmonton Social Planning Council) 5, 4: 5-7.

——— and Brenda Munro

1988 'Farm women/farm work'. *Sex Roles* 19, 3/4: 155-68.

———

1989 'Reducing stress of farm men and women'. *Family Relations* 36, 1: 358-63.

———, Maryanne Dougherty and Brenda Munro

1987 'The whole economy: resouce allocation of Alberta farm women and men'. *Canadian Home Economics Association Journal* 37, 3: 135-9.

———
1978 'Women's participation in the North American Family Farm'. *Women's Studies International Quarterly* 1, 1: 47-54.

Kohl, Seena B.
1976 *Working Together: Women and Family in South Western Saskatchewan*. Toronto: Holt, Rinehart and Winston.

Koski, Susan
1982 *The Employment Practices of Farm Women*. Saskatoon: The National Farmers Union.

Laurin-Frenette, Nicole
1981 'Les femmes dans la sociologie'. *Sociologie et Sociétés* 13, 2: 3-18.

Lee, Julie
1987 'Women as non-family farmworkers', in the Canadian Advisory Council on the Status of Women (ed.), *Growing Strong: Women in Agriculture*. Ottawa.

McGhee, Molly
1984 *Women in Rural Life: The Changing Scene*. Toronto: Government of Ontario, Ministry of Agriculture and Food.

McLaren, Arlene Tigar (ed.)
1988 *Gender and Society: Creating a Canadian Women's Sociology*. Mississauga, Ont.: Copp Clark Pitman.

Meiners, Jane and Geraldine Olson
1987 'Household, paid and unpaid work time of farm women'. *Family Relations* 36, 4: 407-11.

Nieman, Lynne L.
1991 Literature review for 'Broadening Our Horizons', conference sponsored by the Canadian Federation of Agriculture concerning Canadian farm women and decision-making. Ottawa, April.

Phillips, Lynne
1989 'Gender dynamics and rural household strategies'. *Canadian Review of Sociology and Anthropology* 26, 2: 294-310.

Rasmussan, Linda, Lorna Rasmussen, Candace Savage and Anne Wheeler
1976 *A Harvest Yet To Reap: A History of Farm Women*. Toronto: The Women's Press.

Reimer, William
1980 'Sources of farm labour in contemporary Quebec'. *Canadian Review of Sociology and Anthropology* 20, 3: 290-301.

Rose-Lizee, Ruth
1984 *Portrait des Femmes Collaboratrices du Québec*. Saint-Lambert: Association des femmes collaboratrices du Québec.

Rosenfeld, Rachel
1986 'US farm women: their part in farm work and decision-making'. *Work and Occupations* 13, 2: 179-202.

Ross, Lois
1985 *Prairie Lives: The Changing Face of Farming*. Toronto: Between the Lines.

———
1990 *Harvest of Opportunities: New Horizons for Farm Women*. Saskatoon: Western Producer Prairie Books.

Ross, Peggy

1985 'A commentary on research on American farmwomen'. *Agriculture and Human Values* 2, 1: 19-30.

Sachs, Carolyn

1983 *The Invisible Farmers.* Totowa, NJ: Rowman and Allanheld.

Salant, Priscilla

1983 'Farm women: contribution to farm and family'. Washington, DC: US Department of Agriculture Research Report No. 140.

———

1984 'Farm households and the off-farm sector: results from Mississippi and Tennessee'. Washington: US Department of Agriculture Research Report No. 143.

Sawer, Barbara

1973 'Predictors of farm wives' involvement in general management and adoption decisions'. *Rural Sociology* 38, 4: 412-26.

Shaver, Fran

1989 'Women in Canadian agriculture'. Unpublished, revised paper presented to le Congrès de l'Acfas, Montreal, May.

Smith, Pamela

1986 'Not enough hours, our accountant tells me: trends in children's, women's and men's involvement in Canadian agriculture'. *Canadian Journal of Agricultural Economics* 33 (June): 161-95.

———

1987 'What lies within and behind the statistics?: trying to measure women's contribution to Canadian agriculture' in Canadian Advisory Council on the Status of Women (ed.), *Growing Strong: Women in Agriculture.* Ottawa.

———

1988 'Murdoch's, Becker's and Sorochan's challenge: thinking again about the roles of women in primary agriculture' in G.S. Basran and D.A. Hay (eds), *The Political Economy of Agriculture in Western Canada.* Toronto: Garamond Press: 157-72.

———

1989 'Women working on and off the farm: trends across Canada', in N. Johns (ed.), *Canadian Farm Women's Network Newsletter* 2 (Spring): 3-4.

Symes, D. and T. Marsden

1983 'Complementary roles and asymmetrical lives: farmers' wives in a large environment'. *Sociologia Ruralis*, 23, 3-4: 229-41.

Tigges, Leann and Rachel Rosenfeld

1987 'Independent farming: correlates and consequences for women and men'. *Rural Sociology* 52, 3: 345-64.

Villani, Rosemary

1990 'Review of Statistics Canada sources of farm labour data'. Unpublished paper. Ottawa: Statistics Canada, Agriculture Division.

Waring, Marilyn

1988 *If Women Counted: A New Feminist Economics.* San Francisco: Harper & Row.

Whatmore, Sarah
1988 'From women's roles to gender relations: developing perspectives in the analysis of farm women'. *Sociologia Ruralis* 28, 4: 239-47.
Wilkening, Eugene
1981 'Farm husbands and wives in Wisconsin: work roles, decision-making and satisfaction, 1962 and 1979'. Research Bulletin No. R3147. Madison: University of Wisconsin, College of Agriculture and Life Sciences.
Williamson, Lenny
1981 'Farm women'. *Canada Agriculture* 26, 3: 21-2.

Chapter Eleven

Agricultural Institute of Canada
1990 'AIC Presents Sustainable Agriculture Brief'. *AgriScience* (March): 5-7.
Batie, Sandra S.
1989 'Sustainable development: challenges to the profession of agricultural economics'. *American Journal of Agricultural Economics* 71: 1083-101.
Beus, Curtis E., and Riley E. Dunlap
1990 'Conventional versus alternative agriculture: The paradigmatic roots of the debate'. *Rural Sociology* 55: 590-616.
Buttel, Frederick H.
1983 'Beyond the family farm' in Gene F. Summers (ed.), *Technology and Social Change in Rural Areas*. Boulder, CO: Westview Press: 87-107.
——— and Michael E. Gertler
1982 'Agricultural structure, agricultural policy, and environmental quality: some observations on the context of agricultural research in North America'. *Agriculture and Environment* 7: 101-19.
———, Gilbert W. Gillespie, Jr, Rhonda Janke, Brian Caldwell, and Marianne Sarrantonio
1986 'Reduced-input agricultural systems: Rationale and prospects'. *American Journal of Alternative Agriculture* 1, 2: 58-64.
———, Olaf F. Larson, and Gilbert W. Gillespie
1990 'The new sociology of Agriculture' in *The Sociology of Agriculture*. Westport, CT: Greenwood Press, Inc.: 127-70.
——— and Louis E. Swanson
1986 'Soil and water conservation: a farm structural and public policy context' in Stephen B. Lovejoy and Ted L. Napier (eds) *Conserving Soil: Insights from Socioeconomic Research*. Ankeny, Iowa: Soil Conservation Society of America: 26-39.
Cameron, Silver Donald
1990 'Net losses'. *Canadian Geographic* 110, 2: 29-37.
Campbell, C.A., R.P. Zentner, H.H. Janzen, R.D Tinline, and J.R. Byers
1990 'Sustainable agriculture—some complicating interactions' in *New Frontiers in Prairie Agriculture*, Soils and Crops Workshop sponsored by the Saskatchewan Advisory Committee on Soils and Agronomy and the University of Saskatchewan, Saskatoon, 22-23 February: 313-23.

Council on Scientific Affairs, American Medical Association

1991 'Council report: Biotechnology and the American agricultural industry'. *Journal of the American Medical Association* 265, 11: 1429-36.

Cushon, Ian

1991 'Sustainable agriculture resource guide'. *Union Farmer* 42, 4: 10.

Drake, Lars

1989 'Swedish agriculture at a turning point'. *Agriculture and Human Values* 6: 117-26.

Franklin, Ursula

1990 *The Real World of Technology*. CBC Massey Lectures Series. Montreal: CBC Enterprises.

Fuller, Tony, Philip Ehrensaft, and Michael Gertler

1990 'Sustainable rural communities in Canada: issues and prospects' in Michael Gertler and Harold Baker (eds) *Sustainable Rural Communities in Canada*. Proceedings of Rural Policy Seminar #1. Saskatoon: Canadian Agriculture and Rural Restructuring Group: 1-41.

Fulton, Murray, Ken Rosaasen, and Andrew Schmitz

1989 *Canadian Agricultural Policy and Prairie Agriculture*. Study Prepared for the Economic Council of Canada. Ottawa: Supply and Services Canada.

Gertler, Michael E.

1991 'The institutionalization of grower-processor relations in the vegetable industries of Ontario and New York' in William Friedland, Lawrence Busch, Frederick Buttel, and Alan Rudy (eds) *Towards a New Political Economy of Agriculture*. Boulder, CO: Westview Press: 232-55.

———

1987 'Biotechnology and prairie agriculture: Some societal issues' in *Biotechnology: New Thrusts in Prairie Agriculture*, Proceedings from the Agrologist Update, 3-5 November, Saskatoon: 130-43.

——— and Thomas Murphy

1987 'The social economy of Canadian agriculture: family farming and alternative futures' in Boguslaw Galeski and Eugene Wilkening (eds), *Family Farming in Europe and America*. Boulder, CO: Westview Press: 230-69.

Griffin, Keith

1974 *The Political Economy of Agrarian Change*. Cambridge, MA: Harvard University Press.

Kennedy, Des

1990 'The challenge: making paper without pollution'. *Canadian Geographic* 110, 3: 56-63.

Kloppenberg, Jack, Jr

1988 *First the Seed*. New York: Cambridge University Press.

——— and Frederick H. Buttel

1987 'Two blades of grass: the contradictions of agricultural research as state intervention' in Richard G. Braungart and Margaret M. Braungart (eds) *Research in Political Sociology*. Greenwich, CT: JAI Press: 111-35.

Lockeretz, William
1990 'What have we learned about who conserves soil?'. *Journal of Soil and Water Conservation* 45: 517-23.
———, Georgia Shearer, and Daniel H. Kohl
1981 'Organic farming in the Corn Belt'. *Science* 211: 540-7.
——— and Sarah Wernick
1979 'Commercial organic farming in the corn belt in comparison to conventional practices'. *Rural Sociology* 44 (Winter): 773-90.
MacRae, Rod J., Stuart B. Hill, John Henning, and Alison J. Bentley
1990 'Policies, programs, and regulations to support the transition to sustainable agriculture in Canada'. *American Journal of Alternative Agriculture* 5, 2: 76-92.
Madden, Patrick
1988 'Low input/sustainable agricultural research and education-challenges to the agricultural economics profession'. *American Journal of Agricultural Economics* 70: 1167-72.
Manning, Edward W.
1988 'Soil conservation: the barriers to comprehensive national response'. *Prairie Forum* 13: 99-121.
Molotoch, Harvey and John Logan
1984 'Tensions in the growth machine: overcoming resistance to value-free development'. *Social Problems* 31, 5: 483-99.
Nikiforuk, Andrew, and Ed Struzik
1989 'The great forest sell-off'. *Report on Business Magazine* 6, 5: 56 ff.
Pearse, Andrew
1980 *Seeds of Plenty, Seeds of Want*. New York: Oxford University Press.
Perreault, Denis
1982 'L'integration contractuelle: Le cas de la production porcine, 1966-1980'. *Interventions Economiques pour une Alternative Sociale* 9: 115-30.
Redclift, Michael
1987 *Sustainable Development: Exploring the Contradictions*. London: Methuen Publications.
Rosaasen, Ken, Ron Eley, and James Lokken
1990 'Federal government relief programs for grain farmers: rewards for late adjusters?' in *New Frontiers in Prairie Agriculture*, Soils and Crops Workshop sponsored by the Saskatchewan Advisory Committee on Soils and Agronomy and the University of Saskatchewan, Saskatoon, 22-23 February: 354-79.
Shiva, Vandana
1989 'Development, Ecology, and Women' in Judith Plant (ed.) *Healing the Wounds: The Promise of Ecofeminism*. Toronto: Between the Lines: 80-90.
Statistics Canada
1987 'Census of Agriculture: 1986'. *The Daily* (3 June). Catalogue 11-001E.
———
1989 *A Profile of Canadian Agriculture*. Census of Agriculture, 1986. Catalogue 96-113.
Swanson, Louis E., Silvana M. Camboni, and Ted L. Napier
1986 'Barriers to adoption of soil conservation practices on farms' in Stephen B. Lovejoy and Ted L. Napier (eds) *Conserving Soil: Insights from Socioeconomic Research*. Ankeny, Iowa: Soil Conservation Society of America: 108-20.

Taylor, Robert C., and Klaus K. Frohberg

1977 'The welfare effects of erosion control, banning pesticides and limiting fertilizer applications in the Corn Belt'. *American Journal of Agricultural Economics* 59 (February): 23-35.

Thorne, Susan

1990 'Organic food for the masses'. *Food in Canada* 50, 6: 26-9.

Vail, David

1982 'Women and small farm revival: The division of labour and decision-making authority on Maine's organic farms'. *Review of Radical Political Economy* 13, 14 (Winter): 19-32.

van Es, J.C.

1983 'The adoption/diffusion tradition applied to resource conservation: inappropriate use of existing knowledge'. *The Rural Sociologist* 3 (March): 76-82.

Van Kooten, G.C.

1987 'A socioeconomic model of agriculture: a proposal for dealing with environmental problems in rural economy'. *Prairie Forum* 12, 1: 157-68.

Weinberg, Anne C.

1990 'Reducing agricultural pesticide use in Sweden'. *Journal of Soil and Water Conservation* 45, 6: 610-13.

Wernick, Sarah, and William Lockeretz

1977 'Motivations and practices of organic farmers'. *Compost Science* 18, 6: 20-4.

Chapter Twelve

Anderson, D.W.

1987 'Pedogenesis in grasslands and adjacent forests of the Great Plains'. *Advances in Soil Science* 7: 53-93.

Beck, Paul and M. Scafe

1989 'Pesticide monitoring in ground water in Ontario'. Workshop on Pesticide Contamination of Canadian Ground Waters. Saskatoon: National Hydrology Research Institute (abstract).

Beke, G.J. and J.D. Hilchey

1977 'Soils of the Appalachian Region' in G.K. Rutherford, B.P. Warkentin and P.J. Savage (eds) *The Geosciences in Canada, 1977*. Ottawa: Geological Survey of Canada.

Berry, Wendell

1981 *The Gift of Good Land*. San Francisco: North Point Press.

Biederbeck, V.O., C.A. Campbell and R.P. Zentner

1984 'Effect of crop rotation and fertilization on some biological properties of a loam in southwestern Saskatchewan'. *Canadian Journal of Soil Science* 64: 355-67.

Bird, Peter M. and David J. Rapport

1986 'State of the Environment Report for Canada'. Hull: Government Publishing Centre.

Bursa, Marjorie

1975 'The politics of land use'. *Agrologist* 4: 27-9.

Cameron, D.R., R. De Jong and C. Chang
1978 'Nitrogen inputs and losses in tobacco, bean and potato fields in a sandy loam watershed'. *Journal of Environmental Quality* 7: 545-50.

Coote, D.R., J. Dumanski and J.F. Ramsey
1981 'An assessment of the degradation of agricultural lands in Canada'. Ottawa: Land Resource Research Institute Contribution 118.

Dance, K.W. and H.B.N. Hyne
1980 'Some effects of agricultural land use on stream insect communities'. *Environmental Pollution* (Series A) 22: 19-28.

Dormaar, J.F. and U.J. Pittman
1980 'Decomposition of organic residues as affected by various dryland spring wheat-fallow rotations'. *Canadian Journal of Soil Science* 60: 97-106.

Doughty, J.L., F.D. Cook and F.G. Warder
1954 'Effect of cultivation on the organic matter and nitrogen of Brown soils'. *Canadian Journal of Agricultural Science* 34: 406-11.

Dumanski, J.
1986 'Towards a soil conservation strategy for Canada' in D. W. Anderson (ed.) in *In Search of Soil Conservation Strategies in Canada*. Ottawa: Agricultural Institute of Canada.

Farstad, L. and C.A. Rowles
1960 'Soils of the Cordilleran Region'. *Agricultural Institute Review* 15: 23-32.

Federal-Provincial Agriculture Committee on Environmental Sustainability
1990 'Growing together'. Report to Ministers of Agriculture. Ottawa: Agriculture Canada.

Frank, R., H.E. Brown, M. Van Hove Holdrinet, G.J. Simons and R.D. Ripley
1983 'Agriculture and water quality in the Canadian Great Lakes Basin. V. Pesticide use in 11 agricultural watersheds and presence in stream water, 1975-77'. *Journal of Environmental Quality* 11: 497-504.

Gauthier, David A. and J. David Henry
1989 'Misunderstanding the prairies' in Monte Hummel (ed.) *Endangered Species*. Toronto: Key Porter Books.

Greer, K.J.
1989 'Evaluating the soil quality of long-term crop rotations at Indian Head'. MSc thesis. Department of Soil Science, University of Saskatchewan.

Hallberg, George R.
1987 'Agricultural chemicals in ground water: Extent and implications'. *American Journal of Alternative Agriculture* 11, 2: 3-15.

Hedlin, R.A.
1971 'Nitrate contamination of ground water in the Neepawa-Langruth area of Manitoba'. *Canadian Journal of Soil Science* 51: 75-84.

Hind, H.Y.
1959 *Narrative of the Canadian Red River exploring expedition of 1857, and of the Assiniboine and Saskatchewan exploring expedition of 1858*. Edmonton: Hurtig (reprint).

Hogg, T.J. and J.L. Henry
1990 'Waterwell surveys of selected areas in Saskatchewan'. Publication M89. Saskatoon: Saskatchewan Institute of Pedology, University of Saskatchewan.

Janzen, H.H.
1987 'Soil organic matter characteristics after long-term cropping to various spring wheat rotations'. *Canadian Journal of Soil Science* 67: 845-6.

Ketcheson, J.W.
1980 'Long-range effects of cultivation and monoculture on the quality of southern Ontario soils'. *Canadian Journal of Soil Science* 60: 403-10.

——— and D.P. Stonehouse
1983 'Conservation tillage in Ontario'. *Journal of Soil and Water Conservation* 38: 253-4.

Kohut, A.P., S. Sather, J. Kwong and F. Chwojka
1989 'Nitrate contamination of the Abbotsford aquifer, British Columbia'. Symposium on Ground-water Contamination, National Hydrology Research Institute, Saskatoon (abstract).

Lynch-Stewart, Pauline
1983 'Land use change on wetlands in Southern Canada'. Working Paper No. 26. Ottawa: Lands Directorate, Environment Canada.

McCuaig, J.D. and E.W. Manning
1982 'Agricultural land use change in Canada'. Land Use in Canada Series No. 21. Ottawa: Lands Directorate, Environment Canada.

MacEwan, Grant
1986 *Entrusted to My Care*. Saskatoon: Western Producer Prairie Books.

McEwen, F.L. and M.H. Miller
1986 'Environmental effects and strategies to deal with them' in D.W. Anderson (ed.) *In Search of Soil Conservation Strategies in Canada*. Ottawa: Agricultural Institute of Canada.

McGill, W.B., K.R. Cannon, J.A. Robertson and F.D. Cook
1986 'Dynamics of soil microbial biomass and water-soluble organic C in Breton after 50 years of cropping to two rotations'. *Canadian Journal of Soil Science* 66: 1-20.

McKeague, J.A.
1975 'How much land do we have'. *Agrologist* 4: 10-14.

MacRae, H.F.
1986 'The effect of provincial policies and legislation on conservation' in D. W. Anderson (ed.) *In Search of Soil Conservation Strategies in Canada*. Ottawa: Agricultural Institute of Canada.

Martel, Y.A. and A.F. MacKenzie
1980 'Long-term effects of cultivation and land use on soil quality in Quebec'. *Canadian Journal of Soil Science* 60: 411-20.

Masse, L., S.O. Prasher and S.U. Khan
1989 'Leaching of atrazine and its metabolites in soil and ground water'. Symposium on Ground-water Contamination, National Hydrology Research Institute, Saskatoon (abstract).

Mathews, B.C. and R.W. Baril
1960 'Soils of the Great Lakes-St Lawrence Lowlands'. *Agriculture Institute Review* 15: 37-40.

Neilsen, G.H., J.L.B. Culley and D.R. Cameron
1982 'Agriculture and water quality in the Canadian Great Lakes Basin'. *Journal of Environmental Quality* 11: 493-7.

Nicholaichuk, W. and D.W.L. Read

1978 'Nutrient runoff from fertilized and unfertilized fields in Western Canada'. *Journal of Environmental Quality* 7: 542-4.

Ridley, A.O. and R.A. Hedlin

1968 'Soil organic matter and crop yields as influenced by the frequency of summerfallowing'. *Canadian Journal of Soil Science* 48: 315-22.

———

1980 'Crop yields and soil management on the Canadian prairies, past and present'. *Canadian Journal of Soil Science* 60: 393-402.

Rowe, Stan

1990 *Home Place, Essays on Ecology*. Edmonton: NeWest Publishers Ltd.

Saini, G.R. and W.J. Grant

1980 'Long-term effects of intensive cultivation on soil quality in the potato-growing areas of New Brunswick (Canada) and Maine (U.S.A.)'. *Canadian Journal of Soil Science* 60: 411-21.

Sexsmith, W.A.

1989 'Agricultural pesticides in ground water in New Brunswick'. Workshop on Pesticide Contamination of Canadian Ground Waters. Saskatoon: National Hydrology Research Institute (abstract).

Taylor, E.M.

1942 'Land settlement in New Brunswick'. *Scientific Agriculture* 23: 217-19.

Verity, G.E. and D.W. Anderson

1990 'Soil erosion effects on soil quality and yield'. *Canadian Journal of Soil Science* 70: 471-84.

Wall, G.J., W.T. Dickinson, R.P. Rudra and D.R. Coote

1988 'Seasonal soil erodibility variation in southwestern Ontario'. *Canadian Journal of Soil Science* 68: 417-24.

———, Terry J. Logan and Jennifer Ballantine

1989 'Pollution control in the Great Lakes Basin: An international effort'. *Journal of Soil and Water Conservation* 44: 12-15.

———, E.A. Pringle and R.W. Sheard

1991 'Intercropping red clover with silage corn for soil-erosion control'. forth-coming *Canadian Journal of Soil Science* 71: 00-00.

Warren, C. Leigh

1982 'Total land use change in Urban Centred Regions, Winnipeg, 1970-77'. Report No. 14. Ottawa: Lands Directorate, Environment Canada.

———, A. Kerr and A.M. Turner

1989 'Urbanization of rural land in Canada, 1981-86'. SOE Fact Sheet No. 89-1. Ottawa: Lands Directorate, Environment Canada.

——— and P.C. Rump

1981 'The urbanization of rural land in Canada: 1966-71 and 1971-76'. Land Use in Canada Series No. 20. Ottawa: Lands Directorate, Environment Canada.

Zentner, R.P., J.E. Stephenson, P.J. Johnson, C.A. Campbell and G.P. Lafond

1988 'The economics of wheat rotations on a heavy clay Chernozemic soil in the Black soil zone of east-central Saskatchewan'. *Canadian Journal of Plant Science* 68: 389-404.

Chapter Thirteen

Bertin, Oliver
1986 'Farmers Divided Over Free Trade'. *Globe and Mail*, 10 April.
———
1990 'Canada Packers Registers Its First Loss Since 1978'. *Globe and Mail*, 8 May.
Bowker, Marjorie
1988 *On Guard For Thee*. Hull: Voyageur.
Braden, Bonny
1990 'Export Subsidy Option Questioned'. *Star Phoenix*, 9 May.
Briarpatch
1988 'Free Trade Facts'. March.
Burton, Randy
1990 'Cargill Plant Called Danger to City Water Supply'. *Star Phoenix*, 18 April.
Canadian Broadcasting Corporation
1990 'Country Canada'. 12 June.
Canadian Press
1990 'US Pork Producers Want Subsidies'. Washington, 21 March.
Drohan, Madeleine
1989 'Canada's Trade Balances in the Red'. *Globe and Mail*, 14 December.
———
1990a 'Cargill, McCain Find Life Different Under Free Trade Deal'. *Globe and Mail*, 22 March.
———
1990b 'US Harassment Increasing, Senators Say'. *Globe and Mail*, 4 April.
Dryden, Ken
1989 'Oats Removal Erosion of Wheat Board Power'. *Western Producer*, 23 February.
Economist, The
1990 'Analysis'. *Globe and Mail*, 22 May.
External Affairs, Canada
1987 The Canada-US Trade Agreement in Brief. Ottawa.
———
1988 The Canada-US Free Trade Agreement. Ottawa.
Feather, Frank
1990 'G-Forces. Re-Inventing the World'. New York: Summerhill.
Foster, J.B.
1986 *Theory of Monopoly Capitalism*. New York: Monthly Review Press.
Fortune
1989 'The Fortune 500'. 31 July.
Francis, Diane
1990 'Warning Issued on Questionable Insurance'. *Financial Post*, 14 May.
Goulding, Warren
1990 'Intercon Blames Trade War for Layoffs'. *Star Phoenix*, 27 March.
Greenshields, Vern
1990 'Justify Actions or Face Retaliation: Mayer'. *Star Phoenix*, 10 February.
Hay, D.A. and G.S. Basran
1988 'The Western Canadian Farm Sector: Transition and Trends' in G.S. Basran

and D.A. Hay (eds) *The Political Economy of Agriculture in Western Canada*. Toronto: Garamond Press: 3-25.

Herman, Deanna
1988 'Free Trade and Farmers: Cash Crop or Bad Risk?' *Star Phoenix*, 1 November.

Howard, Ross
1990 'Free Trade Opponents Claim 72,000 Jobs Lost During Pact's First Year'. *Globe and Mail*, 18 December.

Johnston, Catharine
1990 'Our Common Future'. *Canadian Business Review*, 17 (Spring): 6.

Jorgensen, Bud
1990 'Street Talk'. *Globe and Mail*, 7 May.

Kidd, Kenneth
1989 'Soft Landing or Hard Fall?' Part 4. *Globe and Mail*, 18 December.

Kneen, Brewster
1989 *From Land to Mouth*. Toronto: NC Press.

Kolko, Joyce
1988 *Restructuring the World Economy*. New York: Pantheon.

Lewington, Jennifer
1989 'US Has Own Subsidies: GATT'. *Globe and Mail*, 15 December.

Lipsey, Richard
1986 'Economic Destiny Now Beyond Our Control'. *Financial Post*, 19 October.

MacEwan, Arthur
1990 *Debt and Disorder*. New York: Monthly Review Press.

MacKenzie, Colin
1990 'Estimates Escalating for Bailout of S&Ls'. *Globe and Mail*, 1 April.

Magdoff, Harry
1971 'Economy, Myths and Imperialism'. *Monthly Review* 23: 1-17.

Masse, Carol
1988 'The Impact of the Free Trade Deal on Agriculture' in Jim Silver and Jesse Vorst (eds), *Why No Free Trade*. Winnipeg: Manitoba Coalition Against Free Trade.

Menzies, Heather
1990 'Solutions That Ignore Reality'. *Globe and Mail*, 4 June.

Mitchell, Fred
1985 'US Market Crucial for Canada'. *Star Phoenix*, 10 December.

Mitchell, Russell
1990 'The Farm Belt is Feeling Its Oats'. *Business Week*, 8 January.

Powell, Johanna
1990 'Few Will Survive Massive Beef Industry Shake-out'. *Financial Post*, 29 January.

Pugh, Terry
1990 'Free Trade Threatens Canadian Wheat Board'. *Canadian Dimension*, June.

Reuters
1990 'Consumers Pay for Agriculture Subsidies'. *Western Producer*, 26 April.

Ricardo, David
1963 *The Principles of Political Economy and Taxation*. Illinois: Irwin.

Rusk, James
1990 'Canadian Firms Losing Labour Cost Edge'. *Globe and Mail*, 5 June.

Saskatchewan Federation of Labour

1990 'What's Happening to Our Province'. Pamphlet.

Schaefer, R.T.

1989 *Sociology*. New York: McGraw-Hill.

Scotton, Geoffrey

1990 'Mexico Muscling In On Free Trade'. *Financial Post*, 16 April.

Sheppard, Robert

1990 'Farmers and Governments Set to Muddle Through Another Summer'. *Globe and Mail*, 9 May.

Shields, John

1988 'The Capitalist State and Class Struggle in the Fruit and Vegetable Industry in British Columbia' in G.S. Basran and D.A. Hay (eds), *The Political Economy of Agriculture in Western Canada*. Toronto: Garamond Press: 87-105.

Sproat, Deborah

1990 'Fertilizer Plant Becomes Political Issue'. *Western Producer*, 7 June.

Sterling, Theodor

1990 'Are the Communists Tossing in the Towel Too Soon?'. *Globe and Mail*, 18 January.

Trade and Investment Saskatchewan

1988 Canada-US Free Trade Agreement. Regina.

Visser, Ron

1990 'Millers Warn CWB to Lower Wheat Prices Once Border Opens'. *Union Farmer*, May.

Warnock, J.W.

1988 *Free Trade and the New Right Agenda*. Vancouver: New Star.

Western Producer

1990a 'EC to Spend $3 billion On Rural Areas'. Reuters, 10 May.

———

1990b 'Hog Producers Could Regret Stabilization'. 12 April.

Wilson, Barry

1989 'Trade Surplus Disappearing'. *Western Producer*, 24 August.

———

1990a 'Canada Defends Itself Against Subsidy Charges'. *Western Producer*, 12 April.

———

1990b 'Cattlemen Seek Shelter From Flood of Beef Imports'. *Western Producer*, 18 January.

———

1990c 'Millers Warn CWB to Lower Wheat Prices Once Border Opens'. *Western Producer*, 7 June.

Zakreski, Dan

1990a 'Most Family Farms Failing as Businesses: Report'. *Star Phoenix*, 7 April.

———

1990b 'Pork Producers Get $23.5 Million'. *Star Phoenix*, 8 May.

Zaracostas, John

1990 'US Turning Up Heat for Liberalized Trade in Services'. *Globe and Mail*, 15 May.

Chapter Fourteen

Arbab, Donna M. and B. Louise Weidner
1986 'Infectious Diseases and Field Water Supply and Sanitation Among Migrant Farm Workers'. *American Journal of Public Health* 76, 6: 694-5.
Arnopoulos, S.M.
1979 *Problems of Immigrant Women in the Canadian Labour Force*. Ottawa: Canadian Advisory Council on the Status of Women.
Bang, K.M., J.E. Lockey and W. Keye, Jr
1983 'Reproductive Hazards in the Work Place'. *Family and Community Health* 6, 1: 44-56.
Barrera, Mario
1979 *Race and Class in the Southwest: A Theory of Racial Inequality*. Notre Dame: University of Notre Dame Press.
Barthel, E.
1981 'Increased Risk of Lung Cancer in Pesticide-exposed Male Agricultural Workers'. *Journal of Toxicology and Environmental Health* 8: 1027-40.
Berger, John and Jean Mohr
1975 *A Seventh Man: Migrant Workers in Europe*. New York: Viking Press.
Bird, P.M. and D.J. Rapport
1986 *State of the Environment Report for Canada*. Ottawa: Minister of Supply and Services.
Blauner, Robert
1972 *Racial Oppression in America*. New York: Harper & Row.
Bohning, W.R.
1974 'Immigration Policies of Western European Countries'. *International Migration Review* 8, 2: 155-63.
Bolaria, B. Singh
1984 'Migrants, Immigrants and the Canadian Labour Force' in John A. Fry (ed.) *Contradictions in Canadian Society*. Toronto: John Wiley and Sons: 130-9.
———
1984 'On the Study of Race Relations' in John A. Fry (ed.) *Contradictions in Canadian Society*. Toronto: John Wiley and Sons: 219-47.
———
1988 'The Health Effects of Powerlessness: Women and Racial Minority Immigrant Workers' in B. Singh Bolaria and Harley D. Dickinson (eds) *Sociology of Health Care in Canada*. Toronto: Harcourt Brace Jovanovich: 439-59.
———
1988 'Profits and Illness: Exporting Health Hazards to the Third World' in B. Singh Bolaria and Harley D. Dickinson (eds), *Sociology of Health Care in Canada*. Toronto: Harcourt Brace Jovanovich: 477-96.
———
1991 'Environment, Work and Illness' in B. Singh Bolaria (ed.) *Social Issues and Contradictions in Canadian Society*. Toronto: Harcourt Brace Jovanovich: 222-46.
———, Harley D. Dickinson and Terry Wotherspoon
1991 'Rural Issues and Problems' in B. Singh Bolaria (ed.) *Social Issues and*

Contradictions in Canadian Society. Toronto: Harcourt Brace Jovanovich: 393-416.

——— and Peter Li

1988 *Racial Oppression in Canada* 2nd ed. Toronto: Garamond Press.

British Columbia Human Rights Commission

1983 'What This Country Did to Us, It Did to Itself'. A report of the BC Human Rights Commission on Farmworkers and Domestic Workers. February.

Brown, Carol A.

1983 'Women Workers in the Health Service Industry' in Elizabeth Fee (ed.) *Women and Health: The Politics of Sex in Medicine*. Farmingdale, New York: Baywood Publishing Co.: 105-16.

Burawoy, Michael

1976 'The Functions and Reproduction of Migrant Labour: Comparative Material from Southern Africa and the United States'. *American Journal of Sociology* 81 (March): 1050-87.

Campbell, Ian

1986 'Health and Safety on the Farm'. *At the Centre* 9, 3: 1, 5, 7.

Canada, Department of Manpower and Immigration

1973 The Seasonal Farm Labour Situation in Southwestern Ontario—a Report. (mimeo).

Canada, Employment and Immigration

1983 Annual Report 1982-83.

———

1984 Immigration Statistics.

Canada Employment and Immigration Commission

1981 Commonwealth Caribbean and Mexican Seasonal Agricultural Workers Program: Review of 1979 Payroll Records. Labour Market Planning and Adjustment Branch. Hull, Quebec. (mimeo).

———

1981 1980 Review of Agricultural Manpower Programs. Labour Market Planning and Adjustment (June). (mimeo).

Canada, Government of

1974 Department of Manpower and Immigration (Green Paper), The Immigration Program: 2.

Canadian Centre for Occupational Health and Safety

1986 'Occupational health and Safety in Agriculture'. *At the Centre* 9, 3 (July).

Canadian Civil Liberties Association

1977 Brief to the House of Commons Standing Committee on Labour, Manpower and Immigration, June 2, regarding Immigration Bill C-24.

Canadian Farmworkers' Union

1980 Support British Columbia Farmworkers. Pamphlet.

Carney, John

1976 'Capital Accumulation and Uneven Development in Europe: Notes on Migrant Labour'. *Antipode* 8, 1: 30-6.

Castells, Manuel
1975 'Immigrant Workers and Class Struggles in Advanced Capitalism: The Western European Experience'. *Politics and Society* 5: 33-66.
Chase, H.P., S. Barnett, N. Welch, F. Briese, and M. Krossner
1973 'Pesticides and US Farm Labour Families'. *Rocky Mountain Medical Journal* 70: 27-31.
Cliff, K.S.
1981 'Agriculture—The Occupational Hazards'. *Public Health* 95: 15-27.
Coye, Molly Joel
1985 'The Health Effect of Agricultural Production: The Health of Agricultural Workers'. *Journal of Public Health Policy* (September): 349-70.
Denis, Wilfrid B.
1988 'Causes of Health and Safety Hazards in Canadian Agriculture'. *International Journal of Health Services* 18, 3: 419-36.
Dosman, J.
1985 *Health and Safety in Agriculture.* Saskatoon: University of Saskatchewan (Conference Proceedings).
Doyal, Lesley and Imogen Pennell
1979 *The Political Economy of Health.* London: Pluto Press.
Economic Council of Canada
1978 *For a Better Future.*
Edwards, Richard, Michael Reich, and David Gordon (eds)
1975 *Labor Market Segmentation.* Lexington, MA: D.C. Heath.
Eitzen, D.S. and M.B. Zinn
1989 *Social Problems*, 4th ed. Boston, MA: Allyn and Bacon.
Epstein, S.
1979 *The Politics of Cancer.* Garden City, NY: Anchor Books.
Eyer, Joseph
1984 'Capitalism, Health and Illness' in John B. McKinlay (ed.) *Issues in the Political Economy of Health Care.* New York: Tavistock Publications.
Fisher, Lloyd
1953 *The Harvest Labor Market in California.* Cambridge, MA: Harvard University Press.
Freudenberg, N.
1989 'The Corporate Assault on Health' in Phil Brown (ed.) *Perspectives in Medical Sociology.* Belmont, CA: Wadsworth: 104-21.
Gallagher, R.F. *et al.*
1985 'Cancer in Farmers and Farm Labourers in British Columbia' in J. Dosman (ed.) *Health and Safety in Agriculture.* Saskatoon: University of Saskatchewan (Conference Proceedings).
George, Anne
1976 *Occupational Health Hazards to Women.* Ottawa: Advisory Council on the Status of Women. October.
Glavin, Terry
1980 'Breaking the Back of Back-Breaking Labour'. *Canadian Dimension*, August: 18-19.
Goff, Colin H. and Charles E. Reasons
1986 'Organizational Crimes Against Employees, Consumers, and the Public' in

Brian D. MacLean (ed.) *The Political Economy of Crime*. Scarborough, Ont.: Prentice-Hall Canada, Inc.

Guttmacher, S.

1984 'Immigrant Workers: Health, Law, and Public Policy'. *Journal of Health Politics, Policy and Law* 9, 3: 503-14.

Harding, J.

1988 'Environmental Degradation and Rising Cancer Rates: Exploring the Links in Canada' in B. Singh Bolaria and Harley D. Dickinson (eds) *Sociology of Health Care in Canada*. Toronto: Harcourt Brace Jovanovich: 411-25.

Hussain, M.

1983 *Pesticide Safety Survey*. Edmonton: Alberta Agriculture.

Johnson, Laura C. and Robert E. Johnson

1981 *The Seam Allowance*. Toronto: Women's Education Press.

Kahn, E.

1976 'Pesticide Related Illness in California Farm Workers'. *Journal of Occupational Medicine* 18: 693-96.

Kelly, Russell

1983 'Bitter Harvest'. *New West Review*, November.

Koch, Tom

1983 'Farm Poison Death Government Fault, Jury Says'. *The Vancouver Province*, 17 March: B1.

Kreckel, R.

1980 'Unequal Opportunity Structure and Labour Market Segmentation'. *Sociology* 14, 4: 525-50.

Kuo, W.H. and Y. Tsai

1986 'Social Networking, Hardiness and Immigrant's Mental Health'. *Journal of Health and Social Behavior* 27 (June): 133-49.

Labonté, Ron

1982-1983 'Of Cockroaches and Berry Blight'. *This Magazine* 15, 6 (December-January): 4-6.

———

1980 'The Plight of the Farmworkers'. *Vancouver Sun*, 25 August.

———

1982 'Racism and Labour: The Struggle of British Columbia's Farmworkers'. *Canadian Forum* June-July.

———

1984 'Chemical Justice: Dioxin's Day in Court'. *This Magazine* 17, 6: 4-9.

Lee, Gloria and John Wrench

1980 'Accident Prone Immigrants: An Assumption Challenged'. *Sociology* 14, 4: 551-6.

Leggett, J.

1968 *Class, Race and Labour: Working Class Consciousness in Detroit*. New York: Oxford University Press.

MacQueen, Ken

1990 'Slim Pickings'. *The Vancouver Sun*, Saturday, 22 September 1990: B1.

Majka, L.C. and T.J. Majka

1982 *Farm Workers, Agribusiness and the State*. Philadelphia: Temple University Press.

Martin, P.L.

1985 'Migrant Labor in Agriculture: An International Comparison'. *International Migration Review* 19, 1: 135-43.

Matsqui, Abbotsford Community Services

1982 'Agricultural Pesticide and Health Survey Results'. A project of the Matsqui, Abbotsford Community Services (October).

Migrant Legal Action Program and Farmworker Justice Fund

1984 Post Hearing Proposed Findings of Fact and Conclusions of Law, In the Matter of: Proposed Farmworker Field Sanitation Standard, On Behalf of A. Phillip Randolph Institute, Arizona Farmworkers Union, and Others, August 30. U.S. Department of Labour, Occupational Safety and Health Administration. (Docket H-308).

Miles, Robert

1982 *Racism and Migrant Labour*. London: Routledge and Kegan Paul.

Miller, A.

1975 'The Wages of Neglect: Death and Disease in the American Work Place'. *American Journal of Public Health* 65, 11: 1217-20.

Milvey, T.H., and D. Wharton

1980 'Epidemiological Assessment of Occupationally Related Chemically Induced Sperm Count Suppression'. *Journal of Occupational Medicine* 22: 77-8.

Montejano, David

1977 *Race, Labor Repression, and Capitalist Agriculture: Notes From South Texas, 1920-1930*. Berkeley, CA: University of California, Institute for the Study of Social Change, Working Papers Series No. 102.

Moore, A.

1984 'Study Shows At Least 7000 Farmers Poisoned by Pesticides Last Year'. *Commonwealth*, 15 March.

North, D.S.

1980 'Non-immigrant Workers: Visiting Labor Force Participants'. *Monthly Labor Review* 103, 10: 26-30.

Omishakin, M.A.

1983 'Assessment of Health Needs of Black Agricultural Workers in Mid-Delta of Mississippi, USA'. *Journal of Royal Society of Health* 103, 6: 239-41.

Ontario Ministry of Agriculture and Food, and Ministry of Labour

1985 Report of the Task Force on Health and Safety in Agriculture. Toronto.

Oppenheimer, M.

1974 'The Sub-Proletariat: Dark Skins and Dirty Work'. *Insurgent Sociologist* 4: 7-20.

Parr, Joy

1985 'Hired Men: Ontario Agricultural/Wage Labour in Historical Perspective'. *Labour/Le Travail* 15 (Spring): 91-103.

Porteous, S.M.

1977 *Migrant Child Welfare: A Review of Literature and Legislation*. Washington, DC: InterAmerica Research Associates.

Portes, Alijandro and Jozsef Borocz

1989 'Contemporary Immigration: Theoretical Perspectives on Its Determinants and Modes of Incorporation'. *International Migration Review* 23, 3: 606-30.

Pynn, Larry
1983 'Exempting Farmers From Safety Rules Attacked'. *The Vancouver Sun*, 11 March.
Reasons, Charles E., Lois Ross and Craig Paterson
1981 'Farming May Be Dangerous to Your Health' in C. Reasons *et al.* (ed.) *Assault on the Workers*. Toronto: Butterworths Canada Ltd.
———
1981 *Assault on the Workers*. Toronto: Butterworths Canada Ltd.
Report of the Special Committee on Visible Minorities in Canadian Society
1984 *Equality Now!* Canada, House of Commons.
Royal Commission, Canada.
1984 Equality in Employment. Ottawa: Minister of Supply and Services.
Rust, George S.
1990 'Health Status of Migrant Farmworkers: A Literature Review and Commentary'. *American Journal of Public Health* 80, 10 (October): 1213–17.
Sakala, Carol
1987 'Migrant and Seasonal Farmworkers in the United States: A Review of Health Hazards, Status, and Policy'. *International Migration Review* 21, 3: 659–87.
Sandborn, Calvin
1983 'Equality for Farmworkers — A Question of Social Conscience'. A submission to the legislative caucus of the provincial New Democratic Party.
———
1986 'OHS on the Canadian Farm: What Is to Be Done?'. *At the Centre* 9, 3: 1–5.
Sanderson, G.
1974 'The Sweatshop Legacy: Still With Us in 1974'. *The Labour Gazette* 74: 400–17.
Sassen-Koob, Saskia
1980 'Immigrant and Minority Workers in the Organization of the Labour Process'. *The Journal of Ethnic Studies* 8, 1: 1–34.
———
1981 'Toward a Conceptualization of Immigrant Labor'. *Social Problems* 29, 1: 65–85.
Satzewich, Vic
1989 'Unfree Labour and Canadian Capitalism: The Incorporation of Polish War Veterans'. *Studies in Political Economy* 28 (Spring): 89–110.
Schatzkin, Arthur
1978 'Health and Labour Power: A Theoretical Investigation'. *International Journal of Health Services* 8, 2: 213–34.
Sharma, Hari
1983 'Race and Class in British Columbia — The Case of BC's Farmworkers'. *South Asian Bulletin* 3: 53–69.
Sharma, Shalendra
1982 'East Indians and the Canadian Ethnic Mosaic: An Overview'. *South Asian Bulletin* 1: 6–18.
Shields, John M.
1988 'The Capitalist State and Class Struggle in the Fruit and Vegetable Industry in British Columbia' in G.S. Basran and D.A. Hay (eds) *The Political Economy of Agriculture in Western Canada*. Toronto: Garamond Press: 87–106.

Simpson, S.G.
1984 'Farm Machinery Injuries'. *The Journal of Trauma* 24, 2: 150-2.
Slesinger, D.P., B.A. Christenson, and E. Cautley
1986 'Health and Mortality of Migrant Farm Children'. *Social Science and Medicine* 23, 1: 65-74.
Stringini, P.
1982 'On the Political Economy of Risk: Farmworkers, Pesticides, and Dollars'. *International Journal of Health Services* 12, 2: 263-92.
Stubbs, H.A., J. Harris and R.C. Spear
1984 'A Proportionate Mortality Analysis of California Agricultural Workers, 1978-79'. *American Journal of Industrial Medicine* 6: 305-20.
Task Force on Immigration Practices and Procedures
1981 *Domestic Workers on Employment Authorizations*. A Report. Government of Canada, Supply and Services.
The Law Union of Ontario
1981 *The Immigrant's Handbook*. Montreal: Black Rose Books.
US Congress
1972 Hearings on Migratory Labor. U.S. Government Printing Office. Washington, DC.
Waitzkin, Howard
1983 *The Second Sickness*. New York: The Free Press.
Waldron, I., M. Nawotarski, M. Freimer, J. Henry, N. Post, and C. Wittin
1982 'Cross-Cultural Variation in Blood Pressure: A Quantative Analysis of the Relationships of Blood Pressure to Cultural Characteristics, Salt Consumption and Body Weight'. *Social Science and Medicine* 16: 419-30.

Chapter Fifteen

Agriculture Canada
1981 *Canada's Agri-food System: An Overview*. Ottawa: Queen's Printer.
———
1977 *A Food Strategy For Canada*. Ottawa: Queen's Printer.
Beatty, David M.
1987 *Putting the Charter to Work: Designing a Constitutional Labour Code*. Montreal: McGill-Queen's University Press.
Beveridge, Karl and Carole Condé
1982 'Canadian Farmworkers Union: The Effects of an Automated Agribusiness on Workers' Lives are Often Hidden'. *Fuse* 5, 10: 317-23.
Bolaria, B. Singh and Peter S. Li
1985 *Racial Oppression in Canada*. Toronto: Garamond Press.
British Columbia Federation of Agriculture (BCFA)
1982 *Year Book*. n.p.
British Columbia Ministry of Agriculture and Food
1985 *Agriculture Statistics Profile 1984*. Victoria, BC: Queen's Printer.
———
1984a *Farm Labour Management in British Columbia*. Victoria, BC: Queen's Printer.
———
1984b *1983 Annual Report*. Victoria, BC: Queen's Printer.

———
1977 *1977 Annual Report*. Victoria, BC: Queen's Printer.

British Columbia Ministry of Labour and Consumer Services
1988 *BC Labour Directory 1988*. Victoria, BC: Queen's Printer.

Burbach, Roger and Patricia Flynn (eds)
1980 *Agribusiness in the Americas*. New York: Monthly Review Press.

Canadian Department of Labour
1960 *Trends in the Agricultural Labour Force in Canada: From 1921 to 1959*. Ottawa: Queen's Printer.

Carroll, J.A.
n.d. 'Foreword' in S.H. Lane and D.R. Campbell, *Farm Labour in Ontario*. Toronto: Department of Agriculture and Economics, Ontario Agricultural College and Ontario Department of Agriculture.

Clement, Wallace
1983 'Property and Proletarianization: Transformation of Simple Commodity Producers in Canadian Farming and Fishing' in *Class, Power and Property: Essays on Canadian Society*. Toronto: Methuen Publications: 225-43.

Dixon, Marlene, Elizabeth Martine and Ed McCaughan
1983 'Chicanos and Mexicans Within a Transnational Working Class'. *Our Socialism* (March): 9-12.

Drache, Daniel
1978 'Rediscovering Canadian Political Economy' in Wallace Clement and Daniel Drache, *A Practical Guide to Canadian Political Economy*. Toronto: James Lorimer and Co., Publishers: 1-53.

Dyck, Rand
1986 *Provincial Politics in Canada*. Scarborough, Ont.: Prentice-Hall Canada, Inc.

Fields, Belden
1982 'The Battle of Sonactra: A Study of an Immigrant Worker Struggle in France'. *New Political Science* 9, 10: 93-112.

Fisher, Anne
1986 'Farming's Mortgaged Future'. *Report on Business Magazine* (May): 24-31.

Fowke, Vernon C.
1978 *Canadian Agricultural Policy: The Historical Pattern*. Toronto: University of Toronto Press.

Friedman, Andrew L.
1978 *Industry and Labour: Class Struggle at Work and Monopoly Capitalism*. London: Macmillan.

Glavin, Terry
1980 'Breaking the Back of Back-Breaking Labour'. *Canadian Dimension* (August): 18-19.

Globe and Mail
1986 'Canada Safeway will buy 23 Woodward's Food Floors'. 24 Dec.

Haythorne, George V.
1960 *Labour in Canadian Agriculture*. Cambridge, MA: Harvard University Press.

Hurd, Richard W.
1974 'Organizing the Working Poor—The California Grape Strike Experience'. *The Review of Radical Political Economics* 6, 1: 50-75.

Hutchison, Bruce
1942 *The Unknown Country*. New York: Coward-McCann.
Jhappan, Carol R.
1983 'Resistance to Exploitation: East Indians and the Rise of the Canadian Farmworkers Union in BC'. MA thesis, Department of Political Science, University of British Columbia.
Labonté, Ronald
1982 'Racism and Labour: The Struggle of British Columbia's Farmworkers'. *The Canadian Forum* 62, 719: 9-11.
McEwan, Kenneth A. and Wayne H. Howard
1989 'Human Resource Management: A Review with Applications to Agriculture'. *Canadian Journal of Agricultural Economics* 37, 4: 733-42.
Macpherson, C.B.
1977 *Democracy in Alberta*. Toronto: University of Toronto Press.
Menzie, E.L.
1980 'Developments in Canadian Agricultural Policy, 1929-79'. *Canadian Farm Economics* 15, 2: 15-9.
Mitchell, Don
1975 *The Politics of Food*. Toronto: James Lorimer and Co., Publishers.
Neilson, Kathryn and Innis Christie
1975 'The Agricultural Labourer in Canada: A Legal Point of View'. *Dalhousie Law Journal* 2, 2: 330-68.
Ontario Ministry of Agriculture and Food
1989 *Agricultural Statistics for Ontario 1988*. Toronto: Queen's Printer.

———

1972 *Corporate Farming and Vertical Integration in Ontario*. Toronto: Queen's Printer.
Ontario Task Force on Hours of Work and Overtime
1987a Farm Workers and Worktime Provisions of Ontario's Employment Standards Act, Research Report. Toronto: Queen's Printer.

———

1987b Working Times: Phase II, The Report of the Ontario Task Force on Hours of Work and Overtime. Toronto: Queen's Printer.
Palmer, Bryan D.
1981 *The Making of E. P. Thompson: Marxism, Humanism, and History*. Toronto: New Hogtown Press.
Pfeffer, Max J.
1983 'Industrial Farming'. *Democracy* 3, 2: 37-49.
Pynn, Larry
1983 'Exempting Farmers from Safety Rules Attacked'. *Vancouver Sun*, 11 March: B8.
Rea, K.J.
1985 *The Prosperous Years: The Economic History of Ontario 1939-75*. Toronto: University of Toronto Press.
Reasons, Charles E., Lois L. Ross and Craig Paterson
1981 *Assault on the Worker: Occupational Health and Safety in Canada*. Toronto: Butterworths Canada Ltd.
Robin, Martin
1978 'British Columbia: The Company Province' in M. Robin (ed.) *Canadian Provincial Politics* 2nd ed. Scarborough, Ont.: Prentice-Hall of Canada: 28-60.

———

1973 'Safeway Canada—Controls the Grocery Business From Thunder Bay to Vancouver' and editorial introduction. *Our Generation* 9, 4: 10–14.

———

1968 'The Social Basis of Party Politics in British Columbia' in W. E. Mann (ed.) *Canada: A Sociological Profile*. Toronto: Copp Clark Publishing Co.: 338–49.

Select Standing Committee on Agriculture

1979a Concentration and Integration in the British Columbia Food Industry. Phase III Research Report, Legislative Assembly, Province of British Columbia.

———

1979b Food Distribution in British Columbia: An Analysis of the Wholesale and Retail Sectors of the Food System. Phase III Research Report, Legislative Assembly, Province of British Columbia.

———

1979c The Impact of Labour on the British Columbia Food Industry. Phase III Research Report, Legislative Assembly, Province of British Columbia.

———

1979d Marketing Boards in British Columbia, Vol. 1. Phase II Research Report, Legislative Assembly, Province of British Columbia.

Shields, John M.

1989 'British Columbia's New Reality: The Politics of Neo-Conservatism and Defensive Defiance'. PhD dissertation, Department of Political Science, University of British Columbia.

———

1988 'The Capitalist State and Class Struggle in the Fruit and Vegetable Industry in British Columbia' in G.S. Basran and D.A. Hay (eds) *The Political Economy of Agriculture in Western Canada*. Toronto: Garamond Press: 87–106.

Skogstad, Grace

1990 'The Farm Policy Community and Public Policy in Ontario and Quebec' in William D. Coleman and Grace Skogstad (eds) *Policy Communities and Public Policy in Canada: A Structural Approach*. Mississauga, Ont.: Copp Clark Pitman Ltd: 159–90.

Smit, Barry, Tom Johnston and Robert Morse

1984 *Employment and Labour Turnover in Agriculture: A Case Study of Flue-cured Tobacco Farms in Southern Ontario*. Guelph: University of Guelph.

Statistics Canada

1989 *Canada Year Book 1990*. Ottawa: Minister of Supply and Services.

Stultz, Erma

1987 'Organizing the Unorganized Farmworkers in Ontario' in R. Argue, C. Cannage and D. Livingstone (eds) *Working People and Hard Times*. Toronto: Garamond Press.

Thompson, John Herd and Allen Seager

1978 'Workers, Growers and Monopolists: The "Labour Problem in the Alberta Beet Sugar Industry During the 1930's" '. *Labour/Le Travailleur* 3: 153–74.

Warnock, John W.

1987 *The Politics of Hunger*. Agincourt, Ont.: Methuen Publications.

———

1986 'Agriculture and the Food Industry' in Warren Magnusson, Charles Doyle, R.

B. J. Walker and John DeMarco (eds) *After Bennett: A New Politics for British Columbia*. Vancouver: New Star Books Ltd: 150-68.

———

1978 *Profit Hungry: The Food Industry in Canada*. Vancouver: New Star Books.

———

1976 'The Political Economy of the Food Industry in Canada: Oligopoly and American Domination'. *Our Generation* 11, 4: 52-72.

———

1975 'Free Trade Fantasies: The Case of Farm Implements Industry'. *This Magazine* 9, 5/6: 36-40.

Weiner, Merle

1978 'Cheap Food, Cheap Labour: California Agriculture in the 1930's'. Essays on the Social Relations of Work and Labour: A Special Issue of *The Insurgent Sociologist* 8, 2/3: 181-90.

Chapter Sixteen

Coughenour, C. Milton and Lawrence Busch

1978 'Alternative futures for rural America' in Thomas R. Ford (ed.) *Rural USA: Persistence and Change*. Ames: Iowa State University Press.

Crown, Robert W. and Earl O. Heady

1972 *Policy Integration in Canadian Agriculture*. Ames: Iowa State University Press.

Eldridge, Eber

1963 Imbalances in Rural America. (unpublished).

Fuller, Tony, Philip Ehrensaft, and Michael Gertler

1990 'Sustainable rural communities in Canada: Issues and prospects' in M. E. Gertler and H. R. Baker (eds) *Proceedings of Rural Policy Seminar #1, Sustainable Rural Communities in Canada*. Saskatoon: The Canadian Agricultural and Rural Restructuring Group: 1-41.

Hall Commission

1979 *Grain and Rail in Western Canada*, Vol. 1. Ottawa: Minister of Supply and Services.

Olsen, Marvin E.

1968 *The Process of Social Organization*. New York: Holt, Rinehart and Winston.

Swanson, Louis E.

1989 'The Rural Development Dilemmas'. *Resources for the Future* 96: 14-16.

Warner, Keith W.

1974 'Rural Society in a Post-Industrial Age'. *Rural Sociology* 39: 306-18.

Warren, Roland L.

1956 'Toward a typology of extra community controls limiting local community autonomy'. *Social Forces* 34: 338-41.

———

1978 *The Community in America*. Boston: Houghton Mifflin.

INDEX